Encyclopedia of INDIANA

GEORGE ROGERS CLARK
Miltary Leader — Revolutionary War

Encyclopedia of INDIANA

–a volume of
ENCYCLOPEDIA OF THE UNITED STATES

SECOND EDITION

>—•—◂

SOMERSET PUBLISHERS, INC.
521 Fifth Ave., 17th Floor
New York, N.Y. 10175

Copyright© 1993, by Somerset Publishers

All rights reserved. No part of this work may be reproduced or utilized in any form or by any means, electronic or mechanical, or by any information storage and retrieval system, without permission in writing from the publisher.

Printed in the United States of America

```
            Library of Congress Cataloging-in-Publication Data


Encyclopedia of Indiana. -- 1993 ed.
         p.   cm. -- (Encyclopedia of the United States)
      Includes bibliographical references and index.
      ISBN 0-403-09998-6
      1. Indiana--Encyclopedias.   I. Somerset Publishers.  II. Series.
   F526.E53   1993
   977.2'003--dc20                                            93-32275
                                                                  CIP
```

FOREWORD

Information on this state is available from many other sources. Histories and geographies abound; there are place-name books, guidebooks and biographical references; many excellent atlases provide map detail; government registers contain in-depth coverage of the political organization.
It is the existance of so many varied sources of information that makes a systematic, encyclopedic reference necessary - a single source for the most useful information about the state.
A secondary purpose of this volume is to play a part in a national reference on all of the states, a systematic approach to referencing the entire nation - an *Encyclopedia of the United States,* with each volume following a planned outline that matches each other volume in the series - with exceptions in the format made only when necessary.
This goal was partly achieved during the Great Depression years with the publication of the WPA Federal Writers' Project State and City Guidebooks, which we are proud to have republished in recent years in their original form.
While containing a wealth of interesting and still useful information they are essentially *tour-guides* rather than general reference books. They were, however, very useful in the planning of this new work.
It is our hope that this Encyclopedia series will have a permanence through the issuance of revised editions at intervals to be determined by a careful watch on the availability of new material. Undoubtedly, changes in the concept will be reflected in later editions as a result of feedback from users and the observations and introspection of our editors.
We wish to acknowledge with great appreciation the cooperation of the many state and local government offices that have furnished or reviewed material.
We are further grateful to the many librarians who have made their facilities so available during the years that this project has been in progress.

LIBRARIANS WHO CONTRIBUTED MATERIAL FOR THIS EDITION

AYRES, SCOTT W. — Flora

BRIGHT, VELMA — Akron

BROWN, DONNA I. — Markle

BROWNING, HERB — Decatur

BURDETT, TONI — Noblesville

DOYLE, VICKY — Loogootee

EKSTROM, DONNA — Tipton

GAINS, DORIS — Kendallville

GOODWIN, ARLENE, — Auburn

HIVELY, ELVA — Roann

HOLDMAN, MRS. V. — Lebanon

HOLMES, MAURICE — Shelbyville

LUDWIG, ELIZABETH A. — Farmland

PERKINS, S. KENT — Fairmont

POTTS, WANDA — Mooresville

RIFE, GAY ANN — Dunkirk

SCHULTZ, LINDA J. — Albion

SHERRILL, NANCY LYNN — Terre Haute

STEWART, ELISABETH — Angola

SULLIVAN, ELLEN M., — Boonville

SUTER, GAIL — Walkerton

WAGNER, CHARLES — Peru

WARGO, TERRI — West London

WEIDEMAN, JANET — Newburgh

WILKINSON, MARJORIE — Knightstown

YOUNG, JEAN ANN — Bristol

ZEBRUN, NANCY — Centerville

CONTENTS

INTRODUCTION.	1
GEOGRAPHICAL CONFIGURATION.	7
PRE-HISTORY AND ARCHEOLOGY.	37
HISTORY.	47
CHRONOLOGY.	77
GOVERNORS.	87
DIRECTORY OF STATE SERVICES.	125
DICTIONARY OF PLACES.	139
INDIANAPOLIS.	345
PICTORIAL SCENES.	355
HISTORICAL PLACES.	376
STATE CONSTITUTION.	405
BOOKS ABOUT INDIANA.	439
INDEX.	443
MAP OF INDIANA.	484

INTRODUCTION

No better introduction to the country's heartland can be found than in Indiana. Blast furnaces and cornfields, urban ethnicity and rural homogeneity, tree-covered hills and unwavering plains, rugged gorges and gentle river valleys clearly set forth the seemingly contradictory nature of mid-America. That peculiar juncture of industry and agriculture, with its attendant commerce and transportation networks, led the Hoosier state in 1937 to adopt as its motto "The Crossroads of America."

As the hub of the Great Lakes region of the United States, the 19th state--admitted to the Union in 1816--is bounded on the north by Lake Michigan, on the east and south by the Ohio River, and on the southwest by the Wabash River. Its neighbors include the states of Michigan, Ohio, Kentucky, and Illinois. Indiana ranks 38th in area, with 36,291 square miles. Its population is concentrated primarily in the capital city of Indianapolis and the four major cities of Gary, South Bend, Evansville, and Fort Wayne.

STATE SYMBOLS

THE NAME

French trappers and soldiers called the northern portion of the land from which present-day Indiana was carved "Canada," its southern portion "Louisiana." English colonials called the region "Ohio Country." American settlers first called it "Virginia," then the "Northwest Territory," and, in 1800, the "Indiana Territory." Eventually, the Indiana Territory formed the states of Illinois, Wisconsin, and parts of Michigan and Minnesota, as well as Indiana.

A myriad of place-names in the Midwest are drawn from the Indian cultures which prevailed prior to the arrival of the first whites late in the 17th century. In fact, the Indian era on that frontier did not end until 1813, when the death of the great Shawnee chief Tecumseh and the resultant defeat of his confederated tribes by federal troops brought about the final cession of Indian lands to the new U.S. government. The Indians were driven westward, their presence in what was to become the state of Indiana--a presence which extended back to prehistoric times--remembered in name only.

It has been said that the U.S. Congress created the name Indiana, meaning *Land of the Indians*, when it created the Indiana Territory out of the Northwest Territory in 1800.

NICKNAMES

If the name "Indiana" has an obvious derivation, the opposite is true of the state's nickname. The use of the term "Hoosier" to denote a native of Indiana can be documented as early as 1831, but its actual origin remains a mystery.

One theory supposes that when a visitor hailed a pioneer at his door, the settler would respond with "Who's yere?" leading to the appelation of "Hoosier" state. A more facetious explanation was offered by the Hoosier poet James Whitcomb Riley, who claimed that the nickname originated in the pugnacious habits of Indiana's early settlers. "They were enthusiastic and vicious fighters who gouged, scratched, and bit off noses and ears. This was so common that a settler coming into a tavern the morning after a fight and seeing an ear on the floor would touch it with his toe and casually ask: "Whose ear?"

While Riley's yarn is more indicative of his state's penchant for tall tales than it is illustrative of the nickname's origin, others have arrived at a similiar conclusion. A popular notion is that Indiana rivermen were so successful in trouncing or "hushing" their adversaries in the brawling that was then common that they became known as "hushers," and eventually as "Hoosiers."

Slightly tamer are the two linguistic theories, the first being that "Hoosier" is derived from *hoosa*, an Indian word for corn. Indiana flatboat men taking corn to New Orleans came to be known as "hoosa men" or "Hoosiers." Unfortunately for this theory, a search of Indian vocabularies has

Introduction

failed to reveal such a word for corn. A second approach noted that "Hoosier" was frequently used in many parts of the South during the 1800s to denote woodsmen or rough hill people. The word was derived from the term "hoozer" which, in the Cumberland dialect of England, referred to a hill dweller or highlander. Immigrants from Cumberland, England, settled in the southern mountains of this country, whose foothills stretch into southern Indiana, and their decendants may have brought the name with them.

Least romantic, but equally plausible, is the theory that a contractor named Hoosier preferred to employ laborers from Indiana to work on the Louisville and Portland Canal. They were called "Hoosier's men", and it is possible that from this term all residents of Indiana were eventually called "Hoosiers."

Whatever its origin, "Hoosier" today is a mark of pride for Indianans, particularly when it is used to refer to the Hoosier hospitality for which the people of the state are known.

THE FLAG

The design of the state flag was adopted in 1917. In 1979, an amendment standardized the size of the flag, but the 1917 law otherwise remains the same.

The flag bears Indiana's colors of blue and gold. The dark blue field provides the background for a golden torch surrounded by 19 stars, one larger than the rest. The torch represents liberty and enlightenment, its rays symbolizing the far-reaching influence of those two concepts. An outer circle of 13 stars stands for the original states, an inner circle of five stars for the five admitted to the Union. The larger, central star is, of course, the 19th state of Indiana. The word *Indiana* is placed in a half circle over and above the star representing Indiana, and midway between it and the star in the center above it.

Encyclopedia of Indiana

THE STATE MOTTO

Crossroads of America was designated by the Indiana legislature in 1937 as the state's official motto.

THE GREAT SEAL

In 1963, Indiana officially adopted its state seal; prior to that, it had been using a territorial seal from 1801 depicting pioneer scenes.

The law reads:

The official seal for the state of Indiana shall be described as follows:

A perfect circle, two and five eighths inches in diameter, inclosed by a plain line. Another circle within the first, two and three eighths inches in diameter, inclosed by a beaded line, leaving a margin of one quarter of an inch. In the top half of this margin are the words 'Seal of the State of Indiana.'

At the bottom center, 1816, flanked on either side by a diamond, with two dots and a leaf of the tulip tree, at both ends of the diamond. The inner circle has two trees in the left background, three hills in the center background with nearly a full sun setting behind and between the first and second hill from the left.

There are fourteen rays from the sun, starting with two short ones on the left, the third being longer and then alter-

Introduction

nating, short and long. There are two sycamore trees on the right, the larger one being nearer the center and having a notch cut nearly half way through, from the left side, a short distance above the ground. The woodsman is wearing a hat and holding his ax nearly perpendicular on his right. The ax blade is turned away from him and is even with his hat.

The buffalo is in the foreground, facing to the left of front. His tail is up, front feet on the ground with back feet in the air--as he jumps over a log.

The ground has shoots of blue grass, in the area of the buffalo and woodsman.

THE STATE FLOWER

The Peony, *Paeonia,* which blooms throughout the state in May and early June, replaced the zinnia as the state flower in 1957.

THE STATE TREE

The Tulip tree, also known as the yellow poplar, became the state tree in 1931. The Indiana Historical Bureau reported that this tree was once the "monarch of the great forests which covered most of Indiana in pioneer times," but has since become "comparatively rare."

THE STATE SONG

In 1913 "On the Banks of the Wabash, Far Away" became the state song of Indiana. Paul Dresser wrote both the words and the music.

THE STATE BIRD

The Historical Bureau added that in 1933 the cardinal, whose "rich and cherry song is heard in Indiana all year round," became the official state bird.

Encyclopedia of Indiana

THE STATE MINERAL

The state mineral is Limestone; it was adopted in 1971.

THE STATE LANGUAGE

The official state language was adopted in 1984; it is English.

THE STATE POEM

The official state poem, chosen in 1963, is "Indiana", written by Arthur Franklin Mapes.

THE CAPITOL BUILDING

In 1824 the Indiana capital was moved to Indianapolis from Corydon, which had been the capital even before Indiana became a state in 1816. The first statehouse, a Greek revival building occupied in 1835, had been outgrown by 1877. Construction of the new Modern Renaissance capitol, designed by local architect Edwin May, began in 1878 and was completed in 1888 at a cost of approximately $2 million. The four-story capitol, constructed of Indiana limestone, contains over twelve acres of floor space. It is distinguished by the dome, 72 feet in diameter, which reaches a height of 234 feet. The inner dome, rising 108 feet above the main floor, is a 48-foot-wide work of stained glass, which was installed in 1887.

GEOGRAPHICAL CONFIGURATION

PHYSICAL FEATURES AND GEOGRAPHY

Indiana has a land area of 36,045 miles. The whole of the state has been glaciated except the south central and southwestern parts. The highest point in the state is in Randolph County, 1,285 feet above sea level, and the lowest is in Point Township, Posey County, at the mouth of the Wabash River, at 313 feet. The average elevation is about 700 feet. Indianapolis has an elevation of 718 feet.

Indiana's northern boundary is Lake Michigan and the state of Michigan along 41 50' north latitude. Its southern boundary is the low water mark of the north bank of the Ohio River, the most southerly point being 37 40' north latitude. In longitude it lies between 84 49' to the east, and 88 2' to the west.

About 90 percent of the state lies between 500 and 1,000 feet above sea level. Most of the state's surface slopes toward the west and south. Most of the surface features were formed by the glaciers that covered the greater part of the area during the Ice Age, approximately 1,000,000 years BP (before the present).

Indiana may be divided into three broad physiographic zones. These are the northern lake plain, the central till plain, and the southern hill and lowlands region.

The Northern Lake Plain. This rolling plain covers the northern third of the state. The evidence of glaciation found throughout this region includes swamps and marshes, lakes, and moraines (low ridges or mounds composed of materials deposited by glaciers). In the northwestern section, the swampland has been drained and the land used for truck farming.

Also in the northwest, along the shores of Lake Michigan, are the Indiana Dunes, which cover a belt about four miles wide at the western end, and a half mile wide at the eastern end. The Michigan Central Railroad tracks run along the southern boundary of the Dunes area.

In Lake County, to the west, the dunes are low, being for the most part from 5 to 15 feet high; dune areas alternate with interdunal flats. In the eastern part of Lake County, the dunes increase in height, with the high dunes region continuing eastward through Porter County to the vicinity of Michigan City. The highest dune is Mount Tom in Dunes State Park, Porter County, which is 192 feet high. The dunes proper consist of almost pure sand, and were formerly well wooded.

Since industry encroached upon the dunes and lakefront areas of northwestern Indiana in the early 20th century, conservationists have been struggling to prevent further encroachments and to preserve the natural beauty of the region. A major move for the preservation of the dunes was made in 1972 when the Indiana Dunes National Lakeshore, a preserve surrounding the Indiana Dunes State Park, was established.

Apart from the dunes, the northern lake plain has a great variety of habitats, ranging from lakes and rivers, bogs and marshes, dry sand and gravelly places, prairies and remnants of prairies, and mesophytic (moderately moist) forest areas. The line which divides the Lake Plain from the Tipton Till Plain to the south runs roughly westward from Fort Wayne to Huntington, Logansport, and Monticello on to the state line.

The Tipton Till Plain. This area is bounded on the north by the Lake Plain, and on the south by the southern boundary of the Wisconsin glacial drift. The southern part of this region consists of decidedly irregular territory. Its surface is comparatively level, however, although marked by many terminal moraines. The Tipton Till Plain contains the best agricultural land of Indiana. It has been cleared of most of the woodlands in the relatively brief period of a little more than a century.

The Till Plain is so named for the till, or jumbled earth materials, left behind by the melting edge of the glaciers. Its mainly level surface is broken in places by low hills and shallow valleys.

The Southern Hills and Lowlands Region. This area manifests many surface features including the Illinoian Drift Area, which lies south of the Tipton Till Plain, north

Geographical Configuration

of the glacial boundary, and east of the Lower Wabash Valley. The drift area is divided into an eastern and a western lobe. The topography varies from level areas to deeply cut ravines. In Clark, Jefferson, Jennings, and Riply counties the land is level, poorly drained, and contains acid soil patches known as "flats."

The Prairie. The prairie area of Indiana is small and actually belongs to the eastern limit of the Great Western Prairie. This section is relatively unimportant in the general division of the physiographic zones.

The Lower Wabash Valley. The valley is part of the southern, unglaciated lowlands of Indiana. The Wabash Lowland is a narrow strip of alluvial land along the Wabash River from Vigo County south to the Ohio River and thence north to Little Pigeon Creek in Warrick County. To it belongs the short, alluvial extensions of the White and Patoka rivers. The lower part of the low lying area includes Gibson, Posey, Vanderburgh, and Warrick counties. The eastern portion of the unglaciated area of the state is mostly hilly and broken and is divided by the broad valley of the White River.

The area contains numerous scenic knobs, deep valleys, sinkholes, underground rivers, caves, and mineral springs. Marengo and Wyandotte caves in Crawford County are among the most beautiful in the United States, as well as being well-known tourist attractions. The mineral springs at French Lick, West Baden, and Martinsville have a historic past.

South central Indiana is the source of the state's best known mineral resource, oolitic limestone. Extensive layers of the stone, however, underlie most of the southern section of Indiana. Indiana still contains approximately $17 billion of unquarried limestone deposits. The type formation, Salem Limestone, was formed about 300,000,000 years ago from compaction of layers of dead plant and animal matter.

The Crawford Upland. This area contains Indiana's most varied topography. The Upland is extremely rugged and inaccessible. It covers an area of approximately 2,900 square miles. Within this region are low and high hills, sharp and rounded ridges, trench-like valleys, flat-bottomed valleys, rock benches, rolling peneplain remnants, sinkholes, escarpments, canyon-like gorges, and caves. Elevations range from 349 to 980 feet. Alternating non-resitant shales, resistant sandstones, and limestones in the unglaciated section, combined with topographic maturity, have resulted in this scenic maze of land forms. Perry County, bordering on the Ohio River, is the most rugged county in Indiana.

The Mitchell Plain. This westward-sloping limestone plain exhibits a well-developed karst (sink- and cave) topography and covers approximately 1,125 square miles. Sinkholes of various sizes are abundant and reach a density of 100 per square mile in some sections. Surface waters drain into subterranean passages and underground rivers through open sinks. Many of the sinks are plugged and form small ponds. The elevation of the plain varies from 600 to 900 feet. Most of Indiana's caves are found on the Mitchell Plain.

The Norman Upland. This elevated section of Indiana encompasses 2,075 square miles of hills and intervening valleys and reaches a maximum width of 40 miles. In Brown County, rugged hills and scenic woodlands make this one of the most scenic and most often visited parts of the state. The maximum elevation of 1,050 feet is at Weedpatch Hill near Nashville. Elsewhere, great local relief is characteristic and uniform dissection by stream action has long been underway. Long, sharp ridges and V-shaped valleys are the result.

The Knobstone Escarpment ("The Knobs") of the Norman Upland is the most prominent relief feature and it extends from southern Jackson County through Harrison County, a distance of 150 miles. In Harrison and Floyd counties, the crest of the escarpment rises 400 to 600 feet above the valley floor. Crests in Clark, Floyd, Scott, and Washington counties reach an altitude of over 1,000 feet.

The Scottsburgh Lowland. Primarily, this lowland is broad, shallow, and of low relief. It is characterized by wide expanses of flat valleys and a notable lack of steep slopes and bluffs. The Lowland covers an area of 950 square miles. Much of the relief is below 600 feet. A deeply dissected upland area of 25 or 30 square miles in Jackson County is known as the "Brownstone Hills", and it repre-

Geographical Configuration

sents an upland mass isolated from the Norman Upland by stream erosion. The upper portion of these hills stood above the continental ice sheet during the Illinois Glacial Stage and today rise 300 feet above the surrounding lowland.

The Musctatuck Regional Slope. The most notable regional slope in Indiana is represented by this area of 1,875 square miles. Its eastern border ranges from 875 to about 1,100 feet in elevation, while the western edge varies from about 500 to 725 feet. Stream valleys of the southern half of the region are canyon-like in character but are never entrenched deeper than 175 feet below the gently inclined plain. In the area of greatest entrenchment, tributary streams are typically quite flat. Most of the streams passing down the center of the eastern part are comparatively less entrenched.

The Dearborn Upland. About 1,925 square miles of the southeastern corner of the state make up this unit. It is an upland composed of drainage basins of the Whitewater River and its tributaries. Elevations range from about 425 feet at the Ohio River to a maximum elevation of 1,100 feet. The streams are short and have a relatively great drop. Local relief is often measured in hundreds of feet; slopes are steep, but bluffs are rare. Long, evenly elevated upland tongues lie between the deeply dissected valleys. Terraces of glacial outwash border the Whitewater River flood plain. In western Dearborn County and eastern Ripley County, a rather extensive upland tract of marked flatness occurs. It rises slightly above the 1,100 foot contour and has not been severly dissected by streams.

Mineral Resources. Indiana is blessed with an abundance of mineral wealth and produces more than 80 percent of the limestone used in the United States. The Salem Limestone has been coveted as an excellent building stone for more than 150 years. It is more porous than other limestones and has a uniform texture and color. It is free from impurities and is easily worked at both the quarry site and at the mill. Although the Salem Limestone outcrops as far north as Owen County and as far south as Washington County, the center for the quarrying industry is in the Bloomington-Bedford area in Monroe and Lawrence counties.

Coal reserves underlie much of southwestern Indiana, and mining of the bituminous variety has long been a major industry. The bulk of Indiana's coal is burned to produce steam for turbine engines in electric power plants. Only about 15 percent is exported to other areas of the country. The coal in general has a low heat value and does not compare in quality to that of the Appalachian coal fields. Coal recovery is concentrated around Sullivan, Pike, and Gibson counties. Lesser centers are in Clay and Vermillion counties. The Indiana coal fields lie at the western edge of the great Illinois Basin which covers nearly all of central and southern Illinois, parts of western Kentucky, and southwestern Indiana. The coal beds lie in blanket formation and were first mined in 1840. Surface strip mines now number 36; they produced a yield of 782,339 tons in 1974. Many of the strip mines have been made part of Indiana's ambitious land reclamation program designed to return strip mines to their natural state. In 1967, a Hoosier reclamation law was passed which required all coal companies to file reclamation plans with the Department of Natural Resources. Reclaimed lands have been replanted in trees. The largest of these areas is the Greene-Sullivan State Forest, south of Dugger. It contains 6,439 acres of woodland and 100 lakes.

On a lesser scale, Indiana's deposits of oil shale have recently been exploited. The shale is capable of yielding a substance very similar to crude oil. The shale is easily mined in southern Indiana and reaches depths of 110 feet. When refined, it produces kerogens, which in turn can be used as oil substitutes. The main drawbacks to full-scale production are the expensive refining process and the lands, containing the shale, which are not zoned for mining.

Other important resources include abundant deposits of peat, clay, sand and gravel, all found throughout the state. Indiana's oil wells are located mainly in the Tri-State area of Illinois, Indiana, and Kentucky. Oil drilling, which began in the 1880s in central Indiana, brought large amounts of natural gas. The supplies of gas, at first thought unlimited, were depleted by the turn of the century.

Geological Formation. All the underlying rock strata found in Indiana are sedimentary, formed in the course of millions of years along the margins and bottoms of the seas.

Geographical Configuration

At one time the Precambrian seas covered the Indiana area, and during this earliest time (about 500,000,000 BP), the first sedimentary rocks were deposited upon the original crust. Rocks formed during this time are not exposed at any place in the state today, but their presence has been verified through rock samples taken during oil drilling.

Except for this basic layer, all rock strata in Indiana were deposited during the Paleozoic Era (500,000,000 to 200,000,000 years BP), a period of time during which most of the lower orders of plants and animals evolved. The Paleozoic Era is divided into 7 sections of time: the Cambrian, Ordovician, Silurian, Devonian, Mississippian, Pennsylvanian, and Permian periods. These periods are identified by their plant and animal fossil type sections.

Indiana was submerged beneath the seas during the Cambrian, Ordovician, and most of the Silurian periods. Late in the Silurian Period, the continent was uplifted and the great interior seas receded. The land rose slowly--an inch perhaps in a century. The first and sharpest uplift in the Indiana region was the formation of what is now known as the Cincinnati Arch. Pressure from below the Earth's crust slowly forced upwards the layers of rock deposited in the preceding periods. The Cincinnati Arch today extends from Cincinnati to Richmond, and south to Kokomo and Logansport, thence east to Chicago. Most of the arch was formed in the late Silurian and Devonian periods, approximately 350,000,000 to 300,000,000 years BP, but the slow upheaval process continued throughout the Paleozoic Era.

In the Mississippian and Pennsylvanian periods, Indiana was steadily elevated; at the close of the Mississippian, the whole region was above sea level. During the Pennsylvanian Period, about 250,000,000 years BP, Indiana was undoubtedly a lush swamp, populated by amphibian creatures and covered with fern-like plants. It was during this time that most of Indiana's present coal-beds were laid down. The climate steadily became cooler, and by the Permian Period, the swamps had dried up.

Paleozoic Formations. In the southeastern corner of the state the surface rocks immediately under the topsoil are of Ordovician Age. Then in order, toward the west, appear belts of Silurian, Devonian, Mississippian, and Pennsylvanian outcrops. A second and smaller Devonian formation to the north indicates the presence in that period of a separate northern basin. Cambrian and Precambrian rocks, though not exposed anywhere in Indiana, underlie these more recent formations. There are no Permian rocks, because Indiana was above sea level during and after this period.

Ordovician rocks were exposed only in the southeastern corner of Indiana, because of the uplift that began at this point to form the Cincinnati Arch. Elsewhere in the state, Ordovician strata was found beneath more recent formations. Next to the Ordovician outcroppings is a belt of Silurian rocks which farther west are overlapped by rocks succeeding periods. Only in the southwestern part of the state are Pennsylvanian rocks found.

Mesozoic Formations. During the many millions of years between the Permian Period and the Pleistocene Glacial Epoch, Indiana experienced three major cycles of erosion. During the Mesozoic Era (200,000,000 to 70,000,000 years BP), the region was above sea level and no rocks of Triassic, Jurassic or Cretaceous age were formed. At the same time, no rocks were formed in Indiana during the Tertiary Period of the Cenozoic Era.

The Pleistocene Glacial Epoch. At the beginning of the Pleistocene or Ice Age (1,000,000,000 BP), Indiana was elevated for the fourth time. The glaciers subsequently advanced and created many of the physical features seen today. During the Ice Age, about 5/6 of the whole region, with the exception of what is now South Central Indiana, was at one time or another under a 2,000 feet thick layer of ice. Geologists say that there were at least three ice invasions into Indiana. The ice at one time extended south of the Ohio River. After each invasion came a warming trend which lasted many thousands of years. The glaciers receded and plants and animals began to flourish.

The most striking effect of the glaciers was the channeling of the Ohio River bed by the melting ice. The glaciers lopped off many hills in the northern part of the state, filled the valleys with the eroded rocks, and smoothed and leveled the entire area. Excellent topsoil was formed from the mixing of the resultant rock flour. Over much of Indi-

Geographical Configuration

ana, the glacial topsoil forms excellent farmland. Glaciers also greatly altered drainage conditions by destroying existing streams and valleys and in turn creating new ones. Water was left in many depressions which formed marshes and lakes. In melting, the glaciers also left extensive deposits of sand and gravel and created many hills in the north by piling up soil and rocks into moranic deposits.

DRAINAGE AND SOILS

Naturally, Indiana is divided into three regions. These are the northern lake country, the central agricultural plain, and the southern hill and lowland section. The boundary of the northern region is the Upper Wabash River, which flows southwestward across the state to Terre Haute. The northern area, which consists of low plains with little stream action, is broken by many marshes and lakes. The northeastern section has hundreds of small bodies of water. It is characterized by low, morainal hills left by glaciers. Farther west, in Kosciusko County, Lake Wawasee occurs as a major drainage basin. It has an extreme length of about six miles.

Northern lake section. In lake country rises the watershed of the St. Lawrence and Mississippi rivers. To the northwest, the Kankakee and Iroquois rivers flow across wide expanses of marshy area to finally empty into the Illinois River. The Tippecanoe empties into the Wabash near Lafayette, while the Eel River rises north of Fort Wayne and flows into the Wabash at Logansport. The St. Joseph River of Michigan flows across northern Indiana through South Bend, then northward again into Lake Michigan, having drained a considerable area. The St. Mary's River rises in Ohio and flows northwest to Fort Wayne. It unites there with another stream, also called the St. Joseph, to form the Maumee River. The Maumee in turn, flows northwestward into the St. Lawrence drainage system. The watershed encompasses Adams and Allen counties, northern Indiana's lake country, and part of Lake Michigan.

The central agricultural section. The most important river here is the White River. The West Fork of the White River has its source in Randolph County and flows quietly southwestward across Indiana to confluence with the Wabash River in Gibson County.

Through the upper part of the plain constitutes important tributaries of the Wabash River. In eastern Indiana, the twin forks of the Whitewater meet to flow southward into the Ohio River.

The South. The upland-lowland drainage system of the southern part of Indiana is drained by scores of tiny streams and creeks which empty into the Ohio River. The major rivers of the basin are the Wabash and White, which in turn drain 2/3 of the entire state.

Man-made reservoirs. During recent years, a large system of man-made dams and reservoirs have been jointly constructed by the State of Indiana and the U.S. Army Corps of Engineers. They are part of an ambitious program which will substantially increase the state's water supplies and recreational facilities.

The largest of these "lakes" is the Monroe Reservoir, a 10,750-acre body of water that sprawls across southeastern Monroe County. It stretches for 22 miles from the Bloomington vicinity to the Monroe-Lawrence County line north of Bedford. The lake, with 85 miles of shoreline, is Indiana's largest. Fourteen projects are planned which will eventually encompass a flood control system that includes the Upper Mississippi, Ohio, and Wabash rivers.

Soils. Soils are derived from various geological materials. Glacial till, limestone, or wind-blown silt undergo changes as a result of a direct effect of climate. The resulting soil depends on the kind of geological material, climate, kinds of vegetation, topography of the land, and the length of time the soil has been forming.

Indiana is blessed with a great variety of parent materials needed to form soil. In roughly the northern 5/6 of the state these deposits have resulted from glaciation. The parent materials of the other 1/6 are largely bedrock formations such as limestone and sandstone which are partially covered by windblown silt. Mostly, the soils of Indiana have formed under a growth of hardwood trees. The resulting soils are light colored on slopes and flats and dark colored in depressions. In a small area the soils that have

Geographical Configuration

formed under prairie grasses are all dark colored. The young soils of northern Indiana are less acid and have more organic matter than the very old soils of southern Indiana. The depth of free lime varies from about three feet in the young soils of northern Indiana to three to fifteen feet in the south.

CLIMATE

Indiana, mainly the northern half, lies within the sweep of winter cold waves from the west and northwest. In the summer, the state is occasionally visited by hot periods which blanket the middle and northern parts of the great central valleys. Its climate, therefore, is largely continental. There are no large bodies of water, except for Lake Michigan, to influence general climatic conditions which very largely with latitude.

Temperature and precipitation. In the southern half of the state considerable irregularities in topography result in many local variations of temperature and precipitation. On damp, clear nights the numerous ravines and valley bottoms often experience considerably lower temperatures than do the slopes and summits of surrounding hills. The difference in spring and fall results in frost, and even damage from freezing, in the lower areas, while the higher grounds escapes harm.

There is a decrease in mean annual temperature and precipitation from north to south. There is also an occasional period of extreme cold during the winter season, although on a whole, the three winter months are characterized mainly by a mean temperature only slightly below the freezing point. A somewhat greater amount of precipitation occurs in the growing season in Indiana, although precipitation in general is fairly evenly distributed throughout the year. There are occasional droughts of considerable severity. There is seldom, however, a complete crop failure.

Frosts. The last killing frost usually occurs around April 15, in the extreme southern and southwestern counties. The date becomes later to the northward, as late as

May 10. In the south there is a large area where the last killing frost occurs between April 20 and 25.

The first frost occurs early in the Kankakee Valley and the extreme northeast, but southward the date becomes later rather steadily, occuring around October 20 along the Ohio and Lower Wabash rivers. The influence of Lake Michigan delays killing frosts until about October 15, around the Indiana shores.

Growing season and precipitation. The average growing season is a little more than 190 days in the extreme southern section, decreasing to about 150 days north to the Kankakee Valley and the northeast. Around Lake Michigan the average is 170 days.

The entire state is well-watered. The percentage of annual precipitation received during a growing season increases from 51 in the extreme south to 57 in the extreme north. This is in reverse of the south-to-north decrease in precipitation for the entire year, and it is probably due largely to the greater frequency of the storm movement to northern Indiana during the season when the Sun is north of the Equator.

Snowfall is heavy in the north, again due to the influence of Lake Michigan. An annual snowfall of 50 inches is not uncommon. Southern Indiana receives far less than the north, about 15-16 inches per year. The state's average is 23 inches. Almost all moisture is drawn from the Gulf of Mexico, with little being received from the west, north, or south. The average annual temperature is about 52 Fahrenheit. July is the hottest month, with an average around 75 F; January is the coldest month, with an average around 30 F.

FLORA AND FAUNA

Indiana has no clearly defined floral and faunal zones. The climate is nearly uniform, and there is no transition from mountain to lowland or from seacoast to interior. Indigenous plants and animals are distributed fairly evenly throughout the state. The Ohio River area in the south and the lake and marsh regions and the dunes in the north are

Geographical Configuration

the most differentiated areas. Most of the plants in these regions, however, can be found elsewhere in the Hoosier state, and even in the whole north central area of the United States. A few plants are restricted to a particular habitat. The persimmon, for instance, is found only in the marshy lowlands of the Ohio River. The black gum tree and the southern cypress are likewise limited to the Ohio's bottomlands.

The marshlands. Years ago, the world "discovered" the northern Indiana swamps (long since cleared and drained) through Hoosier authoress Gene Stratton Porter's novels of the Limberlost. At that time, trees characteristic of the marshy lands were the tamarack and bog willow. Interesting and now rare carnivorous plants abounded; the pitcher plant and the round-leafed sundew could be found in sunny glades of the swamps. The pitcher plant has a deep-purple blossom and cylindrical leaves, or pitchers, which hold water into which unwary insects are lured and absorbed. The round-leaf sundew exudes a sticky fluid onto its leaves which in turn trap insects that are held until the leaves fold over and the insect's body is digested.

Floating pondweeds, bladderwort, and water milfoil are common water plants in the swampy areas. Before the marshes were drained, crops of cranberries and blueberries were raised there. Only peppermint remains as an important product.

The dunelands. This area fosters a wide variety of plant life that is now part of Indiana Dunes State Park. The region has been the focal point of the efforts of conservationists who want to save it from invasion and destruction by industry. The recently developed Indiana Dunes National Lakeshore and an adjoining state preserve cover a total area of 8,700 acres of rare duneland habitats. More than 1,000 species of flowering plants, ferns, and cacti thrive on the sandy slopes and intervening marshlands. White pines and many species of oak are there as well as the jack pine and arctic lichen. Tulip trees, sour gum, and paw paw grow in profusion, and the prickly pear cactus coexists alongside the iris.

Other plant life. Charles C. Deam, former Indiana state forester, lists 134 species of trees in Indiana, 124 of which are native. Prominent among them are the oak, black maple, beech, sycamore, and the tulip tree, the latter of which is also the state tree. Several species of fruit trees are also common, among them the apple, cherry, pear, and peach tree. A beautiful specimen, the golden raintree was brought from China and first planted in New Harmony. It blooms with large cascades of yellow flowers.

Deam lists 163 species of shrubs, including vines. All but one, the Japaneses honeysuckle, are native to the state. Summer, fall, and spring arrivals are the lupine, the rue anemone, pussy willows, jack-in-the-pulpit, and violets. Transition into summer brings the ox-eyed daisy, pink clover, and Queen Anne's lace. The colorful fall with its many-hued trees is further accented by the goldenrod, aster, and sunflower.

Animal life. Indiana is rich in mammals, birds, and fish. Deer have increased and many of the smaller animals such as the rabbit, muskrat, raccoon, woodchuck, opposum, mink, and squirrel are hunted. There are plenty of fish in lakes and streams, including the catfish, pike, pickerel, bass, and sunfish. In addition, several species of blind fish inhabit the subterranean waters of Indiana's cave region, although they are becoming rare.

In the north, near Lake Michigan and the dunes, birds from the far north, the plains, and the deep woods, still roost and rest on their migratory routes. Waterfowl and marsh birds are plentiful south of the dune region and to the Kankakee River. Fish duck, teal, the American golden-eyed duck, mallard, great blue heron, American bittern, and the wild goose are probably the most common species found in these areas. Yellow-winged sparrows and the prairie larks have become endangered species.

In the southeastern part of the state, just north of the Ohio River, are found the Cape May warbler, summer redbird, and black- throated blue warbler. They can be seen nesting in the surrounding oak, maple, and gum trees.

Many orchard and meadow birds are found in the heavily farmed central part of the state. These include the field sparrow, yellow warbler, orchard oriole, robin, and meadow swallow. Winter residents include the junco, shore lark, tree sparrow, sapsucker, white snowbird, snowy owl,

Geographical Configuration

and several species of waterfowl. During very mild winters, some robins, meadow larks, and woodpeckers remain all season. In all, 48 species of birds are native to Indiana.

WILDLIFE AND FISH

The natural habitat for game disappeared as the state underwent economic development through the decades. The situation became so intense that hunting areas available to sportsmen were lost at a rate as high as 200 square miles per year. Encroachment of urban areas into open country and the construction of interstate highways were principal factors in crowding out animal life. North of Indianapolis, for example, huge areas have been engulfed by housing developments. In addition, modern agricultural methods and decreased pasture land have discouraged wildlife. To offset this environmental devastation, the state took constructive measures to provide new habitats. By the mid-1970s, deer, grouse, rabbits, squirrels, and other animals could find refuge. Improvements included the clearing of areas in the forests, the preparation of waterholes, and above all, the encroachment of farmers to increase wildlife on their land.

Restocking the land with vanished and vanishing species of animals has also been effective in making Indiana again a game area. Wild turkeys, deer, and pheasant have proven to be exciting game to hunters. Quail is the most common game bird, while in the north hunters find ducks and geese plentiful. The Fish and Game Division has supervised hunting for the greatest good.

Some 1,000 natural lakes scattered throughout the state, along with man-made lakes, offer opportunity for fishermen. Some of these small bodies of water are on state-owned property where the Fish and Game Division can exercise direct control. A number of fish hatcheries not only provide stock for the lakes and ponds, but serve as a means of selecting the most suitable species of fish for an optimum catch. The most plentiful species attracting sportsmen include bass, catfish, pike, pickerel, and sunfish. The annual purchase of about 750,000 fishing licenses attests to the popularity of sports fishing among Hoosiers and out-of-state fishermen.

Activities of commerical fisheries are limited almost exclusively to the Ohio and Wabash rivers and the Indiana waters of Lake Michigan. Mussel shells from the Wabash River constitute the greatest harvest, but buffalo fish, bullheads, and catfish are the dominant species of fish in the total catch.

WATER AND HYDROELECTRIC RESOURCES

Indiana has an abundant supply of water. The annual average of precipitation ranges from around 32 inches in the north to 46 inches in the south, with a mean of about 40 inches for the state as a whole. Each inch of rain falling within Indiana's boundaries totals more than 632,000,000,000 gallons. A significant proportion sinks into the ground to moisten the soil or is pumped up from wells for domestic use or to water livestock. The remainder, comprising approximately one-third of the total rainfall, known as runoff, drains from the land into rivers and streams. From it an estimated 8,600,000,000 gallons a day is withdrawn for industrial use, mostly for steam electric utilities. Municipalities take about 500,000,000 gallons a day for general use.

As is true throughout the eastern half of the Midwest, precipitation in Indiana from year to year is fairly regular. The maximum generally falls during the warm months when evaporation is highest and the minimum, including snowfall, when loss by evaporation is low. Nevertheless, there are problems of localized floods and drought which disrupt the agrarian economy. Farmers frequently grumble about the lack of enough rain for a good corn crop, or about an overly wet season which jeopardizes their harvest. Erratic climatic behavior, however, has never approached proportions such as those of the Dust Bowl disasters of the Great Plains to the west. The Ohio, Wabash, and White river systems are all subject to high water and flooding, but only in the southern part of the state, especially along the Ohio, are floods of great magnitude common. Because the boundary between Indiana and Kentucky follows the north bank of the Ohio River, Hoosiers do not necessarily con

Geographical Configuration

sider it "their" river, as they do the beloved Wabash, which sweeps through most of the length of the state.

The state's river systems. Indiana lies within two contrasting drainage basins. In the northeast drainage is northward, terminating in the Great Lakes and ultimately the Atlantic Ocean. This watershed, even though significant in the state's hydrological pattern, only covers about three percent of Indiana's territory. Virtually all of the remainder of the state drains into the Gulf of Mexico by the way of the Ohio and Mississippi rivers. A very small section in northwestern Indiana drains directly into Lake Michigan through a series of creeks and ditches. The divide between the two major watersheds is almost imperceptible. In the days of canals and barge traffic, before the railroad era, continous waterways were opened across this divide. One important link connected the Maumee and Wabash rivers near Fort Wayne, and allowed traffic to pass between Lake Erie and the Mississippi.

Two of the state's principal rivers that drain the more northerly drainage basin over short distances are named St. Joseph. One passes through South Bend and crosses the boundary into Michigan, while the other enters the state from Ohio and joins the St. Mary's in Fort Wayne to form the Maumee.

By comparison, the more southerly drainage basin has several rivers that flow long distances in the state and critically influence its economy. Foremost, the Wabash rises in Ohio and forms a great arc in north-central Indiana before flowing south along the western edge of the state to join the Ohio. Next in importance, the White River rises near the Ohio boundary and passes through Indianapolis before joining the Wabash in the southwest near Princeton. In the northwest the Kankakee River and its tributary, the Iroquois, drain a rich corn-growing area, the water eventually reaching the Mississippi via the Illinois River. Although Kentucky, Ohio, and Pennsylvania have great cities on the middle and upper courses of the Ohio River, Indiana has none.

Hydroelectric potential. It is unfortunate that the absence of any high or sharp relief in this well-watered area limits the number of sites suitable for dams. The highest elevation of 1,285 feet occurs along the Ohio boundary, while the lowest point of 313 feet is located at the juncture of the Wabash and the Ohio rivers. From Layfayette in the north to the mouth of the Wabash, a direct distance of 200 miles, the river drops less than 200 feet.

Such gentle gradients explain in large part the lack of opportunity to install power-generating plants with a strong capacity. Of Indiana's 61,674,000,000 kilowatt-hours generated in 1972, only 385, or 0.625 percent, were classfied as hydroelectric, an insignificant proportion. The little that was produced by running water came largely from the southeastern part of the state along the Ohio River and from the west-central region along the Wabash.

Sub-surface water supplies. An important source of water for homes and farms throughout most of Indiana lies beneath the land surface. Especially in the north, where thick layers of glacial drift were deposited during the Ice Age, ground water is trapped in porous layers known as aquifers. With a thickness averaging about 125 feet in depth, the glacial drift may be trapped by wells to supply water for homes and farms. The glaciers did not reach the south, but glacial outwash from the north was deposited in the southern valleys. Two large areas, one in the southwest and one in the north-central part of the state along the Wabash and White rivers, have unusually fine underground strata which hold copious quantities of ground water easily tapped by drilling wells. These sources especially enhance development of the rural landscape.

Water quality. Indiana has quality as well as quantity in its water resources. In the northern glaciated part of the state, the water analyzes favorably, except that it is "hard," a characteristic not good for some purposes but preferred for drinking and cooking. Artesian springs, thought to have had mineral properties of therapeutic value, led to the opening of several spas in the 19th century. The best known and only spa remaining in the late 1970s, French Lick, became an all- year health resort and convention center. In Indiana's early history the spot had been a salt lick for animals and an 18th- century French trading post. In its heyday, French Lick was a Midwest version of elite Saratoga Springs, New York, and Bedford Springs, Pennsylvania.

Geographical Configuration

NATURAL RESOURCES

Any inventory of Indiana's natural resources would reveal a bountiful land. Environmental advantages have led to a stirring economic development and the casting of a solid society symbolic of an American heritage at its best. A limited number of basic resources are found in great abundance, supplemented by a scattering of others. For example, limestone suitable for construction purposes is virtually inexhaustible, while much needed petroleum is in relatively short supply.

Among the 50 states, Indiana ranks about 25th in the production of minerals. The state's forests include hardwoods of high quality, but the production of sawtimber is not great. Even without mountains, seacoasts, or other spectacular physical features, the Hoosiers can still boast of scenic beauty and outdoor recreational features that attract tourists from other states.

Forests, minerals, plentiful water, and wildlife all play major roles in Indiana, not only from an economic point of view, but also because they have a dynamic effect on state politics and contribute to the social well-being of the state's inhabitants.

Coal

Without a doubt, coal is the most basic natural resource associated with the economic development of the United States. Although not known as a "coal state," Indiana has had a remarkably strong record in the production of this mineral. Nearly 1,500,000,000 tons of it have been dug out of the ground by the late 20th century. Of the national production of 595,000,000 short tons of coal, some 26,000,000 or 4.5 percent, came from Indiana mines by the 1970s. This proportion accounted for the state ranking seventh in the country in coal production during that time. By comparison, West Virginia, the foremost coal-producing state, yielded 24 percent of the nation's total in the same period.

Coal constitutes Indiana's most valuable mineral resource. Its impressive reserves are part of the vast deposits reaching from Ohio to northern Missouri through Indiana and Illinois. Coal beds, for the most part lying near the surface, extend through about 6,500 square miles, or 18 percent of Indiana's total area, and amount to untold billions of tons.

Problems of coal mining. All coal mined is classified as bituminous. Of the total state production, more than 90 percent comes from strip mining. This method, suitable to these vertical dimensions, was first practiced in the area in 1866 at Danville, Illinois. In Indiana, the thickness of the coal seams generally ranges from 24 to 57 inches, with some measuring as thick as 82 inches. An overburden, varying from 15 to 97 feet in thickness, must be removed as part of the mining operation. In the early days, this overriding material was removed by horse- drawn plows and hauled away in carts and wheelbarrows.

By the mid-20th century, the operation became much more sophisticated, utilizing elaborate machinery capable of rapidly tearing the earth away from large areas and scooping up the coal. Modern equipment has included power shovels, draglines, front-end loaders, and huge scrapers. Some power shovels have a capacity to lift more than 50 cubic yards at a time. One dragline removing overburden can handle 145 cubic yards, or 215 tons. Most of the coal is transported from the mines by rail and water, with a smaller amount hauled by truck. About one-eighth is converted into electric power near the mine site. In instances where coal is more deeply imbedded in the earth, underground methods are employed. Here the coal seams vary from 71 to 81 inches in thickness, requiring shafts and tunnels and mechanical loading.

Strip mining takes place almost exclusively in the southwestern part of the state, parallel to the lower course of the Wabash River, in the rolling or hilly lands between Terre Haute and Evansville. More specifically, almost all of the mines lie in Warrick, Pike, Sullivan, Greene, Vermillion, and Clay counties, with Warrick County outdistancing all others in production. Coal from underground mines comes from the same general area, with Sullivan County the leading producer.

The problem of strip mining is all the more critical because of the nature of the operation. Initial investments are

Geographical Configuration

relatively low, since tunnels and shafts are unnecessary and movement of the coal is easily performed. Thus, strip mines, unlike underground mines, can be readily put into operation, and companies can go out of business without losing great investment in installations. For example, in one recent year, six new strip mines were opened and ten were abandoned. Control under these circumstances by regulatory methods have often been difficult in the face of slow-moving legislative processes.

Control of strip mining. Areas once subjected to strip mining are rendered useless unless conservation methods are applied to restore the land to productivity. Soil horizons, which have taken centuries to develop by the processes of nature, disappear or are disrupted to the point where they cannot support crops. Indiana residents place much emphasis on preserving their environment, counter to the success of strip mining enterprises. As a result, attempts were made in the Indiana legislature to abolish, or at least control, this particular industry. Quite understandably, political impasses arose between commercial companies engaged in strip mining and those interests--whether government agencies or environmentalist groups such as the Sierra Club--dedicated to preventing the land from being despoiled.

The first strip mine reclamation program is claimed to have taken place in Indiana, where peach and pear orchards were planted on mined land in 1918. Another solution has been to replace the overburden. The process of reclamation on slopes has involved contouring, which reduces the destructive effects of erosion. Much progress has taken place in lessening the ravages of tearing the earth open. The Indiana Coal Association reported that, in recent years, more than 156 square miles had been reclaimed. The principal method was that of afforestation: more than 53,000,000 trees were planted on 113 square miles. Other areas were seeded, while still others were converted into lakes. In these reclamation projects, 8.5 square miles were incorporated into state forests, 23 square miles converted into recreational areas, and 5 square miles utilized for private homes. These statistics testify to some success by the people of Indiana through decades of effort toward controlling the disposition of their land.

With the advancing importance of petroleum in the mid-20th century, the coal industry has become down-graded. Indiana was especially hard hit because the quality of its product was only fair at best, and did not measure up to that of many of the other producing regions in the country. The world crisis in petroleum and domestic shortages of fuel which took place in the 1970s, however, helped the coal mining industry take on some new life.

Production and uses of Indiana coal. Consumption of coal in Indiana, before the energy crisis caused by a worldwide shortage of petroleum, approached 60,000,000 tons, or well over twice the figure of production. Of the total consumption, only 44 percent came from mines within the state. Another 40 percent originated in West Virginia and Virginia. Western Kentucky and Illinois also furnished substantial amounts, while smaller quantities were brought in from Pennsylvania, Montana, and Wyoming. Despite the necessity to import coal from out of the state to meet the demand, almost one-quarter of Indiana's production in turn found its way to other states, especially those nearby.

The preponderant amount of Indiana's coal is used for the generation of electrical energy and heat. Although Indiana coal is not of the type to convert into coke for use in the mammoth iron and steel industry, the state stands as the second largest coke producer in the nation after Pennsylvania. In more recent times, a total of 13,800,000 tons of coal - all of it shipped in from other states - was carbonated to produce 9,100,000 tons of coke. Nearly 93 percent of the coke production was consumed by the steel industry in producing pig iron and steel.

Natural Gas. In the late 1880s and the 1890s, great deposits of natural gas were opened up in a broad area northeast of Indianapolis known as Trenton's Field. Based upon this cheap and seemingly inexhaustible source of energy, numerous industries sprang up in Indianapolis, Muncie, Marion, Anderson, and other cities. By 1902, however, gas lights no longer lit up the sky because judgment had been bad and deposits ran out. Some cities, such as Muncie, developed a sufficient industrial base to survive

Geographical Configuration

the collapse. It might be argued that the famous Indianapolis Speedway and its annual 500-mile automobile race originated because of natural gas. The nearby speedway was built for testing and racing cars and continued to operate with fanfare until the annual race became a national tradition.

When natural gas deposits became more limited, it no longer ranked as a prime resource in the state. Some of the old wells served as storage reservoirs for supplies imported from other states, while other reserves were known to be trapped in association with coal and petroleum formations, requiring more complex and costly methods of extraction. A small production persisted, but was insignificant compared to the former blazing glory of the late 19th century. Production by the 1970s had reached about 350,000,000 cubic feet, nearly all of it coming from two gas fields, one located in an area roughly outlined by boundaries forming a triangle with the angles at Muncie, Kokomo, and Marion, the other located near Connersville in Fayette County. Indiana has belatedly adopted some of the country's most enlightened regulatory measures to control the industry and insure conservation.

Petroleum. Crude petroleum came into production as natural gas declined. Deposits were discovered in the gas fields, but the principal region lies in the southwest in the same general areas as the producing coal mines. Posey, Gibson, Pike, Knox, Vanderburgh, and Green counties had a preponderant proportion of production, although some continued to come from the old natural gas region northeast of Indianapolis. Oil in the southwest counties was discovered between 1940 and 1960, largely accounting for a total of 4,379 individual wells, producing a little more than three-quarters of one percent of those in the United States.

By the late 1960s, the wells were producing about 11,500,000 barrels per year, but this figure dropped to about 6,000,000 barrels before the middle of the next decade, or 0.2 percent of the national total.

Most of the production came from the older wells, but exploratory wells were constantly being drilled. In 1971, for example, among the hundreds of wells drilled, 14 new ones were successively brought in; by 1972 there were 11 new wells. Estimates of proven reserves appear to vary from year to year as geological surveys are made. The Bureau of Mines reported 29,000,000 barrels of reserves in 1972, as compared to an estimated 30,000,000 barrels estimated the year before and 66,000,000 in 1960. Given the rate of production, the state was concerned that underground sources would soon run dry unless geologists discovered new proven resources.

The demand for petroleum in the state continues to be much greater than the supply. Its refineries have been capable of distilling more than 500,000 barrels of crude petroleum per day. As in the case of coal, Indiana industries must look to other states for a substantial proportion of this fuel.

Indiana lies at the heart of a great national network of pipelines that transport crude petroleum, refined oil products, and natural gas. For petroleum, the major lines cross the central part of the state in the west-southwest/east-northeast direction and others focus on the Chicago area, including the industrial cities in northwestern Indiana. Pipelines carrying natural gas form a trellis-like network, the more important lines paralleling a diagonal connecting the southwestern and northeastern extremities of the state.

NON-METALLIC MINERALS

Indiana is favorably endowed with several minerals that extend through vast expanses of its territory. Others are found sparingly in isolated deposits.

Limestone. Probably the most notable nonmetallic resource is limestone, which holds high rank among the state's natural resources, both because of its abundance and because of its many uses. It is considered to be an almost inexhaustible resource. Although the principal deposits are in south-central Indiana, much of the entire southern part of the state is underlain with limestone. Nearly all of the quarries are concentrated in Lawrence, Monroe, Franklin, and Rush counties. Contrary to what might be expected, the preponderant proportion of all limestone quarried is crushed and statistically reported as crushed stone. Of this, nearly

Geographical Configuration

two-thirds is used as foundation or paving material in the construction of highways and roads. Other uses are for manufacturing concrete aggregate, portland cement, and ballast. By weight, only some three percent of the limestone produced in the state comes under the category of building stone, but it is the substance for which Indiana has long been famous. Known as dimension stone, it is quarried for use as building blocks or as slabs to veneer other types of building material. Fine in quality, it is especially good for foundations and walls where a high polish is unnecessary. In addition, as a building stone it is strong, easy to carve, and does not split when cut. It is second only to marble in the designing of architecturally attractive construction, and has dominated in the U.S. building stone market for more than a century. In fact, more than 80 percent of the country's production of dimension stone has come from Indiana, most of it from the great quarries in Lawrence and Monroe counties, where Bedford and Bloomington are centers of the industry.

Much of the stone is quarried around the small city of Oolitic, just north of Bedford, so named for the grainy texture of the limestone. In 1920s, when the industry was at its peak, huge blocks of stone were stacked to heights of 50 to 75 feet, awaiting shipment to cutting mills. Because of competition with concrete, glass, and metal in modern building construction, however, the state's building stone works have declined in importance since the mid-20th century. On a much smaller scale, sandstone and marl, also found in quantity in Indiana, provide stone for construction purposes.

Sand and gravel. Production of sand and gravel ranks a close second in value to stone among Indiana's mineral resources (excluding coal). Deposits exist throughout the state and are commercially exploited in as many as 80 counties, annual production generally exceeding 20,000,000 tons. Each of six counties--Hamilton, Madison, Marion, St. Joseph, Switzerland, and Tippecanoe--normally produce more than 1,000,000 tons. More than half of the total production goes into road building materials, and one-third is used in the building industry. The remainder mainly provides fill material and railroad ballast, or serves as an important ingredient in the manufacture of glass.

Clay, lime, and gypsum. Like those of sand and gravel, deposits of clay are widely scattered over the state. Production takes place in some 20 counties, of which Morgan, Clay, Clark, and Parke provide more than two-thirds. Morgan County alone, just southwest of Indianapolis, accounts for 30 percent. Clay may be of innumerable varieties, depending upon its resistance to heat, presence of impurities, and other characteristics. Most of the types found in Indiana are used in the manufacture of building blocks, portland cement, and items such as sewer pipes, drain tiles, conduits, roofing, and ceramics. One type, known as fireclay, is especially adapted to the fabrication of floor and wall tile, terra-cotta, refractories, and some kinds of pottery. Perhaps clay is the most versatile mineral resource found in Indiana, its uses ranging from a soil type conducive to vegetative growth to the manufacture of highly decorative glazed tile for fancy architectural design.

Lime, a product not industrially associated with limestone or crushed limestone, has special significance in Indiana industry as a flux in iron and steel-making processes. It is used in oxygen, open hearth, and electric arc furnaces. Small amounts also serve to purify water. Virtually all of the lime produced in the state comes from Lake County in the immediate vicinity of Gary, East Chicago, and other iron- and steel-producing cities. As one of the largest consumers of lime and only a small producer of it among the states, Indiana must import much of its supplies.

Indiana ranks high in the country as a producer of gypsum, most of which occurs in underground mines in Martin County in the southwest. Other deposits, particularly the huge one in La Porte County, have been but little worked in recent years. Most of the production of gympsum is used in making wallboard, lath, sheathing, other items of the building industry. A smaller proportion is converted into land plaster for agricultural use.

Other minerals. A few other minerals are of minor importance. Abrasives are quarried in Orange County for making whetstones. Peat, burned as fuel in early years, is now obtained from bogs in the north as peat moss, used primarily for soil improvement and potting soils. It also pro

Geographical Configuration

vides a substance for packing flowers, and can sustain earthworm culture.

BIOLOGICAL RESOURCES

Forests . When the first settlers filtered over the Appalachians in the early 19th century, they found in the Midwest an environment rich in biological resources. Indiana, located in the heart of this pioneer land, was seven-eighths covered with fine stands of timber and inhabited by a variety of wild animals. The broadleafed deciduous forests contained hardwoods such as ash, beech, black walnut, elm, hickory, maple, oak, sycamore, and yellow poplar. Through them roamed deer, bear, elk, wildcats, and timber wolves, not to mention the small fur-bearing animals that had previously attracted French trappers. Early accounts of animals in the region refer to "The Old Buffalo Trail," a route beaten through southern Indiana from Illinois, leading to salt licks in Kentucky. Part of the route is now followed by U.S. Highway 50, which crosses the Wabash River in Vincennes.

Exploitation of the forests. Trees and wild animals offered very little in the way of a livelihood for the breed of settlers who were to become Hoosiers. The land was cleared of forests to make way for crops, and wood was used for housing and fuel. In the process, animals were recklessly killed off or routed. Modern conservationists may look back upon this period as one of environmental devastation, but at the time it was the only logical means of developing the area. With the coming of industry, sawmills increased so rapidly that, by the late 19th century, more than 1,000,000 board feet were produced annually. From 1880 until the end of the century, trees were chopped down until the forests approached extinction. Only 1,500,000 acres remained, about 6.5 percent of the original stand when the white man entered the area with his broadax less than a century before.

The seriousness of the situation was realized and, in 1898, the Indiana Forestry Association was founded and a forestry management program put into operation. In 1919, this organization was merged with others concerned with resources to form a state Department of Conservation. Many reforms have been effected since, including reforestation and the preservation of existing forest lands.

To make the program as effective as possible, the state was divided into 11 forestry districts, each receiving guidance by specialists in conservation methods. As a result, forests generally now grow more timber each year than is cut. Some inequalities remain, however. For example, the black walnut, one of Indiana's finest woods, has been over cut. Also, trees in some of the present growth may not be of the high quality of the original forests. Finally, statistics show that in some years the removal of sawtimber has exceeded annual growth, reflecting the incomplete control of conservationists.

Contemporary conditions. By the mid-20th century, forests covered slightly more than 4,000,000 acres, or a little more than one-sixth of the state's total area. The Department of the Interior estimated that of all forest lands in Indiana, about one-half could be classified as sawtimber and another one-third as pole-timber. Seedlings and second growth occupied the remainder. The great majority of all forests are in private hands. Some 70 percent was held by 100,000 farmers in wood lots for lumber, fence posts, fuel, and other products of value in a rural area. In addition, Hoosiers look upon trees as an aesthetic part of any farm, a tradition inherited from their forefathers. The remainder of the privately owned forests belonged to various organizations or individuals, such as sawmill operators and coal companies, or were on estates. Only seven percent of the state's forest lands were government-owned, either national or state.

The U.S. Forest Service manages some 214,000 acres, including a national forest of 137,000 acres in the south-central part of the state southeast of Bloomington. In turn, the Indiana Department of Natural Resources controls the remaining forest in the public domain, having created a number of state forests. Of the total area in the state, only 58,000 acres have been excluded from cutting in an attempt to preserve the small proportion of remaining virgin stands of timber. Some 130 different kinds of trees have been scattered throughout the state, of which 30 were introduced since the early 19th century. More than two-thirds of the

Geographical Configuration

forests are in the southern part of the state, partly because the northern region offers better agricultural opportunities.

The extent of Indiana's use of its forestry resources, while locally significant, compares poorly with that of Oregon, one of the more richly endowed states. A production of 351,000,000 board feet of sawtimber in 1970, for example, appeared ridiculously low when measured against the 9,700,000,000 board feet produced in Oregon the same year. The Oregon cut, however, was from coniferous, or softwood, trees as compared to Indiana's choice hardwoods that are especially useful as a high-grade building material and in the manufacture of chairs, desks, and other furniture.

OUTDOOR RECREATION

Natural vegetation accounts for much of a state's scenic beauty, which in itself may be considered a resource. In addition to the satisfaction of aesthetic beauty, an appealing landscape featuring trees and foliage produces revenue as a recreational area. Forest management has included this aspect in its program of setting aside and maintaining state parks with facilities for family fun and relaxation.

Tourism. Indiana lies remote from the many national parks and coastal features in the western and eastern parts of the United States. Therefore, an attractive natural environment such as the rolling hills decked with colorful vegetation, the narrow valleys, and the rock-faced cliffs in the limestone countryside of the southern area, have proved popular for in- state vacations. Visitors by the thousands come to the area each year to enjoy the outdoor delights of swimming, fishing, boating, hiking, camping, or just taking it easy under a benevolent Hoosier sun. Facilities for these privileges spring not only from state-sponsorship, but private entrepreneurs as well. All are dependent on a soft and enchanting landscape closely tied to the traditions of the people who have fashioned their "homeland" through multiple generations.

Indiana's state parks. Of the state parks, four are especially noteworthy. Foremost, Brown County State Park has attracted much attention because of its deep gorges and valleys cut by streams and its superb recreational facilities such as bridle paths, hiking trails, and bow-and-arrow hunting grounds. Largest of the parks, it is located near Nashville, and about 45 miles south of Indianapolis. Turkey Run State Park in Parke County, McCormick's Creek State Park near Spencer in Owen County, and Spring Mill State park near Mitchell in Lawrence County reflect the Indiana countryside at its best. Altogether, more than 30 sites have been classified as state parks, memorials, and recreational areas. In addition to specific parks, the southern Indiana landscape offer scenic drives which are appealing to residents of the somewhat monotonous glacial plains of the northern part of the state. Winter sports enliven recreation in the northeast when the myriad of small lakes freeze over from December to March.

The Indiana Dunes. The Indiana Dunes along the shores of Lake Michigan are by far the leading attraction for the nearby metropolitan area of Chicago. Unique in the entire country, the dunes contain one of the most varied plant collections in the world, with species ranging from Arctic bogs to tropical orchids and examples of wetland as well as desert environments. The Indiana Dune State Park was established in 1925, comprising 2,182 acres along the immediate shore front. An ever-expanding industrial complex on the west, however, threatened the natural setting of the park by polluting the air and water and encroaching land use. In 1966, after a long fight by conservationists, the Indiana Dunes National Lakeshore was authorized, adding another 8,720 acres which enveloped the original state park on its land sides.

PRE-HISTORY

Sucessive groups of Indians lived in Indiana prior to the arrival of the white man in the 17th century. They belonged to many archaeological stages -- Paleo-Indian Stage, Archaic Stage, Woodland Stage, and Late Prehistoric Stage -- and many cultures - - Indian Knoll culture, Adena culture, Hopewell culture, and Mississippi culture.

PALEO-INDIAN STAGE

Indiana remains an anomaly as to the exact time when Paleo- Indians inhabited this area. Radio-carbon dating of sites and classification of fluted arrow and spear points found throughout the state suggest that the region was probably inhabited 20,000 years ago. Little is known about these Paleo-Indians, except that they were probably nomadic hunters of the then plentiful bison, mammoth, and mastodon. The Plleistocene ice sheet was in a recessional stage. As the ice melted, early man followed the animals which lived on the tundra ice fringe. When the animals became extinct, the nomadic hunters moved on and the last traces of them disappeared around 5000 BC. Replacing them were the more sedentary and agricultural people of the Archaic Stage.

ARCHAIC STAGE

The earliest inhabitants of the Indian Knoll and Glacial Kame cultures of the Archaic Stage lived in Indiana beginning around 7000 BC. The stage includes hunting and gathering cultures which preceded the introduction and development of agriculture and ceramics. The stage is characterized by full exploitation of the environment. The Indian Knoll culture is named for a site in Kentucky and began about 500 BC. The Glacial Kame culture has been found in northeastern Indiana.

Subsistence activities. Subsistence activities increased as these people became increasingly familiar with local environments. There is evidence of fishing, and taking of shellfish, and of hunting. Archaic peoples also gathered wild plants, nuts, berries, and seeds. Agriculture was unknown, and the dog was the only domesticated animal.

Technology. As changes occurred in subsistence activities, so did changes occur in technology. Artifacts include stone projectile points, knives, scrapers, and bone fishhooks. As time went on, atlatl weights, grinding stones, and woodworking tools were added to the inventory. The atlatl, consisting of a wooden shaft tipped with a socketed antler hook, became the principal weapon. It was, in essence, a primitive spear thrower.

Settlement patterns. Villages were placed along river banks on top of refuse shell mounds. Discarded shells of river clams and other garbage was thrown on the floors of the shelters or on the ground outside. Over a period of time, the garbage pile became a huge mound of clam shells, animal and bird bones, and other refuse. The villagers continued to live on top of the mounds in shelters resembling arbors. The shelters were covered with skins and thatching.

Religious and aesthetic activities. Ceremonialism surrounding death and burial is well represented during the Archaic Stage, and the Indian Knoll and Glacial Kame cultures were no exception. Indian Knoll dead were placed in circular burial pits with the skeletons usually flexed. Sometimes red ocher and other offerings were placed in the graves. The inclusion of dog skeletons with those of the humans suggests that the Indian Knoll peoples held this animal in high esteem. Glacial Kame dead were buried in pits and the bodies were usually in a flexed position and accompanied by grave goods. The development of art and aesthetics is evident. Clothing was ornamented with snail-shell beads, and necklaces of shell beads, bone beads, and perforated teeth were worn. The principal articles of clothing were woven breechcloths and skin robes.

WOODLAND STAGE

Adena culture. The Adena culture was in existence from 500 BC until shortly after the beginning of the Christian era in the central Ohio Valley, including Indiana. Adena is the major Ohio Valley representative of the Early Woodland Stage which arose from the Archaic Stage. During the Early Woodland Period, there was a gradual introduction of early domesticated plants, ultimately derived from Mesoamerica. Burial mounds were constructed as monuments and cemeteries for the dead.

Pre-History

Settlement patterns. Most Adena people lived in villages, although a few rock shelters have been found. The houses were generally round and about 25 to 30 feet in diameter, with walls made of paired sapling poles placed in the ground and slanted outward. The most conspicuous architectural features of Adena are large conical burial mounds of earth, usually in groups, although single mounds are not uncommon.

Burial characteristics. The corpse was normally buried in a subfloor pit or the floor of the mound. The dead were usually either extended or flexed, although disarticulated bundles also occur. Cremations were normal and burials were accompanied by grave goods such as tubular pipes, bracelets, beads, celts, and adzes.

Subsistence activities. Adena people depended on hunting, fishing, collecting, and cultivation for their livelihood. Nuts, seeds, wild plants, and berries were gathered, and some gourds and squash were apparently raised. Cultivated plants were not a significant part of their diet.

HOPEWELL CULTURE

Although southern Ohio was the center of the Hopewell culture, there were subsidiary centers in Indiana, Illinois, Michigan, Pennsylvania, New York, Tennessee, Wisconsin, Iowa and Kansas. The Hopewell culture was largely responsible for the legend of a "mound builder" race that preceded the Indians in North America. Archaeological investigations, however, have shown this to be a myth. The culture was evidently at its height about 100 AD.

Hopewell mounds. The large conical burial mounds and the earthwork patterns continue in the Hopewell culture. The earthen mounds are, however, larger than those of Adena time. The mounds show an elaborate cult of the dead, evidenced by rich funerary offerings. Excellent examples of these mounds can be found near the bluffs overlooking the White River in Mounds State Park near Anderson, Indiana. Hopewell mounds tend to be two- stage. The first stage is essentially a low platform prepared to contain a single log tomb or a series of crematory basins. The burials are generally accompanied by tools and elaborate ornaments. The second stage, or mantle, is applied so that the final earthwork is a conical mound of earth as much as 100 feet in diameter and from 10 to 70 feet high. Since archaeologists have not extensively explored Hopewell village sites, concentrating instead on mounds, little is known of their subsistence activities.

Aesthetic activities. Hopewell artisans were superior in their craftmanship. Earspools, head and breast ornaments, bracelets, rings, and panpipes were made of copper. Mica sheets were cut into head dresses, delicate ornaments, and geometric designs. Conch shells were carved into bowls, beads, and gorgets. The craftmen also made stone platform pipes decorated with naturalistic animal and human sculptures.

Much of the Hopewell pottery was standard Woodland -- conchoidal in form, with a wide mouth, the surface roughened with cord paddle, and grit-tempered. A small but distinctive percentage was used in their burial ritual; it was quite ornate and unique. Common designs were the raptorial duck and bird, along with a variety of geometric and cursive elements.

LATE PREHISTORIC STAGE

The Mississippian Period. The Mississipian Period of Indiana was classified into Upper, Middle, and Lower units, with the Upper Mississippian culture predominating. Although the period began around 500 AD, it seems to have reached its zenith about 1400 AD. The Fort Ancient and Tennessee-Cumberland variants (c. 1400-1650) of the Upper Mississippian Period are clearly evident in the mound structures along the Ohio River and in the lower Wabash Valley.

Fort Ancient variant. Habitation sites of the Fort Ancient culture near the mounds are large, and the great accumulation of debris attests to the sedentary and agricultural nature of the inhabitants. Although these people used burial mounds, shallow earth-and-stone lined graves have been substituted in many instances. The pottery of this group is distinctive, being unpainted to tan, gray, black, or reddish-brown. The jars and vases are characteristically squat and globular with rounded bottoms, broad mouths, and equipped with strap handles. These early artisans were also fond of working in bone. Stone tools were rarely used.

Tennessee-Cumberland variant. The Tennessee-Cumberland variant is primarily developed in Posey, Sullivan,

Pre-History

Knox, and Vanderburgh counties in southwestern Indiana. Terraced, flat-topped mounds are characteristic of this culture, which also was sedentary and agricultural.

The houses were built of wattle work and cane and mud combinations. They used copper for both tools and ornaments. Stone, especially flint, was utilized for both tools and weapons.

Merom of the Wabash River. The site contains a three-sided defensive enclosure measuring 2,450 feet in circumference. Within its confines are 5 mounds and 45 pits.

Conclusive evidence is lacking that these mound builders were ancestors of the Miami Indians which lived in Indiana in pioneer days. It has definitely been shown, on the other hand, that they are not the ancestors or descendants of the Aztecs. They were, in point of fact, the first true Indiana Indians.

INDIANS OF EXPLORATIONS

There was considerable movement of Indians in Indiana during the 17th and 18th centuries. The three most important historic tribes were the Miami, Potawatomi, and Delaware. Many lesser tribes such as the Kickapoo, Mascontin, Piankashaw, and Winnebago coexisted with the others, but played a minor role in shaping Indiana's history. Limited information is available because the Indians lacked a written language prior to the arrival of the French and English in the 1600s.

THE MIAMI INDIANS

The Miamis lived mainly in northeastern Indiana in the upper Wabash, Mississinewa, and Saint Joseph river valleys. Their headquarters were at Kekionga (present-day Fort Wayne). The claims of the Miami to aboriginal occupancy were most clearly set forth by a famous leader of the tribe, Little Turtle, but his claims are uncertain, as it appears that several other tribes, including the Kickapoo, Potawatomi, and Huron lived there at the same time. The language of the Miami was Algonquian, but varied in dialect from neighboring tribes who also spoke the same tongue.

Subsistence activities. The Miami led a semisedentary life, had fixed villages, but lived away from them on the hunt. Their staple crop was corn, which was supplemented by wild roots, tubers, pumpkins, and beans. They depended largely on hunting and fishing and ate all manner of wild fowl except raven, crow, and loon.

Social structure. The Miami Nation was divided into ten groups or gentes, each bearing a designate name such as Turtle, Snow, Moon, or Raccoon. A member could not marry within his own gens but had to take a mate from one of the others. Personal names of members of each gens usually contained a reference to the gens designation. Each Miami village was headed by several officials. Men as well as women could serve as village funcionaries. In addition, there was a male civil chief, a female civil chief, and several lesser officials. Traditionally, female officials held less power than their male counterparts.

Little Turtle. Perhaps the most influential of all the Miami leaders was Little Turtle. This great war chief was able to keep the nation strong and unified in the ensuing battles which took place in the 1700s between his tribe and the Americans. Until 1794 he was able to keep his lands from falling into enemy possession, but that year he met with disaster at the Battle of Fallen Timbers. Although he fought a savage battle against General "Mad" Anthony Wayne and his soldiers, his defenses were finally weakened and he was forced to withdraw his people from their land. Following a subsequent treaty in 1795, the Miami managed to live for 15 years in relatively peaceful coexistence with the Americans. In the final analysis, they had been reduced to 1,100 in number.

THE DELAWARE INDIANS

The Delaware Nation lived in the wide valley between the Ohio and White rivers, having been pushed westward in the 1770s by white settlers who claimed their lands. Although written records are sketchy, the tribe managed to keep an account of its wanderings from early times by means of pictographic paintings on sticks. A Moravian mission was established among them in 1801. Its aim of converting them to Christianity failed and the mission was soon abandoned. The Delaware left Indiana in 1818, releasing their lands on the White River to the United States. At that time they numbered about 800 people.

Pre-History

THE POTAWATOMI INDIANS

The Potawatomi tribe was the largest one in Indiana even though it had been the last one to cross its borders. By 1800 the Potawatomi had numerous settlements in northern Indiana from the Kankakee River all the way East across the state.

Social structure. As with many other tribes, the Potawatomi were divided into gentes. In addition to the gentes, they were also divided into two moieties (halves) designated as either Oskush or Kishko. The order of birth of children in a gens predetermined to which moiety each would belong. The eldest child always became part of the Oskush moiety. Traditionally, the Oskush moiety contained the warriors.

WESTWARD MIGRATION OF INDIANS

With the Potawatomi, the migration of Indian groups to Indiana ended. The advance of white settlers brought the usurpation of Indian lands, and most of the Indians had crossed west of Mississippi by 1838. Only a few scattered Miami remained behind. Today, except for a few musical place names like Kokomo, Maumee, Mississinewa, and Wawasee, rare traces of their vanished life remain.

THE FRENCH PERIOD

The first white men to enter Indiana were probably French Jesuits who came in hopes of establishing missions and converting the Indians to Christianity. The first white man to actually explore Indiana was Robert Cavalier Sieur De La Salle who crossed the Saint Joseph-Dankakee protage near South Bend. Two years after his discovery of the portage on December 3, 1679. LaSalle returned to the site to sign a treaty with the Miami Indians. Overly ambitious and demanding, LaSalle was assassinated in 1687 by one of his subordinates.

Early settlement patterns and Indian conflicts. By this time, white infiltration was pretty well established and the first permanent settlement, Ouiatenon (Lafayette), was begun in 1720. Kekionga (Fort Wayne) and Vincennes followed. Vincennes became the largest and most powerful settlement of the French occupancy. Much of its historic past is still preserved today. The quest for furs became the primary goal of the French. The Indians around Kekionga and Vincennes were invited to trade their pelts in exchange for whiskey and tools. Many, because of a large illiteracy rate, were heavily shortchanged or cheated by their so-called white friends. The alliance held, in spite of that problem. The Miami Nation was party to the frontier holocaust on June 21, 1752 which grew into the eleven-year French and Indian War, so named because the French and Indians allied themselves against the British, who were now beginning to take over Indian lands and the fur trade. The Indians developed a growing dislike for the British who earlier, unlike the French, had refused to bring gifts to the tribal chiefs. Indian hostility toward the British continued to grow throughout the whole Northwest Territory.

Treaty of Paris. An Indian war instigated by Pontiac, chief of the Ottawa Nation, broke out in 1763. The fury of Indian attacks upon the British were in vain against the powerful enemy garrisons, and on February 10, 1763 the Treaty of Paris was signed, ceding all French land holdings to Great Britain. Under the treaty, the British attempted to pacify the Indians and to secure the profitable fur trade. The Indians were subsequently made wards of the British government and were granted all the land located between the Alleghenies and the Mississippi River. This action also served to keep out land-hungry white speculators and homeseekers from the American colonies. Avarice of the colonists for the rich lands of the Ohio Valley and the equal determination of the Indians to hold on to them were prime factors of the Revolutionary War which followed. The Indians, who previously had been enemies of the British, now either supported and fought with them against the Americans or remained neutral.

George Rogers Clark and Indiana's part in the Revolution. Indiana entered the conflict in 1778 when Virginia dispatched young Colonel George Rogers Clark and 200 men on a secret expedition to capture and hold territory which Virginia claimed under its colonial grants. Clark was able to take Fort Sackville at Vincennes in a bloodless strike in July, 1778. A local priest, beloved by the town residents, arranged for the coup when the French militia, who held the fort for the British, turned it over to Clark.

Pre-History

Unfortunately, Governor Henry Hamilton, the British commander at Detroit, recaptured Vincennes the following year. Hearing of this development, Clark returned in February, 1779 with 130 men, made an incredible 18 day journey through 240 miles of drowned, ice-laden swamplands in the dead of winter, and launched an attack on Vincennes. Taken by surprise and having underestimated the size of Clark's army, Hamilton formally surrendered. The flag that Clark subsequently raised was the first American flag ever seen on Indiana soil. Hamilton was sent to Virginia as a prisoner. George Rogers Clark became a hero of the Revolution.

Peaceful beginnings in the Northwest Territory. Warfare continued intermittenly until 1783 when, under a second Treaty of Paris, the Northwest Territory, which included Indiana, was added to the United States. Clarksville (q.v.), first American settlement of the Territory, was founded by George Rogers Clark's former soldiers. It was here that Clark himself established his residence and built a saw-and-grist-mill. In the next few years townships and towns were planned, laid out, and populated throughout the entire Territory in hopes of an orderly settlement. The former backwoods empire became the "public domain", and in 1787 Congress adopted the ordinance which would provide for a legal government of the Northwest Territory.

HISTORY

The first white men to set foot in Indiana were French Jesuits. By the first half of the seventeenth century, French colonies in the St. Lawrence Valley had been founded and firmly established, and the French began to push westward into the unknown country beyond Lake Erie. The Jesuits, who hoped to build missions and convert the Indians to Christianity, took the lead in this move. Along with them were representatives of the government of New France, who were interested in the Indian fur trade, in reported copper mines, and in the great western river which the Indians had told them was the "Father of Waters." They believed this river might be the long-sought outlet to the Pacific.

However, neither the Jesuits nor the traders were primarily interested in the territory which later became Indiana. Father Marquette may have crossed the dune country of northern Indiana in 1675. His successor, Father Allouez, almost certainly followed the St. Joseph Valley in his wanderings. But the French were seeking Indian villages, and in the last half of the century, Indiana was practically deserted.

The English also hoped to profit from the fur trade and to counteract French influence in the interior. They encouraged the powerful Iroquois nation to go on the warpath against tribes of the Great Lakes region. If any Indians had inhabited the Indiana area before this time, they probably retreated to escape the attacks of the better-armed and better-organized Iroquois.

The Iroquois onslaught temporarily forced Indiana Indians from their traditional homes. It was the first move in the French-British rivalry that was to shape the development of the Northwest for 100 years. France formally took possession of "the West" at Sault Saint Marie on June 14, 1671, in a ceremony designed to impress the Indians.

Less than three months later, English explorers held a similar ceremony on the headwaters of the Ohio, and took possession of the interior in the name of Charles II, the King of England. These ceremonies meant less than nothing, since neither nation had even a faint idea of what "the West" was, but they symbolized the opening of a struggle that was to continue until the close of the French and Indian War in 1763, when England gained sole title to the Mississippi Valley.

The first white man who actually explored the Indiana region was Robert Cavelier, Sieur le la Salle, a French fur trader and traveler. He advocated building a series of forts from Lake Ontario to the mouth of the Mississippi to protect the western Indians against Iroquois raids.

FRENCH EXPLORERS DISCOVER INDIANA REGION

On December 3, 1679, La Salle and a party of explorers ascended the St. Joseph in canoes until they reached the south bend of the river, where the city of South Bend now stands. The next day, they portaged across to the Kankakee River and continued their journey down the Kankakee toward the Illinois.

La Salle came again to the south bend in the spring of 1681, holding a council with the Miami and Illinois Indians under the great tree known later as the Council Oak. In the next few years, he explored the Indiana region extensively. Though his attempt to form an anti-Iroquois confederacy was not altogether successful, by 1700 the Iroquois joined with other tribes in signing an agreement to live at peace. Soon thereafter, the Miami and other tribes reoccupied the valleys of the St. Joseph, the Maumee, and the Wabash. La Salle died in Texas in 1687, but his dream of a chain of protective forts was later carried out by the governors of New Frnace.

After the Indians returned to Indiana, many fur traders arrived to offer trinkets, whisky, and blankets in exchange for pelts. Licenced traders, or *voyageurs*, traveled with a permit from the king; wandering smugglers, or *coureurs de bois*, also ventured into the wilds to pick up what trade they could, but when they returned to Canada, they were sometimes arrested as outlaws.

By 1720, dozens of French traders had filtered into Indiana. They were scattered for the most part along the Wabash and its tributaries, since Indian villages were most numerous there. For 40 years, French policy in the west

History

was dominated by a determination to protect their traders against English competition, and to keep open the vital Wabash-Maumee line across Indiana, an all-important link between Lake Erie and the Mississippi.

To this end, three principal forts were established in the Indiana region: Fort Miami, Fort Ouiatenon, and Fort Vincennes. The forts were part of the chain envisioned 40 year earlier by La Salle. Stretched from Detroit to New Orleans, they were the first permanent white settlements in Indiana.

Authorities differ on which of the forts is oldest, for there is no conclusive evidence of the dates of their founding. However, it is likely that a military post was established in 1720, on the site of the Indian village at Ouiatenon, four miles below the present city of LaFayette. Fort Miami, at the site of Fort Wayne, may have been built even earlier, because in 1722, a new fort was constructed there. Neither of these forts became stable white settlements with real community life, and after the French were driven out, they reverted to the Indians.

DEVELOPMENT OF COMMUNITY LIFE

Vincennes alone was a permanent community. There is considerable dispute about the date of the founding of this post, which grew into a beautiful town of great cultural and historic interest. Important church records found by Bishop Brute indicated that both the town of Vincennes (not then known by that name) and the church of St. Francis Xavier were in existence as early as 1708. And letters written by French commanders and traders in 1720, 1724, and 1725 indicate that settlers had arrived before 1727, and that a fort was already built by 1732.

Vincennes was named for the French officer in command during the early period, Francois Morgane de Vincennes. During the next fifty years, Vincennes became a trading post and a center of French life. Here lived the Catholic families from Canada, some belonging to the gentry, many of them sturdy peasants, conservative and law-abiding. They lived in whitewashed log houses on narrow streets, built picket fences around their orchards and gardens, and cultivated long, narrow plots with wooden plows. Their houses were one-story, four-room cabins, with dormer windows and porches, furnished with homemade rustic furniture, Indian mats, and sacred pictures.

Social as well as religious life centered largely in the Church. On feast days and Sundays after mass, there were visiting, dancing, and cards, and the priest was often present. Mardi Gras brought its feast and dancing and contests. Sugar- making time was a season of great merriment. There was a good deal of hard drinking at taverns, and gambling and cockfighting were popular sports. Such characteristic French gaiety was misunderstood by English visitors. George Croghan, an Indian agent who spent many years in the region, reported that the inhabitants were a "parcel of French renegadoes, worse than the Indians."

BRITISH AND FRENCH TRADERS VIE FOR GOODS

Croghan's remark was probably inspired by British rivalry. Although English traders were in the region from the beginning, for many years they were outstripped by the French in the struggle for furs. They were handicapped in their dealings with the Indians by their feeling of arrogance and racial superiority, while the French laughed, played, and even intermarried with the Indians, imposing on them no racial discrimination.

However, by the middle of the century, two important factors began to tip the scales in British favor. First, the English were willing to give the Indians firearms, a practice which French policy had always opposed. And, even more important, the English, because of superior manufacturing and shipping methods, could pay higher prices for furs and charge lower prices for whisky, cloth, and other trade goods than could the French.

The outcome of the struggle, however, was not determined in the Indiana region. On the high seas, in the remote valleys of India, and on the battlefields of Canada, French and British imperialists came to blows. By the Treaty of Paris in 1763, the French agreed to give up the western territory to the English. French garrisons were to be withdrawn and the posts delivered over to the English as soon as possible.

History

INDIANS UPRISE AGAINST BRITISH DOMINATION

But the English had reckoned without the Indians, who hated them and regarded the French as their friends. The arrogance of British traders soon brought Indian hostility to a head. Under Pontiac, chief of the Ottawa nation, the Senecas in the east and the Ottawa-Ojibway-Potawatomi confederacy in the west joined forces in 1763 in a mighty uprising to drive the English out of the territory forever.

From May 1763 to August the following year, the region from Canada to the Ohio was ravaged by bands of Indian warriors, who butchered garrisons at Sandusky, Fort. St. Joseph, and Michilimackinac. In Indiana, Pontiac's men forced Lieutenant Jenkins and the Ouiatenon garrison to surrender and destroyed the post. At Fort Miami, they murdered Ensign Holmes and most of his company.

But the fury of Pontiac's army dashed itself in vain against the palisades of Detroit, which received English reinforcements on August 1764; the troops were able gradually to restore peace throughout the territory. In the fall of 1764, Colonel Bouquet set out from Fort Pitt with a strong army. By threats and a show of force, he compelled the return of 206 white prisoners, many of whom had been held in Ohio and Indiana. For a time, the power of the Indians was broken.

Now masters of the Northwest, the British attempted to pacify the Indians in order to secure a profitable fur trade. Even before Pontiac's war, the king had issued the Proclamation of 1763, ceding to the Indians the land "beyond the heads of the Atlantic rivers." The Proclamation was an effort to win Indian friendship by adopting the former French policy of trading rather than settlement.

Shrewdly recognizing the superior power of the new English government, the Indians joined forces with British fur traders and soldiers in a common hostility toward the pioneer, the growth of whose farms and towns threatened hunter and trader alike. For a time, except for an influx of lawless elements and squatters, the immigration of land-hungry settlers was checked.

Because it was considered a part of Louisiana, the post at Vincennes had not been turned over to the English. In

1765, General Gage sent George Croghan to conciliate the Indiana Indians. They made one mistake, however. They failed to establish any civil government in the territory north of the Ohio, a region not included in any of the provinces formed by the Proclamation of 1763. They even failed to send a garrison to the Wabash forts, with the result that Fort Miami and Fort Ouiatenon ceased to exist, and the stockade posts at Vincennes rotted down and disappeared.

Vincennes became more and more lawless, overrun with drunken Indians and arrogant traders. In those days, French and English suffered together, and discontent was acute.

NORTHWEST FRONTIER DEVELOPS

For ten years after 1763, wealthy colonists of Virginia and Pennsylvania moved intensely into the Northwest. Various land companies were formed, which vainly petitioned for land grants from the crown. Although a few British statesmen saw the need for a farming population to support the garrisons and to furnish a wider market for British manufactures, most royal governors opposed any move that would encourage settlement.

Meanwhile there was unauthorized purchase of land from the Indians, unregulated fur trade, and absence of any protection for property or lives.

The Quebec Act of 1774 was an effort to bring order out of chaos. Placing the Ohio Valley under the jurisdiction of the Province of Quebec, the act promised the region a stable government and pacified the French by protecting their religious and civil law. Before it could be given a fair trial, however, the American Revolution changed the entire situation.

At the outbreak of the American Revolution, there was no English garrison in Indiana. Throughout the Northwest, however, the English were contending with the Americans for Indian friendship, and encouraging them to make punitive raids upon pioneer settlements. In Detroit, Governor Henry Hamilton became so notorious in his bargains with the Indians for American scalps that he won the unpleasant title of "hair buyer."

History

Early in 1777, Hamilton sent Lieutenant Governor Edward Abbot to Vincennes to rebuild the fort and organize the French and Indians for an attack on the frontier. The Indians were willing, naturally enough, since American settlement meant ruin for them. But the French were not eager to join their recent enemies against the friendly pioneers. Abbot returned to Canada in 1778, leaving Vincennes without a military command.

British influence succeeded in stirring the Indians into many savage outbreaks during 1777, long remembered as the "bloody year." Terror hung over the West, the frontier was in a fever, forts and blockhouses were hastily constructed.

During that summer, George Rogers Clark, a militia officer who represented the county of Kentucky in Virginia's legislature, learned through spies that English forts at Kaskaskia and Vincennes were poorly guarded, and that the people of those towns were not devoted to the English. Seeing clearly that the colonies were unsafe as long as the English held the frontier forts, Clark hastened to lay his plans before Governor Patrick Henry. After a conference at Williamsburg, he was commissioned to raise an army to capture the Northwest, which Virginia claimed by her charter of 1609.

In May 1778, Clark and his band of 175 frontiersmen started down the Ohio to the mouth of the Tennessee and struck across country to Kaskaskia, arriving July 4, 1778. The town and fort fell without a struggle, and the French helped to take other posts along the Mississippi. Having won the good will of Pierre Gibault, an influential priest, Clark sent him to Vincennes (which was now without an English garrison) to explain the Treaty of Alliance recently made between France and the United States. Father Gibault was trusted and beloved, and the inhabitants of Vincennes soon raised the American flag, with Clark's best officer, Captain Leonard Helm, in command of the fort.

But the news of Clark's victories finally reached Detroit, and in December 1778, Hamilton arrived with 600 men and recaptured Vincennes. He repaired Fort Sackville and kept a small garrison. Supposing himself safe from attack during the winter months, he dismissed most of his soldiers until spring. News of this folly would not have reached Clark but for the heroic journey of Francis Vigo, a rich trader of Vincennes, who fled in a canoe to Kaskaskia with the news.

Clark was in a difficult position. The spring would undoubtably bring revenge and victory to Hamilton, as soon as his scattered soldiers and Indians reported for duty. On the other hand, the wilderness was grim and almost impassable during the winter months.

Clark gathered together 170 French and American volunteers and set out on the long march of 240 miles in the dead of winter. Across icy swamps and flooded rivers, the men marched to reach Warrior's Island, just out of Vincennes. Here they sent a message to the citizens, warning them of the attack and urging friendly Americans to stay quietly in their homes. By the time Clark's men had surrounded the fort in the darkness, and were ready to attack, they had received dry powder and supplies from the town's inhabitants.

Wholly taken by surprise, the British tried to retaliate, but their cannon did no damage in the darkness. The frontiersmen were deadly marksmen and, with the coming of daylight, rained a hail of bullets that silenced the artillery of the fort. On February 25, 1779, the garrison surrendered. Fort Sackville became Fort Patrick Henry. Protected by Virginian arms, 20,000 settlers poured into Kentucky during the next two years.

Clark's exploit seriously crippled the British rear attack upon the settlers for the rest of the war. Undoubtedly, it also had much to do with England's surrender of the lands west of the mountains in 1783. For a time, Virginia claimed the territory, but under the stress of revolutionary conditions, it proved as incapable of governing it as the British had been. In 1784, recognizing the need for a stable government in what had become a lawless region, the Old Dominion relinquished its title. The backwoods empire became the "Public Domain."

CONTINENTAL CONGRESS ADOPTS ORDINANCE

In 1787, the Continental Congress enacted the famous "Ordinance for the Government of the Territory Northwest

History

of the River Ohio." Embracing the present states of Wisconsin, Michigan, Illinois, Indiana, Ohio, and part of Minnesota, the Territory was to be ruled by a govenor and three judges, who were to adopt laws and enforce them. The ordinance prohibited slavery, encouraged public education, and guaranteed religious freedom and civil rights to all the people.

The first governor, General Arthur St. Clair, was a veteran of the American Revolution. The seat of government was established at Marietta, Ohio. Within a year after the Territory was organized, 20,000 home-seekers came down the Ohio.

Settlers had been coming for the past 20 years, drifting down the great river in flatboats. At first, every settler built his own crude boat, a cabined raft with a long oar for a rudder. But as the flow of colonists increased, a class of professional boatsmen developed. A robust breed of drinkers and brawlers, the river boatsmen had to be skillful enough to combat the elements-- ice, sandbars, and rapids-- and brave enough to fight cutthroats, robbers, and Indians. Many pioneer families owed their safe arrival to the resourcefulness of the river guides.

After 1787, the influx of colonists thoroughly alarmed the Indians, who still had the support of the British. In defiance of the Treaty of 1783, British traders had not given up their posts and forts and were still scattered here and there, slyly suggesting that England would continue to protect the Indians if they fought bravely against the American invaders.

INDIAN RESISTANCE ESCALATES

The first task of the new government was to "pacify" the Indians. In 1789, Congress authorized St. Clair to call out the militia of adjoining states whenever necessary. But at first, he sought to quiet the Indians by peaceful means.

In the spring of 1790, Antoine Gamelin, a Vincennes trader who knew the Indians well, was sent to the Wabash country with a message of friendship. The older warriors listened, but the young braves spoke of the British commander at Detroit. Gamelin returned to Vincennes with his mission a failure.

St. Clair then determined to strike the Indians so ruthlessly that they would never again dare to launch another war party. Three military expeditions were hurled rapidly against the most powerful and influential tribes in the Territory. In October 1790, General Josiah Harmar destroyed the deserted Maumee towns, but suffered two severe defeats, the second in the hands of Little Turtle, the ablest war chief of the Miami. In the spring of 1791, President George Washington sent General Charles Scott into the Territory to quell disorder by destroying the Wea towns near the present site of LaFayette. When Scott's troops returned, St. Clair sent the Kentucky milita, under General James Wilkinson, to overthrow the Eel River Miami. The outcome of this effort, however, was the wanton destruction of the Indians' corn crops. Expeditions such as this only enraged the Indians, and provoked further destruction.

The Indians' ruined crops and flaming villages forced them into the Wabash confederacy, led by the Miami, which also included the Lake Indians. The allied tribes had already killed hundreds of settlers.

Late in the autumn, St. Clair himself set out with an undisciplined expeditionary army. As the troops moved toward Miami-town, they were unaware that an Indian army was stalking them. Near the headwaters of the Wabash, on the morning of November 4, the Indians gave the war cry to signal an attack. The regular troops held firm, but suffered a crushing defeat by Little Turtle. St. Clair and his shattered troops reached Cincinnati on November 8, 1791.

This disaster forced President Washington to send General Anthony Wayne to the troubled West. Wayne realized that the end of these struggles would require a decisive defeat to the Indians. He drilled an army for more than a year and, early in 1974, marched boldly through Indian country and built Fort Greenville, Fort Defiance, and Fort Recovery. The hostile tribes fell back before him, watching eagerly and vainly for a chance to surprise his army.

By this time, Little Turtle saw that defeating this "army that never sleeps" would be far more difficult than scattering the troops of Harmar and St. Clair. He counseled his people to accept Wayne's offer of a peace treaty. The Wea had already concluded such a treaty. But the Miami, still

History

under British influence and confident from their victories, remained unyielding. The fact that Governor Simcoe of Canada had built them a fort at the Maumee rapids, and supplied them with arm and ammunition, made them believe they were protected.

A short distance from the fort at Maumee was a dense forest strewn with fallen trees, an excellent spot for ambush. Little Turtle determined to wait for General Wayne here, and in the ensuing Battle of Fallen Timbers, the Miami confederacy met its doom. In the early morning hours of August 20, 1794, the American army approached in battle formation. As soon as scouts located Little Turtle's warriors, Wayne's men charged with bayonets and close rifle fire. The army drove the Indians from their position and scattered them through the dense woods. The fort did the Indians little good, for the Americans got there first as well.

Although actually fought on the soil of what is now Ohio, this battle proved an important event in Indiana history. The allies of the Miami, worn out and convinced that further resistance was futile, went home to their own hunting grounds. After destroying all the propery in the area--both Indian and English--Wayne marched up the Maumee (ravaging as he went), to the confluence of the St. Mary's and St. Joseph rivers. Here he built Fort Wayne, then returned with his army to winter quarters in Greenville. Defeated, robbed of their grain, broken in spirit, the Indians subsisted that winter on British charity. One after another, Buckongahelas, Blue Jacket, Little Turtle, and other chieftains visited Wayne and promised to come to a council to be held at Greenville the following summer.

TREATY CEDES INDIAN LANDS

They kept their word. In August 1795, the Treaty of Greenville, ratified by tribal chiefs, ceded much of what is now Ohio to the settlers. Only a narrow strip of eastern Indiana was at that time opened up for settlement, but the Indians promised to cease their war parties. It now seemed certain that peace would prevail on the frontier. British agents, for the most part, withdrew to Canada, where they continued their agitation against the United States.

Peace prevailed for about 15 years, and settlers kept pouring in. In 1800, however, there were only 50,000 whites in the whole Northwest Territory, and about 45,000 were in Ohio. In that year, William Henry Harrison, the Congressional delegate from the Northwest, secured passage of a bill which split off Ohio and created Indiana Territory, embracing the present states of Wisconsin, Michigan, Illinois, and Indiana. Vincennes became the capital, and President Adams appointed Harrison the first governor.

In 1805, Michigan was separated from Indiana Territory and, in 1809, Illinois Territory was formed, which included all the western region; Indiana was reduced to its present area.

The first ten years of Governor Harrison's reign was peaceful. However, frontier govenment was difficult. The settlements had to be defended; the problem was solved by the militia, and every able-bodied man was involved. Laws were adopted and enforced, at first by the governor and three judges, later by a council of elected delegates. Indians had to be protected from dishonest traders. Efforts were needed to regulate the whisky traffic.

Slavery also presented a problem. Forbidden by the Ordinance of 1787, the institution was still approved by most of the early settlers. In 1805, the judges and the governor adopted a law allowing masters who owned slaves to make an agreement with them for lifelong slavery. Thus, the machinery of civil government was set in motion.

More important than civil government was the perennial Indian problem. By a treaty in 1784, the Ohio River had become the Indian boundary. But by 1795, aggressive squatters had scattered over Ohio and penetrated Indiana. Beyond the new boundary set by the Treaty of Greenville, however, the Indians were the legal owners of most of Indiana. Only a few patches of land had been granted to the whites: small tracts at Fort Wayne, Ouiatonon, and Vincennes, and 149,000 acres at the Falls of the Ohio, known as Clark's Grant. In these areas lived a few hundred settlers, surrounded by Indians who outnumbered them many times over.

History

The situation was tense when Harrison arrived early in 1801. Indiana Territory looked rich and promising to many veterans of the American Revolution, who were not inclined to honor the land claims of a few "miserable savages." Hundreds of squatters entered southern Indian land in open defiance of the Treaty. Unless a solution could speedily be found, another Indian war was inevitable.

To restrain and dam the tides of immigration in the East and preserve the wilderness empire of a few thousand primitive people was inconceivable to the settlers. Governor Harrison therefore resolved to purchase southern Indiana from the Indians, and take their lands by legal means. Before the close of 1809, in a series of questionable triumphs, he won most of the southern third of Indiana. The Treaty of Fort Wayne was ratified on September 30, 1809 by chiefs of the Miami, Wea, and Delaware. By the agreement, Harrison bought (for $10,000 and a small annuity) 3,000,000 acres of land between the Wabash and White rivers. The northern boundary of this purchase was the famous "Ten O'Clock" line, so-called because the Indians insisted the line be determined by the shadow cast by the sun at 10 a.m. on the day the treaty was signed.

INDIAN CONFLICT INTENSIFIES

But Indian resistance was growing. Although Little Turtle counseled the Indians to face the inevitable, live amiably with the white men, and learn their ways, younger leaders believed the counsels to be a bitter mockery. Among the dissenters were the Shawnee brothers, Tecumseh and the Prophet.

The dissenters' theory was simple. If the Indians were to survive, they had to avoid the white man's whisky and degenerate ways, and return to their ancestral mode of life; they must not sell any more land, for the land belonged to all in common.

This theory of "cultural conservatism" was the contribution of one-eyed Laulewasikau, known as the Prophet. A man of great physical strength and oratorical ability, he was a strange mixture of savagery and gentleness, chicanery and apostolic fervor. He rekindled the ancient flame of Indian religion, thus creating an emotional unity to the scattered peoples his brother attempted to lead. Tecumseh was also remarkable, a fearless, upright, generous man who had a deep love for his troubled race, and an unusual grasp of the necessity for political unity and cooperation among the scattered Algonquian tribes.

The confederation of the Shawnee leaders sought for an agreement of all the tribes not to sell any more land. But the tribal chieftains hated to give up, even in the face of a common threat, their traditional rights to sell land and make treaties. The Shawnee were a refugee tribe, they argued, who had no real claims to the territories the Indians were selling. Shawnees had no right to dictate to the ancient owners of these lands. The Treaty of Fort Wayne was a repudiation of Tecumseh by these cheiftains.

Meanwhile, Laulewasikau built a village on the north bank of the Wabash, near the mouth of the Tippecanoe. Known as Prophet's Town, this village soon became a rendezvous for discontented Indians from every tribe in Indiana who were breaking away from the chieftains and joining the Shawnee leaders. It was also a center of British influence, as the Prophet himself finally admitted.

During the winter of 1809-1810, feeling ran high among the Wabash Indians. Under Little Turtle, the Miami maintained an offical attitude of friendship throughout the troubled era; they had signed the Treaty of Greenville and sought to keep the faith. The Delaware also remained pacifists. But the Shawnee, Wyandot, Potawatomi, and bands of deserters from other tribes were in a state of angry unrest, threatening to kill the chiefs who had signed the Fort Wayne Treaty. As the mass meetings became more turbulent, Governor Harrison became more alarmed.

A grand council in the summer of 1810 proved futile. Neither Harrison nor Tecumseh would yield on the question of land sales. Later that year, Tecumseh went South in an attempt to enlist other allies in his confederacy. In his absence, Harrison received orders from President Madison to break up the Indian rendezvous at Prophet's town.

Tecumseh was gone an entire year before Harrison was able to set out. With an army of less than 1,000 men, with whom he intended to establish a post farther up the Wabash, he reached the highlands at Terre Haute on October 3, 1811.

History

He built Fort Harrison here, which soon became the target for Indian hostilities. A sentinel was shot, and frightened bands of Miami and Delaware came to protest their own friendship and to report that Prophet's Town was preparing for war. The reports offered Harrison the excuse he needed for a military invasion of Indian territory. On October 29, he began to march toward Prophet's Town.

As Harrison's troops neared the Prophet's stronghold on the Tippecanoe, Indian scouts began to hover threateningly on their flanks. When they were within a mile of the town, an Indian deputation came out and begged for a truce. After exchanging promisies that no fighting would be engaged until the following day, the Indians returned to Prophet's Town and Harrison led his army into camp.

Harrison was not deceived by the Indian's promise, and gave all necessary orders in anticipation of a night attack. In Prophet's town, the Indians were in turmoil. Women and children prepared to flee if the Prophet's counterattack should fail. According to tradition, the Prophet called his warriors together and brought out the magic bowl and others talismans to protect them against wounds and death. After war songs and dances, the Indians seized their weapons and rushed out to make the attack.

The Battle of Tippecanoe was begun before dawn on November 7, 1811. In a chilly drizzle, the two enemies fought in a deadly struggle. After heavy losses on both sides, the Indians broke and fled soon after daylight. Harrison destroyed Prophet's Town with all its supplies and made his way back to Vincennes.

Tippecanoe was a death blow to the Prophet's image. He had promised his warriors a magical immunity from wounds and death, but 38 were left dead on the field, and the number of gravely wounded was very great. His town on the Wabash was destroyed, and with it, the confidence Indiana tribes had placed on the Shawnee confederacy. The Delaware and Miami renewed their pledge not to fight the whites. When Tecumseh returned, ten years of work lay in ruins.

The Prophet did not lightly relinquish his hope for victory, however. Leaving the Wabash town, he started on a long tour among the Kickapoo, Potawatomi, and other Northern tribes. At the same time, relations between the United States and Great Britain were becoming more strained. Soon bands of the Indians began to raid areas of Chicago and the more remote Indiana towns, and the settlers retreated southward into more populous regions. In April 1812, Governor Harrison gave orders for the militia to hold themselves in readiness, and a row of blockhouses was built from Vincennes to Greenville.

British influence was still strong in Indian activity at the time. The British sought to create an Indian buffer state to the rear of the American colonies, a state which would be both highly profitable to English fur traders and an effective barrier to American expansion. Although many other factors also led up to the War of 1812, this aspect of British policy alone was destined to provoke armed conflict.

WAR OF 1812 DECISIVE IN NORTHWEST DOMINATION

War was declared in the summer of 1812. The first disaster took place in Chicago, when the commander of the fort evacuated under orders and attempted to march to Detroit. The garrison and accompanying civilians were captured and massacred, and Detroit itself was surrendered the following day. These events were the signal for a general uprising among the Indiana Indians. Even the Miami took the warpath, only a few in Little Turtle's village remaining friendly to the whites.

Tecumseh traveled from tribe to tribe, urging unified action. On September 3, in order to terrorize the border and, if possible, prevent a northward movement of troops, a small band of warriors attacked and massacred the peaceful Little Pigeon Roost settlement in the northern part of what is now Scott County. Two days later, an army of Indians and British attacked Fort Wayne, which held out desperately until Governor Harrison arrived with fresh toops on September 12. Meanwhile, Fort Harrison was attacked and partly burned by an Indian war party.

In retaliation, Harrison sent troops to destroy Little Turtle's town of Eel River, the Potawatomi village on the Elkhart, and the strong Miami and Kickapoo towns at the

History

forks of the Wabash. Their villages and granaries in flames, the Miami gathered in the towns of the Mississinewa. That December, they attacked with desperate fury another army that was sent out to destroy them.

This was the last real battle fought on Indiana soil. Except for petty raiding parties, the Indians were quiet in the next year. The settlers huddled in blockhouses until the militia restored order. But Indiana kept 4,160 men under arms in 1813, for home defense and for duty on the northern front.

Meanwhile the Indians, desolate after their bitter defeats, began to leave the Territory. Many bands of Miami and Delaware who had not taken a prominent part in the fighting fled into Ohio. The Shawnee, with most of the tribes that had followed Tecumseh and the Prophet, went to Detroit to place themselves under British protection. The British surrendered Detroit in September 1813. A few days later, Harrison defeated Tecumseh and the British general, Proctor, in the Battle of the Thames. Tecumseh was killed in the battle.

The war was over. After the Treaty of Ghent two years later, the British gave up hope of dominating the Northwest Territory.

TERRITORY SETTLEMENT EXPANDS

In the first year of the nineteenth century, there had been only about 1,000 people in Indiana, scattered along the Ohio River and the lower Wabash. In addition, there was a scattering of hunters and trappers. As newcomers invaded the region and found locations, they became squatters. When a land office was opened, they became settlers. Where they congregated, a simple beginning of government sprang up, and they became citizens. By 1813, with the exception of a small settlement up the Whitewater Valley, the frontier extended east from Vincennes to where Madison now stands. Further north, there were no whites except traders at Fort Wayne, Anderson, and South Bend.

From 1800 to 1813, Vincennes was the capital of Indiana Territory. By 1805, there were enough people in Indiana to elect a legislature under the terms of the Ordinance of 1787. When Harrison resigned the governorship in 1812 to take part in the war against England, the population had grown to nearly 30,000. Harrison was succeeded by John Gibson, secretary of the Territory and, in 1813, the capital was moved to Corydon, with General Thomas Posey as governor. By 1816, Indiana had reached a population of more than 60,000.

Land offices at Vincennes and Jeffersonville were besieged daily by dozens of new settlers, many of whom laid claim to the same quarter-section. Difficulties of administering the sale of land and dealing with the defeated Indians were strong arguments for Indiana's needing a stable government.

The Territorial legislature met in December 1815 and framed a petition for statehood. In April 1816, Congress passed the Enabling Act. The act designated May 13 as the day for an election of delegates to a constitutional convention. It would be the first time in the Territory's history that no property qualification would be required for voting. Under the terms of Ordinance of 1787, slavery had been excluded, but this question was controversial from the beginning. Most of the early pioneers came from the South, and resented the restrictions of the Ordinance. In fact, it was not until 1843 that slavery ended in Indiana; until then, many slaves were held under the fiction of "voluntary servitude."

Indiana delegates met from June 10 to June 29, 1816, in the old Statehouse at Corydon. They framed a constitution modeled closely after those operating in neighboring states. The document did contain one notable innovation, however. Acticle IX expressly recognized the State's obligation to educate all its citizens. In the August election, Jonathon Jennings was elected Indiana's governor. Congress formally declared Indiana a member of the Union on December 11, 1816.

The new State had many difficulties. Its comparatively small population was made up of poor farmers, with a sprinkling of tradesmen and artisans in Vincennes, Jeffersonville, Brookville, Madison, and other small towns in southern Indiana. There was little state revenue except for land tax, but settlers were exempt from this tax for five years after they bought their land from the federal govern-

History

ment. Two-thirds of Indiana was still wildnerness owned by the Indians, and it was deemed necessary to open up the central region of the State for further settlement.

In 1818, three commissioners, including Governor Jennings, met with Indian chieftains in St. Marys Ohio, and bought from them the entire central portion of Indiana. This territory, long known as the "New Purchase," was opened in 1820 and quickly settled. As soon as it was surveyed, the legislature appointed ten men to select a site for the permanent capital, for which purpose Congress had already granted Indiana four sections of government land. In June 1820, the commissioners selected a tiny squatter village where Indianapolis now stands. A city was laid out and settlers began to come in. By 1824, the seat of government was moved from Corydon and had established a temporary residence in the Marion County courthouse.

SETTLEMENT POPULATION MULTIPLIES

The population of Indiana in 1820 was nearly 150,000, and it continued to grow rapidly. Men, women, and children came into the state on foot, on horseback, or in wagons drawn by ox teams or horses. From the South, especially the North Carolina Piedmont, poured a stream of pioneers who were largely of English and Scottish origin. Between 1820 and 1840, many immigrants arrived from England, a band of Swiss founded Vevay on the Ohio, and a number of Irish laborers came to work on the Wabash and Erie Canal. Farmers and and small traders from New England, of English and Scotch-Irish ancestry, filtered into the northern section of Indiana. The influx continued for nearly 30 years.

Transportation at this time was so costly and difficult that pioneer families were forced to manufacture most of their necessities at home. Clothing was made almost entirely of furs and skins. But soon, linsey cloth took the place of skins and, by the 1830s, homespun dresses in summer and woolen shawls in winter were common. Shoepacks were worn in winter, but many went barefoot in the summer months.

By 1822, Indianapolis stores were advertising goods, including Eastern broadcloth, muslins, calico, hats, bonnets, shoes, silverware, tools, and glassware. Merchants were also selling tea, coffee, medicine, soap, tobacco, musical instruments, clocks, stoves, and plows. Those prosperous enough to buy these products were the envy of their neighbors. To the average farmer, however, even if his crops were abundant, such luxuries were unobtainable. Because wheat, corn, and hogs had to be transported a long distance to market, they were worth little in exchange for manufactured goods.

SOCIAL AND POLITICAL ISSUES DOMINATE

These factors determined almost all the political struggles in Indiana for nearly 20 years. Even in the era of so-called "good feeling" between 1816 and 1824, politics in Indiana revolved largely around the need for roads and waterways, although there was also considerable conflict from the poorer settlers concerning the policy of the federal government toward public lands. For those who bought their land on credit and found the payments difficult to make, Congress issued due bills to be used in future land purchases if the original holdings were lost.

After 1824, internal policies continued to focus on the need for roads and canals. Opposition came from people who were already well-located on navigable waters and objected to paying taxes for the benefit of less-fortunate citizens, but their objections were inevitably overruled.

Good roads were eventually built, making wagon transportation both less costly and less difficult. For many years, wagon travel made tavern-keeping profitable, and the most lively centers of social and political life were the houses of entertainment along all the principal highways. The first important road was the National Road (now US 40), which ran from Cumberland, Maryland to Vandalia, Illinois, crossing central Indiana from Richmond to Terre Haute. It was never fully improved by the federal government beyond Indianapolis, and the Indiana section reverted to the State in 1839. At one time, twelve stage lines operated over this road, and for two decades, it was a powerful factor in binding the East and West together.

The main north-south highway was the Michigan Road, extending from Michigan City through South Bend, Logansport, Indianapolis, and Greenburg to Madison. The north-

History

ern section of the route was obtained from the Potawatomi Indians in 1826. Poor as it was, this road carried heavy traffic in pioneer days, the inhabitants of 35 communities using it to reach Indianapolis. Other State roads were also built in this period, with money from the three percent fund provided by Congress from the sale of public lands. The available money, however, permitted only the clearing of timber, and roads were at times almost impassable.

With the growth of population and wealth, State roads improved and, in 1879, a system of free, tax-supported county roads was inaugurated.

The waterways were not neglected. In 1827, Congress granted Indiana a strip of land for the purpose of constructing a canal utilizing the Maumee and Wabash rivers. In 1836, Governor Noble signed the Mammoth Internal Improvement Bill, which appropriated $13,000,000 for three canals, two railroads, and various road improvements. The bill mortgaged the State for many years. Work on the Wabash and Erie Canal cost nearly $25,000,000 and continued until 1852. Its total length was 460 miles; 380 miles were in Indiana, and 80 miles were in Ohio. Although the canal was eventually completed and proved an important outlet to the East for northern Indiana, most of the projects undertaken under the Mammoth Bill were failures. Costly for such a poor and young State, graft and inefficiency only added to the financial disaster.

Work on the canals and railroads ceased in August 1839. Contractors who had put their money into the projects were forced to take huge losses, and laborers were deprived of their means of livelihood. Bondholders pressed for their money in vain; in 1840, the State debt was more than $13,000,000. In the meantime, a flurry of litigation arose as bondholders tried to realize something on their investments. They grouped together and hired a New York attorney, Charles Butler, to represent them. Butler conferred with a joint committee of the General Assembly, but was unable to find a solution for his clients for a long time. Finally, he succeeded in getting a bill through the General Assembly which provided that the unfinished railroads and canals be turned over to the bondholders, although the State did assume some part of the debt. This debt was not paid, however, and eventually the investors lost more than half their money. As late as 1871, the General Assembly passed a bill forbidding any payment of the debt.

POLITICAL CONTESTS SPLIT LOYALTIES

As Indiana citizens became more interested in the State's politics, they also became more involved in national politics, especially after the elections of 1824. A large proportion of early settles were mechanics or poor farmers from the East and South, enterprising persons who sought to better themselves in a region of cheap land and good opportunity, and who often went into debt to buy their 160 acres of uncleared forest. A majority of them were loyal to the Jefferson party. But another group of settlers had also come to Indiana: prosperous Quakers who left the South partly because they objected to slavery and partly because they could buy land less expensively in the new country; land speculators who had a ready supply of cash to enable them to amass a fortune in a few years; business people who saw a chance to make money in a region of rising values. As this prosperous group grew, it formed the backbone of the emerging Whig party in Indiana.

The first real political contest in Indiana was between supporters of Clay, Adams, and Jackson in 1824. Jackson opposed the tariff, which was blamed for the high price of Eastern goods. He also opposed the Bank of the United States as politically controlled and undemocratic.

When Adams was elected, in spite of opposition by a majority of frontiersmen, dissatisfied citizens in Indiana turned to the Jacksonian Democratic party. The principles of a wider democracy and more universal participation in government appealed to many of the settlers. By 1826, the Democrats had completed county and township organizations and most offices were in their hands.

For some years, Jacksonian Democrats were dominant; however, the Whigs' power grew steadily as the State's commerce and industry developed. After Jackson's political victories in 1828 and 1832, the Whigs began to search for a candidate who would appeal to the West as Jackson had. In 1836, they chose William Henry Harrison, who had spent much of his life on the frontier. But, with Jackson's influence, Martin Van Buren was elected.

Still, the Whigs had gained power in Indiana. And, in 1840, with Van Buren and Harrison again the candidates, the Whigs won national success.

RELIGIOUS COMMUNITIES ORGANIZE

In Indiana's early period, religion was an important factor. The first preachers were circuit-riders who held camp meetings in fields encircled by tents and wagons. Before long, meeting houses were built, and stable religious communities developed. The communities founded and supported academies and colleges, and exerted a restraining influence against the taverns.

Baptists were the first Protestant group in the State; in 1801, they organized their first church. The Indiana Baptist convention met in 1833, and in 1837, the Indiana Baptist Manual Labor Institute--now Franklin College--was opened. Shortly after the Baptists, Methodists began to organize, and became the most popular religious group in Indiana. They founded Indiana Asbury College, now DePauw University, in 1837.

The Presbyterians came to Indiana from Kentucky. The group was small, but members were generally prosperous. They founded Hanover College in 1827, and Wabash University in 1832. Charges were made that they sought to dominate higher education, and other denominations founded their own colleges to offset Presbyterian influence.

Other fairly large religious groups in Indiana were the Disciples of Christ (Christians), the Society of Friends (Quakers), and the Roman Catholic Church.

The first settlers in Indiana were French Catholic at Vincennes, and the first chapel was built soon after the town was founded. Bishop Gabriel Brute from Vincennes traveled over his diocese to organize Catholic settlers into parishes. By 1837, the Church was well organized in the State.

The outbreak of the Mexican War was important to the State. Many families had relatives who had gone West to colonize, and felt a vital interest in the Texas Declaration of Independence, in the 1845 annexation, and in the declaration of war. Indiana sent about 5,000 volunteers to the conflict; about 540 were killed.

TRADE AND CREDIT INCREASE PROSPERITY

Great economic and social changes took place in the 1830s and 1840s. Log cabins were replaced by brick or white frame houses. Former squatters often gained wealth and rose to membership in the General Assembly. Imported goods gained in importance, and clothing became more colorful and ornate: ruffled shirts, taffetas, and hats trimmed with flowers began to be common dress of prosperous farmers and townspeople from the late 1830s to the Civil War.

The decade before the war, economic factors were emerging that would shape Indiana's future. Railroads were the most important, as they allowed produce from Indiana to be sent to the East, where the important markets were located. Mines and quarries were opened, and mills and factories were built. The bonds of trade and credit began to link Indiana to the North and East. Merchants, manufacturers, and bankers grew increasingly powerful.

These changes were reflected in the political climate of the period. The Jefferson and Jackson party were no longer considered as serving the majority of the people. Although the Middle West was weakening it allegiance to the Democratic party, there was little indication that the Whig party was capable of formulating a platform to meet changing conditions.

The increasing conflict in the South, where a majority of Indiana's citizens had come from, stirred up all sorts of partisan and sectional loyalties. There was strong suspicion that abolitionists were at the core of dissagreement with the South. Sympathies and loyalites battled with economic realities, and the political atmosphere was charged with tension.

In 1849, voters called for a new State constitution. It met in Indianapolis in 1850, with 150 delegates, and remained in session for 18 weeks. Principal changes were that most govenmental business was turned over to counties, and the number of legislators was increased; it was also decided that some officials would be elected rather

History

than appointed, and the foundation was laid for a modern school system. Robert Dale Owen tried to win equal rights for women, but he was only partly successful.

The State officially frowned upon the Underground Railroad method of helping fugitive slaves. Laws were enacted to ban former slaves from settling in the State, to void any contracts with blacks, and to fine any person who employed or otherwise encouraged slaves to remain in Indiana. This provision was struck out in 1881.

After the first election under the new constitution, several new parties began to emerge, including the Free-Soilers, Abolitionists, and the Know-Nothings. In 1854, a convention of anti-Democrats made up of temperance sympathizers, antislavery proponents, Know-Nothings, and former Whigs was held in Indianapolis. Out of this emerged the People's party, soon to be transformed into the Republican party. Passage of the Kansas-Nebraska Bill in 1854, which repealed the Missouri Compromise and opened the territories to slavery, drove many hesitant people into Republican ranks. The Democrats nonetheless won the 1856 election.

The National Republican Convention held in Chicago in 1860 was well-represented by Indiana. Headed by Henry Smith Lane, his devotion to Lincoln aided in Lincoln's nomination, and the Republicans scored a sweeping success. When the Assembly of 1861 sent Governor Lane to the United States Senate, Lieutenant Governor Oliver P. Morton became governor of the State.

CIVIL WAR SOLIDIFIES SENTIMENTS

From this time until April 12, when Confederate troops fired upon Fort Sumter, uncertainty hung over Indiana. Some Democrats and Republicans held that states who wished to secede should be allowed to do so, since this outcome was better than coercion and a bloody civil war. Some hoped that Southern secession would eventually carry the old Northwest with it. Governor Morton and his followers felt that "coercion" was merely "enforcement of the law," and that the President had no choice but to crush the rebellion in South Carolina before it went further.

The onset of the Civil War solidified the sentiments of

many Indiana citizens. Morton's views were embraced by those who wished the Union to be preserved intact. Indiana was, however, unprepared to carry on its part of the burden of war. Merchants, banks, and others, invested funds. The legislature met in a special session to authorize a $2,000,000 war loan. Other difficulties soon developed. Enlistment was inadequate, desertion common, and conscription became necessary.

The 1862 election voted into office an administration hostile to Governor Morton. His prosecution of the war and the unpopularity of the draft contributed to defeat of the Republican party. Democrats proposed removing him from office, charging that he used the State militia for political purposes. Morton ran the State government for two years without legislative support.

No fighting took place in Indiana until 1863, when General John Hunt Morgan and 2,500 Confederate cavalrymen crossed the Ohio into Harrison County and raided Corydon, Salem, Dupont, and Versailles. When he learned that his force was in danger of being surrounded and captured, Morgan crossed the state line into Ohio, and was there captured by Union troops.

As the war dragged on, opposition became open. Political demonstrations, resistance to the draft, and attacks on newspapers were common. An outbreak of violence occurred in some 30 counties of the State. The most serious opposition came from the Knights of the Golden Circle. This secret organization envisioned the conquest of Mexico and the setting up of a vast empire around the Gulf based on cotton and slavery. The organization grew; by 1863, about 5,000 members existed in Indiana. In 1864, the U.S. government broke up the group through arrest and conviction of its leaders. The order disintegrated, and the idea of ending the Civil War by revolution was abandoned.

By the close of the war, economic and social conditions in Indiana had changed greatly. Prices rose, making merchants and manufacturers wealthy, but creating hardships for the majority of people. Other changes also took place. Indianapolis had grown from a quiet town to a large city. Over half the residents were newcomers. The simple ways had all but vanished; demoralization had taken place during the war, and crime and drunkenness increased.

RECONSTRUCTION CREATES FURTHER UNREST

As in the rest of the country, post-war politics in Indiana were dominated by Reconstruction issues for the next decade. Opposing political factions fought bitterly. George W. Julian, a Quaker, abolitionist, and member of Congress from eastern Indiana, began a vigorous campaign that again split the country into two hosile camps. He advocated punishment for the leaders of the Confederacy and enfranchisement of the blacks.

The 1866 election was won by radical Republicans, not only in Indiana, but throughout most of the north. The Fourteenth Amendment and Fifteenth Amendment were ratified in the next three years. Political strife continued well into 1872, when the Democratic party began to recover its peace-time role of the "popular representative of the masses."

The momentous economic and social changes that took place in Indiana were reflected by the many diversified manufacturing enterprises, the utilization of natural resources on a large scale, and the rapid development of roads and railways in the State.

Farmers suffered most from these advancements. Improved machinery led to a self-defeating scramble to mortgage the farm in order to buy new plows and tractors, which increased agricultural production and drove down prices. Tariffs, high freight rates, and profiteering middle men victimized the already economically burdened farmer. The hope and excitement of the pioneer era were gone, and farming families faced a bleak, hard life.

Many new political parties also sought to gain power in the 1870s. The Grange, a semipolitical fraternal order, organized the Independent party in 1874; their platform advocated railroad regulation, the curtailment of land and grain monopolies, banking reforms, and the substitution of a paper currency for the gold standard. The National Greenback party influenced State politics for a time, especially due to their position on currency reform. The Populist party, with its platform calling for increased Federal control of currency, free silver, a graduated income tax, and government ownership of railroads and utilities, found support among Indiana workers and farmers.

INDUSTRIALIZATION EXPANDS OPPORTUNITIES

By 1890, the frontier had all but disappeared. Industrialization became more widely spread, and smaller towns and counties acquired mills and factories.

But a depression in 1893-1894 caused further suffering. Labor conflicts and factory closings brought about the organization of labor unions, among them the United Mine Workers and the American and State Federations of Labor. Eugene V. Debs came into national prominence and started his career in the Labor and Socialist movements.

The close of the nineteenth century brought about marked changes and social and cultural opportunities unknown before the Civil War. The standard of living rose, streets were paved, gas lighting illuminated homes and neighborhood streets. Many people had more leisure time, and social and cultural endeavors were pursued vigorously.

This transition period was altered almost before it took shape, however. The twentieth century ushered in mass production and a boom in heavy industry. The automobile began to replace horse-drawn carriages, thousands of industrial employees began to work in large factories, competition sharpened, and the pace of business life stepped up dramatically.

In Indiana, a sparsely settled region of wasteland on the shore of Lake Michigan was converted into one of the great industrial centers of the world. Standard Oil, Inland Steel, and the United States Steel Corporation transformed the northwest area of the State into a vast metropolitan area.

To provide labor for the new industries, thousands of immigrants were brought in. Germans were the largest group, but other Europeans also were attracted to Indiana. Soon areas such as Gary, Whiting, and South Bend all had important colonies of Hungarians, Italians, Poles, Danes, Swedes, and other nationalites.

History

DEMAND INCREASES PRODUCTION OF MANUFACTURED GOODS

World War I further stimulated Indiana's industrialization. Goods needed for the war effort increased production. European demands for American agriculture moved prices to the highest levels in history. Land values increased, and farmers began to realize profits. They bought automobiles, new farm machinery, improved strains of livestock, and built new barns and homes. Many of them mortgaged their farms, intending to pay off debts from future income.

With the end of the war, however, came the end of high prices in produce and a steep drop in land value. By 1921, the entire nation was caught in a sudden, deep depression. Farmers found their land mortgaged for more than its total worth, and farming became and increasingly expensive enterprise.

For Indiana as a whole, however, the 1920s were years of some prosperity. The State was no longer predominately agricultural. Factories eventually absorbed thousands of men and women who had been raised on farms. The State's rural population dropped sharply, and its urban population steadily increased.

The Ku Klux Klan became prominent in Indiana during this time. Under the leadership of D.C. Stephenson, the organization dictated the election of at least one governor, several U.S. senators, mayors, and thousands of lesser officials. Stephenson was convicted in 1925 of the murder of a young woman in Indianapolis. Early in 1928, the attorney general of Indiana took the offensive against the Klan in two suits asking for its dissolution. Although the suits were never tried, public opinion began to veer. A savage campaign waged by the Indianapolis Times against the Klan, for which the newspaper was awarded a Pulitzer prize in 1928, brought about the end of the Klan as a political power in the State.

Although Indiana's legislature attempted to exclude freedman, the State gradually began to provide economic opportunities to the steadily growing black population. By 1910, there were 60,000 blacks in Indiana, four-fifths of them in the cities. After World War I, many blacks moved from the tobacco and cotton fields and into higher paid factory work. By 1920, 80,000 blacks resided in the State. And by 1930, Indiana's black population numbered nearly 112,000, all but 9,000 living in larger cities.

Like other states, Indiana suffered in the Great Depression that followed the financial collapse of 1929. Farmers lost their land, thousands were unemployed, and private charities could not withstand the burden of supporting indigents. Hardest hit were the southern counties, which depended on coal mining or stone quarrying for their economic welfare. As much as 50 percent of the population was without a means of support in some areas of the State.

INDIANA CHALLENGED BY POST-DEPRESSION ECONOMY

Public welfare programs underwent great changes after 1929. Many State-funded organizations, whose services had been considered adequate for many years, now needed additional support. Starting in 1933, the federal government began to supplement the work of private charities and State-supported agencies, providing some relief to Indiana's citizens.

Since the 1930s, numerous other changes have taken place in Indiana's history. In 1933, the State legislature adopted a gross income tax that combined income tax with sales tax to help those hardest hit by the Great Depression. By 1949, schools in the State were desegregated. The Studebaker automobile plant in South Bend closed in 1965, after 63 years of production. And in 1967, Richard H. Hatcher of Gary became the first black mayor of an Indiana city.

Indiana's cities and suburbs have continued to grow, technology has replaced some industry, political power has changed hands many times over. Tourism has become increasingly more important to the State's economy. And many of the structures built early in Indiana's history have now become landmarks, calling forth a time when Indiana first began to undergo the vast transformations that have made the Hoosier State what it is today.

CHRONOLOGY

1609 — Northwest country is granted to Virginia by charter.

1679 — Robert Cavelier, Sieur de La Salle, reaches the approximate site of South Bend, on his way to the Illinois River; he and his party are the first known white men in the area.

1680 — Father Allouez discovers Wea village in St. Joseph River in northern Indiana.

1681 — La Salle holds a council with Miami and Illinois Indians at Council Oak, present site of South Bend.

1708 — Possible founding date of Vincennes, the center of French settlement in present-day Indiana.

1720 — A fort is built at Ouiatenon, near present day Lafayette.

1722 — The French build Fort Miami at the site of present-day Fort Wayne.

1732-33 — Francois Morgane de Vincennes builds stockage fort on present site of Vincennes.

1749 — Beginning of extant records in Vincennes Roman Catholic Church, first church in Indiana.

1760 — British take Montreal; French relinquish all claim to western country, including Indiana. Ouiatenon and Fort Miami become British posts.

1763 — By the terms of the Treaty of Paris, which ends the French and Indian War, France cedes to Great Britain the territory that includes present-day Indiana.

King George sets aside region west of Alleghenies as Indian reserve.

Pontiac leads Indian tribes into war against frontier in Ohio Valley and beyond; Fort Miami captured.

1765 — George Croghan, Indian agent for British, makes treaties of conciliation with Indiana Indians.

1774 — 'Quebec Act' places all lands in northwest country under jurisdiction of of British province of Quebec.

1778 — Virginian George Rogers Clark, aided by disaffected French settlers, takes Vincennes from the British. It is recaptured on December 17.

Virginia organizes all lands northwest of the Ohio River as Illinois County.

1779 — February 25. British troops at Vincennes surrender to 170 American and French volunteers serving under Clark.

1779-80 — Virginia legislature presents 150,000 acres of land in Indiana to Colonel Clark and his regiment.

1781 — Don Pierro, Spanish commander of St. Louis, captures British post of St. Joseph, laying basis for Spanish claim to all territory northwest of Ohio River.

Encyclopedia of Indiana

1784 — Virginia conveys territory northwest of the Ohio River to United States.

1787 — Congress passes ordinance providing for government of 'Territory Northwest of the River Ohio.'

1790 — Hartmar destroys Indian villages along Maumee River; part of his force, under Colonel John Hardin, is annihilated by Little Turtle's Indians.

1791 — Miami war chief, Little Turtle, defeats federal troops and militia near Fort Miami; close to 1,000 are killed or wounded.

1792 — Brigadier General Rufus Putnam concludes treaty of peace with Indians at Vincennes.

1794 — The defeat of the Miami in the Battle of Fallen Timbers, near present-day Toledo, Ohio, opens the way for white settlement in Indiana.

Fort near junction of St. Joseph and St. Mary's rivers completed on site of English fort built in 1764; it is named Fort Wayne.

1795 — August 3. By the Treaty of Greenville, Indians cede lands that include a portion of what is now east-southeast Indiana.

1800 — May 7. Indiana Territory is created, with Vincennes as its capital. Population in the Territory numbers about 5,500.

William Henry Harrison is appointed governor of Indiana Territory; population of Territory is 5,641.

1801 — Harrison arrives at Vincennes.

1802 — Harrison concludes first of treaties with Indians, designed to extinguish all Indian titles in Indiana.

1803 — Swiss colonists settle in Switzerland County and introduce grape culture into Indiana.

1804 — First issue of Indiana Gazette, later called Western Sun, the first newspaper in Indiana, appears in Vincennes.

Electorate of Territory votes for representative form of government in place of government by governor and judges.

1805 — January 11. Michigan is detached from Indiana Territory.

Territorial legislature convenes for the first time.

Treaty signed at Grouseland, near Vincennes, gives U.S. title to Indian lands in eastern Indiana.

1806 —

1807 — First federal land sale takes place in Indiana, in Vincennes.

1808 — Harrison County organized; Corydon established as seat of government.

1809 — February 9. Illinois Territory is organized, reducing Indiana to its present borders.

Chronology

1810 —	Harrison and Tecumseh hold a council at Vincennes. Territory population is 24,520.
1811 —	Harrison defeats the Shawnee confederacy, led by Tecumseh's brother, the Prophet, at the Battle of Tippecanoe.
1812 —	War with England begins. Little Turtle, leader of Miami Confederacy, dies. Miami Indians are defeated in battle fought on the banks of Mississinewa River near Peru; it is the last battle fought in Indiana.
1813 —	Territorial capital moved from Vincennes to Corydon.
1814 —	Farmers and Mechanics Bank at Madison and Bank of Vincennes are chartered.
1815 —	Rappites settle in New Harmony.
1816 —	State Constitution is adopted by convention held in Corydon. First State election is held; Jonathon Jennings elected governor. Indiana admitted to the Union as 19th state. The constitution excludes slavery. Lincoln family moves into Indiana; Abraham is seven years old.
1817 —	First Medical Society in State organized by physicians of Vincennes.
1818 —	By Treaty of St. Mary's, most of central Indiana lying south of the Wabash River is purchased from Wea, Potawatomi, and Delaware Indians by Governor Jennings.
1820 —	Indianapolis replaces Corydon as the permanent State capital. U.S. Census population is 147,178.
1821 —	First sale of town lots in Indianapolis.
1824 —	U.S. mail stage between Vincennes and Louisville begins operation. Indiana Seminary opens at Bloomington.
1825 —	The colony of New Harmony is founded by Robert Owen.
1826 —	Treaty of Wabash signed, whereby Indians cede most of their lands north and west of the Wabash River.
1827 —	Presbyterians establish Hanover College, first denominational college in Indiana.
1828 —	Stage route established between Madison and Indianapolis.
1829 —	Indiana Colonization Society founded at Indianapolis for purpose of sending blacks to Liberia.
1830 —	Lincoln family moves from Spencer County to Illinois. Work is begun on Michigan Road. Population is 343,000.
1831 —	Underground Railroad begins operations in Indiana at Cabin Creek, in Randolph County.

Encyclopedia of Indiana

1832 — Construction of Wabash and Erie Canal begins at Fort Wayne.

Black Hawk's War arouses sentiment against Indians; the agitation initiates their removal from State.

1833 — Wabash College opens at Crawfordville; formerly founded in 1832 as Wabash Manual Labor College and Teachers' Seminary.

1834 — First railroad track in Indiana laid at Shelbyville; it is one mile long.

1835 — Capitol building at Indianapolis completed.

1836 — Legislature passes Mammoth Internal Improvement Bill, appropriating $13 million for internal improvements.

1837 — First coal is mined near Cannelton for river steamers.

Indiana Baptist Manual Labor Institute, now Franklin College, opens.

1838 — A group of 859 Potawatomi is forcibly expelled from Indiana. The expulsion virtually clears the State of Indians.

Indiana University is founded.

1840 — St. Mary-of-the-Woods is founded in Terre Haute.

Population is 685,800.

1842 — University of Notre Dame is founded at South Bend; chartered in 1844.

1843 — Wabash and Erie Canal formally opens in Fort Wayne.

1844 — Whig Convention held in Indianapolis.

1845 — Common school convention is held in Indianapolis; it is the beginning of movement for free schools.

1847 — Electorate votes for free public school system for Indiana.

1848 — First meeting of Indiana Education Society held in Indianapolis.

1849 — Electorate votes for constitutional convention.

James Whitcomb Riley is born is Greenfield, Indiana.

1850 — Constitutional Convention held in Indianapolis October 7; it runs through February 10, 1851.

State School for Deaf is established.

Population of Indiana is 988,500.

1851 — State Board of Agriculture is established.

New State constitution is ratified by electorate; it contains a provision that no blacks be allowed to settle in Indiana.

1852 — New school law creates tax-supported public school system for Indiana.

Studebaker brothers come to South Bend.

1853 — Wabash and Erie Canal is opened; links Toledo, Ohio on Lake Erie, with Evansville on the Ohio River.

First Union Station in U.S. is built in Indianapolis.

Chronology

1854 —	First large coal mine opens in Sulivan County.
	Monon Railroad, connecting New Albany and Michigan City, is completed.
1855 —	Northwestern Christian University, now Butler University, opens in Indianapolis.
	Eugene V. Debs, labor leader, is born in Terre Haute.
1856 —	Oliver P. Morton is nominated for governor on Republican ticket; it is the first act of Republican party in Indiana.
1857 —	St. Meinrad's College in Spencer County is opened.
1858 —	Indiana Academy of Science is organized in Indianapolis.
1859 —	Minerva Club, first women's club in U.S. with constitution and by-laws, is founded in New Harmony.
1860 —	Rail mileage rises from 212 (in 1855) to 2,163 miles.
	Indiana Republican delegates at Wigwam convention held in Chicago nominate Abraham Lincoln for president.
	The State's population, numbering 1,350,428, ranks sixth.
1861-65 —	Indiana contributes 196,363 men to the Union cause in the Civil War. 25,028 die in the war effort. Indiana troops are involved in 308 engagements.
1861 —	Oliver P. Morton becomes governor of Indiana.
	Governor Morton issues call for six regiments of soldiers in response to Lincoln's appeal to halt rebellion in South.
1862 —	Knights of the Golden Circle become active in Indiana.
1863 —	Confederate cavalrymen, under General John Hunt Morgan, raid southern Indiana.
1864 —	First streetcars in State begin operating in Indianapolis.
1865 —	Lincoln's body lies in state in capitol building in Indianapolis.
1866 —	National convention of Grand Army of the Rebublic held at Indianapolis.
1867 —	Indiana University opens its doors to women, receives State funds for its support.
1868 —	James Oliver of South Bend invents chilled-steel plow.
1869 —	Indianapolis News founded by John Holliday.
	Legislation is enacted, admitting black children to public schools on same basis as white children.
1870 —	Indiana State Teachers College opens in Terre Haute.
	Population is 1,680,630.
1871 —	Theodore Dreiser, novelist, is born in Terre Haute.
	Edward Eggleston's The Hoosier Schoolmaster is published.
1872 —	State grange of Indiana is organized.

Encyclopedia of Indiana

1873 — First belt railroad in U.S. is built around Indianapolis.
Purdue University, chartered in 1862, opens in Lafayette.

1874 — Rose Polytechnic Institute is founded in Terre Haute.

1877 — James Whitcomb Riley becomes a regular contributor of verse to the Indianapolis Journal, establishing a career as the State's virtual poet laureate.

1878 — Knights of Labor become active in Indiana.

1879 — Legislation provides for mine inspection and safety.

1880 — Cornerstone of new statehouse is laid in Indianapolis.
General Lew Wallace's book Ben-Hur is published.
Population is 1,978,300.

1881 — Conference at Terre Haute launches American Federation of Labor.

1883 — May Wright Sewall founds Art Association of Indianapolis.
The Old Swimmin' Hole by James Whitcomb Riley is published.

1885 — Indianapolis Conference of Indiana trade unions organizes first State Federation of Labor in U.S.

1886 — Natural gas well comes in at Portland.

1888 — Indianapolis resident Benjamin Harris, former senator, is elected president of the United States.

1889 — Standard Oil Company builds world's largest oil refinery in Whiting.

1890 — United Mine Workers organize and become powerful in Indiana.
Population is 2,192,400.

1893 — Eugene V. Debs organizes American Railway Union, the first industrial union in U.S. labor history.
Inland Steel Corp. moves its mills to Calumet region.

1894 — Elwood Haynes, early automobile pioneer, successfully tests his horseless carriage in Kokomo.

1897 — First compulsory education law passed.
United Mine Workers call coal strike.

1898 — Indiana regiments mustered into service for duty in Spanish-American War.
Eugene V. Debs founds Social Democratic Party.

1899 — Booth Tarkington's The Gentleman from Indiana is published.

1900 — Peak number of farms in Indiana stands at 221,897.
Meredith Nicholson's The Hoosiers is published.
Population is 2,516,460.

1901 — Compulsory education law amended to compel children ages seven through 16 to attend school throughout school year.

Chronology

1902 — George Ade's Fables in Slang begin to appear.

1904 — Largest interurban terminal station in U.S. opens at Indianapolis.

Debs polls 402,312 votes for President.

Kin (Frank McKinney) Hubbard's first 'Abe Martin' cartoon appears in Indiana News.

1905 — Gary is founded.

U.S. Steel Corporation's largest plant is built in Calumet region.

1907 — High schools become part of State public school system.

1910 — Population is 2,7000,900

1911 — May 30. First Indianapolis 500 Memorial Day weekend auto race is held.

Legislation is passed making employers responsible for industrial safety.

1914 — State Workmen's Compensation Act is passed.

1915 — Little Theater Society of Indiana is organized, with George Ade as president.

Indiana Historical Bureau is established.

1916 — First State primary election is held.

Centennial Exposition is held.

1917 — Governor appoints members of local draft boards; U.S. enters World War I.

Registration of men ages 21 to 31 for selective service begins.

1918 — Registration of men ages 18 to 45 for selective service begins.

1919 — Indiana ranks third among states in iron and steel production.

Nation-wide steel and coal strikes affect thousands in Indiana.

1920 — Debs is in prison for opposing the draft; he polls 915,302 votes for President.

Life of John Marshall, by Albert J. Beveridge, wins Pulitzer Prize.

Population is 2,930,390.

1921 — President Harding frees Debs.

1923 — The Ku Klux Klan has 300,000 members in Indiana.

1925 — Murder trial of D.C. Stevenson results in expose of corrupt role of Ku Klux Klan in Indiana politics; its political power weakens.

1926 — J. Arthur MacLean excavates a mound on Albee farm in Sullivan County, the first scientific archaeological excavation in State.

Encyclopedia of Indiana

1928— Indianapolis News receives Pulitzer Prize for campaign against Ku Klux Klan.

Albert J. Beveridge's Life of Abraham Lincoln is published posthumously.

1930— Population is 3,238,500.

1931— Indianapolis News wins Pulitzer Prize for advocating tax reforms.

1932— Full effects of Great Depression felt in Indiana; dozens of banks fail, thousands unemployed, mining and quarrying industries collapse, farm prices drop.

1933— The State legislature adopts a gross income tax, combining income and sales tax, to finance the needy of the Great Depression.

1934— John Dillinger is shot and killed outside Chicago's Biograph Theater, ending his gang's string of Indiana bank robberies.

1935— General strike in Terre Haute.

1936— Legislature passes social security and unemployment compensation acts.

State Department of Public Welfare is established.

1937— Ohio River reaches highest level ever recorded in Indiana history; entire cities are flooded; hundreds drown; property damage estimated at $500 million.

1940— Wendell Willkie nominated for President by Republican Party; he polls more than 22 million votes and carries Indiana, but is defeated by Franklin D. Roosevelt.

Population is 3,427,800.

1948— Alfred Kinsey, Indiana University biologist, stirs controversy with publication of first of two surveys on human sexual behavior.

1949— Indiana's schools are desegregated.

1957— A state right-to-work law abolishes the closed and union shops.

1965— The Studebaker automobile plant in South Bend shuts its doors after 63 years of producing automobiles.

1967— Richard D. Hatcher of Gary, Indiana, becomes the first black mayor of any city in the State.

1970— Indianapolis and its suburbs are consolidated, raising the city's population to 736,800.

1971— Justice Department files criminal charges against Mobil Oil Corp. and Blaw-Knox, an East Chicago firm in State, for polluting the Indiana Harbor Canal.

Terre Haute added to U.S. Labor Dept. list of "substantial unemployment areas."

1973— U.S. District Court Judge S. Hugh Dillin finds Indiana guilty of maintaining segregated school systems; State legislature is ordered to devise permanent integration plan for Indianapolis schools.

Chronology

1974 — Tornadoes kill about 48 people and cause property damage of more than $200 million dollars.

1974 — E.P.A. reports findings of organic chemicals, some carcinogenic, in Evansville drinking water.

1976 — U.S. House approves enlargement of Indiana Dunes National Lakeshore.

Uniroyal plant in Mishawaka reported by U.S. Labor Department as discriminating against women and minorities.

1978 — Midwest blizzard kills residents in parts of Indiana.

Legionnaire's Disease affects Bloomington; three die, 18 others become ill; bacteria discovered in cooling tower on top of Indiana University student union hotel.

1979 — Demonstration held at nuclear plant under construction in State.

Bobby Knight, head basketball coach at Indiana University, sentenced to six months in jail for conduct during Pan Am games in Puerto Rico.

1980 — Tornadoes hit 13 Midwest states, killing four and injuring more than 100; two are reported in Indiana.

Black civil rights leader, Vernon E. Jordan, is critically shot in Fort Wayne motel parking lot.

1982 — Unemployment in Fort Wayne is 10.5 percent and rising.

Unfinished bridge in East Chicago collapses; 12 workers killed, 17 injured.

Severe flooding hits Fort Wayne; it is declared a disaster area.

1983 — Fifty-seven counties in Indiana are declared eligible for Federal aid for drought disaster assistance.

Fort Wayne newspaper, the News Sentinal, is awarded Pulitzer Prize for coverage of area flooding.

1984 — Professional football's Baltimore Colts move to Indianapolis and begin playing in the city's Hoosier Dome.

1985 — Warsaw, Indiana court jury convicts Faith Assembly member James H. Menne of reckless homicide and criminal recklessness in the death of his daughter for untreated kidney failure.

William E. Vandiver is electrocuted in Michigan City for murder of his father-in-law.

1987 — Gary named one of nine urban areas nationally with airborne lead concentration in excess of Federal clear air standards.

Gary's jobless rate reported at 20 percent.

1988 — State lottery is approved.

Newport Army Ammunition Plant in State named one of five U.S. sites for production of chemical weapons.

1989 — United Mine Workers coal strike spreads into Indiana.

1991 — Gary resident Christopher D. Peterson is charged in connection with shotgun killings that terrorized northwestern Indi-

Encyclopedia of Indiana

ana from October through December 1990.

State population is more than 5,500,000; Indianapolis population isalmost 1,250,000, a 7.1 percent jump from 1980 figures.

1992 — Boxer Mike Tyson is convicted in rape trial.

GOVERNORS

JENNINGS, JONATHAN (1787-1834), first state governor of Indiana (1816-1822), was born in 1787, in the area of Hunterdon County, New Jersey, the son of Jacob and Mary (Kennedy) Jennings. As a boy, he received a common school education and attended grammar school in Canonsburg, Pennsylvania.

At the age of nineteen, he went west to the Indiana Territory and settled in Clark County. He was admitted to the bar in 1807 and served as a land clerk and as a member of the Board of Vincennes University.

In 1809, he ran for territorial delegate to Congress on the anti-slavery platform, defeating Thomas Randolph, then Attorney- General of the Indiana Territory. Jennings was reelected in 1811, 1812, and 1814. During his terms as a delegate, he concerned himself with such matters as internal improvements to the Territory, land purchases, and protection of settlers from Indian attacks.

In 1815, Jennings presented a petition to Congress from the Indiana Territorial Legislature which requested statehood. The Enabling Act, passed the following year, made provisions for a constitutional convention to begin the process of statehood. Jennings served as president of the convention. In the same year, 1816, he was elected governor of the new state, defeating Thomas Posey, Indiana Territorial Governor.

As governor, Jennings worked to establish a banking system and an educational system. He supported the enactment of laws to protect free blacks, and assisted in the negotiation of treaties with the Delaware, Wea, Potawatomi, and Miami Indians. He was reelected to the governorship and served until 1822, when he became a member of Congress. He remained in Congress until 1830, then retired to his farm near Charlestown, where he died four years later, on July 26, 1834.

Jennings was married to Ann Gillmore Hay on August 8, 1811. She died in 1826. The following year, he married Clarissa Barbee. He had no children.

BOON, RATLIFF (1781-1844), second governor of Indiana (1822), was born on January 18, 1781 in North Carolina, the son of Jesse and Kessiah Boon. He was educated at public schools in Danville, Kentucky, and later worked as a gunsmith.

In 1809, he went to live in Warrick County, Indiana Territory. Four years later, he became the first Treasurer of Warrick County. He was subsequently elected to the Indiana House of Representatives, and served from 1816 to 1817. He was a member of the Indiana Senate in 1818.

In 1819, Boon ran for lieutenant governor on the ticket with Governor Jonathan Jennings, and was elected. Three years later, Jennings resigned to take a seat in the U.S. Congress, and Boon became governor, serving out the final months of Jennings' unexpired term.

He once again became lieutenant governor, this time under Governor William Hendricks. Boon resigned his office in January, 1824 and was elected to the U.S. Congress later that year. As a congressman, Boon lobbied for legislation regarding public lands. He remained in Congress until 1827, when Thomas H. Blake defeated his bid for office by a mere eighty-four votes. Boon regained his seat in 1829, and served for ten more years.

After leaving Washington, Boon moved to Missouri, where he remained active in politics. He died there on November 20, 1844. Boon was married to Deliah Anderson. The couple had seven children.

HENDRICKS, WILLIAM (1782-1850), third governor of Indiana (1822- 1825), was born in Westmoreland County, Pennsylvania on November 12, 1782, the son of Abraham and Ann (Jamison) Hendricks.

He attended school in Canonsburg, Pennsylvania and, while still a young man, moved to Cincinnati. After studying law, he was admitted to the bar and practiced for a short time. He moved to Madison, Indiana Territory and, with a partner, Seth M. Levenworth, published the newspaper, *Western Eagle* from 1813 to 1815.

In 1814, he was a member of the House of Representatives of Indiana Territory. He became involved in the Territory's bid for statehood, serving in 1816 as secretary of the Indiana Constitutional Convention. Later that year, he was elected the new State's first state representative to the U.S. Congress. As a congressman, he was a strong proponent of public works, particularly the building of roads and canals.

After three terms in Congress, Hendricks ran for governor of Indiana and was elected on August 5, 1822. As governor, he saw an increase in population in the State, as settlers moved north from the Ohio River. He also supervised the moving of the State capital from Corydon to Indianapolis in 1824. Hendricks resigned the governorship in 1825 to take a seat in the U.S. Senate. He served in that body until 1837, then retired to his estate in Jefferson County. He died there on May 16, 1850.

Hendricks was married in 1816 to Ann Parker Paul. They had nine children.

RAY, JAMES BROWN (1794-1848), fourth governor of Indiana (1825- 1831), was born on February 19. 1794 in Jefferson County, Kentucky, the son of William and Phebe Ann (Brown) Ray. As a young man, he read law in Cincinnati. In 1818, he moved to Indiana, where he was admitted to the bar.

Ray ran for state representative and, in 1821, was elected to the Indiana House. The following year he served in the State Senate. In 1824, Lt. Governor Boon resigned his office and Ray became president pro tempore of the Senate. He was reelected the following year.

When, in 1825, Governor Hendricks resigned to take a seat in the U.S. Senate, Ray was named governor of Indiana. Later that year, he was elected governor in his own right. He served two terms. During his administration, the construction of the Michigan Road from the Michigan border to the Ohio River, and the Wabash and Erie Canal were major objectives. In 1826, Ray served as a commissioner in negotiating land concessions from the Miami and Potawatomi Indians.

Ray had strong opposition from the Legislature during his second term; his attempts to revise the penal code were overridden, and his appointments to the State Supreme

Court were challenged. He left office in 1831 and practiced law in Indianapolis. In 1833, with business partner, W. M. Tannehill, he started the Greencastle, Indiana newspaper *The Hoosier*. Ray died of cholera on August 4, 1848 in Cincinnati.

Ray was twice married, first to Mary Riddle in 1818, who died in 1823, and second, to Esther Brooker in 1825. Ray had six children.

NOBLE, NOAH (1794-1844), fifth governor of Indiana (1831-1837), was born on January 14, 1794 in Berryville, Virginia, the son of Dr. Thomas and Elizabeth (Sedgewick) Noble. His family moved to Kentucky around 1800, and Noble attended common schools there.

He settled in Brookville, Indiana in 1816. The next year, he was commissioned a lieutenant colonel in the Indiana Militia. In 1820, he was promoted to the rank of colonel.

While in Brookville, Noble was involved in various business endeavors, including wool carding, a fulling mill, and real estate speculation. He was elected sheriff of Franklin County in 1820 and 1822. In 1824, he won a seat in the Indiana House of Representatives and, in 1825, was named receiver general of public monies for the Indianapolis Land Office, a post he held for four years. Nobel was a commissioner, and assisted in the locating of the Michigan Road in 1830.

In 1831, Noble was elected governor of Indiana. Accomplishments during his administration included the construction of new roads and canals, and the revision of the tax law.

Noble left office in 1837. He was a candidate for U.S. Senate in 1836 and 1838, but lost both times. He did, however, continue to serve in public posts. From 1839 to 1840, he served on the Internal Improvements Board and, in 1841, he was fund commissioner.

Noble died on February 8, 1844 in Indianapolis. He was married to Catherine Stull Van Swearington. The couple had one son and one daughter.

Governors

WALLACE, DAVID (1799-1859), sixth governor of Indiana (1837- 1840), was born on April 4, 1799 in Mifflin County, Pennsylvania, the son of Andrew and Eleanor (Jones) Wallace. His family moved to Ohio in 1807 and Wallace attended school in Troy. In 1817, he entered West Point and studied for four years, graduating in 1821 with the rank of second lieutenant. He taught at West Point for a year, then returned to Brookville, Indiana, where his family was living.

In Brookville, he studied law and was admitted to the bar. He also served in the 7th Regiment of the Indiana Militia where, in 1827, he rose to the rank of colonel.

Wallace ran for state representative, was elected to the Indiana House, and served from 1828 to 1831. Campaigning on a ticket with Noah Noble in 1831, and again in 1834, he was elected lieutenant governor. In 1837, he ran for the governorship and won over his opponent, John Dumont, by nearly 10,000 votes. Wallace's administration was marked by an economic collapse in the State's internal improvement program, and the removal of the Potawatomi Indians onto reservations.

In 1840, at the close of his term, Wallace began a law practice in Indianapolis. He ran for U.S. Congress in 1841 and served a single term in Washington, then returned to Indianapolis. He was a member of the Indiana Constitutional Convention in 1850, and was a judge in Marion County from 1856 to 1859. Wallace died in Indianapolis on September 4, 1859.

Wallace was married twice. He married Esther French Text in 1824, with whom he had four sons. After her death, he married a second time, to Zeralda Sanders in 1836, with whom he had two daughters and a son.

BIGGER, SAMUEL (1802-1846), seventh governor of Indiana (1840- 1843), was born on March 20, 1802 in Warren County, Ohio, the son of John Bigger. He received his A.B. and A.M. degrees at Ohio University, then studied law.

In 1829, he moved to Indiana, settling first in Liberty, and later in Rushville. He ran for the Indiana House of Representatives in 1833 and 1834, and was elected both times. In 1836, the State Legislature named him presiding judge of the Sixth Judicial Court, a position he held until 1840, when he was nominated for governor by the Whigs.

Bigger won the gubernatorial election and took office in December of 1840. During his term, Indiana suffered under an enormous debt, due mainly to a breakdown in the internal improvements program. Bigger took few steps to alleviate these financial problems. His administration supported the revision of state's laws.

Bigger opposed, on religious grounds, the establishment of Methodist Ashbury College; it was believed that this opposition caused his defeat in a subsequent campaign for reelection.

Bigger left office in 1843 and moved to Fort Wayne to practice law. He died there on September 9, 1846. He was married in 1830 to Ellen Williamson.

WHITCOMB, JAMES (1795-1852), eighth governor of Indiana (1843- 1848), was born on December 1, 1795 in Windsor, Vermont, the son of John and Lydia (Parameter) Whitcomb. He attended Transylvania University, then studied law and was admitted to the Kentucky bar in 1822.

In 1824, he moved to Indiana and practiced law in Bloomington. Six years later, he was elected to the Indiana Senate, where he served for two terms.

President Andrew Jackson appointed Whitcomb commissioner of the General Land Office in October, 1836. President Van Buren reappointed him for a subsequent term, and he remained at this post until 1841. He returned to Indiana and practiced law in
Terre Haute until 1843, when he won the Democratic nomination for governor. He was elected to the office later that year.

As governor, Whitcomb worked to alleviate debts accrued by the internal improvements program, and approached the State Bank for loans to bolster state finances. With help from these loans, in 1846, the State raised five regiments of infantry for the war with Mexico. Also during Whitcomb's term, the Indiana Asylum for the Education of the Deaf and the Indiana Hospital for the Insane were established.

Whitcomb resigned as governor in 1848 after the Legislature elected him to the U.S. Senate. His term as senator, however, was interrupted by poor health. He died in New York on October 4, 1852.

James Whitcomb was married to Ann Renick Hurst; the couple had one daughter.

DUNNING, PARIS C. (1806-1884), ninth governor of Indiana (1848- 1849), was born near Greensboro, North Carolina on March 15, 1806, the son of James and Rachel (North) Dunning. He attended school in Greensboro and, after the death of his father in 1823, moved to Indiana with his family.

As a young man, he attended medical school in Louisville, Kentucky, then switched to law and returned to Bloomington, Indiana and studied in the office of Governor Whitcomb. He soon entered politics, winning a seat in the State House of Representatives in 1833, and again in 1834 and 1835. In 1836, he was elected to the Indiana Senate and served for four years. He was a member of the Board of Trustees of Indiana State College from 1838 to 1841.

Dunning was the Democrat's nominee for lieutenant governor in 1846, winning by a margin of about 3,000 votes. He remained in this office until 1848, when he became governor, upon James Whitcomb's resignation to take a U.S. Senate seat.

Dunning served out the remainder of Whitcomb's term and left office in 1849. He continued to play an active role in state politics. In 1863, he was elected to the Indiana Senate and served for one term. Dunning died on May 9, 1884 in Bloomington.

He was married twice; first, to Sarah Alexander in 1826, who died in 1863, and second, to Ellen Lane Ashford in 1865. He had five children.

WRIGHT, JOSEPH A. (1810-1867), tenth governor of Indiana (1849- 1857), was born on April 17, 1810 in Washington, Pennsylvania, the son of John and Rachel (Seaman)

Wright. While he was still a child, his family moved to Bloomington, Indiana. Wright received his education at Indiana Seminary, studied law, and passed the bar in 1829.

He practiced his profession in Rockville until 1833, when he was elected to the Indiana House of Representatives. In 1836, he was reelected. He served a term in the State Senate, and then in the U.S. Congress from 1843 to 1845.

The Democrats nominated Wright for governor of Indiana in 1849, and he was elected. Due to changes in the State constitution, he was the first Indiana governor chosen for a four-year term. During his administration, the State formally adopted the new constitution. Strides were made in education: The first State Board of Education was established, and Indiana cities began to collect taxes for educational purposes. In 1851, Indiana had its first State Fair and, in 1852, a State Board of Agriculture was formed, with Wright as its president.

Governor Wright left office in 1857 and went to Prussia as U.S. minister until 1862, at which time he returned to Washington for an appointment to the U.S. Senate. He served for one year. In 1863, he was named commissioner of the Hamburg Exposition. Two years later, he went back to Prussia as U.S. minister, and remained at that post until his death on March 11, 1867.

Wright was married three times and was the father of four children.

WILLARD, ASHBEL P. (1820-1860), eleventh governor of Indiana (1857-1860), was born in Oneida County, New York on October 31, 1820, the son of Erastus and Sarah (Parsons) Willard. He graduated from Hamilton College in 1842, subsequently studied law, and was admitted to the bar. Over the new few years, he lived for short time in several parts of the country: Michigan, Texas, and Kentucky.

He settled in New Albany, Indiana in 1845, and worked as an attorney. Five years later, he was elected to the Indiana House of Representatives and served for one term. He ran for lieutenant governor in 1852 as a Democrat, and won by a margin of more than 15,000 votes.

Willard was elected governor of Indiana in 1857. During his term, he often found himself at odds with the State Legislature. He was critical of the Legislature's focus on national issues rather than state problems, and of its failure to make sufficient appropriations for government expenses. Indiana was faced with such financial crises during Willard's tenure that, when the Legislature was adjourned, he was forced to take out a loan to pay the interest on the state debt.

While governor, Willard's brother-in-law, John E. Cook, was arrested and eventually tried and put to death for his part in the famous raid on Harper's Ferry. Although Willard's attempts to help Cook were unsuccessful, his efforts in the matter brought him increased constituent approval at home.

Willard left Indiana in failing health and went to St. Paul, Minnesota where he died on October 3, 1860, while he was still governor. He was married in 1847 to Caroline Cook and had three children.

HAMMOND, ABRAM A. (1814-1874), twelfth governor of Indiana (1860- 1861), was born on March 21, 1814 in Brattleboro, Vermont, the son of Nathaniel and Patty (Ball) Hammond. His family moved to Brookville, Indiana when he was six years old. As a young man, Hammond studied law and was admitted to the bar. He practiced his profession in Greenfield, and later in Columbus, where he was prosecuting attorney. He subsequently lived and worked in Indianapolis, Cincinnati, San Francisco, and Terre Haute. In 1849, in Indianapolis, he was judge of the Court of Common Pleas.

Hammond was elected lieutenant governor of Indiana in 1856 and served under Governor Ashbel Willard. When Willard died in office on October 3, 1860, Hammond succeeded him as governor and served out the remainder of his term. With a mere three months in office, Hammond had little chance to leave his mark. Appearing before the Legislature, however, he urged its establishment of a refuge house for juvenile offenders, an institution that was founded several years later.

Hammond left office in January of 1861 in poor health. He was never to regain his former stamina, and lived out his final days in Colorado.

Hammond died in Denver on August 27, 1874. He was married to Mary Amsden; the couple had one son.

LANE, HENRY S. (1811-1881), thirteenth governor of Indiana (1861), was born on February 11, 1811 in Kentucky, the son of James and Mary (Higgins) Lane. He was educated at home by tutors, and later studied law and was admitted to the bar.

In 1835, he moved to Crawfordsville, Indiana and practiced law. Soon after, he won a seat in the Indiana House of Representatives, serving from 1837 to 1838. He ran for U.S. Congress in a special election in 1840, and won a seat. The following year, he was reelected. However, in the 1849 congressional election, Lane lost to his opponent, Joseph McDonald.

When the Mexican War began in 1846, Lane mustered volunteers and became major of the First Indiana Regiment. He rose to the rank of lieutenant colonel before completing his service in 1848.

Returning to Indiana, Lane became a major promoter of the new Republican Party and, in 1860, was nominated governor by the Republicans. In the election that followed, he defeated Democrat Thomas A. Hendricks by 10,000 votes.

He took office on January 14, 1861, but resigned after only two days, when the Legislature elected him to the U.S. Senate.

In the Senate, Lane supported the Union as the Civil War raged throughout the country. He served until 1867, then returned to his home state. From 1869 to 1871, he was special Indian commissioner in Indiana and, in 1872, served as commissioner for improvement of the Mississippi River.

Lane died on June 19, 1881 in Crawfordsville, Indiana. He was married twice: in 1833 to Pamela Bledsoe Jameson,

Governors

who died in 1842, and to Joanna Elston in 1845.

MORTON, OLIVER P. (1823-1877), fourteenth governor of Indiana (1861-1867), was born on August 4, 1823 in Salisbury, Indiana, the son of James and Sarah (Miller) Morton. He attended Miami University in Oxford, Ohio from 1843 to 1845, then studied law and was admitted to the bar.

In 1852, he became circuit court judge in Centreville. He was an early supporter of the Republican Party and, in 1856, was chosen as the Republican nominee for governor. Democrat Ashbel P. Willard defeated him in the general election. Four years later, Morton returned as the Republican contender for lieutenant governor. Just two days after inauguration, the new Republican governor, Henry S. Lane, resigned to take a seat in the U.S. Senate, and Morton was sworn in as governor. Morton was elected governor in his own right in 1864.

During the Civil War, Morton's administration managed to answer the Union call for troops despite a lack of funds and only mixed support for the war among Indiana residents. The Legislature voted against war appropriations, so Morton obtained the capital to outfit troops by taking out loans of nearly a million dollars. Governor Morton suffered a stroke in 1865 and was unable to perform his duties as governor for a time. During his recovery, Lieutenant Governor Conrad Baker assumed executive responsibilities.

After he recuperated from his stroke in 1867, Governor Morton won a seat in the U.S. Senate. He resigned the governorship on January 24, 1867. In 1872, he was reelected to the Senate. When his term ended, he returned to live in Indianapolis. He died there on November 1, 1877.

Morton was married in 1843 to Lucinda Burbank. The couple had five children.

BAKER, CONRAD (1817-1885), fifteenth governor of Indiana (1867- 1873), was born on February 12, 1817 in Franklin County, Pennsylvania, the son of Conrad and Catherine (Winterheimer) Baker. He attended Pennsylvania College in

Gettysburg, then studied law and was admitted to the bar.

After practicing for two years, he moved to Evansville, Indiana. He served a term in the Indiana House of Representatives, from 1845 to 1846. Active in Republican politics, he won the Republican nomination for lieutenant governor in 1856, but was defeated in the general election.

When the Civil War began in 1861, Baker joined the Union forces as colonel of the First Cavalry, 28th Regiment of Indiana Volunteers. He served until 1864, when he once again received the Republican nomination for lieutenant governor. Campaigning on a ticket with Oliver P. Morton, Baker won the lieutenant governorship and took office in January, 1865. Later that year, when Governor Morton suffered a stroke, Baker carried out the executive duties until the Governor regained his health.

In January, 1867, when Morton resigned to take a seat in the U.S. Senate, Baker was sworn in to serve out the remainder of his predecessor's gubernatorial term. Baker was elected to a full term as governor in 1868. His administration was marked by the establishment of various institutions, including a normal school in Terre Haute, a women's prison, a refuge house for juvenile offenders, and a retirement home for soldiers.

After leaving office in 1873, Baker practiced law in Indianapolis. He died on April 28, 1885.

Baker was married to Matilda Sommers in 1838; she died in 1855. The couple had two children. He married a second time in 1858, to Charlotte Chute, with whom he had four children.

HENDRICKS, THOMAS (1819-1885), sixteenth governor of Indiana (1873-1877), was born on September 7, 1819 in Zanesville, Ohio, the son of John and Jane (Thompson) Hendricks. He graduated from Hanover College in 1841, then studied law in Chambersburg, Pennsylvania.

After completing his studies, he moved to Shelbyville, Indiana and, in 1848, won a seat in the State House of Representatives. Hendricks was a member of the Indiana Constitutional Convention in 1851, and was elected to Congress in 1851 and 1852. From 1855 to 1859, he was commissioner of the General Land Office. He served in the U.S. Senate from 1863 to 1869.

An active member of the Democratic Party in the State, Hendricks received the Democratic nomination for governor three times: first in 1860, when he was defeated by Henry S. Lane; second in 1868, when he lost to Conrad Baker; and third, in 1872, when he won over Republican, Thomas M. Browne.

During his term as governor, Hendricks signed the Baxter Prohibition Law , but saw it repealed just two years later. He also worked to mediate labor disputes in Clay County and Logansport.

In 1876, while he was still governor, Hendricks ran as the Democratic candidate for vice president with Samuel J. Tilden, but was not elected. He completed his term as governor of Indiana in January 1877. In 1884, Hendricks ran again as a candidate for vice president, this time with Grover Cleveland, and won. He was sworn in as vice president in 1885, but served only about eight months. On November 25, 1885, he died in Indiana.

Hendricks was married in 1845 to Eliza Morgan. The couple had one son, who died at the age of three.

WILLIAMS, JAMES D. (1808-1880), seventeenth governor of Indiana (1877-1880), was born on January 16, 1808 in Pickaway County, Ohio, the son of George Williams. He grew up on farms and was educated in the common schools of the area.

About 1831, he moved to the Wheatland region and bought a farm of his own. He entered state politics as a Democrat and served numerous terms in the Indiana House of Representatives: 1843-44, 1847-48, 1851-52, 1857, and 1869. He was elected several times to the State Senate, and filled that office from 1859 to 1865, in 1871, and again in 1875. During this period, Williams was also a member of the Indiana State Board of Agriculture.

Williams was nominated for governor by the Democrats in 1872, but lost to Oliver P. Morton in the general election. In 1874, he was elected to the U.S. Congress and served until 1876, when he was elected governor of Indiana.

Williams' term was marred by labor disputes. A railroad strike paralyzed much of the Midwest, and worker unrest in Indianapolis escalated. Construction of the Indiana State House began in 1878 during Williams' administration.

Throughout his political life, Williams was known by the nickname, "Blue Jeans", because he wore blue jeans in nearly all except the hottest months of the year.

Williams died on November 20, 1880, while still governor. He was married in 1831 to Nancy Huffman, with whom he had four children.

GRAY, ISAAC P. (1828-1895), eighteenth and twentieth governor of Indiana (1880-1881 and 1885-1889), was born on October 18, 1828 in Chester County, Pennsylvania, the son of John and Hannah (Worthington) Gray. As a boy, Gray attended common schools.

His family moved to Ohio in 1839. When he was older, Gray moved to Union City, Indiana, and worked in the dry goods business, then as a banker. He eventually studied law and became an attorney.

At the outbreak of the Civil War, Gray entered the military and served as a colonel of the 4th Indiana Cavalry for six months. In July 1863, he served for a week as colonel of the 106th Regiment, which took part in the Indiana raid against John H. Morgan. The regiment was disbanded on July 17, 1863. Gray later mustered the 147th Regiment in the spring of 1865.

Following the Civil War, in 1866, Gray ran for U.S. Congress and was defeated. Two years later, however, he won a seat in the Indiana Senate, and served until 1872. Originally a Republican, Gray's views changed over time, and he aligned himself with the Liberal Republicans. The party later joined with the Democrats.

Gray was nominated for lieutenant governor by the Democratic Party in 1876 and was elected, serving under James D. Williams. On November 20, 1880, Governor Williams died, and Gray became governor for the remaining six weeks of Williams' term. Gray was defeated in a second bid for lieutenant governor in 1880, but returned strong in the 1884 election, and won the governorship from his Republican opponent, William Calkins.

During Gray's term, appropriations were made for several institutions, including a school for the mentally handicapped in Fort Wayne, and the reconstruction of the Soldiers' Orphan Home in Knightstown. Monies were also provided for the Indiana Soldiers and Sailors' Monument in Indianapolis.

Gray left office in 1889 and practiced law in the capital for four years. In 1893, he was sent to Mexico City as U.S. minister. He died there on February 14, 1895. Gray was married to Eliza Jaqua in 1850. The couple had four sons, two of whom died in childhood.

PORTER, ALBERT G. (1824-1897), nineteenth governor of Indiana (1881-1885), was born on April 20, 1824 in Lawrenceburg, Indiana, the son of Thomas and Miranda (Tousey) Porter. He received his education at Hanover College and Indiana Asbury College. After graduation in 1843, he moved to Indianapolis, where he worked as an attorney. From 1853 to 1857, he was a reporter for the State Supreme Court.

Originally a Democrat, Porter changed his affiliation upon the rise of the new Republican Party. He ran for U.S. Congress as a Republican, and was elected in 1858 and 1860. He also served as controller of the U.S. Treasury from 1878 to 1880.

In 1880, Porter received the Republican nomination for governor of Indiana. In the general election later that year, he won against Democrat Franklin Landers. As governor, Porter gave attention to the issue of medical care in Indiana. Hospitals were erected in Richmond, Evansville, and Logansport, and the State Board of Health was established. A drive to clear up swamplands was put into action, and the Kankakee Swamp and other marshlands were drained.

After leaving office, Porter was named U.S. minister to Italy and served there from 1889 to 1892. He returned to Indiana and lived his final years in Indianapolis. He died on May 3, 1897.

Porter was married in 1846 to Minerva Brown, with whom he had four children; she died in 1875. In 1881, he married a second time to Cornelia Stone.

HOVEY, ALVIN P. (1821-1891), twentieth governor of Indiana (1889- 1891), was born on September 6, 1821 in Posey County, Indiana, the son of Abiel and Frances (Peterson) Hovey. As a boy, Hovey received his education at common schools. He later studied law, was admitted to the bar, and began to practice in Mount Vernon, Indiana.

During the Mexican War, he was commissioned first lieutenant in a company of the 2nd Indiana Regiment, but his company was never called into service. From 1850 to 1854, he was a circuit court judge. When a seat was left vacant on the State Supreme Court, Hovey was appointed to fill the position; he served from May 1854 to December 1855. In 1856, he was named U.S. district attorney and served for two years.

Although Hovey was a supporter of the Democratic Party during his early years, in about 1858, he joined the Republicans. Soon after, he ran as a Republican candidate for Congress, but was not elected. When the Civil War began in 1861, he returned to military service as a colonel of the 1st Regiment, 1st Brigade Indiana Legion. Later that summer, he took command of the 24th Indiana Regiment. Less than a year after that, he was promoted to brigadier general and, two years later, to major general. He served until October 1865.

In December of 1865, Hovey was sent to Peru as U.S. minister to that country. He remained in Lima until 1870. Returning to Indiana, he practiced law in Mount Vernon. The Republicans offered him the nomination for governor in 1872, but he declined. Instead he continued his law practice and, in 1886, began a term in the U.S. Congress. In 1888, the Republicans again offered him the gubernatorial nomination, and this time he accepted. He won by a narrow margin in the general election.

During his administration, Hovey was at odds with the Democrat-controlled Legislature, especially on the issue of appointive powers. Also, changes were made in public

Governors

school policy, as the State Board of Education was given responsibility for selecting textbooks.

Hovey died while still governor, on November 23, 1891. He was married twice, first to Mary Ann James in 1844, who died in 1863, and then to Rose Alice Smith Carey in 1865. He had four children from his first marriage.

CHASE, IRA (1834-1895), twenty-second governor of Indiana (1891- 1893), was born in Monroe County, New York on December 7, 1834, the son of Benjamin and Lorinda (Mix) Chase. His family moved to Milan, Ohio when he was twelve years old, and Chase studied at the Milan Seminary. As a young man, he returned to New York to attend Medina Academy.

After graduation, he settled in Barrington, Illinois, where his family was then living, and worked as a school teacher. In 1861, at the outbreak of the Civil War, Chase signed on for military service in the 19th Illinois Regiment. A year after enlisting in the regiment, however, he had to be discharged due to poor health.

Back in Barrington, he tried his luck in the hardware business, but his store failed after a short time. He then turned to the Christian Church and became a minister, preaching over the next several years to congregations in Danville; Wabash; Mishawaka; LaPorte, Indiana; Peoria, Illinois; and Pittsburgh, Pennsylvania. In 1886, Chase served as chaplain for the Indiana G.A.R. The following year, he became department commander.

During his time in the ministry, Chase was vocal in political matters and strong in his support of the Republican Party. In 1888, the Republicans made him their nominee for lieutenant governor and, later that year, Chase won over Democrat William R. Myers.

Chase served under Governor Alvin P. Hovey, and when Hovey died on November 23, 1891, Chase was sworn in to complete the Governor's unexpired term. As Indiana governor, Chase supported appropriations for public works, particularly for the construction of new roads. He then ran for a term as governor in 1892, but lost to the Democratic candidate, Claude Matthews.

Chase left office in 1893 and returned to the ministry and the lecture circuit. Two years later, in Maine, he died on May 11. Chase was married to Rhoda Castle in 1859. They had four children.

MATTHEWS, CLAUDE (1845-1898), twenty-third governor of Indiana (1893-1897), was born on December 14, 1845 in Bethel, Kentucky, the son of Thomas and Eliza (Fletcher) Matthews. He attended Centre College in Danville, Kentucky and graduated in 1867. Soon after, he moved to Indiana, bought a farm, and began to breed fine livestock.

He won his first public office in 1876 when he was elected a Democrat representative in the Indiana House. He made a bid for the State Senate in 1882, but lost the election.

In between his political service, Matthews continued on his farm with the breeding of livestock. From 1891 to 1893, he was the Indiana Secretary of State. He received the Democratic nomination for governor in 1892, and later that year was elected, defeating the Republican candidate, Ira Chase.

While governor, Matthews was called upon to deal with various labor disputes. During a bitter coal miners' strike, the Governor ordered out the National Guard to restore the peace. Matthew's administration was also taken up by his campaign against the formal organization and promotion of prize fighting and racing, which he only managed to suppress against heavy opposition.

Matthews left office in 1897. He died the following year, on April 28. He was married in 1868 to Martha Whitcomb and had three children.

MOUNT, JAMES A. (1843-1901), twenty-fourth governor of Indiana (1897-1901), was born in Montgomery County, Indiana on March 24, 1843, the son of Atwell and Lucinda (Fullenwider) Mount. When he was a child, he lived on a farm and was educated at common schools.

He served in Company D of the 72nd Indiana Regiment for three years during the Civil War, and attained the rank of sergeant. After the war, he returned to Lebanon, Indiana and attended the Presbyterian Academy. He bought a farm soon after, and became a well-respected lecturer on agricultural matters. Mount's appearances on the lecture circuit led him to seek public office and, in 1888, he ran as a Republican for the Indiana Senate, and was elected. He lost a bid for U.S. Congress in 1890, but in 1896, he made a political comeback and won the Indiana governorship by a margin of 6,000 votes.

Mount served as governor during the Spanish-American War. While in office, he worked to overhaul the prison system. He also saw the establishment of the Medical Examining Board and the Office of Labor Commissioner.

Mount completed his term in January, 1901. He died only a few days after leaving office, on January 16. He was married in 1867 to Catharine Boyd; the couple had three children.

DURBIN, WINFIELD (1847-1928), twenty-fifth governor of Indiana (1901-1905), was born on May 4, 1847 in Lawrenceburg, Indiana, the son of William and Eliza (Sparks) Durbin. His father owned a tannery. While Winfield Durbin was young, his family moved to New Philadelphia, Indiana and he attended public schools.

During the Civil War, he served for five months in the 139th Regiment. He moved to St. Louis shortly after the war, and pursued studies at a commercial college. Following college, he taught school and worked during the summers at his father's tannery.

Over the next several years, Durbin participated in various business ventures: a dry goods company in Indianapolis; the Citizens' Bank in Anderson; and a paper mill in Anderson. He returned to military duty in 1898 during the Spanish-American War, and served for ten months as a colonel in the 161st Indiana Regiment.

In 1900, he was nominated for governor by the Republican Party, and won easily over his Democratic opponent, John Worth Kern, in the general election. While in office,

Durbin worked to defeat legislation he saw as benefiting the few rather than the many, and ruffled some Republican supporters as a consequence. He was in favor of luring industry to Indiana, and advocated highway improvements as a means to that end.

Durbin left office in 1905. He ran for governor a second time in 1912 on the Republican ticket, but lost to Democrat Samuel M. Ralston.

Durbin returned to live and work in Anderson, Indiana, and died there on December 18, 1928. He was married in 1875 to Bertha McCullough, with whom he had a son and a daughter.

HANLY, JAMES FRANKLIN (1863-1920), twenty-sixth governor of Indiana (1905-1909), was born on April 4, 1863 in Champaign County, Indiana, the son of Elijah and Ann (Calton) Hanly. He grew up on a farm and received an intermittent education at rural schools. In 1879, he moved to Williamsport and worked as a teacher in the common school. Over the next several years, he taught and did manual labor in the summers.

He studied law, passed the Warren County Bar in 1889, and started a law practice in Williamsport. Through his legal work, Hanly, or J. Frank Hanly, was he came to be known, became involved in Republican politics. He was elected to the State Senate in 1890, and to the U.S. Congress in 1894.

In 1904, the Republicans nominated him for governor; he won by a wide victory over John Worth Kern, the Democratic contender. Several public structures were built during Hanly's term: the Coliseum at the Indiana State Fairgrounds, a tuberculosis clinic near Rockville, and the Industrial School for Girls in Clermont. A temperance law was passed during his administration, and moves were made to curb gambling and vice in Indiana. Ethics was a major issue, and a number of state officials were charged in a financial scandal and forced to give up their jobs.

After Hanly completed his term in 1909, he remained active in the temperance movement. He helped establish what was known as the "Flying Squadron," a group that traveled throughout the United States and gave anti-saloon lectures. In 1916, Hanly ran for president of the U.S. as a Prohibition candidate, but was not elected.

He continued to be active in politics until his death August 1, 1920 in Denison, Ohio, when his car was hit by a train. Hanly was married to Eva Simmer in 1881, with whom he had one daughter.

MARSHALL, THOMAS R. (1854-1925), twenty-seventh governor of Indiana (1909-1913), was born in North Manchester, Indiana on March 14, 1854, the son of Daniel and Martha (Patterson) Marshall. As a boy, he lived in Illinois, Missouri, Kansas, and Indiana. He received his education at public schools and at Wabash College, from which he graduated in 1873.

Following college, he studied law in Fort Wayne and Columbia City, and passed the bar. An attorney, Marshall soon became known for his abilities as a public speaker. He was an ardent Democrat, and in 1908 ran for governor of Indiana on the Democratic ticket. He won over Republican James Watson by nearly 15,000 votes.

Marshall worked for a new state constitution during his administration, terming the old one obsolete due to changes in the way business was conducted in the State. His efforts, however, were not successful. Marshall also had no success with his attempts to pass legislation to protect bank and trust company depositors, and to require that building and loan companies be examined by the state. His accomplishments included the passage of the Child Labor Law, and strides in enforcement of the State's anti-gambling laws.

Marshall ran on the ticket with Woodrow Wilson in 1912 and 1916, and was elected vice president of the United States. At the end of his two terms, he returned to Indianapolis to write his memoirs, which were published in 1925 under the title, *Recollections.* He also toured the country, giving lectures, and served on the Board of Trustees of Wabash College.

Marshall died on June 1, 1925 in Washington, D.C. He

was married in 1895 to Lois Kimsey. The couple adopted a son who died in early childhood.

RALSTON, SAMUEL (1857-1925), twenty-eighth governor of Indiana (1913-1917), was born on December 1, 1857 in New Cumberland, Ohio, the son of John and Sarah (Scott) Ralston. His family was in Ohio during the Civil War, but immediately thereafter moved to Owen County in Indiana. Ralston attended public schools and achieved a good record. Still not twenty, he began teaching school, but within a few years had matriculated into the Central Normal College at Danville, Indiana. While at school, he met and married Mary Josephine Backous who tragically died the following year.

Graduating in 1884, Ralston began to study law, and was admitted to the Indiana bar in 1886. For the next fourteen years, he successfully practiced the legal profession in Lebanon, Indiana. Shortly after his fortieth birthday in 1898, Ralston decided to go into politics. He became the Democratic Party's candidate for secretary of state, but lost to his Republican rival. This defeat ended his political career until 1908, when he ran as the Democratic nomination for governor, but lost to fellow Democrat Thomas R. Marshall. A third attempt at high office succeeded four years later in 1912, when he was nominated by the Democrats for governor, and he went on to win in the general election.

Coming to office at the peak of the Progressive era in politics, Ralston initiated a number of reform measures. Following disastrous floods in 1913, he backed legislation for state flood control efforts. He appointed a non-partisan commission to plan the building of public roads, and began the State Park System. With his prodding, the Legislature passed a Workmen's Compensation Law, and provided aid to the blind. His administration was considered successful by the people of Indiana, who subsequently elected him their Senator in 1922.

Senator Ralston died in 1925, while he was still holding his seat in the U.S. Senate. He was married to Jennie Craven in 1889; the couple had three children.

Governors

GOODRICH, JAMES P. (1864-1940), twenty-ninth governor of Indiana (1917-1921), was born on February 18, 1864 in Winchester, Indiana, the son of John and Elizabeth (Edger) Goodrich. He grew up in Winchester, attended public schools, and after high school, enrolled at DePauw University.

By the age of twenty-three, he had gained admittance to the bar; he began a highly successful practice in his home town. Over the next two decades, Goodrich amassed a large fortune before moving his office to Indianapolis in 1910.

With wealth had come political connections, and he served as Republican state chairman from 1901 until 1910. From 1912 until 1916, he served as Republican national committeeman, but resigned the same year to run for governor. Despite a close race, he defeated his Democratic rival, and assumed office just as the United States entered World War I.

During his term of office, a Department of Conservation was organized, more state parks were added to the system, and the highways were improved.

After his successor's inauguration, James Goodrich toured Europe as part of the American Relief Administration, and served on the commission which brought succor to numerous Russian famine districts. Upon his return home in 1923, he worked on the Indiana Deep Waterway Commission and, in 1924, accepted an appointment to the International St. Lawrence Waterways Commission.

In the last decade of his life, Goodrich became a prominent philanthropist and donated significant sums to a number of Indiana Colleges. He died in his home town of Winchester on August 15, 1940. He was married to Cora I. Prist, with whom he had one son.

MCCRAY, WARREN (1865-1938), thirtieth governor of Indiana, was born on February 4, 1865 near Kentland, Indiana, the son of Greenberry and Martha (Galey) McCray. He grew up in Kentland, where his father had gone into the banking business. By the age of fifteen, he joined his father's firm as a bank teller, and gradually rose in its administration. In addition to his banking business, McCray ran a grain elevator business in northern Indiana, and became a highly successful breeder of Hereford cattle.

As a prominent businessman, he served on the Indiana Board of Agriculture from 1912 until 1916. During World War I, he was chairman of Indiana's Food Conservation Committee and, shortly thereafter, a trustee of Purdue University.

Setting his sights on politics, McCray ran for and was elected governor of Indiana in 1920, after defeating his Democratic opponent, Carleton McCulloch. Unfortunately, his administration paralleled Warren Harding's scandal-ridden national administration.

McCray resigned from office on April 29, 1924, following his conviction in a mail fraud case. He served the next three years in a federal prison, finally gaining release in 1927. Considered to have paid his debt, McCray received a pardon from President Herbert Hoover in 1930.

McCray died on December 19, 1938 near his hometown of Kentland. He was married to Ella M. Ade, and fathered three children.

BRANCH, EMMETT (1874-1932), thirty-first governor of Indiana (1924-25), was born in Martinsville, Indiana on May 16, 1874, the son of Elliott and Alice (Parks) Branch. He attended the local public schools and, after graduation from high school, enrolled at Indiana University. Following graduation from the University in 1896, he decided to study law.

Two years later, however, the Spanish-American War broke out and he enlisted in the Army. Although he achieved the rank of first lieutenant by the time of his discharge a year later, Branch saw no action in the conflict.

He resumed his studies and passed the Indiana bar in 1899. Four years later, with a successful legal practice underway, Branch decided to enter politics. He ran for and was elected to the Indiana House of Representatives in 1903, and was reelected in 1905 and 1907.

In 1909, he resumed his law practice and remained a private citizen until 1916, when he served as a lieutenant

Governors

colonel on the Mexican Border campaign. He continued his service when American participation in World War I began, and was promoted to colonel during this time.

Returning home, Branch reentered politics and was elected lieutenant governor on the Republican ticket with Warren McCray. McCray's resignation in 1924 elevated him to the governor's office for a period of eight months. During his short tenure, Governor Branch urged a comprehensive program to improve the public road system and the schools.

Emmett Branch died in his hometown on February 23, 1932. He was married to Katherine Bain in 1905, with whom he had one son.

JACKSON, EDWARD (1873-1954), thirty-second governor of Indiana (1925-1929), was born on December 27, 1873 in Howard County, Indiana, the son of Presley and Mary (Howell) Jackson. Jackson attended local public schools and, after graduation, decided to study law. He passed the bar in the early 1890's, and opened an office in Kennard, Indiana.

Jackson became the prosecuting attorney for Henry County in 1901, and remained at that post for five years. By 1907, he had been appointed judge of the Henry County Circuit Court. The following year, he won election to that office and continued as a judge for the next six years. Seeking higher office in 1916, he won the election for secretary of state. His tenure in office, however, ended in 1917 when he resigned to become a captain in the Army during World War I.

After two years of military service, Jackson resumed his law career in Lafayette. He had been barely settled when, early in 1920, the State Administration reappointed him secretary of state. Destined, it seemed, to hold this office, Jackson was reelected in November, 1920.

In 1924, the Republican Party nominated him for governor, and he went on to win the election. Governor Jackson continued his predecessor's expansion of the State Park system, and began the George Rogers Clark Memorial in Vincennes.

After his tenure ended, he retired to his farm near Orleans, Indiana. Jackson died on November 18, 1954. He was married to Rosa Wilkinson in 1897; the couple had two children.

LESLIE, HARRY G. (1878-1937), thirty-third governor of Indiana (1929-1933), was born in West Lafayette, Indiana on August 6, 1878, the son of Daniel and Mary Ann (Burkhardt) Leslie. He attended local schools and was a successful student. He worked several years before entering Purdue University in 1901.

After graduation in 1905, he attended Indiana University Law School and received a law degree in 1907. Leslie settled in Lafayette, and began a profitable law practice.

At the age of thirty-four, he was elected treasurer of Tippecanoe County, an office he faithfully executed for the next five years. In 1923, Leslie ran for and was elected to the Indiana House of Representatives. He rose quickly and became the speaker of the House in 1925.

At fifty, Leslie ran for governor on the Republican ticket, and defeated his Democratic opponent. Although his administration started out in the Great Bull stock market, the Depression arrived in 1930. He struggled with issues of public relief and, in 1932, called a special session of the Legislature to reduce property taxes.

After his term ended in 1932, he organized the Standard Life Insurance Company of Indiana. Leslie died in Miami, Florida on December 10, 1937. He was married to Martha Morgan in 1910, and they had three sons.

MCNUTT, PAUL (1891-1955), thirty-fourth governor of Indiana (1933-1937), was born in Franklin, Indiana on August 6, 1878, the son of John and Ruth (Neely) McNutt. In 1898, when he was eight, his family moved to Martinsville, Indiana, where he attended local schools. After high school, McNutt enrolled at the University of Indiana, and graduated four years later. He was accepted to Harvard Law School and received his J.D. degree in 1916.

He practiced law with his father for one year in Martinsville before accepting a position as an assistant professor at the University of Indiana Law School. Dr. McNutt's budding career was interrupted when the United States entered World War I. He promptly joined the Army and became a Captain in the Field Artillery. By the end of his active service in 1919, he had attained the rank of Major.

He resumed his teaching duties at the University, and became dean of the Law School in 1925. McNutt was active in the American Legion, and served as its National Commander in 1928-29. As the Depression deepened, he was drawn into politics. In 1932, he ran for governor, and was elected in the Democratic landslide of that year.

Governor McNutt sprang into action with the passage of emergency relief laws, and quickly followed with new regulatory legislation to control the operations of banks and insurance companies. In 1936, he called a special session of the Legislature which brought Indiana state law into conformity with Federal legislation on issues of social security and welfare.

The national administration tapped his abilities after his term of office in 1937; he spent the next two years as high commissioner of the Philippines. Upon returning to the United States, Roosevelt appointed him an administrator of the Federal Security Administration.

When World War II broke out, he became the Chairman of the War Manpower Commission. After V-J Day, McNutt became the first U.S. ambassador to the new Philippine Republic. In 1947, he returned to the United States and set up a practice in New York City.

McNutt died on March 24, 1955 in New York City. He was married to Kathleen Timolatin 1918, and the couple had one child.

TOWNSEND, M. CLIFFORD (1884-1954), thirty-fifth governor of Indiana (1937-1941), was born in Blackford County, Indiana on August 11, 1884, the son of David and Lydia (Glancy) Townsend. While young, he lived on a farm and received his education at the common schools. He attended Marion College and graduated in 1907.

In the years that followed, he worked as a teacher and a farmer. From 1909 to 1919, he was superintendent of

Blackford County Schools. From 1925 to 1929, he was superintendent of Grant County Schools. At the start of the Great Depression, Townsend became director of the Indiana Farm Bureau.

During the years he worked in education, Townsend was also active in Democratic politics. In 1923, he was a member of the State House of Representatives and, in 1928, he ran for U.S. Congress, but was defeated. He was nominated by the Democrats for lieutenant governor in 1932, and won, running on a ticket with Paul McNutt. While Townsend was lieutenant governor, the Legislature voted to make his office full-time, and he was accordingly given responsibilities to act as commissioner of agriculture in addition to his regular duties.

Townsend ran for governor in 1936 and won over his Republican rival, Raymond E. Springer, by nearly 200,000 votes. During his administration, severe flooding occurred in Indiana, and Townsend set up a relief program to help disaster victims. His term was also marked by the creation of a pension fund for firefighters, establishment of the Division of Labor, and passage of legislation requiring an exam before the issuance of drivers' licenses.

Townsend left office at the beginning of World War II, and became director of the Office of Agricultural War Relations. From 1942 to 1943, he served as an administrator for the Agricultural Conservation and Adjustment Administration and later, in 1943, he was named director of the Food Production Administration. In 1946, after the war, Townsend ran for the U.S. Senate, but was defeated.

Townsend died in Hartford City, Indiana on November 11, 1954. He was married in 1910 to Nora Harris. The couple had three children.

SCHRICKER, HENRY F. (1883-1966), thirty-sixth and thirty-eighth governor of Indiana (1941-1945 and 1949-1953), was born in North Judson, Indiana on August 20, 1883, the son of Christopher and Magdalena (Meyer) Schricker. He received his early education at common schools in Starke County.

At the age of twenty-five, he took over publication of

Governors

the *Starke County Democrat,* a Knox, Indiana weekly newspaper. He continued with the paper for nine years, selling it in 1919 to take a position with the Farmers' Bank and Trust Company. In 1932, he ran for State Senate and was elected. Four years later, the Democrats chose him as their candidate for lieutenant governor. He won the election, and served under Governor Townsend.

Schricker ran for governor in 1940, and was elected by a margin of 4,000 votes over his Republican opponent, Glenn Hills. During his administration, he was at odds with the Republican- controlled Legislature. In 1941, the Legislature attempted to centralize state government and revoke the Governor's appointive powers as laid out in laws passed in 1933. Governor Schricker rejected this, and the Indiana Supreme Court agreed with him, striking down the new legislation as unconstitutional.

Schricker was elected to another gubernatorial term in 1948. During his second administration, he faced a Republican- controlled Legislature once again. He worked to make welfare available to the needy and sought, in a special session of the Legislature, to preserve federal funding for the State.

Schricker left office in 1953 and became associated with the Wabash Fire and Casualty Company in Indianapolis. He died at the age of eighty-three in Knox, Indiana on December 28, 1966. Schricker was married in 1914 to Maude L. Brown, with whom he had three children.

GATES, RALPH F. (1893-   ), thirty-seventh governor of Indiana (1945-1949), was born on February 24, 1893 in Columbia City, Indiana, the son of Benton and Alice (Fessler) Gates. He attended the University of Michigan and received his A.B. degree in 1915 and his LL.B. in 1917.

During World War I, he served as an ensign in the Pay Corps of the Naval Reserves. He was assigned to the War Risk Insurance Bureau as a lieutenant, junior grade, and was sent overseas from December 1917 to April 1919.

Gates returned home to Columbia City after the war and worked as an attorney with his father's law firm. He became interested in politics, and aligned himself with the Republicans. From 1941 to 1944, he was chairman of the Republican Party.

In 1944, he ran for governor of Indiana and won over his Democratic rival, Samuel D. Jackson, by more than 45,000 votes. Gates took office just as World War II came to a close. His administration was concerned with the reorganization of state government. A number of new public offices were established, including the Department of Veteran Affairs, the Department of Revenue, the Flood Control Commission, and the Traffic Safety Commission. During his term, a retirement pension plan for public employees was also begun.

Gates left office in 1949 and returned to Columbia City, where he practiced law and remained active in Republican politics. He was married in 1919 to Helene Edwards, and the couple had two children.

CRAIG, GEORGE N. (1909-   ), thirty-ninth governor of Indiana (1953-1957), was born in Brazil, Indiana on August 6, 1909, the son of Bernard and Clo (Branson) Craig. As a young man, he enrolled at Culver Military Academy, then went on to the University of Indiana, where he received his LL.B. degree in 1932.

He returned home to Brazil and practiced law with his father's firm. He also worked as an attorney in Indianapolis until 1942. When the United States entered World War II, Craig began military service and was sent to Europe. During his four years in the armed forces, he rose to the rank of lieutenant colonel. He was discharged in 1946.

In the years after the war, he was an active member of the American Legion in Indiana, and served as national commander of the Legion from 1949 to 1950. He also participated in Republican politics, and practiced law until 1953.

Craig became governor of Indiana in 1953. Serving during the post-war boom, Craig supported plans for various public works, including the creation of an Indiana port on Lake Michigan, the construction of the Indiana Toll

Road, and the implementation of such ay safety features as widened bridges and roads. Several state offices were reorganized within the Department of Health, and the Department of Corrections was established to manage the state prison system.

Craig completed his term in 1957 and went to Washington, D.C., where he practiced law. He later moved his law practice to California, and then back to his hometown of Brazil, Indiana. He was married in 1931 to Kathryn Heiliger and had two children.

HANDLEY, HAROLD W. (1909-1972), fortieth governor of Indiana (1957-1961), was born on November 27, 1909 in LaPorte, Indiana, the son of Harold L. and Lottie (Brackbill) Handley. He attended Indiana University and graduated with an A.B. degree in 1932.

After graduation, he worked with his father at the Rustic Furniture Company in LaPorte, and then became a sales representative for the Unagusta Furniture Corporation of Hazelwood, North Carolina. In 1941, he entered the State Senate and served for a single session. With the entry of the United States into World War II, he enlisted in the army and served in the 85th Division, attaining the rank of lieutenant colonel.

After his return from duty, he was elected a second time to the Indiana Senate and served from 1949 to 1952. In 1952, Handley was the Republican nominee for lieutenant governor on the ticket with George N. Craig. He was elected and served for four years.

In 1956 Handley ran for governor, winning easily over his Democratic opponent, Ralph Tucker. He entered office in January, 1957. During his administration, funding was appropriated for a Lake Michigan port, a new highrise state office building was erected, and the Purdue University Veterinary School was founded. Handley refused to approve controversial "right to work"legislation, and it was put into effect without his signature.

After completion of his term in 1961, Handley joined an Indianapolis public relations firm and served in the capacity of president. Handley died on August 30, 1972.

He was married in 1944 to Barbara Winterble, with whom he had a son and a daughter.

WELSH, MATTHEW E. (1912-   ), forty-first governor of Indiana (1961-65), was born in Detroit, Michigan on September 15, 1912, the son of Matthew and Inez (Empson) Welsh. The family lived in Michigan until Welsh was 12 years old, when they moved to Vincennes, Indiana.

After graduation from high school in 1930, Welsh attended the University of Pennsylvania. Following college, he enrolled at the University of Chicago Law School, and received his J.D. degree there three years later.

He returned to Vincennes and began a successful law practice. As World War II approached, Welsh ran as a Democrat for a seat in the Indiana House of Representatives, and was elected. His term ended in 1943, and he joined the Navy with the rank of lieutenant. Upon demobilization in 1946, he resumed his law practice. In 1950, Welsh became the United States attorney for the Southern District of Indiana. Four years later, the people of his district elected him to the State Senate.

Welsh ran for but lost the Democratic nomination for governor in 1956, but achieved that goal in 1960. He went on to defeat his Republican opponent by a 22,000 vote margin. Once in office, he quickly responded to a pressing need for more state revenue by enacting a two percent sales tax. Heeding the growing Civil Rights movement, he also created the Indiana Fair Employment Commission, and set up youth training centers.

After his term ended, Welsh rejoined his law firm. Seven years later, he ran for governor again, but was defeated by the Republican candidate.

Welsh married Virginia Homann in 1937, with whom he had two children.

BRANIGIN, ROGER D. (1902-1975), forty-second governor of Indiana (1965-1969), was born in Franklin, Indiana on July 26, 1902, the son of Elba and Zula (Francis) Branigin. After graduation from high school, he enrolled at Franklin College, and attained his A.B. degree in 1923. He immediately went to Harvard University and acquired an LL.B. degree in 1926.

His formal education now over, Branigin returned to Franklin and practiced law for the next three years. In 1930, he moved to Louisville, Kentucky to serve as counsel for the Federal Land Bank and Farm Credit Administration. When that job ended in 1938, he returned to Indiana and set up his practice in Lafayette.

During World War II Branigin held the office of chief of the Legal Division, Army Transport Corps, with the rank of lieutenant colonel. At the end of the war, he resumed his practice in Lafayette, and became a trustee of both Franklin College and Purdue University.

In 1964, Branigin ran for governor on the Democratic ticket, and beat his Republican challenger. His administration abolished the poll tax, and began the state's first taxpayer-supported college scholarship program. He terminated the "right to work" law, expanded the powers of the Civil Rights Commission, and set up the Department of Natural Resources. Finishing his term at the age of 67, he went back to Lafayette and once again practiced law.

Branigin died on November 19, 1975. He was married to Josephine Mardis in 1929, and the couple had two children.

WHITCOMB, EDGAR D. (1917-   ), forty-third governor of Indiana (1969-1973), was born in Hayden, Indiana on November 6, 1917, the son of John and Louise (Doud) Whitcomb. He attended local schools, and enrolled at the University of Indiana after high school graduation. When he became financially unable to continue his studies, he left academics and took a job to support himself.

Whitcomb joined the Army Air Force in 1940, and after training as a navigator for bombers, was posted to the Philippines in October 1941. The Japanese took him prisoner at the fall of Corregidor on May 7, 1942. After several thwarted attempts, he escaped the Philippines and returned to the United States in December, 1943. He flew transport missions in Europe and returned to the Philippines in May 1945.

Following his heroic efforts during the war, he enrolled at the University of Indiana, and attained his L.L.B. degree in 1950. Two years later, at the age of 35, he was admitted to the bar. In 1951, Whitcomb was elected to the Indiana State Senate, and held that office until his appointment as assistant U.S. attorney for the Southern District of Indiana in 1955. He continued his law practice until 1966, when he became Indiana's Secretary of State.

In 1968, while the country was debating the war in Vietnam, Whitcomb ran for governor of the State on the Republican ticket, and was elected. His administration held the line on taxes, and appointed a Economy Task Force to reduce waste and duplication in government. The "pocket veto" was declared unconstitutional during his administration.

After leaving office, Whitcomb became a director of the Mid- America World Trade Association in Indianapolis. He was married to Patricia Dolfuss in 1951, and had five children.

BOWEN, OTIS R. (1918-   ), forty-fourth governor of Indiana (1973-1981), was born in Rochester, Indiana on February 26, 1918, the son of Vernie and Pearl (Wright) Bowen. His family moved several times during his youth, and finally settled in Francesville, where he graduated from high school in 1935. Bowen enrolled at the University of Indiana at Bloomington and received a B.A. degree in Chemistry in 1939. He immediately went to medical school and was awarded an M.D. in 1942. Given the times, the young doctor joined the U.S. Army Medical Corps, and served in the Pacific Theater.

After the war, he set up a family practice in Bremen, and served on the staffs of several local hospitals. Public service called, and he became Marshall County coroner from 1952 until 1956. In that year, he ran for and was elected to the Indiana General Assembly. Bowen served only one term and lost reelection by only four votes. Determined to try again, Bowen won election to the Indiana House of Representatives in 1960. He loyally served the Republican Party and his constituents and, in 1972, won the Republican nomination for governor.

Governors

He defeated his Democratic opponent by his political stand on issues of property tax relief and control of government spending at all levels. The State Constitution was amended in 1972 to allow a governor to hold more than one term, and Bowen took advantage of this fact to run for governor again in 1976; he was subsequently reelected.

His second term was a continuation of the success of his first. He managed to lower taxes, deal with a number of natural disasters, and finish Indiana's part of the National Highway System earlier than projected. Additionally, he supported Indiana's ratification of the Equal Rights Amendment.

After leaving office, he resumed his medical career and took a professorship with the Indiana University School of Medicine. He was married to Elizabeth Steinmann in 1939, with whom he had four children. After his wife's death in 1981, he married a second time, to Rose M. Hochstetler.

ORR, ROBERT D. (1917-), forty-fifth governor of Indiana (1981-1989), was born on November 17, 1917 in Ann Arbor, Michigan, the son of Samuel Lowry and Louis (Dunkerson) Orr. His family lived in Evansville, Indiana, and he received his early education in Evansville and at Hotchkiss School in Connecticut. He went on to Yale University, where he graduated with a B.A. in history in 1940, and then entered the Harvard Graduate School of Business Administration. During World War II, he enlisted in the Army and served in the Pacific.

In 1946, after the war, Orr returned to Evansville and worked as a manager for the Orr Iron Company, his family's business. He also became involved in other business ventures in Evansville, and served on the boards of various companies, including Sign Crafters, Hahn, Erie Investments, Sterling Brewers, Product Analysis and Research Industries, and Evansville Metal Products.

Starting in 1965, Orr served as chairman of the Vanderburgh County Republican Central Committee for the next six years. In 1968, he won a seat in the Indiana State Senate. He was nominated for lieutenant governor by the Republicans in 1972; running on a ticket with Otis R.

Bowen, he won in the general election later that year. In 1976, he was reelected and served for a second time under Governor Otis.

At the end of two terms, in 1980, Governor Otis endorsed Orr as the Republican gubernatorial candidate, and Orr won a smashing victory over his Democratic rival, John Hillenbrand II, in the fall election. He was subsequently reelected in 1984.

Entering office in the midst of a recession, Orr saw the State's surplus quickly become a deficit. As unemployment rose to 20 percent in parts of the State, public dissatisfaction grew. Orr attempted to ameliorate these problems by pushing for job creation and opposing tax increases. By 1983, however, Indiana's deficit exceeded $450 million, and Orr called a special session of the Legislature which resulted in an increase in the state income tax from 1.9 percent to 3 percent, and state sales tax from 4 percent to 5 percent.

Orr's second administration struggled to help the State recover economically by improving educational programs and luring foreign investors. In 1988, Indiana was successful in bringing the Isuzu/Subaru light truck and auto plant to the State. Orr left office in January, 1989 and was succeeded by Birch Evan Bayh III.

Robert Orr was married in 1944 to Joanne "Josie" Wallace, with whom he had three children.

BAYH, EVAN (1955-   ), forty-sixth governor of Indiana (1989-   ), was born Birch Evan Bayh III in Terre Haute, Indiana on December 26, 1955, son of Birch and Marvella Bayh. While growing up, he lived in Bloomington, Terre Haute, and on the family farm in Shirkieville, Vigo County.

In 1962, his father was elected to the U.S. Senate, and the family moved to Washington, D.C. After high school, Evan Bayh returned to his home state and attended Indiana University in Bloomington, where he received his B.S. in business economics in 1978. He went on to study at the University of Virginia, Charlottesville, and graduated with a law degree in 1981.

Governors

After law school, Bayh returned once again to Indiana, and practiced law with the Indianapolis firm of Bingham Summers Welsh and Spilman. His father's successful political career motivated Bayh to also become interested in Democratic Party politics.

In 1986, he was elected the secretary of state for Indiana; he began serving on December 1, 1986. Two years later, he was elected governor of the State. He entered office on January 9, 1989, at the age of 33, becoming the third youngest governor in Indiana history.

Evan Bayh met his wife, Susan, in 1981. The couple was married on April 13, 1985.

DIRECTORY OF STATE SERVICES

ADJUTANT GENERAL
2002 S. Holt Rd.
Mail to: PO Box 41326
Indianapolis, IN 46241-0326

ADMINISTRATION, DEPARTMENT OF
State Office Building., Rm. 507
100 N. Senate Ave.
Indianapolis, IN 46204

AERONAUTICS, DEPARTMENT OF
143 W. Market St., Suite 300
Indianapolis, IN 46204

AGING, DEPARTMENT OF
251 N. Illinois St.
Mail to: PO Box 7083
Indianapolis, IN 46207-7083

AGRICULTURE, DEPARTMENT OF
State House
200 W. Washington St.
Indianapolis, IN 46204

AIR POLLUTION CONTROL, DEPARTMENT OF
Chesapeake Bldg., Rm. 203
105 S. Meridian St.
Mail to: PO Box 6015
Indianapolis, IN 46206-6015

ALCOHOLISM, DEPARTMENT OF
117 E. Washington St.
Indianapolis, IN 46204-3647

ARCHIVES & RECORDS, DEPARTMENT OF
Library & Historical Bldg.
140 N. Senate Ave.
Indianapolis, IN 46204

ARTS & HUMANITIES
47 S. Pennsylvania St., 6th Floor
Indianapolis, IN 46204

ATHLETICS, DEPARTMENT OF
State Office Bldg., Rm. 1021
100 N. Senate Ave.
Indianapolis, IN 46204-2246

ATTORNEY GENERAL
State House, Rm. 219
200 W. Washington St.
Indianapolis, IN 46204

AUDIT
State Office Bldg., Rm. 912
100 N. Senate Ave.
Indianapolis, IN 46204-2281

BANKING, DEPARTMENT OF
State Office Bldg., Rm. 1024
100 N. Senate Ave.
Indianapolis, IN 46204

BUDGET
200 W. Washington St.
Indianapolis, IN 46204

State Services

CHILD WELFARE, DEPARTMENT OF
141 S. Meridian St., 6th Floor
Indianapolis, IN 46225

CIVIL DEFENSE, DEPARTMENT OF
State Office Bldg., Room 90B
100 N. Senate Ave.
Indianapolis, IN 46204

CLERK OF THE HOUSE
State House, House Chamber, Rm. 3A-8
200 W. Washington St.
Indianapolis, IN 46204

COMMERCE, DEPARTMENT OF
One N. Capitol Ave., Ste., 700
Indianapolis, IN 46204-2288

COMMUNITY AFFAIRS, DEPARTMENT OF
251 N. Illinois St.
Mail to: PO Box 7083
Indianapolis, IN 46207-7083

CONFLICT OF INTEREST
State Office Bldg., Suite 444
One N Capitol
Indianapolis, IN 46204

CONSUMER AFFAIRS
State House, Rm. 219
200 W. Washington St.
Indianapolis, IN 46204

CORRECTIONS, DEPARTMENT OF
State Office Bldg., Rm. 804
100 N. Senate Ave.
Indianapolis, IN 46204

COURT ADMINISTRATION
State House, Rm. 312
200 W. Washington St.
Indianapolis, IN 46204

DATA PROCESSING, DEPARTMENT OF
State Office Bldg., Rm. 1004
100 N. Senate Ave.
Indianapolis, IN 46204

DEVELOPMENTAL DISABILITIES
117 E. Washington St.
Indianapolis, IN 46204

DRUG ABUSE, DEPARTMENT OF
117 E. Washington St.
Indianapolis, IN 46204-3647

ECONOMIC DEVELOPMENT, DEPARTMENT OF
One N. Capitol Ave.
Indianapolis, IN 46204-2288

EDUCATION (HIGHER)
101 W. Ohio St., Suite 550
Indianapolis, IN 46204

EDUCATION (PRIMARY, SECONDARY, & VOCATIONAL), DEPARTMENT OF
State House, Rm. 229
Indianapolis, IN 46204-2798

State Services

ELECTIONS
850 N. Meridian St., 2nd Fl.
Indianapolis, IN 46204

EMPLOYMENT SECURITY, DIVISION OF
10 N. Senate Ave., Room 331
Indianapolis, IN 46204

ENERGY, DEPARTMENT OF
Commerce Center, Rm. 700
One N. Capitol St.
Indianapolis, IN 46204-2288

ENVIRONMENTAL AFFAIRS, DEPARTMENT OF
105 S. Meridian St.
Indianapolis, IN 46225

FEDERAL-STATE RELATIONS
Hall of the States, Rm. 242
444 N. Capitol St., NW
Washington, DC 20001

FINANCE, DEPARTMENT OF
State House, Rm. 212
200 W. Washington St.
Indianapolis, IN 46204

FISH & GAME, DEPARTMENT OF
State Office Bldg., Rm. 607
100 N. Senate Ave.
Indianapolis, IN 46204

FOOD & DRUGS, DEPARTMENT OF
Health Bldg., Room 303S
1330 W. Michigan St.
Indianapolis, IN 46206

FORESTERY, DEPARTMENT OF
State Office Bldg., Rm. 613
100 N. Senate Ave.
Indianapolis, IN 46204

GENERAL SERVICES, DEPARTMENT OF
State Office Bldg., Rm. 507
100 N. Senate Ave.
Indianapolis, IN 46204

GEOLOGY, DEPARTMENT OF
Geological Survey Bldg., Rm. S-409A
611 N. Walnut Grove
Bloomington, IN 47405

HANDICAPPED
Department of Human Services
2511 N. Illinois St.
Mail to: PO Box 7083
Indianapolis, IN 46207-7083

HAZARDOUS MATERIALS
105 S. Meridan St.
Indianapolis, IN 46225

HEALTH, DEPARTMENT OF
1330 W. Michigan St.
Mail to: PO Box 1964
Indianapolis, IN 46206-1964

HIGHWAY SAFETY, DEPARTMENT OF
State Office Bldg., Rm. 801
100 N. Senate Ave.
Indianapolis, IN 46204

State Services

HIGHWAYS, DEPARTMENT OF
State Office Bldg., Rm. 1101
100 N. Senate Ave.
Indianapolis, IN 46204

HISTORIC PRESERVATION, DEPARTMENT OF
201 E. Ohio St., Suite 880
Indianapolis, IN 46204

HOUSING, DEPARTMENT OF
251 N. Illinois
Mail to: PO Box 7082
Indianapolis, IN 46207

HUMAN RIGHTS, DEPARTMENT OF
32 E. Washington St., Suite 900
Indianapolis, IN 46204

INSURANCE, DEPARTMENT OF
311 W. Washington St., Suite 300
Indianapolis, IN 46204

JUVENILE DELINQUENCY, DEPARTMENT OF
State Office Bldg., Rm. 804
100 N. Senate Ave.
Indianapolis, IN 46204

LABOR, DEPARTMENT OF
State Office Bldg., Rm. 1013
100 N. Senate Ave.
Indianapolis, IN 46204

LAW ENFORCEMENT PLANNING
101 W. Ohio St., Suite 1030
Indianapolis, IN 46204

LEGISLATIVE RESEARCH
State House, Room 302
200 W. Washington St.
Indianapolis, IN 46204

LIBRARY SERVICES, DEPARTMENT OF
Library & Historical Bldg.
140 N. Senate Ave.
Indianapolis, IN 46204

LICENSING (CORPORATE)
State House, Room 201
Indianapolis, IN 46204

LICENSING (OCCUPATIONAL & PROFESSIONAL)
State Office Bldg., Rm. 1021
100 N. Senate Ave.
Indianapolis, IN 46204-2246

LIQUOR CONTROL, DEPARTMENT OF
251 N. Illinois, Suite 900
Indianapolis, IN 46204

MASS TRANSIT, DEPARTMENT OF
100 N. Senate Ave., Room 218
Indianapolis, IN 46204

MENTAL HEALTH, DEPARTMENT OF
117 E. Washington St.
Indianapolis, IN 46204-3647

MINING, DEPARTMENT OF
6 NE 21st St.
Washington, IN 47501

State Services

MOTOR VEHICLES, DEPARTMENT OF
State Office Bldg., Rm. 401
100 N. Senate Ave.
Indianapolis, IN 46204

NATURAL RESOURCES, DEPARTMENT OF
State Office Bldg., Rm. 608
100 N. Senate Ave.
Indianapolis, IN 46204

NUCLEAR ENERGY, DEPARTMENT OF
State Office Bldg., Rm. 913
100 N. Senate Ave.
Indianapolis, IN 46204

OCCUPATIONAL SAFETY & HEALTH, DEPARTMENT OF
Health Bldg.
1330 W. Michigan St.
Indianapolis, IN 46206

OIL & GAS, DEPARTMENT OF
Old Trails Bldg., Suite 601
309 W. Washington St.
Indianapolis, IN 46204-2267

OMBUDSMAN
One N. Capitol St., Suite 700
Indianapolis, IN 46204

PARKS, DEPARTMENT OF
State Office Bldg., Rm. 616
100 N. Senate Ave.
Indianapolis, IN 46204

PERSONNEL, DEPARTMENT OF
State Office Bldg., Rm. 513
100 N. Senate Ave.
Indianapolis, IN 46204

POLICE, DEPARTMENT OF
State Office Bldg., Rm. 301
100 N. Senate Ave.
Indianapolis, IN 46204

PRINTING & PUBLISHING, DEPARTMENT OF
State Office Bldg., Rm. 88
100 N. Senate Ave.
Indianapolis, IN 46204

PROBATION & PAROLE
State Office Bldg., Room 804
100 N. Senate Ave.
Indianapolis, IN 46204

PUBLIC DEFENDER
309 W. Washington St., Suite 501
Indianapolis, IN 46204-2726

PUBLIC UTILITIES
State Office Bldg., Rm. 913
100 N. Senate Ave.
Indianapolis, IN 46204-2284

PUBLIC WORKS, DEPARTMENT OF
State Office Bldg., Rm. 510
100 N. Senate Ave.
Indianapolis, IN 46204

State Services

PURCHASING, DEPARTMENT OF
State Office Bldg., Rm. 507
100 N. Senate Ave.
Indianapolis, IN 46204

RAILROADS, DIVISION OF
143 W. Market St., Suite 300
Indianapolis, IN 46204

REAL ESTATE
State Office Bldg., Rm. 1021
100 N. Senate Ave.
Indianapolis, IN 46204-2246

REFUGEE RESETTLEMENT, DEPARTMENT OF
238 S. Meridian St., 4th Fl.
Indianapolis, IN 46225

RETIREMENT
Harrison Bldg., Rm. 800
143 W. Market St.
Indianapolis, IN 46204

SECRETARY OF STATE, OFFICE OF
State House, Rm. 201
200 W. Washington St.
Indianapolis, IN 46204

SECRETARY OF THE SENATE
State House, Senate Chambers
200 W. Washington St.
Indianapolis, IN 46204

SECURITIES, DIVISION OF
One N. Capitol St., Ste. 560
Indianapolis, IN 46204

Encyclopedia of Indiana

SOCIAL SERVICES, DEPARTMENT OF
251 N. Illinois St.
Mail to: PO Box 7083
Indianapolis, IN 46207-7083

SOLID WASTE MANAGEMENT, DEPARTMENT OF
105 S. Meridian St.
Indianapolis, IN 46225

STATE-LOCAL RELATIONS
State House, Rm. 206
Indianapolis, IN 46204

SURPLUS PROPERTY, DEPARTMENT OF
545 W. McCarty St.
Indianapolis, IN 46225

TAXATION & REVENUE, DEPARTMENT
State Office Bldg., Rm. 202
100 N. Senate Ave.
Indianapolis, IN 46204

TEXTBOOKS, DEPARTMENT OF
State House, Rm. 229
200 W. Washington St.
Indianapolis, IN 46204-2798

TOURISM, DEPARTMENT OF
One N Capitol, St., Suite 700
Indianapolis, IN 46204-2288

TRANSPORTATION, DEPARTMENT OF
Harrison Bldg., Rm. 300
143 W. Market St.
Indianapolis, IN 46204

State Services

TREASURER, DEPARTMENT OF
State House, Rm. 242
200 W. Washington St.
Indianapolis, IN 46204

UNCLAIMED PROPERTY, DIVISION OF
State House, Rm. 219
200 W. Washington St.
Indianapolis, IN 46204

UNEMPLOYMENT, DIVISION OF
10 N. Senate Ave., Rm. 209
Indianapolis, IN 46204

VETERANS' AFFAIRS, DEPARTMENT OF
State Office Bldg., Rm. 707
100 N. Senate Ave.
Indianapolis, IN 46204

VITAL RECORDS & STATISTICS
1330 W. Michigan St., Rm. 236
Mail to: PO Box 1964
Indianapolis, IN 46206-1964

WATER POLLUTION CONTROL, DEPARTMENT OF
105 S. Meridian St.
Indianapolis, IN 46225

WATER RESOURCES, DIVISION OF
2475 Directors Row
Indianapolis, IN 46241

WEIGHTS & MEASURES, DIVISION OF
Health Bldg., Rm. 136
1330 W. Michigan St.
Indianapolis, IN 46206

WELFARE, DEPARTMENT OF
State Office BLdg., Room 701
100 N. Senate Ave.
Indianapolis, IN 46204

WOMEN
32 E. Washington St. Suite 900
Indianapolis, IN 46204

WORKERS' COMPENSATION
State Office Bldg., Rm. 601
100 N. Senate Ave.
Indianapolis, IN 46204

DICTIONARY
OF PLACES

This is a gazetteer of geographical places in the state.

It contains listings of all of the *incorporated* populated places (1990 census figures); prominent physical features and cultural locations. Many points of interest are included as well as the names of Nationally recognized Historical Sites. Details on the Historical Places can be found in the section of the book titled Historical Places. They are arranged in that section by County, so it will be necessary to note the name of the County when cross-referencing.

It is anticipated that additional populated places and other geographical entities not included in this edition will appear in subsequent editions, along with updating, correcting and expanding entries presented here.

ACTON, Town; Pop. 650; Marion County; central Indiana; Zip Code 46259; within the Indianapolis Metropolitan Area. The town is basically a rural community specializing in the cultivation of corn hybrids and feeds, and the manufacture of poultry loaders.

ADAMS, County; Pop. 26,871; E Indiana; area 345 sq. mi.; on the E by the Ohio state line, and drained by the Wabash and St. Mary's rivers and Longlois Creek. Adams County is primarily agricultural, but has some diversified industry such as food processing. Decatur is the county seat.

ADVANCE, Town; Pop. 561; Boone County; central Indiana; Zip Code 46102, 16 mo. ESE of Crawfordsville, in a grain and live stock area.

AKRON, Town; Pop. 1,001; Fulton County; N Cen. Indiana; Zip Code 46910; 45 mi. SSE of South Bend; in a grain and livestock area; also industrial town with three factories. Founded by Dr. Joseph Sippy in 1836. The first settlers who arrived by covered wagon in July of 1836, were from

Ohio, so they named it after Akron, Ohio; previous name was Newark, but there was already another Newark, Indiana. Agriculture includes corn, soybeans, hay, and wheat. Manufacturing includes paper tubes, hardwood lumber, and small electrical power tools. There are a number of lakes, and tourist attractions include hunting, fishing, swimming, and boating.

ALBANY, City; Pop. 2,357; Delaware County; central Indiana; Zip Code 47320; 12 mi. NE of Munice. Located in an agricultural region noted for feed grains and livestock, Albany is a manufac turing center and producer of dyes, lumber, wire products and sheet metal.

ALBION, Town; Pop. 1,823; seat of Noble County; NE Indiana; Zip Code 46701; 26 mi. NNW of Fort Wayne. The name is derived from Albion, New York, suggested by an early settler who had lived there; it's another name for England or Britain; previous name was The Center. The town was settled in November of 1846 by Abel Barnum, Samuel Hanna, William Engle, John White, James Worden, Warren Chaffee, F. A. Black, and S. C. Spencer. It is within the Albion Township, which is said to be the smallest township in the United States.

Although the tourist trade dominates the economy, the production of furniture, lumber, tiles, and dairy products is also important, as well as electrical components, wire, automobile parts, brass fittings, and plastic products. Nearby is Chain O' Lakes State Park (q.v.) comprised of a string of nine natural, connecting lakes.

ALEXANDRIA, City; Pop. 5,709; Madison County; E central In diana; Zip Code 46001; on Pipe Creek, 40 mi. NE of Indianapolis. Alexandria's main industry is the production of rock wool; the Johns-Manville Company plant was the first rock-wool insulation factory in the world. Argillaceous limestone, essential to the manufacture of rock wool, is taken out of local quarries. Gloves, asbestos, and magnesium products are also manufactured.

ALFORDSVILLE, Town; Pop. 74; Daviess County; SW Indiana; Zip Code 47511; 7 mi. S of Loogootee, in an agricul-

Dictionary of Places

tural and lumbering area.

ALLEN, County; Pop. 280,455; NE Indiana; area 671 sq. mi. It is bounded on the east by Ohio, and drained by the Maumee, St. Joseph, and St. Mary's rivers. Formed in 1823, it was named for John Allen. Allen County is noted for stock raising, farming, and dairying. Fort Wayne is the county seat.

ALTONA, Town; Pop. 156; DeKalb County; NE Indiana; Zip Code 46738; 19 mi. N of Fort Wayne. The town is in a predominantly agricultural region, noted for the production of grain and livestock.

AMBIA, Town; Pop. 249; Benton County; W Indiana; Zip Code 47917; about 18 mi. SW of Fowler. In an agricultural area noted for its corn cultivation, the town is a producer of fertilizer and grain feed.

AMBOY, Town; Pop. 370; Miami County; N central Indiana; Zip Code 46911; 13 mi. SE of Peru in a primarily agricultural region.

AMISHVILLE, Amish community; Adams County; NE Indiana; 5 mi. SE of Berne. The unincorporated community of "Plain People", so called because of their religious beliefs, contains no automobiles, motors, plumbing, or other modern conveniences. For transportation the population uses horse-drawn buggies, or sleighs in winter.

AMO, Town; Pop. 380; Hendricks County; central Indiana; Zip Code 46103. On Mill Creek, it lies 25 mi. WSW of Indianapolis in a primarily agricultural region.

ANDERSON, City; Pop. 59,459; seat of Madison County; E central Indiana; Zip Code 46000; 34 mi. NE of Indianapolis.

Picturesquely located in the low hills along the White River, Anderson lies on the site of an old Delaware Indian village. Chief Anderson, for whom the city is named, lived in a double log cabin located at present Eight and Central avenues. In 1801, Moravian missionaries arrived at the village in hopes of converting the Indians to Christianity.

Their efforts failed, and they returned to their headquarters in 1806. The first white settler, William Conner, owned much of the land around the present site and sold it to John Berry, who platted the town in 1823. In 1827, the town, then known as Andersontown, became the county seat. Growth was initially slow, but increased rapidly when it was announced that a canal from Logansport to Indianapolis, which would pass through Andersontown, was planned. An influx of workers almost doubled the population in one year. Bankruptcy hit Indiana in 1838, however, and the canal project was abandoned. Andersontown began to deteriorate, but its economy was saved when the first railroad station was established in 1852. Andersontown became Anderson; incorporation to city status came in 1865.

In 1887, natural gas was discovered, bringing fame and prosperity to Anderson. Shortly the city became known as the "Queen City of the Gas Belt." "Old Vesuvius," one of the largest producing wells in the country, was piped into the White River and lighted to burn night and day for the benefit of visitors, who would see it roaring skyward from the water. The gas boom brought much industry into the area. Almost 40 fac tories, as well as financial institutions and publishing com panies, were established because of the promise of a seemingly endless supply of gas. The gas did diminish, however, and by 1917 the boom was over. Anderson settled into a less frenetic pace. Later developments were largely based on the automobile industry. The car factories are gone, but production of automobile equip ment continues to play a large role. Two subsidiaries of General Motors--Delco-Remy and Guide Lamp--are located in Anderson. Other manufactures include files and rasps, fire trucks, corrugated boxes, copper wire, and packaging machinery. Anderson is also an important grain and livestock distribution center.

Anderson College (1917), affiliated with the Church of God, is a coeducational liberal arts college. On campus is a large collection of artifacts from the Holy Land. Nearby is Mounds State Park *(q.v.)*, a scenic archaeological site along the White River that contains a cluster of prehistoric Indian mounds.

Dictionary of Places

●HISTORICAL PLACES... (See Hist. Places Sect for details.)
Mounds State Park.

ANDREWS, Town; Pop. 1,118; Huntington County; central Indiana; Zip Code 46701; 6 mi. WSW of Huntington. Andrews is the birthplace of Ellwood Patterson Cubberley, the well-known educator who presented Stanford University with a building to house a school of education in 1938. The local economy is based on agriculture.

ANGEL MOUNDS STATE MEMORIAL, state memorial in Vanderburgh County, SW Indiana, just E of Evansville. The mounds are named after the Angel family, on whose property they are located. Angel Mounds is the largest group of historic Indian mounds in Indiana, covering 100 acres. Excavation began in 1939 under the leadership of Glenn A. Black, an archaeologist and anthropologist from In dianapolis. The mounds are conical in shape. They were built by prehistoric Indians of the Mississippi culture (AD 500-AD 1650) as burial places or as elevations for temples and palaces.

Since the early diggings, the Angel Mounds have yielded nearly 2,000,000 artifacts, which prove that about 1,000 people inhabited the area between 1400 and 1600. Evidence shows that a wooden stockade enclosed the settlement, which contained houses, a town square, and temples. A series of archaeological studies sponsored by the Indiana Historical Society and Indiana Univer sity was underway in the 1970s. A visitor center funded by the Lilly Foundation includes a museum which houses a large collec tion of artifacts, including stone implements, pottery, jewelry, and effigies.

ANGOLA, City; Pop. 5,824; seat of Steuben County; NE Indiana; Zip Code 46703; 45 mi. NE of Fort Wayne. Named for a city and county in New York State. It was platted by Thomas Gale and Cornelius Gilmore on June 28, 1838, and incorporated on October 1, 1866. Tri-State University was founded here in 1884. Angola is described as a quiet college town located in a scenic, hilly region of woods and lakes.

The first white settlers came from mostly New England states such as New York, Pennsylvania, New Hampshire, and Vermont, and many also came from Ohio. Before they arrived, the area was a hunting ground for the Potawatomi Indians of the north and the Miami Indians of the south.

The city is still a strong agricultural area, with such crops as soybeans, corn, oats, wheat, clover, mushrooms and mint. Angola also has more than 300 commercial businesses, and over sixty industrial plants, many of the latter located in two industrial parks. Some of the products manufactured are feed, brick, tiles, electronic equipment, construction materials, and automobile parts. There are also a handful of businesses remaining from the last century. In addition, Angola depends largely on the tourist trade, both in summer and winter.

The building of the Indiana Toll Road, in conjunction with Interstate 69, has made Angola directly accessible to Chicago, Detroit, Cleveland and Indianapolis.

Nearby are Crooked and Silver lakes and Pokagon State Park *(q.v.)*. The city hosts an annual Winter Snow Festival in January, and a Farm and Home Expo every March.

ARCADIA, Town; Pop. 1,468; Hamilton County; central Indiana; Zip Code 46030; 29 mi. N of Indianapolis. The town's economy is based on agriculture.

ARGOS, Town; Pop. 1,642; Marshall County; N Indiana, Zip Code 46501; 30 mi. S of South Bend. Argos began as a stagecoach stop and flourished as a regional dairy farming center. The town has a fish hatchery and a lumber mill. Nearby is scenic Lake Maxinkuckee.

ARLINGTON, Town; Pop. 500; W central Rush County; E Indiana; Zip Code 46104; 25 mi. SE of Indianapolis in a primarily agricultural area. Of note is the Beckner-Nelson House, built in Classic Italian style in 1853.

Dictionary of Places

ASHLEY, Town; Pop. 767 on the DeKalb-Steuben county line, NE Indiana. Zip Code 46705, 33 mi. N of Fort Wayne. The economy is based on agriculture and some manufacturing. Products include canned goods and cement.

ATLANTA, Town; Pop. 703; Hamilton County; central Indiana; Zip Code 46031; 32 mi. N of Indianapolis in a primarily agricultural region.

ATTICA, City; Pop. 3,457; Fountain County; W Indiana; Zip Code 47918; on the Wabash River; 21 mi. WSW of Lafayette. The city originally was the site of a Potawatomi village, and contained the home of Chief Topenbee, who signed the Treaty of Greenville in 1795. Here, Tecumseh gathered tribal chiefs to form an alliance to fight the advance of white settlers; the site is marked on Perry Street. Attica was officially founded in 1825 and grew rapidly with the coming of the Wabash and Erie Canal. Incorporation came in 1866.

The magnificent scenery of the gorges and escarpments dis sected by the Wabash River has earned Attica the name of "Gem City." It inspired the state song written by Paul Dreiser and his brother Theodore Dreiser, "On the Banks of the Wabash."

Attica is an agricultural and industrial trading center; manufactures include cement products, steel castings, canned goods, and railroad equipment. Bear Creek Canyon and a natural arch are nearby.

ATWOOD, Town; Pop. 250; Kosciusko County; N central Indiana; Zip Code 46502; 7 mi. W of Warsaw in an agricultural area. The town is a manufacturing center for copper and aluminum bits and fracture equipment.

AUBURN, City; Pop. 9,379; seat of DeKalb County; NE Indiana; Zip Code 46706; 21 mi. N of Fort Wayne in a gently rolling prairie region shaped by glacial drift. Founded in 1836 by Wesley Park, and incorporated in 1848, Auburn was the home of early American automobiles. The Auburn and the Cord were manufactured there, and on the Saturday before Labor Day, the city holds its annual Auburn-Cord-Duesenburg rally. The event attracts owners of more than 100 of these classic cars. There is also an Auburn-Cord-Duesenberg Museum, which features over 140 antique, classic and special interest cars, and which is listed in the National Register of Historic Places.

Auburn is a trading center for livestock, dairy products, corn, soybeans, wheat, automobile parts, rubber specialties, lumber, and stationery.

●HISTORICAL PLACES... (See Hist. Places Sect for details.)

Cornell, William, Homestead.

AURORA, City; Pop. 3,825; Dearborn County; SE Indiana; Zip Code 47007; on the Ohio River; 22 mi. WSW of Cincinnati, Ohio.

Founded in 1819, the city was named for the Roman goddess of dawn. Houseboats are plentiful along the river, and rustic houses cling precariously to the hillsides. The city was hard-hit by the flood of 1937, which raised the water level to a height of more than 80 ft. and ruined the homes of 3,000 inhabitants. Industry includes a few lumber mills and a furniture factory. Mainly agricultural, Aurora is a center for livestock and tobacco.

●HISTORICAL PLACES... (See Hist. Places Sect for details.)

Hillforest (Forest Hill); Veraestau.

AUSTIN, Village; Pop. 4,310; Scott County; SE Indiana; Zip Code 47102; 32 mi. N of New Albany. Sometimes called the "canning center of Indiana," Austin markets millions of dollars worth of canned goods each year. Morgan Packing Company and the American Can Company have plants there. The town was platted in 1853.

AVILLA, Town; Pop. 1,366; Noble County; NE Indiana; Zip Code 46710; 21 mi. NNW of Fort Wayne in a primarily agricultural region.

AVOCA, Village; Pop. 300; Lawrence County; S central Indiana; Zip Code 47420; 4 mi. NW of Bedford. Bluegill, redear, sunfish, crappies, and bass are bred annually at the

Dictionary of Places

the hatchery pools.

BAINBRIDGE, Town; Pop. 703; Putnam County; W central Indiana; Zip Code 46105; 35 mi. W of Indianapolis in a scenic, wooded valley devoted mainly to agriculture.

BARGERSVILLE, Town; Pop. 1,681; Johnson County; central Indiana; Zip Code 46106; 17 mi. S of Indianapolis in an agricultural area noted for feed grains and livestock. Manufactures include lumber, dyes, and special machinery.

BARTHOLOMEW, County; Pop. 57,022; S central Indiana; area 402 sq. mi. Founded in 1821 by Gen. Joseph Bartholomew and Gen. John Tipton. The county is drained by the White River and its tributaries and is a primarily agricultural region. Columbus is the county seat.

BASS LAKE, Town; Pop. 300; Starke County; NW Indiana; 6 mi S of Knox. It is a popular fishing resort near Bass Lake State Beach (*g. v.*).

BASS LAKE HATCHERY, state fishery in Starke County, NW Indiana, on the shores of Bass Lake. The hatchery is the largest and most productive of its kind in Indiana.

BASS LAKE STATE BEACH, Starke County; NW Indiana; on the shores of Bass Lake and 5 mi. S of Knox. Bass Lake, Indiana's fourth largest natural lake, was named for its former abundance of black and silver bass. It is a popular resort and, although the bass have been depleted, it remains an abundant fishing ground for bluegills, yellow perch, and wall-eyed pike.

BATESVILLE, City; Pop. 4,720; Ripley County; SE Indiana; 40 mi. SSW of Richmond. The large German population is employed primarily in one of the city's six furniture factories. Other products include hospital equipment, tiles, and mirrors.

BATTLE GROUND, Town; Pop. 806; Tippecanoe County; W central Indiana; Zip Code 47920; 7 mi. N of Lafayette. On Nov. 7, 1811, Battle Ground was the scene of the Battle of Tippecanoe, where Gen. William Henry Harrison defeated the Indians led by Tenskwatawa, the Shawnee

Prophet, brother of Tecumseh. A 100 foot shaft marks the battle site. Other markers show exactly where of ficers fell in battle. National fame came to Harrison as a result of the victory, and 30 years later he was elected to the U.S. presidency on the slogan "Tippecanoe and Tyler Too." Today, most of the town's population is involved in small business and agriculture.

BECK'S MILLS, site of a water-powered mill built in 1865, Washington County; S Indiana; 9 mi. S of Salem. The mill is one of few in Indiana which have survived with their water wheels intact. The water source is a dammed cave spring above the mill. The original mill site was developed in 1808 by George Beck, a prospector along the Buffalo Trace.

BEDFORD, City; Pop. 13,817; seat of Lawrence County; S Indiana; Zip Code 47421; 22 mi. S of Bloomington.

Bedford was platted in 1825 and, by the 1850s, had become the state's leading limestone quarrying center. The beautiful lime stone, with excellent cleavage and carving properties, has been used in many famous buildings throughout the U.S., including the Empire State Building in New York City. Indiana supplies 80 per cent of the nation's limestone, much of which is cut in the quarries of the Indiana Limestone Corporation. Each block averages 4 ft. thick by 10 ft. wide by 50-120 ft. long. There are three major stone mills with an average employment of 5,000 workers. The production of grain and fruit also plays a major role in Bedford's economy.

Bedford is the seat of Hoosier National Forest. The Lawrence County Historical Museum houses a fine collection of Indiana limestone, Indian artifacts, and Civil War memorabilia.

BEECH GROVE, City; Pop. 13,383; Marion County; central Indiana; Zip Code 46107; SE of Indianapolis. Located on the Tipton Till Plain, the city was named for the many beech and maple trees that thrive on the unassorted glacial soils. Beech Grove was founded in 1900 and incorporated as a town in 1906 and as a city in 1935. Mainly residential, the city has extensive railroad shops. It is the seat of Indiana Central College (1902).

BELLEVILLE, Town; Pop. 400; Hendricks County; 5 mi W of Plainfield in an agricultural and tourist area.

BENJAMIN HARRISON MEMORIAL HOME, Indianapolis; Marion County; Indiana. The home was built by Harrison in 1872, 18 years after his arrival in Indianapolis to practice law. It remained his home until his death in 1901, except for the years he resided in Washington, D.C. as a U.S. senator (1881-87), and the 23rd president of the U.S. (1889-93). The home has been restored as a national shrine and contains a collection of clothes worn by Harrison's first wife, Caroline Lavinia Scott, and some of the original furniture.

BENTON, County; Pop. 11,262; W Indiana; area 409 sq. mi.; bounded on the W by the Illinois state line. Benton was organized in 1840 and was named for Thomas H. Benton. The county is drained by Sugar and Pine creeks and is a primarily agricultural region. The county has several canneries and poultry hatcheries. Fowler is the county seat.

BENTONVILLE, Town; Pop. 85; Fayette County; E central Indiana; Zip Code 47322; 13 mi. NW of Connersville in an agricultural area noted for the production of livestock and feed grains.

BERNE, City; Pop. 3,559; Adams County; E Indiana; Zip Code 46711; 31 mi. SSE of Fort Wayne.

Settled in 1840 by Swiss immigrants from Alsace-Lorraine, Berne has become known for its large Amish population and for its authentic Amish farm, "Amishville," which is a popular tourist attraction. The largest Mennonite church in the U.S. is located there, and Amish and Mennonite farmers work side by side on the surrounding farmlands using only horse-drawn plows. Little of the Amish lifestyle has changed since the 1940s. Their religion dictates that they must live frugally and have no automobiles or other modern conveniences. All of their clothes are plain and home-made. The men are bearded and wear black hats, and the women wear shawls and bonnets. There are four large furniture plants in the town. Other products include dairy foods and work clothes. The Mennonite Book Concern (1893) is the largest publisher and distributor for the Mennonite faith in the U.S. and Canada.

BEVERLY SHORES, Town; Pop. 622; Porter County; NW Indiana; Zip Code 46301; in a resort, farming, and industrial area. In the 1920's, the town was part of a giant land speculation scheme in

which 8,000 acres of land were acquired along Lake Michigan. Lots were bought and sold on a grand scale and savings were invested, only to be lost during the Great Depression. Prior to this time, Beverly Shores was a center for cranberry and blueberry farming. Tourism aided the economy and the town became a summer resort for Chicagoans. Three-quarters of the town has become part of the In diana Dunes National Lakeshore and the rest is to be included in future park expansion.

Of note are the several vintage houses brought by barge in 1933 from the Chicago Century of Progress complex. They include the House of Tomorrow, Old North Church, and Paul Revere House. The town is surrounded by quiet marsh- and dunelands, and is an ideal focus for nature studies and hiking.

BICKNELL, City Pop. 3,357; Knox County; SW Indiana; Zip Code 47512, 13 mi. NE of Vincennes. The town was founded in 1875 after the opening of the first bituminous coal mine in Indiana. Mining is still important, although other industries have begun to predominate. Leading products include lumber, women's clothing, and mobile homes. A mine rescue station is also located in the city.

BIDDLE'S ISLAND, Island in the Wabash River at Logansport; N central Indiana. On the island is the home of Judge Horace Biddle (1811-1900), jurist, writer, illustrator, and painter. In the yard of the mansion is the grave of No'Kamena, a Miami chieftain. The judge permitted the burial of the chief on this spot because it was his original home site.

BIG BLUE RIVER, central Indiana; rises in Henry County and flows for 75 mi. SW past New Castle and Shelbyville.

Dictionary of Places

BIRDSEYE, Town; Pop. 472; Dubois County; SW Indiana; Zip Code 47513; 14 mi. ESE of Jasper. It is an important agricultural and bituminous coal-mining center.

BLACKFORD, County; Pop. 15,888; E Indiana; area 167 sq. mi. Formed in 1838, it was named for Judge Isaac Blackford, the noted pioneer jurist. The county is drained by the Salamonie River and0Lick Creek. Mining and agriculture are the main economic ac tivities. Hartford City is the county seat.

BLOOMFIELD, Town; Pop. 2,592; seat of Greene County; SW Indiana; Zip Code 47424; approximately 40 mi. SE of Terre Haute. The land around Bloomfield was originally donated by Peter Van Slyke, a settler. The town grew as a manufacturing center specializing in furniture, metal products, and silos.

BLOOMINGDALE, Town; Pop. 341; Parke County; W Indiana; Zip Code 473832, 28 mi. NNE of Terre Haute. A marker for a stop on the Underground Railway is just north of town. The economy is based on agriculture and coal-mining. In town is the beautiful Friends Church (1865) which has many historic pictures and record books on display.

BLOOMINGTON, City; Pop. 60,633; seat of Monroe County; S central Indiana, Zip Code 47401; 45 mi. SSW of Indianapolis in an industrial, farming, and quarrying area. Bloomington was founded in 1818 and, two years later, became the seat of Indiana Univer sity, the second oldest state university W of the Alleghenies. The beautiful campus encompasses 1,850 acres and boasts the Daily Art Collection and the Thomas Hart Benton murals.

Bloomington owes its initial growth to the development of the stone industry. It is a center for oolitic limestone quarrying and has more than 30 quarries and stone mills, some of which are open to the public. Other industries include the manufacture of screw machine items, beverages, printed circuits, iron, metal, refrigerators, elevators, plastics, molds, and escalators.

The city is a popular stop-over for tourists who come to visit the nearby state parks, six of which are located within 25 miles of Bloomington. They include Spring Mill and Brown County state parks *(g.v.)*, and Lake Monroe, the state's largest lake.

●HISTORICAL PLACES... (See Hist. Places Sect for details.)

Stout, Daniel, House.

BLUE RIVER, S Indiana; rises in Washington County and flows about 50 mi. SW and S past Salem to the Ohio River near Leavenworth.

BLUFFTON, City; Pop. 9,020; seat of Wells County; E Indiana, Zip Code 46714, on the Wabash River and 24 mi. S of Fort Wayne.

Bluffton was settled in 1829 and incorporated in 1858. The city is built on the bluffs overlooking the Wabash River and con tains several century-old houses. Of note are a tulipwood log cabin (1855) preserved in its original state, and the courthouse (1889), which has a Richardson Romanesque architecture. Bluffton manufactures pianos, windmills, and machinery, and has some lime stone quarrying.

The city contains a large arboretum and the Wells County His torical Museum. Southwest of Bluffton, peat bogs are preserved as a rare reminder of the marshlands immortalized by Gene Stratton Porter in her novel *A Girl of the Limberlost.* Porter was Indiana's most widely-read authoress from 1893 to 1913. Ouabache State Recreational Area is nearby.

BOGGSTOWN, Town; Pop. 286; Shelby County; central Indiana, Zip Code 46110, 9 mi. NW of Shelbyville in an agricultural and manufacturing area.

BOONE, County; Pop. 30,870; central Indiana; area 427 sq. mi.; drained by Sugar and Raccoon creeks and the Eel River. Boone County was formed in 1830 and named in honor of Daniel Boone, the famous pioneer and Indian fighter. It is situated on a ridge of what was once known as the dividing swamps between the White and Wabash rivers. The area was the headquarters of the Eel River tribe of the

Dictionary of Places

Miami Indians. The Indians left the area in 1835, three years after Lebanon became the county seat. Agriculture is the mainstate of the economy, although manufacturing (metal con tainers, heating equipment) plays a large role in some areas.

BOONE GROVE, Town; Pop. 200; Porter County; NW Indiana; Zip Code 46302; 10 mi. SW of Valparaiso in an agricultural area noted for livestock and feed grains.

BOONE'S POND STATE FISHING AREA, S Boone County; central Indiana; 5 mi. NE of Indianapolis. The 28-acre lake has facilities for fishing and boating.

BOONVILLE, City; Pop. 6,724; seat of Warrick County; SW In diana; Zip Code 47601; 18 mi. ENE of Evansville. Platted in 1818, the city was named for Jesse Boon, a relative of the frontiersman Daniel Boone, and father of Ratliff Boon, who was the second governor of Indiana. Ratliff Boon was the first Warrick County Representative in the legislature; he was a Congressman for 16 years, and was twice elected lieutenant governor before serving as governor. Boon Township is named after him, and his one-story cabin is well-preserved on First Street.

Abraham Lincoln, in his early years as a lawyer, used to walk to Boonville to listen to courtroom oratory. The townspeople enjoyed a relatively quiet existence until the coming of the railroad in 1880. Manufacturing plants sprang up, and Boonville became a center for tobacco-growing, flour-milling, and the production of bricks and tiles. Now there is also coal mining, the manufacture of aluminum, and an agricultural industry that includes corn, soybeans, and wheat.

Scales Lake State Forest, a reclaimed strip-mining region with an artificial lake, is two miles from town.

BORDEN, Town; Pop. 426; Clark County; S Indiana; Zip Code 47106; 22 mi. NW of Jeffersonville in a farming and lumbering area. Borden is a manufacturing center for wooden cabinets, of fice furniture, dyes, jigs and fixtures.

Encyclopedia of Indiana

●HISTORICAL PLACES... (See Hist. Places Sect for details.)
Borden Institute.

BOSTON, Town Pop. 159; Wayne County; E Indiana; Zip Code 47324; near the Ohio border and 7 mi. S of Richmond.

BOSWELL, Town; Pop. 767; Benton County; W Indiana; Zip Code 47921; 26 mi. WNW of Lafayette. The town is a popular truck stop.

BOURBON, Town; Pop. 1,672; Marshall County; N Indiana; Zip Code 46504; 26 mi. SSW of South Bend in an agricultural area noted for livestock, feed grains, and poultry. There is some manufacturing, including the production of iron castings, truck caps, roofing materials, heater wire, and automatic screw machine products. In town is a monument of the Old Town Pump, first source of a water supply for the townspeople.

BOWLING GREEN, Town; Pop. 235; Clay County; W central Indiana; Zip Code 47833; 15 mi. SE of Brazil in an agricultural and lumbering area. The town has a sawmill.

BRAZIL, City; Pop. 7,640; seat of Clay County; W Indiana; Zip Code 47834; on Birch Creek; 16 mi. ENE of Terre Haute. The city was named for the country of Brazil by William Stewart. It became a leader in interurban transportation in 1893, when one of the first electric interurban coaches was put into operation between Brazil and Harmony. Brazil is a mining and agricultural center, but is best known for its building brick, tile, and block coal. The area has ten clay plants and several huge strip mines of bituminous coal.

In 1953, Brazil was presented with a 27' tall by 45' wide monument of Brazilian granite by the country of Brazil, South America, as a token of international friendship and in honor of the city's being the first and largest U.S. city to take the name of the South American Republic. The monument was installed near the entrance of Forest Park on the south edge of the city and dedicated in 1956. It is an exact size duplicate of a fountain in Oura Preto, Mines in Brazil.

Dictionary of Places

BREMEN, Town; Pop. 4,725; Marshall County; N Indiana; Zip Code 46806; 15 mi. SSE of South Bend. It is a center for the mint- growing belt and has a spearmint and peppermint extraction plant. Manufactures include feed, flour, building materials, and clothes.

BRIDGEPORT, Town; Pop. 700; Marion County; central Indiana; Zip Code 46231; 9 mi. W of Indianapolis in an agricultural and farming area. Major manufactures include the production of aircraft components and assemblies.

BRIDGETON, Town; Pop. 350; SE Parke County; SW Indiana; Zip Code 47836; on Raccoon Creek. Of note is the covered bridge, built in 1868 and typical of the 36 covered bridges that remain in Parke County.

BRIMFIELD, Town; Pop. 253; Noble County; NE Indiana; Zip Code 46720; 6 mi. N of Albion in an agricultural area noted for feed grains and livestock. The town is a manufacturer of electro- harnesses for refrigerator units.

BRINGHURST, Town; Pop. 275; Carroll County; N Indiana; Zip Code 46913; 11 mi. SE of Delphi in an agricultural area noted for feed grains and sweet corn. Kirk's Popcorn Company manufactures popcorn machines and bags, boxes, and oils for popcorn.

BRISTOL, Town; Pop. 1,133; Elkhart County; N Indiana; Zip Code 46507; on the Saint Joseph River; 9 mi. ENE of Elkhart. The derivation of the name is from Bristol, England. At one time, a part of the town was called Sidneyham. Bristol was founded in the early 1830's by George Judson, and was incorporated in 1869. The town's agriculture includes corn, soybeans, dairy, hogs, beef, hay chickens, and ducks. It is also the manufacturer of canned vegetables and electrical pumps. East of town is the Bonneyville Mill, one of Indiana's oldest continuously operating mills. In September, the town holds its annual Storytelling Festival.

BRISTOW, Town; Pop. 100; Perry County; S Indiana; Zip Code 47515; 20 mi. N of Cannelton in a bituminous coal-mining and farming area.

BROADVIEW, Village; Pop. 2,362; Monroe County; central Indiana, just S of Bloomington in a limestone quarrying and agricultural area.

BRONSON CAVE, Lawrence County; S Indiana; near Mitchell. Bronson Cave is one of many in a system of interconnecting caverns within Spring Mill State Park *(q.v.)*. It is especially dangerous for spelunkers because water flows into it rather than out of it. Boat trips are on occasion taken through the cave.

BROOK, Town; Pop. 899; Newton County; NW Indiana; Zip Code 47922; 40 mi. NW of Lafayette in an agricultural area. Brook is the home of the Hess Manufacturing Company, which makes cosmetics. Beginning as a one-man operation, the company grew to a daily production of 20,000 packages. The historical Hazeldon Home of author and playwright George Ade has been restored. Ade became known in the early 20th century for his *Fables in Slang*.

BROOKLYN, Town; Pop. 1,162; Morgan County; central Indiana; Zip Code 46111; on the Whitelick River; 20 mi. SW of Indianapolis. A covered bridge spans the Whitelick River near Brooklyn. Two tile and brick plants are supplied with raw materials from vast deposits of fire clay at the south edge of town.

Lake Jewell, formed from a drained and dammed swamp, is located at Bethany Park. In the park is Gold Creek, the scene of a minor gold rush in the 1900s. Analysis of the creek's water indicated that the spot had enormous gold resources. About 3,000,000 shares of stock were sold, but after the gold pans were found to yield only 25 cents worth of gold per day, the enterprise was quickly abandoned.

BROOKSTON, Town; Pop. 1,804; White County; NW central Indiana; Zip Code 47923; 13 mi. N of Lafayette in an agricultural area noted for livestock and feed grains. There is some industry including the manufacture of industrial batteries, paper boxes, dyes, and farm supplies.

BROOKVILLE, Town; Pop. 2,529; seat of Franklin County; SE Indiana, Zip Code 47012; on the Whitewater

Dictionary of Places

River and 21 mi. SSW of Richmond. Brookville was platted in 1808 by Jesse Brooks Thomas and Amos Butler; it was named for Thomas' mother, whose maiden name was Brooks. Amos Butler has been called the "father of social work in Indiana." Brookville contains many of the original houses built by the Quakers in the 1790s. It is also the home of four Indiana governors and four men who were to become governors of other states. Lew Wallace, author of *Ben Hur,* was born there. Commercially, Brookville is a trading center for grain, tobacco, furniture, and fiber boxes.

Nearby is the Whitewater Canal, which still offers boat rides reminiscent of the days when canal and river boat traffic was at its peak. (*See* Whitewater Canal State Memorial.)

Three mi. S of Brookville is the Little Cedar Grove Baptist Church (1811), the oldest church in Indiana still standing on its original foundation. A series of earthquakes in 1811 reminded the pioneers of their religious responsibilities, and they began work on their church. Although carpenters were hired, much of the labor was donated by the parishioners themselves. The original timbers are still in place, as are the bricks which were kneaded by oxen. The church was rededicated in 1955 to the faith and spirit of early pioneers in this part of the country.

- HISTORICAL PLACES... (See Hist. Places Sect for details.)

Franklin County Seminary.

BROOKVILLE RESERVOIR, Union and Franklin counties; E Indiana; at the northern edge of Brookville. The Brookville Reservoir was developed jointly by the state of Indiana and the U.S. Army Corps of Engineers and covers an area of 16,445 acres. Both Mounds State Park and White Water State Park *(q.q.v.)* are near its eastern shore. Recreational facilities are available for hiking, picnicking, fishing, camping, boating, hunting, and swimming.

BROWN, County; Pop. 9,057; S central Indiana; area 324-sq. mi. Founded in 1836, it was named for Gen. Jacob Brown, a hero of the War of 1812. It is known as the "most picturesque county in the Midwest," with its rugged hills and rustic, century- old cabins that are scattered throughout the area. Brown County is drained by Salt Creek and is mainly agricultural in character. Nashville is the county seat.

BROWN COUNTY STATE PARK, 15,428-acre state park in Brown County; S Indiana; 2 mi. S of Nashville. Largest of the state's parks, it has scenic vistas of lakes and wooded hills. Inside the boundaries are a game preserve and an 80-foot observation tower. From the tower is a magnificent view of Weed Patch Hill (alt. 1,167 feet; *g. v.*), highest point in southern Indiana.

The park has been called a "sampler" from which the tourist can get a taste of all that Brown County has to offer in its breath-taking vistas of hills, woods, rivers, and lakes. The park is traversed by 27 miles of blacktop roads, along which there are 15 lookouts providing magnificent scenic panoramas. The park also provides horseback riding, an archery range, fishing, wildlife and floral exhibits, nature trails, and camping. The park contains a 110-site horsemen's campground in the Greenhorn Valley sections of the park. Indiana's oldest covered bridge, the Ramp Bridge (1838), spans the North Fork of Salt Creek at the north entrance to the park.

BROWNSBURG, Town; Pop. 7,628; Hendricks County; central Indiana; Zip Code 46112, 14 mi. WNW of Indianapolis. The original name of the town in 1835 was Harrisburg, because William Harris had settled in Lincoln Township and sold land to other settlers. Indians also lived in Lincoln Township, near White Lick Creek. The Post Office was established in 1836.

James B. Brown was the first settler in Brown Township in 1824, which was later (in 1863) split into Brown and Lincoln townships. Brownsburg is in Lincoln Township. The name changed to Brownsburg because there was already a Harrisburg in Indiana. Between 1840 and 1860, the town's population almost tripled, and in 1848, it had its first election. The economy is based on agriculture, including corn, soybeans and pumpkins. The town has a vegetable canning plant, and also manufactures automobile

Dictionary of Places

parts. Part of the 1986 film {Hoosiers} was filmed in one of the town's high schools.

BROWNSTOWN, Town; Pop. 2,872; seat of Jackson County; S Indiana; Zip Code 47220; near the East Fork of the White River, 24 mi. E of Bedford. The town was platted in 1816 and is picturesquely located among the low hills of southern Indiana. A land survey in 1809 was conducted to obtain 3,000,000 acres of land from the Indians. Brownstown lies along the historic "Ten O'Clock Line," so called because the Indians insisted the land border be drawn where the sun cast its shadow at 10 A.M. on the day the cession treaty was signed. Nearby is Jackson State Forest and Skyline Drive which winds its way through some of the most breathtaking areas of Indiana's hill and valley country.

Commercially, Brownstown is a trading center for agricultural products and for silverware, brick, lumber, and canned goods.

BROWNSTOWN STATE FISHING AREA, Jackson County; S Indiana; 3 mi. W of Brownstown. The 11-acre lake has a boat-launching ramp and excellent fishing facilities.

BRUCEVILLE, Town; Pop. 471; Knox County; SW Indiana; Zip Code 47516; 8 mi. NE of Vincennes in an agricultural area noted for feed grains and livestock. The town was platted in 1811 and was named for its founder, Maj. William Bruce. It prospered as a mining town for a short while after the first mine was sunk in 1914. Following a mine disaster in 1923, the operations were shut down, and the village has remained a peaceful farming community.

Abraham Lincoln once spoke at the Bruce House in behalf of Henry Clay, Whig candidate for the presidency.

BUCK CREEK, Village Pop. 276; Tippecanoe County; N Indiana; Zip Code 47924; 11 mi. NE of Lafayette in a farming area. Buck Creek is a trade center for grain, feeds, fertilizer, and seeds.

BUFFALO TRACE, ancient buffalo path and later settlers' trail across S Indiana, from Ohio Falls, Kentucky to

Vincennes, Indiana. The route was often traveled by Gen. William Henry Harrison, Col. Francis Vigo, and Gen. John Gibson.

BUNKER HILL, Town; Pop. 1,010; Knox County; SW Indiana; Zip Code 46914; just S of Vincennes in a coal-mining and agricultural region.

BURKET, Town; Pop. 200; Kosciusko County; N Indiana; Zip Code 46508; 40 mi. SSE of South Bend in a farming area.

BURLINGTON, Town; Pop. 568; Carroll County; NW central Indiana; Zip Code 46915, 24 mi. SE of Delphi in a gently rolling, agricultural area. The town was founded in 1832 and long served as a stagecoach stop. It was named for Chief Burlington of the Wyandotte Indians, who lived in the vicinity for many years. Industries include the manufacturing of bricks, pet food, concrete blocks, and hog sausage.

BURNETTSVILLE, Town; Pop. 401; White County; NW central Indiana; Zip Code 47926; 12 mi. W of Logansport. Burnettsville is a center for custom-blended fertilizers, herbicides, and insecticides and has the distinction of being the seat of the first normal school in Indiana (1852). The old school building is now used for storage.

BURNEY, Town; Pop. 250; Decatur County; SE Indiana; Zip Code 47222; 10 mi. SW of Greensburg in an agricultural area noted for feed grains and livestock.

BURNS HARBOR, Town; Pop. 788; Porter County; NW Indiana; Zip Code 46368; in the Calumet Industrial District. Incorporated as a town in 1967, Burns Harbor is the newest community in Porter County. The Bethlehem plant, which opened in 1964, employs a large portion of the population and is one of the most modern steel-making facilities in the U.S. The plant houses the largest blast furnace in the Western Hemisphere.

BUSH CREEK STATE FISH AND WILDLIFE AREA, Jennings County; SE Indiana; 1 mi. N of Butlerville. Public access is provided at the wildlife area, which contains a

Dictionary of Places

180-acre lake. Boating and fishing are available.

BUTLER, City; Pop. 2,601; DeKalb County; NE Indiana; Zip Code 46721; 29 mi. NE of Fort Wayne. Butler's economy is based on small businesses that specialize in such diversified products as leather jackets, windmills, pumps, and condensed milk. It is also an agricultural trading center.

BUTLERVILLE, Town; Pop. 350; Jennings County; S Indiana; Zip Code 47223; 13 mi. W of Versailles. Just E of town is the Jefferson Proving Ground. Between North Vernon and Butlerville is the Quaker cemetery, which contains the grave of former U.S. president Richard Nixon's great-grandfather, Joshua Milhouse. Nearby is Bush Creek State Fish and Wildlife Area, a popular recreation area which has a 180-acre lake.

CAMBRIDGE CITY, Town; Pop. 2,481; Wayne County; E Indiana; Zip Code 47327; 15 mi. W of Richmond. The word "city" was added to the name, as there was already another Cambridge, Indiana. The land in this area was bought in 1813 by John Hawkins. Some of the early settlers included his son William, and the Simon Powell family. Located on the banks of the Whitewater River, the Whitewater Canal was created in the 1840's. Cumberland Road, which runs through Cambridge City, was completed in 1827, and the city was platted in 1836. Cambridge City retains many fine homes from the early 1800s. It was the home of Gen. Solomon Concise Meredith, leader of the Iron Brigade that fought in the Battle of Gettysburg.

The town serves a large grain, dairy, and livestock area, and is a manufacturer of feed, metal products, chairs, pottery, dairy equipment, truck bodies, caskets, meat processing, wall and ceiling finishes, and industrial coatings.

In the early 1900's, the Single G, a world famous pacer, made Cambridge City famous in racing circles. In the mid-1950's, a manufacturing firm built the heavy machinery needed to form the hull of the first atomic submarine. The six Overbeck sisters gained international fame for their pottery, and the town has an Overbeck House, and an Overbeck Museum.

CAMBY, Town; Pop. 200; Marion County; Central Indiana; Zip Code 46113; 7 mi. from Indianapolis in a farming and manufacturing area. Camby is a manufacturing center for electronic coils and windings.

CAMDEN, Town; Pop. 607; Carroll County; N Indiana; Zip Code 46917; 8 mi. E of Delphi in an agricultural area noted for grains, feeds, and poultry. Camden is a trade center for fertilizer, coal, salt, and eggs.

CAMPBELLSBURG, Town; Pop. 606; Washington County, S Indiana, Zip Code 47108; 20 mi. SE of Bedford. Located in the scenic unglaciated hills of southern Indiana, the town is the gateway to the Cave River Valley. A park, enclosing a major portion of the valley, has its headquarters in a restored 150-year-old cabin that sits on the site of once prosperous Hammer's Mill. A river winds its way through the deep canyon into River Cave.

Campbellsburg serves a large agricultural area, but depends in large measure on the tourist trade. A popular event is the annual Strawberry Festival, which attracts visitors from other regions of Indiana.

CANNELBURG, Town; Pop. 97; Daviess County; SW Indiana; Zip Code 47519; 28 mi. E of Vincennes in a primarily agricultural area.

CANNELTON, City; Pop. 1,786; seat of Perry County; S Indiana; Zip Code 47520; on the Ohio River, 50 mi. E of Evansville. Founded in 1837, the city was named for the nearby deposits of canned coal (coal with a fine texture and large amounts of volatile matter). During the mining days, Cannelton was one of the most important Ohio River ports, but its economy dwindled as the coal supply was exhausted. Today the city depends mainly upon sandstone quarrying and the manufacture of cotton cloth, furniture, toys, and caskets. The city gives an impression of great age and, as such, is an attraction to tourists. Rough-hewn century-old buildings mingle with the new. Cannelton Cotton Mill

Dictionary of Places

(1849), a factory with twin towers, was once Indiana's largest industry, housing 10,800 spindles and 372 looms.

East of Cannelton is Lafayette Springs, which contains a shallow cave with an active spring. Gen. Lafayette landed there after his steamboat "Mechanic" capsized and was lost, along with all its baggage and $8,000 worth of gold. Off Hwy. 166 is the Electra Memorial, which marks the site where a plane went down in 1960, killing 63 people.

CARBON, Town; Pop. 350; Clay County; W Indiana; Zip Code 47837; 19 mi. NE of Terre Haute in a coal-mining area.

CARLISLE, Town; Pop. 613; Sullivan County; SW Indiana; Zip Code 47838; 21 mi. NNE of Vincennes. One of the oldest towns in Indiana, it was settled in 1803 and platted in 1812 by Samuel Ledgerwood. It was an important coal-mining center until its deposits were exhausted. Today the town is a producer of lumber, canned goods, and liniment.

In Carlisle is the Treaty Elm, an old elm tree under which a treaty was negotiated to acquire additional lands.

CARLOS, Village; Pop. 100; Randolph County; E central; Indiana; Zip Code 47329; 12 mi. SW of Winchester. Carlos is a trade center for butter, flour, and feed, and is a manufacturer of casket shells, dolls, and stampings.

CARMEL, City; Pop. 25,380; Hamilton County; central Indiana; Zip Code 46032; 10 mi. N of Indianapolis; Carmel was founded by Daniel Warren, a native of North Carolina. He and his wife Mary were the first white settlers in the area. In 1837, Warren and three neighboring farmers, Alexander Mills, John Phelps, and Seth Green, platted and recorded land under the name of Bethlehem. Later, when the town was incorporated, the name was changed to Carmel.

Among later residents to bring recognition to Carmel was Leslie Haines. He manufactured and installed what is believed to be the country's first automatic traffic signal at the intersection of Main Street and Rangeline Road on April 19, 1924.

Carmel was the fastest growing city in the United States during the 1970's, having tripled its population in eleven years. It is an agricultural area noted for feed grains and livestock, and its manufacturing includes such products as ready-mix concrete, elevators, safety belts, radio manufacturing and design, computer equipment, dental equipment, automatic screw machine products, and electric cords. The town also has two newspapers and a typesetting plant.

CARROLL, County; Pop. 17,734; N. central Indiana; area 374 sq. mi., drained by the Tippecanoe River and Wildcat and Deer creeks. Carroll County was organized in 1828 and named for Charles Carroll, the only surviving signer of the Declaration of Independence. In the past, Shawnee and Miami Indians claimed the area as their own, and many Indian relics can still be found.

Prehistoric Indian mounds are also located in the NW sector of the county. Delphi became the county seat in May, 1828. Carroll County's economic progress was enhanced in the 1800s by the trade facilities provided by the Wabash and Erie Canal. Today it is a leader in agricultural products, meat and poultry packing, lumber milling, and plumbing fixture fittings.

CARTHAGE, Town; Pop. 887; Rush County; E central Indiana; Zip Code 46115; 32 mi. E of Indianapolis. It is a marketing center for the paper industry and an agricultural center for livestock, poultry, and grain.

CASS, County; Pop. 40,456; N central Indiana; area 415 sq. mi.; drained by the Eel River and Deer Creek. The county was organized in 1829 and named for Lewis Cass, governor of Michigan Territory (1813-31) and the 1848 Democratic presidential candidate. Cass County is noted for livestock, grain, fruit, poultry, truck and dairy products, plant nurseries, and timber. Manufactures include electrical wire assemblies, wire springs, rubber and plastic products, and machinery. Logansport is the county seat.

CASTLETON, Town; Pop. 37; Marion County; central Indiana; Zip Code 46250; 12 mi. NE of Indianaplolis in an ag-

Dictionary of Places

ricultural and manufacturing area. Castleton manufactures cabinets, clutches, couplings, and leather apparel.

CAYUGA, Town; Pop. 1,083; Vermillion County; W Indiana; Zip Code 47928; near the Wabash River and 34 mi. N of Terre Haute in a coal-mining and agricultural region.

CEDAR LAKE, Town; Pop. 8,885; Lake County; NW Indiana, Zip Code 46303; 7 mi. SW of Crown Point. Cedar Lake became a popular resort for the wealthy in the 1890s. The Monon Railroad was instrumental in its development, carrying trainloads of Chicagoans to the community, which sits on the edge of a forest-rimmed lake. The boom days ended in 1929 with the beginning of the Great Depression. The cottages remain, but many of them are now dilapidated.

Cedar Lake still attracts thousands of visitors every weekend, who enjoy the lake's excellent bathing, boating, and fishing facilities. The Moody Bible Institute holds sacred music concerts every Saturday during July and August on the site of Old Monon Park. Of note to visitors is the Indian Mound Cemetery which has tombstones of early settlers and an old Indian burial ground. Industry is light, including only the manufacture of violin strings and ironwork.

CEDAR GROVE, Town; Pop. 248; Franklin County; SE Indiana; Zip Code 47016; 6 mi. SE of Brookville in an agricultural area noted for feed grains and livestock.

CENTER POINT, Town; Pop. 278; Clay County; W Indiana; Zip Code 47840; 18 mi. ESE of Terre Haute in an agricultural and bituminous coal-mining region. Dietz Lake, a popular recreational spot, is nearby.

CENTERVILLE, Town; Pop. 2,380; Wayne County; E Indiana; Zip Code 47330; 6 mi. W of Richmond. Centerville, the second oldest town in the county, was platted on October 20, 1814 by Henry Bryan, and incorporated on January 2, 1815. The land was originally donated by Israel Elliott and Nathan Stone of Cincinnati.

Centerville is well-known for its fine old homes. Arches and fancy architecture abound on Main Street. The

George W. Julian House (1846) is built in Georgian style and was later remodeled in the Italian Renaissance and Greek Revival styles. Julian was a radical leader of the Indiana Congress (1849-51). The Salisbury Courthouse (1811) is the oldest standing log courthouse in Indiana.

The town, which sustained a major fire in 1969, was placed in the National Register of Historic Places in 1971. It is a marketing center for livestock and dairy farmers, and its agriculture includes such products as corn and soybeans. The town's manufacturing includes furniture, canned goods, commercial water sealant products, and tool and die.

●HISTORICAL PLACES... (See Hist. Places Sect for details.)
Centerville Historic District.

CHAIN O'LAKES STATE PARK, Noble County; NE Indiana; 5 mi. SE of Albion. The park, so named because of its many interconnecting lakes, encompasses 2,731 acres of woods and water. Recreational facilities are available for bathing, boating, fishing, picnicking. horseback riding, hiking, and camping.

CHALMERS, Town; Pop. 525; White County; NW central Indiana; Zip Code 47929; 17 mi. N of Lafayette in an agricultural area.

CHANDLER, Village; Pop. 3,099; Warrick County; SW Indiana; Zip Code 47610; 13 mi. ENE of Evansville in an agricultural and bituminous coal-mining region. The Wabash and Erie Canal passed through Chandler; the canal bed can still be seen west of the town.

CHARLESTOWN, City; Pop. 5,889; Clark County; SE Indiana; Zip Code 47111; 15 mi. NE of New Albany. Charlestown was platted in 1808 and was the county seat from 1811 to 1878. A gradual economic decline ended in 1940, when E.I. duPont de Nemours and Company built a powder plant at the edge of town. The subsequent arrival of the Goodyear Tire and Rubber Company brought an influx of people into Charlestown and resulted in the biggest boom in its history. Although industry has taken over, much of the his toric past has been preserved. The first Methodist Church in In diana was moved to Charlestown, and other

Dictionary of Places

century-old buildings remain. Near the church is the grave of Jonathan Jennings (1784- 1834), first governor of Indiana. Old Tunnel Mill (1820) operated until 1854; its giant wheel and foundation are preserved in a picnic area.

On military property atop a 180-ft. ridge between Fourteen Mile Creek and the Ohio River lie Indian earthworks thought to have been built by the Mound Builders of the Mississippian culture.

CHARLOTTESVILLE, Town; Pop. 400; Hancock County; central Indiana; Zip Code 46117; 29 mi. E of Indianapolis in a farming and dairy area. The town is a producer of steel pipe, farm supplies, and liquid fertilizers.

CHESTERFIELD, Town; Pop. 2,730; Madison County; central In diana; Zip Code 46017; 39mi. NE of Indianapolis. It was named for an Indian trader called McChester, who had a cabin near Mill Creek. Several settlers arrived and built three mills, one of which was a carding mill that brought some measure of prosperity to the town. Chesterfield was organized in 1830, but was not in corporated until 1858. In 1890, the State Spiritualist Associa tion built a camp and a 500-seat auditorium nearby. Every August, thousands of visitors arrive for the meeting of the Spiritualist faith.

CHESTERTON, Town; Pop. 9,124; Porter County; NW Indiana; Zip Code 46304; 15 mi. E of Gary. Chesterton is a center for poultry, fruit, and dairy products, and is a manufacturer of printer's supplies. North of Chesterton is a series of giant sand dunes created by centuries of beach erosion along the shore of Lake Michigan.

CHRISNEY, Town; Pop. 511; Spencer County; SW Indiana; Zip Code 47611; 30 mi. E of Evansville is mainly an agricultural area. Chrisney City Lake, in the town, is a popular fishing and boating spot for the local populace.

CHURUBUSCO Town; Pop. 1,781; Whitley County; NE Indiana; Zip Code 46723; 15 mi. NW of Fort Wayne. Named for the Mexican town of Churubusco, it is a farming community and a shipping point for vegetables. Blue Lake, a 239-acre recreational site, is located 3 mi. NW of the town.

CICERO, Town; Pop. 3,268; Hamilton County; central Indiana, Zip Code 46034; 27 mi. NNE of Indianapolis. Named for a Delaware Indian chief, it is a headquarters for the Seventh-Day Adventists who have a camp nearby. The town is a center for agricultural products.

CLARK, County; Pop. 75,876; SE Indiana; area 384 sq. mi.; bounded SE by the Ohio River and drained by Silver Creek. Clark County was founded in 1801 and named for George Rogers Clark, a Revolutionary War hero. The county is mainly agricultural in character, but has some manufacturing at Charlestown, Clarksville, and Jeffersonville (q.g.v.).

CLARKSBURG, Town; Pop. 300; Decatur County; SE Indiana; Zip Code 47225; 12 mi. NE of Greensburg in an agricultural area noted for feed grains and livestock.

CLARKS HILL, Town; Pop. 716; Tippecanoe County; W central Indiana; Zip Code 47930; 15 mi. SSE of Lafayette. The town economy is based on agriculture and farming.

CLARK STATE FOREST, Scott and Clark counties; SE Indiana; near Henryville in the scenic Hoosier Hills. Clark State Forest covers an area of 22,871 acres and contains several lakes which are stocked with game fish. The forest contains facilities for camping, picnicking, boating, fishing, hiking, and horseback riding.

Clark State Forest is the oldest and one of the largest state forests in Indiana. Much of the land was once part of Clark's Grant, given to George Rogers Clark in the Virginia Cession of

Claims to the Northwest Territory after the Revolutionary War. Virgin stands of maple and beech are abundant, and the many rocky, fern-clad ravines make the area attractive to visitors.

CLARKSVILLE, Town; Pop. 19,833; Clark County; SE Indiana; Zip Code 47130; just E of New Albany. Clarksville was founded in 1783 by George Rogers Clark. Located on the Ohio River, the original settlement overlooked Corn Island, on which Clark established his first military outpost.

Dictionary of Places

After creating the town, however, he did not develop it, and it soon fell into decay. Since Clarks' death in 1818. Clarksville has merged with the Louisville, Kentucky, metropolitan area and has benefited from its industrial economy. The Colgate-Palmolive plant lies along the river and has the world's second largest clock on its roof. In town is the Howard Steamboat Museum, which has memorabilia of the Howard Shipyards (1834-1941), which built some of the most famous steamboats.

• HISTORICAL PLACES... (See Hist. Places Sect for details.)
Old Clarksville Site.

CLAY, County; Pop. 23,933; W Indiana; area 364 sq. mi.; drained by the Eel River and Birch Creek. Clay County was organized in the 1800s and named for Henry Clay, the famous statesman. At the time, Clay County ranked as the largest producer of coal in the state, but the supply was largely exhausted. Mining is still carried out in some areas. Leading industries are clay products and brick manufacturing. Agriculture (livestock, feed grains) is the economic mainstay. Brazil is the county seat.

CLAY CITY, Town; Pop. 929; Clay County; W Indiana; Zip Code 47841; 22 mi. SE of Terre Haute. Clay City was founded in 1873 and was incorporated in 1888. Manufacturing began with the build ing of a pottery plant; the old works still remain and are popular with visitors. Pottery is still produced, but other in dustries which manufacture concrete products and preserves have emerged. Coal mines and clay pits are nearby.

CLAYPOOL, Town; Pop. 411; Kosciusko County; N. Indiana; Zip Code 46510; 45 mi. SSE of South Bend. Located in the northern lake and moraine region, it is a center for feed grains and live stock in one of the best agricultural areas of the state.

CLAYTON, Town; Pop. 736; Hendricks County; central Indiana; Zip Code 46118; 22 mi. WSW of Indianapolis. It is a center for flour, timber, fruit, and grain.

CLEAR CREEK, Village Pop. 250; Monroe County; S Indiana; Zip Code 47426; 4 mi. S of Bloomington in an agricultural and limestone quarrying area. Concrete products are manufactured in the village.

CLERMONT, Town Pop. 1,678; Marion County; central Indiana; Zip Code; 46119. Clermont was platted in 1849. The oldest remaining log cabin in Marion County is outside the town. The cabin was built in 1821, and is dedicated to the pioneers of the county. Historical memorabilia are on display. Most of the population are employed in Indianapolis, and the remainder rely on mining and agriculture.

CLIFFORD, Town Pop. 308; Bartholomew County; S central Indiana; Zip Code 47226; 37 mi. SSE of Indianapolis. Clifford is an agricultural area. Crops include corn, wheat, and soybeans.

CLIFTY FALLS STATE PARK, Jefferson County; SE Indiana; 1 mi. W of Madison. The park, situated on a high wooded plateau, is one of the most beautiful in Indiana. Encompassing 1,200 acres of hills and woods, Clifty Falls offers a striking view of the Ohio River from a point 400 feet above the shoreline. Scenic waterfalls along Clifty Creek and Little Clifty Creek, and a deep, boulder- strewn canyon are popular attractions for thousands of tourists who visit the park annually. In 1974, a tornado damaged the forest and guest facilities near the park's southern end.

CLINTON, County; Pop. 30,547; central Indiana; area 407 sq. mi., drained by Sugar and Wildcat creeks. The county was or ganized in 1830 and named after DeWitt Clinton, early governor of New York. Frankfort became the county seat the following year, when the first court was held in the new log courthouse. The land is generally rolling and the numerous streams afford good drainage, making the entire region conducive to farming and live stock raising. Many areas have large deposits of excellent clay, which is used in the manufacture of bricks, tiles, and pottery. Leading industries are food processing and the manufacture of electronic components and plumbing fixtures.

CLINTON, City; Pop. 5,040; Vermillion County; W Indiana; Zip Code 47842; on the Wabash River, 14 mi. N of Terre Haute. Clinton was platted in 1829 after the discovery

Dictionary of Places

of large coal deposits in the area. It was named for DeWitt Clinton, a governor of New York. Early in its existence, Clinton was an important river port and packing center. Coal mining is still the leading activity, but the manufacture of flour, meat products, and overalls is also important.

CLOVERDALE, Town; Pop. 1,681; Putnam County; W central Indiana; Zip Code 46120; 33 mi. E of Terre Haute in a hog-raising and general farming area. Cloverdale is located close to Lieber State Park *(q. v.)* and Cataract Lake.

COAL CITY, Town Pop. 235; Owen County; central Indiana; 20 mi. W of Spencer in an agricultural and mining area.

COATESVILLE, Town; Pop 469; Hendricks County; central Indiana; Zip COde 46121; 28 mi. WSW of Indianapolis in a primary agricultural area specializing in dairy, grain, and livestock farming. A large area of beech-maple forest growth has been a natural asset for the town's thriving timber business.

COLFAX, Town; Pop 727; Clinton County; central Indiana; Zip Code 46035; 19 mi. SSE of Lafayette in a grain and livestock area. There is some furniture manufacture and mining of bituminous coal.

COLLEGEVILLE, Village; Pop. 1,400; Jasper County; NW Indiana; Zip Code 47978; on the Iroquois River, 45 mi. S of Gary in a dairy and livestock region. The village is the seat of St. Joseph's College, a junior college for men founded in 1891.

COLUMBIA CITY, City; Pop 5,706; seat of Whitley County; NE Indiana; Zip Code 46725; 20 mi. WNW of Fort Wayne. Columbia City is distinguished for its many famous residents. Thomas Riley Marshall (1854-1925), U.S. vice-president under Woodrow Wilson and governor of Indiana (1909-13), once practiced law there. He is well-known for his adage: "What this country really needs is a good five-cent cigar." His home has been preserved as a museum by the Whitley County Historical Society. The city was also the home of Maj. Gen. Merritt W. Ireland, surgeon-general of the U.S. Army (1918-23). Lloyd C. Douglas, author of *The Magnificent Obsession* and *The Robe*, was born in Columbia City in 1877.

The Miami Indian chief, Little Turtle, one of the signers of the Treaty of Greenville (1795), had his village on the Eel River near the site of Columbia City.

The city has diversified manufacturing, producing clothes, flour, condiments, automotive parts, and woolen goods. Whitley County Hospital and a school for retarded children are located in the city.

COLUMBIA, Town; Pop. 70; Fayette County; E Indiana; about 8 mi. E of Rushville in an agricultural area noted for wheat and corn production. One mile north of town is the 654-acre Mary Gray Bird Sanctuary, which harbors more than 60 species of birds.

COLUMBUS, City; Pop. 31,802; seat of Bartholomew Count;, S central Indiana; Zip Code 47210; on the White River, 40 mi. SSE of Indianapolis. The site was first settled in 1820 by Gen. John Tipton, John Lindsay, and Luke Bonesteel, who built cabins along the White River. The following year, Tipton donated 30 acres of his property for the county seat, with the understanding that the town be named for him. The county commissioners, however, named the town Columbus. Tipton left hastily and settled in northern Indiana.

Economic progress was initially slow because the town was lo cated in a swampy area where malaria killed many of the resi dents. It was many years before health conditions were corrected.

Often called the "Athens of the Prairie," Columbus has some of the most outstanding architecture in the country. An ambitious project was begun in the 1930s, when Eliel Saarinen, the Finnish architect, was commissioned to design a church. Since then, 40 additional buildings have been designed by such world famous architects as Eero Saarinen, Eliel's son; John Carl Warnecke; Harry Weese; I.M. Pei; and Kevin Roche. The Columbus Chamber of Commerce operates daily tours of the buildings. The First Christian Church, designed by Eliel Saarinen, is an outstanding ex-

Dictionary of Places

ample of Fundamentalist architecture; its 166-ft. chimes tower can be seen for miles. The North Christian Church is an hexagonal structure that tapers to a spire topped by a golden cross. Other outstanding examples are the Irwin Union Bank, the Cleo Rogers Memorial Library, the post office, and the Cummins Engine Factory.

Large numbers of parks and landscaped areas are scattered throughout the city's business district. Irwin's Sunken Gardens are contained in three-quarters of a city square and harbor hundreds of flowers and some rare historical items. The garden's sundial was made in England in 1699, the fountains came from Vienna, and the coping of the rock wall is from a ruined Italian city once buried in lava. At the west end of Third Street is Tipton Knoll, one of the largest prehistoric Indian mounds in the state; a house occupies the site. Nearby are several developed fishing sites, including Azabia, Grouse Ridge, Lowell Bridge, and Millrace.

Columbus has a dual farming and industrial economy that helped the city survive the Great Depression. The Cummins Diesel Engine Company is the world's largest producer of diesel engines for locomotives, boats, trucks, and cars. Other manufactures include metal products furniture, clothing, cement products, and canned goods.

Columbus has the dubious honor of being the home of the Reeves Octoauto. Invented in the early 1900s, its four additional wheels were said to act as "a shock absorber beyond the dreams of the neurotic." This oddity was later reduced to the Sextoauto, but was hastily abandoned for its impracticality.

CONNER PRAIRIE, Hamilton County; central Indiana; 4 mi. S of Noblesville. A restored pioneer settlement, Conner Prairie contains the brick mansion and farm buildings of William Conner, a Hoosier fur-trader and businessman who settled there in 1823. Other log buildings are on the grounds, and the settlement has been called "a living museum area of Indiana's earliest days."

CONNERSVILLE, City; Pop.15,550; seat of Fayette County; E Indiana; Zip Code 47331, on the Whitewater

River, 55 mi. E of Indianapolis. Connersville was a fur trading post in 1808, run by John Connor, a white man who had been raised by the Delaware In dians. He founded Connersville in 1813, and became its first sheriff. He was one of the nine men to select Indianapolis as the state capital.

Connersville has been called "Little Detroit" because it formerly manufactured ten classic automobiles, among them the McFarlan, Kelsey, Auburn, and Cord. Today, the automobile industry is gone, but automobile parts are still manufactured. Other products include machine-shop equipment, refrigerators, air conditioners, and metal and enamel items.

A major tourist attraction is the office of the Whitewater Canal Company and the Elmhurst mansion, which was built in 1831.
- HISTORICAL PLACES... (See Hist. Places Sect for details.)
Canal House.

CONVERSE, Town; Pop. 1,144; Miami County; N central Indiana; Zip Code 46919; 10 mi. W of Marion. A center for livestock and grain, it is also a manufacturer of canned goods, mops, and milk-bottle caps.

CORTLAND, Village Pop. 170; Jackson County; S Indiana; Zip Code 47228; 10 mi. NE of Brownstown in an agricultural area. The village is a trade center and shipping point for eggs, chickens, feeds, and fertilizer.

CORUNNA, Town; Pop. 241; DeKalb County; NE Indiana; Zip Code 46730; 26 mi. N of Fort Wayne. Located in the northern moraine region, the town is in a primary agricultural area producing feed grains and livestock.

CORYDON, Town; Pop. 2,661; Harrison County; S Indiana; Zip Code 47112; 17 mi. WSW of New Albany. Corydon was founded by William Henry Harrison in 1808. When Indiana Territory was established in 1813, Corydon was named the territorial capital. Under the "Constitution Elm", the 44 Indiana delegates met in 1816 to draft Indiana's first constitution and named Corydon the first state capital. The huge

Dictionary of Places

tree once stood 50 ft. tall and measured 5 ft. in diameter. By 1925, however, it was totally dead, and its trunk was later surrounded by a sandstone memorial. Corydon remained the state capital until 1825, when the government was moved to Indianapolis. The Battle of Corydon (July 8, 1863) was the only battle of the Civil War to take place in Indiana. Confederate raiders occupied the town for a short time while holding the home guard captive.

Corydon is a center for lumber and grain, dairy, and poultry farming. The town has some stone quarries and natural gas reservoirs. Much of its prosperity, however, is due to the tourist trade. Not only is the town attractive in itself, but it is centrally located to several popular sight-seeing attractions: Wyandotte Cave, Squire Boone Caverns, the Hayswood Nature Reserve, and the Zimmerman Art Glass Factory. The Harrison County Fair is held annually in Corydon, and features harness racing and agricultural exhibits. *(See* also Squire Boone Caverns; Corydon Capitol State Memorial.)

●HISTORICAL PLACES... (See Hist. Places Sect for details.)

Corydon Historic District.

CORYDON CAPITOL STATE MEMORIAL, Corydon; Harrison County; Indiana, on Old Capitol Avenue. Completed in 1812 at a cost of $3,000, the blue limestone building originally served as a court house for Harrison County's territorial assembly. Corydon became the territorial capital when Vincennes relinquished its seat in 1813. Corydon became the first state capital in 1816, and the building served as the capitol until 1825. The capitol was re stored in 1929, and houses memorabilia of Indiana's history.

COVINGTON, City; Pop. 2,747; seat of Franklin County; W Indiana; Zip Code 47932; 50 mi. N of Terre Haute. Covington was laid out in 1826 along the east bank of the Wabash River. Beautiful scenery is part of the town; many streams flow through magnificent, deep gorges into the Wabash River. In town is the house of Edward A. Hannegan (1807-1859), U.S. senator and minister to Prussia. He coined the phrase "Fifty-Four Forty or Fight" during the

Northwest Boundary dispute. Lew Wallace, author of *Ben Hur*, one lived in Covington; his house remains on Eighth and Crockett streets. The town is a center for agriculture (farm produce, fruit) and the coal-mining industry. Sand and gravel pits are nearby.

CRANDALL, Town; Pop 147; Harrison County; S Indiana; Zip Code 47114; on Indian Creek; 14 mi. W of Albany. Crandall is on the sandy Mitchell Plain which has virgin stands of beech and maple. Much of the landscape is given over to grazing. Agriculture and the raising of cattle, hogs, and pigs are the main activities.

CRAWFORD, County; Pop. 8,033; S Indiana; area 312 sq. mi.; bounded on the S by the Ohio River and drained by the Blue and Little Blue rivers. Crawford County was founded in 1818 and named for Col. William Crawford, the land agent of Gen. George Washington, who was captured by Indians and burned at the stake in 1782. English is the county seat.

The county is very picturesque, being almost totally covered by rugged hills and scenic forests. Rich in natural resources, Crawford County is a leading producer of livestock, feed grains, tobacco, timber. and limestone. Manufactures include concrete blocks, lime, cement, wagon parts, and canned goods. Within the county are two of the Midwest's finest caves--Wyandotte and Marengo.

CRAWFORDSVILLE, City; Pop. 13,584; seat of Montgomery County; W central Indiana; Zip Code 47933; 27 mi. S of Lafayette. Crawfordsville, the "Athens of Indiana," was platted in 1822 and named for William Crawford, a land agent who was killed by Indians in 1782.

Several nationally famous authors made their homes in Craw fordsville, among them Lew Wallace, Maurice Thompson, and Meredith Nicholson. The Lew Wallace Study, a tower-like struc ture, is centrally located on a beautifully landscaped three and one-half acre site. *Ben Hur* was Wallace's most famous novel, and the Ben Hur Museum, now part of a park, contains many mementos of the author's life

Dictionary of Places

as a writer, soldier, and painter. Crawfordsville is the seat of Wabash College (1832), a nonsectarian liberal arts college for men.

The city is a commercial center for agricultural products, farm implements, fences, caskets, bricks, conduits, and nails. The Milligan Park Gold Course is in town. Shades State Park *(g.v.)*, a 2,900-acre tract of semi-virgin oak and hickory forest, is nearby. The annual Sugar Creek Canoe Race begins at Darlington, passes through Crawfordsville, and finishes at Shades State Park.

CRAWFORD UPLAND, wooded hill region of S Indiana which contains some of the most spectacular scenery in the state. It stretches from Parke County to the Ohio River, trending generally N to S, and is intersected by hills, sharp ridges, knolls, val leys, wall-like bluffs, gorges, natural bridges, caves, and waterfalls. Its best-known features are Wyandotte and Marengo caves and Jug Rock and the Pinnacle (natural pillars of rock) near Shoals *(q.v.)* in Martin County.

Geologically, the upland is part of the Cincinnati Arch, which was formed during the Silurian and Devonian periods in a time of great upheaval. The region is generally unglaciated and is underlain by sandstones, shales, clays, limestones, and thin coals. The area has traditionally been noted for bituminous coal mining and limestone quarrying. The Crawford Upland is drained by the White River and its tributaries.

CROMWELL, Town; Pop. 520; Noble County; NE Indiana; Zip Code 46732; 33 mi. NW of Fort Wayne in a mainly agricultural area (soybeans, corn, wheat, livestock).

CROSLEY FISH AND WILDLIFE AREA, Jennings County; SE Indiana; 4 mi. S of North Vernon. Fishing is provided in Otter Creek, which flows through the 4,042-acre wildlife area. There are facilities for hiking, picnicking, fishing, camping, hunting, and boating.

CROTHERSVILLE, Town; Pop 1,687; Jackson County; S Indiana; Zip Code47226; 28 mi. S of Columbus in an agricultural area.

CROWN POINT, City; Pop. 17,728; seat of Lake County; NW Indiana; Zip Code 46307; 12 mi. S of Gary. Crown Point was founded in 1832 by Solon Robinson, a settler who came from Connecticut and later left the town to become the agricultural editor for the New York *Tribune*. A historical marker is located on the site of his log cabin. Lake County jail is famous for one of its nortorious boarders, John Dillinger, who escaped from the prison only to be killed in Chicago, Illinois, by federal agents.

Crown Point is a manufacturing center in its own right, and has refused to become incorporated in the metropolitan areas of Gary and Hammons. It is a producer of monuments, signs, leather goods, and grinders.
  ●HISTORICAL PLACES... (See Hist. Places Sect for details.)
  Lake County Courthouse.

CULVER, Town; Pop. 1,404; Marshall County; N Indiana; Zip Code 46511; on Lake Maxinkuckee; 32 mi. SSW of South Bend. Culver is the seat of the Culver Military Academy (1894), which is situated on the shores of the lake. Cadets of the world famous Black Horse Troop are trained there. The academy is oriented toward a four-year military program, with an optional two-year junior college course. Opposite the academy is the Culver Bird Sanctuary. Culver is a trade center for livestock, dairy products, and apples.

CYNTHIANA, Town; Pop. 669; Posey County; SW Indiana; Zip Code 47612; 17 mi. NNW of Evansville in an agricultural region.

DALE, Town; Pop. 1,553; Spencer County; SW Indiana; Zip Code 47523; 36 mi. ENE of Evansville. Named for the philanthropist, industrialist, and social reformer Robert Dale Owen, the town is a center for the production of lumber, cheese, and canned foods. Near the sawmill is the O.V. Brown Home, which contains historical memorabilia of pioneer days.

DALEVILLE, Town; Pop. 1,681; Madison County E central Indiana; Zip Code 47334; just S of Anderson. Daleville was platted in 1838 when plans to build a canal and dam were

Dictionary of Places

announced. The canal project was dropped, but the arrival of the railroad in 1852 helped to temporarily boost the economy. The Trenton oil and gas field is in the vicinity, but the main source of income is small private business and agriculture (corn, soybeans, wheat, livestock).

DANA, Town; Pop. 612; Vermillion County; W Indiana; Zip Code 47047; 24 mi. NNW of Terre Haute near the Illinois border. Dana is an agricultural community and contains the largest round barn in the state. Ernie Pyle, the nationally known World War II correspondent, was born there in 1900. Also located in the town is the Ernie Pyle Rest Park, which contains a covered bridge built in 1876.

DANVILLE, Town; Pop. 4,345; seat of Hendricks County; central Indiana; Zip Code 46122; 20 mi. W of Indianapolis. The town was founded in 1824 and named for Daniel Clark, a local justice of the peace.

In 1878, Central Normal College was relocated from Ladoga to Danville in a unique and direct manner. When a group of Danville citizens failed to purchase the college, they "kidnapped" it. At the break of dawn on May 10, 1878, they hauled the students, library, and laboratory equipment away in their carriages and drays, and were well on their way before Ladoga realized what had happened. The relocated institution in Danville continued to operate as Central Normal College until 1946, when the trustees relinquished control to the board of newly-renamed Canterbury College. Canterbury College encountered financial difficulty in 1951 and, despite attempts by the town to raise the necessary funds, it closed its doors that year.

Danville is a trading center for flour, oil dispensers, and cement blocks. It has often been called "Gable Town" because many of the small businesses are located in old buildings that have gabled roofs. The mainstay of the economy is farming (livestock, feed grains).

DARLINGTON, Town; Pop. 740; Montgomery County; W central Indiana; Zip Code 47940; 9 mi. NE of Crawfordsville in an agricultural area. Of note is the Darlington

Covered Bridge, spanning Sugar Creek, which is a favorite spot for fishermen.

DAVIESS, County; Pop. 26,602; SW Indiana; area 430 sq.mi.; bounded on the S by the East Fork and on the W by the West Fork of the White River. It is drained by the tributaries of the White River. Daviess County was organized in 1817 and named for Joseph Hamilton Daviess, a lawyer who was killed in the Battle of Tip pecanoe (Nov. 7, 1811). Washington has remained the county seat since the county's formation.

The Wabash and Erie Canal, which runs the full length of the county, was later supplanted by a railroad. The railroad was built along the towpaths of the canal in order to save money and gas and has been called, on occasion, the "Crooked Wonder of the World." Daviess County is rich in natural resources. Perhaps its greatest asset is coal, but farming, nursery plantations, and oil and gas wells are also important. Principal industries are the manufacture of air conditioners and air conditioner parts.

DEAM LAKE STATE RECREATION AREA, Clark County; SE Indiana; 6 mi. E of Borden in the scenic "Hoosier Hills." Deam Lake is located within Clark State Forest. It covers 200 acres and has a maximum depth of 35 feet. The state recreation area has 1,000 acres of beech and maple forest, and excellent facilities for camping, picnicking, fishing, boating, and swimming.

DEARBORN, County; Pop. 29,430; SE Indiana; area 306 sq.mi.; bounded on the E by the Ohio line and on the SE by Kentucky. It is drained by the Whitewater River and Laughery Creek.

The county was organized in 1803 and named for Gen. Henry Dearborn, secretary of war of the U.S. Lawrenceburg is the county seat. The county is filled with archaeological remains, some of which are believed to be more than 2,000 years old. It is basically an agricultural area given over to livestock, tobacco, and truck farming. There is some manufacturing; the leading in dustries produce distilled liquors and glass containers.

Dictionary of Places

DECATUR, City; Pop. 8,644; seat of Adams County; NE Indiana; Zip Code 46733; 21 mi. SSE of Fort Wayne. Located on the St. Mary's River, the town was settled in 1836 by Samuel L. Rugg, who named it in honor of Stephen Decatur, a U.S. naval hero. It was incorporated on September 5, 1882. The city's agriculture production consists of corn, soybeans, and wheat. It is also an industrial center for RV's, power boats, motors, iron castings, wood and cement products, ice cream, paint, styrofoam products, and soybean products.

A monument to Gene Stratton Porter, authoress of *A Girl of the Limberlost,* who lived in the city for three years, is in the courthouse yard. The Peace Monument, the first war memorial in the U.S. dedicated to peace, is also in the yard.

DECATUR, County; Pop. 22,738; SE central Indiana; area 370 sq.mi.; drained by Flatrock, Duck, Clifty, and Sand creeks. The county was organized in 1821 and was named for Stephen Decatur. Shortly thereafter, Greensburg became the county seat. The county is especially adapted to agriculture and has a large grain, tobacco, and livestock market. Some of the finest limestone quarries are located there, as are several oil and gas wells.

●HISTORICAL PLACES... (See Hist. Places Sect for details.)

Decatur County Courthouse.

DECKER, Town; Pop. 281; Knox County; SW Indiana; Zip Code 47524; on the White River, 11 mi. S of Vincennes. It is in an

agricultural area that produces grains (especially wheat) and livestock.

DEKALB, County; Pop. 30,837; NE Indiana; area 366 sq. mi.; bounded on the E by the Ohio line. It is drained by the St. Joseph River and Cedar and Fish creeks. The county was organized in 1837 and named for Baron DeKalb, a German nobleman who fought in the American Revolution. Auburn became the county seat the same year.

DeKalb is a leading agricultural county, and most of the land is under some form of cultivation or pasture. Livestock, truck, poultry, soybeans, corn, wheat, oats, and dairy items are the leading agricultural products. There is diversified manufacturing in some of the larger cities such as Auburn, Butler, and Garrett; products include automobile parts, hand tools, rubber parts, and castings.

DELAWARE, County, Pop. 129,219; E Indiana; area 396 sq. mi.; drained by the Mississinewa River, the West Fork of the White River, and Kilbuck, Bell, and Buck creeks. The county was organized in 1827 and named for the Delaware Indians. Muncie became the county seat and developed into a leading industrial center for the county. The land is mostly level or gently undulating, and most of the soils are well adapted to the cultivation of corn, feed grains, soybeans, and tomatoes. The raising of livestock (especially hogs) is also prevalent. Major industries produce automobile parts, glass containers, packaged meats, canned goods, steel wire, iron castings, and transformers. Delaware County is located within the Trenton oil and gas field and was part of the great natural gas boom of 1887.

DELPHI, City; Pop. 2,531; seat of Carroll County; NW central Indiana; Zip Code 46923; on Deer Creek; 17 mi. NE of Lafayette. Delphi was named by Samuel Milroy, a member of the state constitutional convention; it was laid out in 1828. A bustling port during the heyday of the Wabash and Erie Canal, it is now an agricultural and farming community. Manufactures include decoys, food products, and automobile bodies. The Carroll County Historical Society operates the Historical Museum, which is in the courthouse. The Carroll County Country Club and nine- hole golf course are in town.

DEMOTTE, Town; Pop. 2,482; Jasper County; NW Indiana; Zip Code 46310; about 28 mi. SW of Valparaiso in an agricultural area.

DENVER, Town; Pop. 504; Miami County; N central Indiana; Zip Code 46926; on the Eel River, 8 mi. N of Peru in an agricultural area. A farming community, it specializes in poultry, fruit, and dairy products.

Dictionary of Places

DEPUTY, Village; Pop. 250; Jefferson County; S Indiana; Zip Code 47230; 19 mi. NW of Madison in a farming and lumbering area. The village is a trade center for lumber, pallets, and wood products.

DERBY, Village; Pop. 60; Perry County; S Indiana; Zip Code 47525, 18 mi. NE of Cannelton in a mining and quarrying area. The village has one stone quarry which produces crushed stone and agricultural limestone and riprap.

DEVIL'S BACKBONE, natural ridge in the hills of Lawrence County; S Indiana. The view from the high, narrow summit takes in a breathtaking panorama from both sides.

DILLSBORO, Town; Pop. 1,200; Dearborn County; SE Indiana; Zip Code 47018; 32 mi. SE of Greensburg in an agricultural region. The town is the seat of Dillsboro Sanatorium, a 100-room hotel in which patients suffering from arthritis, rheumatism, and nervous disorders are treated with medicinal waters. Two miles west of town is Lake Dilldear, a favorite resort and fishing spot.

DUBLIN, Town; Pop. 805; Wayne County; E Indiana; Zip Code 47335; 17 mi. W of Richmond. The first women's suffrage group in Indiana was formed by Amanda Way in Dublin in 1851. Their result ing petition, which was recorded at the Indiana General Assembly, was filed away as being "inexpedient at this time."

Dublin is a peaceful rural community which relies heavily on feed grain cultivation and livestock farming. The Maples, a tavern in town, is a historic building of homemade brick which dates back to 1825. It was one of the most popular inns along the National Road in the early 19th century.

DUBOIS, Town Pop. 520; Dubois County; S Indiana; Zip Code 47527; 9 mi. NE of Jasper in an agricultural and lumbering area. The town is a manufacturing center for furniture, custom cabinets, and poultry products.

DUBOIS, County; Pop. 30,934; SW Indiana; area 433 sq.mi.; bounded partially by the East Fork of the White River and drained by the Patoka River and Huntley, Little

Pigeon, and Pokeberry creeks. It was organized in 1817 and named for Toussaint Dubois, a French soldier who had charge of the spies and guards in the Battle of Tippecanoe (Nov. 7, 1811). Jasper was selected as the second and permanent county seat because of its central location. Dubois County is noted for its large number of manufacturing plants, which produce wood office, school, and household furni ture. It is also the fourth ranking county in the U.S. for the production of turkeys. Bituminous coal mining, lumbering, and stone quarrying aid the economy.

DUGGER, Town; Pop. 936; Sullivan County; SW Indiana; Zip Code 47848; 8 mi. E of Sullivan is an agricultural area dotted with small lakes. The town has a stone crushing plant. Several popular fishing spots are at nearby Briarwood, County Line, Dugger Boat, and Hi-Pit lakes.

DUNE ACRES, Pop 263; Porter County; NW Indiana; 6 mi. N of Chesterton on Lake Michigan. Dune Acres is a select community of summer homes and rambling estates nestled between steel mills and Porter Beach. Headquartered there is the Richardson Wildlife Foundation. Cowles Bog, a remnant of an ancient marshland, is an excellent outdoor study area of marsh, bog, and transitional swamplands. Centuries-old matted moss floats there on an under ground lake.

DUNKIRK, City; Pop. 3,465; on the border of Jay and Blackford counties; E Indiana; Zip Code 47336; 18 mi. NNE of Muncie. The city, originally called Quincy, was founded in 1853 by Isaiah Sutton. Dunkirk is an agricultural and manufacturing (brick, tile, glass) community. One of their tourist attractions is The Glass Museum, which contains 5,000 items from 100 factories, both domestic and foreign.

DUNLAP, Village; Pop. 2,000; Elkhart County; N Indiana; 4 mi. SE of Elkhart in an agricultural area. Most of the residents commute to Elkhart to work. Nearby is the Kunderd Gladiolus Farm, a 175-acre tract used for the commercial cultivation of gladioli.

DUNREITH, Town; Pop. 205; Henry County; E central Indiana; Zip Code 47337; 16 mi. E of Greenfield in an agri-

Dictionary of Places

cultural area noted for feed grains and livestock. The town is a manufacturing center for sanitary well seals.

DUPONT, Town; Pop. 391; Jefferson County; S Indiana; Zip Code 47231; 14 mi. NW of Madison in an agricultural area.

DYER, Town; Pop. 10,923; Lake County; NW Indiana; Zip Code 46311; 10 mi. S of Hammond in an agricultural region. Dyer is the site of State Line House (1838), a tavern which has been used as a hostelry since the early 1800s.

EARLHAM, Unincorporated community; Wayne County; E Indiana; Zip Code 47374; adjacent to Richmond. The community is the site of Earlham College, founded by Quakers in 1847 and chartered in 1859. The college includes Indiana's first natural history col lection and the first astronomical observatory (1861) in the state.

EARL PARK, Town; Pop. 443; Benton County; W Indiana; Zip Code 47942; 34 mi. NW of Lafayette in an agricultural area (feed grains, livestock). Towering old maple trees have been preserved throughout the town. Parish Grove, near the western edge of town, is named for Chief Parish, a Kickapoo Indian who fell to his death from one of the trees.

EAST CHICAGO, City; Pop. 33,892; Lake County; NW Indiana; Zip Code 46312; SSE of Chicago, on Lake Michigan.

East Chicago was founded in 1888 and incorporated as a town in 1889, at which time its population numbered about 1,300. With the ever-increasing demand for steel in the early 1900s, the city found its niche. Its strategic location at the lower end of Lake Michigan made it a perfect site for a harbor and industrial com plex. In 1901, the Block Brothers built a small steel mill in the bleak dunes region north of town. A harbor needed to obtain ore shipments was then constructed, and the industrial revolution in East Chicago began. By 1928, the first mill had expanded to 100 times its original size. Affiliated industries began to pour into the city, among them Inland Steel and Youngstown Sheet and Tube Company, which today are among the largest in the steel industry. The Indiana Harbor, connected to the Grand Calumet River by a three-mile ship canal, is the state's largest port.

East Chicago is part of the Calumet district, one of the largest industrial complexes in the country. It is included in the Chicago-Gary-Hammond-East Chicago standard metropolitan statistical area. Among other diversified industries are oil refineries, meat-packing plants, railroad repair shops, chemical plants, automobile factories, hardware shops, and a tank and valve factory. East Chicago contains Washington Park, with the only zoo in the Calumet district. The city is the seat of the Calumet Extension Center of Indiana University.

EAST GREY, Town; Pop. 9,858; Lake County; NW Indiana; Zip Code 46405; a SE suburb of Gary. East Gary is part of the Calumet district, one of the largest industrial complexes in the country. Its main industrial products include surgical instruments, food products, and cement blocks.

EATON, Town; Pop. 1,614; Delaware County; E Indiana; Zip Code 47338; on the Mississinewa River; 11 mi. N of Muncie. Eaton was the major location of the natural gas boom in Delaware County. In 1876, while boring for coal near the town, miners struck a natural gas pocket. The hole was plugged and forgotten until 1887, when the demand for natural gas began to rise in Indiana's cities. Eaton, located well within the Trenton gas field, was remembered. The old hole was uncapped, and a well was sunk. The roar from the escaping gas was heard and the burning flame seen in Muncie. The gas boom in both Delaware and neighboring Madison counties brought many industries into the area.

Manufacturing is still important in Eaton, the major products being paper, canned goods, and glass jars. Natural beech and maple vegetation and productive soils have made Eaton a center for livestock grazing and feed grains, especially oats and corn.

ECKERTY, Town; Pop. 150; Crawford County; S Indiana; Zip Code 47116; 9 mi. W of English in a limestone quarry

Dictionary of Places

ing and agricultural area. Eckerty is a producer of crushed stone, sand, and lumber.

ECONOMY, Town; Pop. 151; Wayne County; E Indiana; Zip Code 47339; 15 mi. NW of Richmond. The area in and around Economy was originally settled in the early 1800s by Quakers who farmed the land around the Whitewater River. Agriculture is still the leading activity in Economy. Cattle and hogs, feed grains, and soybeans are the main farm products.

EDGERTON, Village; Pop. 125; Allen County; N Indiana, Zip Code 46797; in an agricultural area noted for feed grains and livestock. Edgerton is a trade center for grain, feed, seeds, and fertilizer.

EDGEWOOD, Town; Pop. 2,057; Madison County; E central Indiana; Zip Code 46000; just W of Anderson. Edgewood is a restricted suburb of Anderson, and most of the population is composed of executives and employees who commute to manufacturing plants in the neighboring city.

EDINBURG, Town; Pop. 4,536; on the border of Johnson and Bartholomew counties; S central Indiana; Zip Code 46124; 31 mi. SSE of Indianapolis. Edinburg is a manufacturing and agricultural community (livestock, wood products, canned goods) and has a large veneer mill. The Roth Museum has memorabilia of Edinburg's pioneer days. Nearby is the Atterbury State Fish and Game Area, a conservation and recreational site.

EDWARDSPORT, Town; Pop. 380; Knox County; SW Indiana; Zip Code 47528; 17 mi. ENE of Vincennes. The village is located on the West Fork of the White River and was previously a leading port for flatboats. Edwardsport is centrally located in a region rich in natural resources. Within easy reach are fertile farmlands and deposits of oil, natural gas, and bituminous coal. The electric power plant in town, which also serves the surrounding area, is supplied with coal from near-by strip mines.

EEL RIVER, W central and SW Indiana, rises in Boone County and flows generally SW past Greencastle to SW central Clay County, then SE to join the West Fork of the

White River at Worthington. The 110-mile long river was once the site of Potawatomi and Delaware Indian villages. It was named the Shakamak (meaning "snakefish" or "eel") by the Delaware. It still abounds with eels.

ELBERFIELD, Town; Pop. 635; Warrick County, SW Indiana; Zip Code 47613; 14 mi. NNE of Evansville in a primarily agricultural area.

ELIZABETH, Town; Pop. 153; Zip Code 47117; Harrison County; S Indiana; 14 mi SW of New Albany in an agricultural area.

ELIZABETHTOWN, Town; Pop. 495; Bartholomew County; S central Indiana; Zip Code 47232; 8 mi SE of Columbus in an agricultural area.

ELK CREEK STATE FISH AND GAME AREA, Washington County; S Indiana; 15 mi. NE of Salem. The state property covers 421 acres and has a boat launching ramp and excellent fishing.

ELKHART, City; Pop 43,627; Elkhart County; N Indiana; Zip Code 46514; at the confluence of the Elkhart and Saint Joseph's rivers, 15 mi. E of South Bend. The city was named by the Indians for an island in the Elkhart River, the shape of which resembled an elk's heart. Among the first settlers was a Baptist missionary who adopted the name in 1822. The site was a popular one with the Indians and lay at the junction of some of their trails.

Elkhart was platted in 1832, whereupon its population grew rapidly. After the arrival of the first railroad company in 1850, the growth of the town was closely linked with railroad development, especially that of the New York Central system. Incorporation came in 1877, and industrialization continued at a rapid rate.

Elkhart is the world center for the manufacture of mobile homes. Miles Laboratories began in Elkhart as a small drug business in the late 19th century, and grew to be one of the largest such concerns in the world. In 1875, Charles G. Conn, a small-town band instrument craftsman, set up shop in Elkhart after he had successfully invented a soft

Dictionary of Places

rubber mouthpiece for cornets. Today, Elkhart is the world leader in the manufacture of band instruments. In all, the city had more than 550 industrial plants by the mid-1970s. Other manufactured products include components, construction machinery, fishing tackle, and rubber goods.

Elkhart was the boyhood home of noted journalist and short story writer Ambrose Bierce. His house has been reconstructed in town. The Elkhart Institute of Technology is also located there. Recreational facilities are found at nearby Heaton and Simonton lakes.

ELKHART, County; Pop 126,529; N. Indiana; area 468 sq. mi.; bounded on the N by the Elkhart and St. Joseph rivers. The county was formed in January 1830 and Goshen was platted and chosen as the county seat in 1831. Elkhart County is one Indiana's leading industrial areas and is a center for the manufacture of mobile homes, automobile parts, fabricated metals, pharmaceutical, furniture, and electrical components. It is also a leading agricultural area given over to dairying, livestock, soybeans, corn, wheat, oats, potatoes, hay, mint, and onions.

ELKHART RIVER, N Indiana; rises in Elkhart County and flows about 50 mi. NW to SE across the county to Goshen. It is the site of the Elkhart County River Preserve and the Elkhart River Hydroelectric Canals which supply power for local industries.

ELLETTSVILLE, Town; Pop. 3,275; Monroe County; S central Indiana; Zip Code 47429; 6 mi. NW of Bloomington. A mining town, it has produced some of the finest limestone stonework in the country. The town was named for Edward Ellets, an early resident. The Matthews Mansion (1865), in French Mansard style, has four carved heads above its entrance which are said to depict the builder's children. Bizarre stone carvings are displayed in a park at the rear.

ELNORA, Town; Pop. 679; Daviess County; SW Indiana; Zip Code 47529; 28 mi. ENE of Vincennes in an agricultural area. There is some industry (concrete products, flour, packed poultry).

ELWOOD, City; Pop. 9,494; Madison County; E central Indiana; Zip Code 46036; 15 mi. NW of Anderson. The town was platted in 1853 along the S bank of Duck Creek. The settlement was first known as Duck Creek, then as Quincy, and finally was named Elwood in 1869.

Incorporation followed in 1872. Elwood began to prosper in 1887 with the discovery of natural gas, and became the second largest town in the county. Among the many industries that were fostered by the gas boom were the American Sheet and Tinplate Company, Pittsburgh Plate Glass and Window Glass, foundries, machine shops, and saw mills. Like so many other towns in the county, Elwood's prosperity dwindled with the gas supply, and the populations decreased. Elwood settled down to a more peaceful existence, and farming began to take precedence over industry.

The city is now a center for agriculture, especially tomatoes, and is a manufacturer of canned good, mobile homes, and glassware. Wendell L. Willkie, the Republican presidential candidate of 1940, was born in the town in 1892. His father, Herman F. Willkie, was principal of the high school. A memorial park contains a granite monument to the famous politician.

ENGLISH, Town; Pop. 614; seat of Crawford County; S Indiana; Zip Code 47118; 40 mi. W of New Albany. English was platted in 1839 by W. W. Cummins, and the following year, it was rgiven the name of Hartford. The town was later named after William Hayden English, a vice presidential candidate in 1880. It did not begin to prosper until it became the county seat in 1893. The town's first post office opened on April 1, 1856, with James A. Brown as the first postmaster.

Wilderness surrounds the town, which is picturesquely situated in a deep, wooded valley. Timber and lumbering are the leading industries, followed by agriculture and livestock.

ETNA GREEN, Town; Pop. 578; Kosciusko County; N Indiana; Zip Code 46524; 30 mi. SSE of South Bend. It is a

Dictionary of Places

small shipping and trading center for agricultural products.

EVANSVILLE, City; Pop. 126,272; seat of Vanderburgh County; SW Indiana; Zip Code 47708; on the Ohio River; 145 mi. SSW of Indianapolis.

The site on which Evansville is located was once occupied by a prehistoric Indian village. The inhabitants lived there for 200 years, abandoned it for unknown reasons, and today the site, known as Angel Mounds, is one of the finest archaeological localities in the Ohio Valley (*see* Angel Mounds State Memorial).

The Evansville area remained untouched by white men until March 27, 1812, when Col. Hugh McGary built his cabin on a bend of the Ohio River. Realizing the natural potential of the area, McGary purchased 200 acres from the Vincennes Land Office. He started a ferry service, and more settlers filtered into the vicinity. In 1814, the growing village became the seat of newly- formed Warrick County. McGary later sold 130 acres of his holding to Col. Robert M. Evans and James W. Jones, who replatted the village and named it Evansville. In 1818, Evansville became the seat of Vanderburgh County, which was formed when Warrick County was split into three sections. Incorporation to town status came the following year, and McGary was named president of the first board of trustees. The population then numbered 101.

An influx of new settlers began in 1824 when salt was discovered beneath the town. New jobs were created for mining the salt, but it was subsequently found to be brackish and unsuitable for preserving purposes. The town began to decay; there were no industries, not even a mill, and an epidemic of illness took its toll on the population. In 1832, four disastrous spring floods inundated Evansville, cutting it off from river trade and temporarily making the town an island. In that summer, 391 people died from cholera. The town again began to grow with the announcement in 1834 that it was to become the southern terminus for the Wabash and Erie Canal. Sawmills were erected on Pigeon Creek to supply timber to shipbuilding and fuel for steamboats. In dustry began to flourish, and on Jan. 27, 1847, Evansville was incorporated as a city. The first mayor, James G. Jones, was a son of the earliest proprietors. The riverfront was improved and a fire department was added.

By 1850, Evansville boasted a cabinet shop, sawmill, pottery works, tobacco plant, foundries, and an iron casting factory. By 1853, river traffic business was booming. Down the Ohio River had come such famous steamboats as the "Robert Fulton," "Robert E. Lee," and "Eclipse." Although the canal project was abandoned in 1860, it had brought business into the city. By 1880, Evansville was the greatest hardwood market center in the U.S. and, by 1895, had become the future manufacturing capital of the nation.

River traffic was limited to freight shipments, which declined appreciably after the coming of the railroad in 1853. By 1900, more than 300 iron, steel, and furniture manufacturing businesses flourished there, as did two of the nation's largest cotton mills. Periods of economic recession were followed by periods of growth. Vast coal deposits and oil fields were discovered in the vicinity, which provided new sources of energy for industries. The city is located in the center of the Illinois Oil Basin, and annually produces 65,000,000 barrels of crude oil.

By the 1970's, Evansville stood alone as the major industrial, transportation, and trade center of southern Indiana. Whirlpool Corporation was the largest single employer, followed closely by Arkla Air Conditioning, Burch Plow, Alcoa, Mead Johnson and Company, and Coca-Cola Bottling. There were a total of about 450 industries, and manufactures included agricultural implements, bathroom fixtures, soft drinks, canvas products, casters and furniture hardware, furniture, clothing, road excavation equipment, paint, plastics, uniforms, and sheet metal products. Agriculture forms a solid economic foundation, as the soils around Evansville are ideally suited for feed grains, melons, apples, peaches, potatoes, and small fruits.

Evansville combines the old with the new. A community center was completed in 1972. A civic center, which includes an auditorium, convention center, and government

Dictionary of Places

buildings, was completed in 1969. Evansville remains the second largest convention center in Indiana. Many of the old 19th century mansions from the riverboat days have been restored. Admirable examples are the Morgan Manor (1853) in Georgian style; the Sonntag-Bayard-Kiechle House (1863) owned by Samuel Bayard, founder of the city's library system; the Rudd-Miller House (1865); the Viele-Koch House (1854) of French Imperial style, which had a ballroom papered in gold leaf; the courthouse (1888), one of the finest examples of Baroque-Dresden style in the U.S.; and the post office (1876).

The people of Evansville are devoted to cultural activities. The city has an excellent museum of arts and sciences, a philharmonic orchestra, and six fine arts theaters. The press and media were represented in the 1970s by three newspapers, four television stations, and six radio stations. Mesker Zoo in Mesker Park is one of the most modern zoos in the country, and the largest in Indiana. There are no cages around the animals; their areas are surrounded by hidden moats giving the illusion of a natural setting. More than 1,000 animals are housed there.

Evansville has excellent educational facilities. It is the seat of the University of Evansville (1854), a private, coeducational, four-year college with an average enrollment of 5,500 students. Indiana State University, a branch of Terre Haute institution, opened its doors to 2,700 students in 1965. Other vocational institutions include Indiana Vocational Technical College (1968), ITT Business and Technical Institute, Lain Technical Institute, and Lockyear College of Business.

The city's economy is aided by the tourist trade. Evansville attractions, including southern Indiana's scenic beauty, Angel Mounds; the Lincoln Heritage Trail; the New Harmony State Memorial; and Burdette Park, have made it a primary visitor's center throughout the year. Water recreation can be found at Lost Lake, 7 mi. SW of the city.

●HISTORICAL PLACES... (See Hist. Places Sect for details.)
Evansville Post Office; Former Vanderburgh County Sheriff's Residence; Old Vanderburgh County Courthouse;

Rietz, John Augustus, House; Willard Library; Angel Mounds.

FAIRFAX STATE RECREATION AREA, Monroe County; S central Indiana; approximately 16 mi. S of Bloomington. It is actually one of two recreational facilities that encompass 22,500 acres on the Monroe Dam and Reservoir, which was dedicated in 1965. Fairfax, the southern unit, offers swimming, picnicking, boating, camping, fishing, and hunting.

FAIRLAND, Town; Pop. 1,159; Shelby County; central Indiana; Zip Code 46126; 7 mi. NW of Shelbyville in an industrial and agricultural area. The town is a trade center for fertilizer, lumber products, and farm machinery. It has several industries, among them the production of concrete, trailer skirts, lathe specialties, and precision machinery.

FAIRMOUNT, Town; Pop. 3,130; Grant County; central Indiana; Zip Code 46928; 10 mi. S of Marion. The town was established in 1830 by Quakers, who originally gave it the name of Pucket; its name was changed to Fairmount in 1870.

Basically a farming community, its agricultural production includes corn, soybeans, wheat, hogs, and livestock. The town manufacturing includes wire products, and wood pallets. It is also a center for the Wesleyan and Methodist state conferences. The population is comprised largely of Quakers, whose simple frame churches are scattered throughout the town.

The town may be best known for its yearly tribute to its native son, the late actor, James Dean. Along with the establishment of the James Dean Gallery, a James Dean celebration is held the last weekend of every September, and draws thousands of people, many coming from across the United States.

FAIRVIEW PARK, Town; Pop. 1,446; Vermillion County; W Indiana; Zip Code 47808; 17 mi. N of Terre Haute in an agricultural and coal-mining region.

FARMERSBURG, Town; Pop 1,159; Sullivan County; SW Indiana; Zip Code 47850; 15 mi. S of Terre Haute. Named

Dictionary of Places

for its large concentration of farmers, the town was settled in 1854 and incorporated in 1871. Natural resources are plentiful in the area, and Farmersburg has become a small center for the production of oil and natural gas, lumber, and coal.

FARMLAND, Town; Pop. 1,412; Randolph County; E Indiana; Zip Code 47340; 13 mi. E of Muncie. The town was founded in 1852 by Andrew and Richard Parker, platted by Henry Huffman and William Macy, and incorporated in 1867. It is said to be the only town in the United States with this name. A trading and agricultural community, it produces corn, soybeans, wheat, rye and tomatoes. It also manufactures auto cranes and canned goods.

FAYETTE, County; Pop 26,216; E Indiana; area 215 sq. mi.; drained by the Whitewater River. The county was organized in 1818 and named for the Marquis de Lafayette. Connersville became the county seat. Much of the county is composed of drained bottom lands which are highly suitable for the cultivation of feed grains. Manufactures include refrigerators, hardware, porcelained panels, and industrial blowers.

FERDINAND, Town; Pop. 2,318; Dubois County; SW Indiana; Zip Code 47532, 45 mi. ENE of Evansville. The town is almost entirely composed of the descendants of German settlers who continue to speak a unique mixture of German and English. Agriculture is important, and some manufacturing has developed in town. A furniture factory which makes products that reflect Old World craftsmanship, and a foundry, employ a large portion of the population. Stone quarries are nearby.

Ferdinand is the seat of the Immaculate Conception Convent and Girl's Academy (1859), the buildings of which resemble a medieval castle. The church has an imposing 37 ft. dome, topped by a gold cross. The Ferdinand Railroad Company, which began operations in 1909, is one of the shortest, self-supporting railroads in the U.S. It runs for a mere 7 miles between Ferdinand and Huntingburg.

Recreational facilities (boating, camping, swimming) can be found 6 miles E of Ferdinand at the 87,000-acre Ferdinand State Forest.

FERDINAND STATE FOREST, Dubois County, S Indiana; 2 mi. N of Rochester. The forest encompasses 7,875 acres of beech and maple woods, and contains the Ferdinand State Fish Hatchery, which stocks lakes in the state with game fish. Water recreation is available on a 4,200-acre lake, and there are excellent facilities for camping.

FILLMORE, Town; Pop. 497; Putnam County; central Indiana; Zip Code 46126; 6 mi. NE of Greencastle in an agricultural area noted for feed grains and livestock. The town has a sawmill and a limestone quarry which produces crushed stone and agricultural limestone.

FISHERS, Town; Pop. 7,508; Hamilton County, central Indiana; Zip Code 46038; 15 mi. NE of Indianapolis in an agricultural area. The town is also known as Fishers Station.

FLAT ROCK, Town; Pop. 250; Shelby County; central Indiana; Zip Code 47234; 12 mi. S of Shelbyville in an agricultural and industrial area. Flat Rock is a manufacturer of crushed limestone and food-processing equipment.

FLORA, Town; Pop. 2,179; Carroll County; W central Indiana; Zip Code 46929; 22 mi. ENE of Lafayette in an agricultural region. Flora is number one in state hog production, and number three in corn production. Other agriculture includes soybeans, poultry, veal, and condensed milk. Its manufactures include lumber, cement, cabinetry, metal fabricating and plumbing products.

FLOYD, County; Pop. 26,216; S Indiana; area 149 sq. mi.; bounded on the S by the Ohio River and drained by its small tributaries. The county was organized in 1819 and named for Col. John Floyd, a member of a Virginia family that had been ambushed by Indians across the Ohio River from the county. New Albany became the county seat in 1819.

Floyd County is a hilly region which is best suited for stock raising, dairying, lumbering, and fruit orchards. There

Dictionary of Places

is also some manufacturing (wood products, mens's apparel, foods) in the larger towns. A scenic range of hills known as the Knobs runs the entire length of the county from N to S, making the entire region a popular summer vacation spot.

FLOYDS KNOBS, Town; Pop. 300; Floyd County; S Indiana; Zip Code 47119; 4 mi. NW of New Albany. The town is a center for strawberry-growing and is located in a valley surrounded by high scenic hills known as The Knobs. It was founded in 1815 when James Moore from New York State built a gristmill on the site. The present name was adopted in 1843 in honor of Col. Davis Floyd of nearby Jeffersonville, who was a member of the first General Assembly of Indiana Territory.

Floyds Knobs is a manufacturing center for wooden furniture, cabinets, welded items, and conveyors.

FOREST, Town; Pop. 400; Clinton County; N Indiana; Zip Code 46039; 13 mi. NE of Frankfort in an agricultural area noted for livestock and feed grains. Forest is a trade center for feeds, grain, fertilizer, and seeds.

FORT BRANCH, Town; Pop. 2,447; Gibson County; Hancock County; central Indiana; Zip Code 47533; 19 mi. N of Evansville. The town is located on the site of a fort built in 1811. There is a 50 ft. monument depicting the history of the fort as a defense against Indian attack. Agriculture and the manufacture of concrete blocks are the leading activities.

FORTVILLE, Town; Pop. 2,690; Hancock County, central Indiana; Zip Code 46040; 20 mi. NE of Indianapolis. The town was platted by Cephas Fort in 1849. It has a manufacturing economy; products include chemicals and automobile parts. Nearby is Fort Benjamin Harrison, a U.S. Army post established in 1903.

FORT WAYNE, City; Pop. 173,072; seat of Allen County; NE Indiana; Zip Code 46802; at the confluence of the St. Marys and St. Joseph rivers, forming the Maumee. Fort Wayne is the state's third largest city and is located approximately 105 mi. NE of Indianapolis in a rich farming and dairying region. In the 1600s and 1700s, the site was a meeting place for two powerful Indian tribes, the Miami and the Potawatomi, who called it Kekionga.

Fort Miami, the first fortified outpost, was built by the French in 1682, where the aqueduct now stands. The settlement was under the jurisdiction of the governor of Louisiana, who managed a large section of that part of the country. As a result of the French and Indian Wars, the fort was surrendered to the English in 1760. Until the close of the American Revolution, the site at the rivers' confluence was a lawless settlement known as Miami Town. It remained a stronghold for the surrounding Indian tribes, who resisted settlement of the area by the white man. Chief Little Turtle of the Miami became famous for this valiant efforts of resistance against white soldiers. Little Turtle was finally defeated in 1794 by Gen. "Mad Anthony" Wayne in the Battle of Fallen Timbers at Maumee, Ohio. The Americans erected a fort at Miami Town in Wayne's honor, giving the city its present name.

The settlement flourished as a peaceful fur-trading center after the end of the Indian fighting in the War of 1812. The fur trade remained the principal enterprise of the town for many years. Fort Wayne was incorporated as a town in 1829, and acquired city status in 1840.

Fort Wayne's industrial growth was stimulated by the building of the Wabash and Erie Canal. The Canal teemed with ladened boats, and a business district of sizeable proportions sprang up around it. The real boom, however, did not start until the coming of the railroads, the first of which arrived in 1854. The next five years saw the arrival of other railroad companies and the building of huge railroad repair shops, which came to do the largest business of its kind in the U.S. Diversified manufacturing was introduced into Fort Wayne following the Civil War. The lumber business was outstanding until the hardwood forests of the region were exhausted. Branch industries included the production of wagon wheels, organs, and pianos.

The city had been lighted with gas in 1855, but modernization brought electric lighting. Fort Wayne claims to be the originator of night baseball games. On a balmy Saturday

Dictionary of Places

night in June 1883, League Park was lighted with 17 low-intensity arc lights for the game, which was witnessed by 2,000 spectators.

Fort Wayne contains the grave of John Chapman, better known as Johnny Appleseed, who was a plant nurseryman, preacher, and herb doctor. He came to the area in the 1800s, after wandering for thousands of miles distributing and planting appleseeds and sprouts. He was 70 years old when he died near Fort Wayne in 1845. His grave site overlooks Memorial Coliseum.

Fort Wayne today is a modern industrial and manufacturing center. The gasoline tank and pump industry originated there, and the city has two of the nation's largest manufacturers of these products.

Other manufactures include electrical appliances, mining equipment, truck bodies, tools, paint, paper, clothing, and processed food. The International Harvester Company, one of the largest in the nation, gives tours through the axle and transmission machine division, forge and die shops, and heat treating department.

Fort Wayne is the seat of several institutions of higher learning, among them Concordia College (1839), a four-year liberal arts school; Indiana Institute of Technology (1930); St. Francis College (1890); St. Benedict's College; Fort Wayne Bible School; and the Fort Wayne School of Fine Arts.

The Lincoln Library and Museum, regarded as the best museum for research on the subject in the United States, is operated by the Lincoln National Life Foundation and contains more than 10,000 items of Lincoln memorabilia, including books, paintings, original photographs, and autographs. Cultural institutions are an important part of Fort Wayne. Of note are the Allen County- Fort Wayne Historical Society Museum, the Jack D. Diehm Museum of Natural History, the Fort Wayne Art Institute, the Festival Music Theater, and the Fort Wayne Civic Theater. The city has three parks which provide recreational facilities for horseback riding, hiking, picnicking, and tennis. Of note is

Franke Park, which contains a large bird sanctuary and a children's zoo. Other points of interest include the Cathedral of Immaculate Conception, with its beautiful Bavarian stained glass windows and carved wood altar, and the old hotel from which William Jennings Bryan spoke in 1898 during his campaign for the presidency.

● HISTORICAL PLACES... (See Hist. Places Sect for details.)

Fort Wayne City Hall; Johnny Appleseed Memorial Park.

FOUNTAIN, County; Pop. 18257; W Indiana; area 397 sq. mi.; bounded on the W and N by the Wabash River and drained by Coal Creek. The county was organized in December 1825 and Covington was named the county seat a few months later. The county was named for Maj. Fountain of Kentucky, who was killed in the Battle of Maumee (1790) near Fort Wayne.

Fountain County has a diversified agricultural, industrial, and mining economy, with most of the manufacturing taking place in Attica, Covington, and Veedersburg. Major manufactures include steel castings, electronic components, and storage batteries.

FOUNTAIN CITY, Town; Pop. 766; Wayne County; E Indiana; Zip Code 47341; 10 mi. N of Richmond. Originally known as Newport, its name was changed in 1834 when a subterranean lake was discovered under the town. Pipes driven into the ground caused an immediate rise in the water level, and gave the town its name.

Fountain City became famous for its role as the "grand central station" of the "freedom train" for runaway slaves. The so-called Underground Railroad was run by Levi Coffin, a Quaker, who helped 2,000 slaves escape to Canada in the years 1827 to 1847. Levi Coffin and the rest of the large Quaker population were ardent abolitionists, and they gave many slaves work until they could be sent north or to Canada. Today, Fountain City is a quiet farming community, and descendants of fugitive slaves still live there.

FOWLER, Town; Pop.2,333; seat of Benton County, W Indiana; Zip Code 47944; 27 mi. NW of Lafayette. Fowler was laid out in 1871 at an attractive site covered with vir-

Dictionary of Places

gin forest. Remnants of this forest can be seen in the stately old trees that line downtown sidewalks. The town was named for Moses Fowler, who contributed money for the courthouse. Fowler is a center for corn, soybeans, grain, livestock, and poultry. Just outside the town is the Benton County Country Club.

FOWLERTON, Town; Pop.306; Grant County, E central Indiana; Zip Code 46930; 18 mi. NNW of Muncie in an agricultural region noted for feed grains and livestock. The town is a producer of catsup.

FRANCES SLOCUM STATE FOREST, Wabash County; N Indiana; 17 mi. SW of Wabash. Located on the east side of the Mississinewa River, it is one of the best state forests developed for recreational purposes. It encompasses 1,089 acres of woods and water, and has expanded its facilities to meet the need for new campgrounds and picnic areas. Excellent fishing, swimming, and horseback riding are available. The grave of Frances Slocum, for whom the forest is named, is across the river. A white woman, she lived with the Miami Indians after they captured her at the age of five.

FRANCESVILLE, Town; Pop. 969; Pulaski County; NW Indiana; Zip Code 47946; 40 mi. N of Lafayette. It is a center for flour and machine shop production, and is a shipping point for milk and grain.

FRANCISCO, Town; Pop. 560; Gibson County; SW Indiana; Zip Code 47534; 7 mi. ESE of Princeton in a region rich in natural resources (fertile soils, oil, natural gas, bituminous coal). The town was named for a Spanish worker on the Wabash and Erie Canal.

FRANKFORT, City; Pop. 14,754; seat of Clinton County; central Indiana; Zip Code 46041; 40 mi. NNW of Indianapolis. Frankfort was platted in 1830. It was named for Frankfurt-am- Main, Germany, which was the home of the grandfather of the Pence brothers who owned the land around the present site.

Frankfort is a modern commercial and shipping center. It is strategically located in an apple-growing district and is a leading distributor of the fruit. The city is second in the state for hog-producing, and also produces corn and soybeans. Manufactures include automotive parts, electronic components, plumbing supplies, printing inks, enameled sheet metal, clothing, and brass fittings. Railroad repair shops and an oil refinery are in the city. Frankfort was once the home of the world's largest handle factory.

The Goodwin Funeral Home Museum has a large collection of classic cars and Lincoln memorabilia, as well as pioneer artifacts. Just west of town is the Peter-Paul Candy Factory, which offers tours to visitors. North of Frankfort is the country club, which features an 18-hole golf course.

FRANKLIN, City; Pop. 12,907; seat of Johnson County, central Indiana; Zip Code 46131; 20 mi. SSE of Indianapolis. Founded in 1822, the city was named after Benjamin Franklin, and features a stone-brick courthouse built in 1883. History pervades the town, making it a popular tourist attraction. There are monuments honoring heroes of the Revolutionary, Civil, Spanish- American, and World wars. The Methodist Home, the Indiana Masonic Home, a museum of local pioneer history, and the original log cabin (1834) from which Franklin College grew, are all there. Franklin was the home of two distinguished citizens, Paul V. McNutt, 34th governor of Indiana, and William M. Chase, noted 19th-century painter.

Franklin College, east of the courthouse, began as the Indiana Baptist Manual Labor Institute in 1834. It became the first coeducational college in the state after a financial crisis in 1842. Basically a liberal arts college, its 8-acre campus features a library, gymnasium, dormitories, science hall, and auditorium.

Franklin is a trading center and leading manufacturer for automobile parts, air compressors, aluminum products, household appliances, furniture, lumber, wood products, glue, paint, plastics, canned goods, and flour. There is also some agriculture production of corn, soybeans, and wheat.

FRANKLIN, County, Pop. 16,943; SE Indiana; area 394 sq. mi.; bounded on the E by Ohio and drained by the Whitewater River and its East Fork. The county was organ-

Dictionary of Places

ized in February 1811 and named in honor of Benjamin Franklin. Shortly thereafter, Brookville became the county seat. The topography is generally rolling; the best agricultural areas are found in the bottomlands of the Whitewater River. Tobacco and feed grains are cultivated, and higher elevations have been turned over to pasture for livestock and dairy animals.

● HISTORICAL PLACES... (See Hist. Places Sect for details.)
Whitewater Canal Historic District.

FRANKTON, Town; Pop. 1,736; Madison County, E central Indiana; Zip Code 46044; on Pipe Creek; 10 mi. NNW of Anderson. The town was founded in the 1830s by Jacob Sigler, an early settler who blazed a trail across the first 80 acres of the present site. The original sawmill is still standing. Development was aided by the Panhandle Railroad. The glassworks and rolling mill were located next to the tracks and were able to easily distribute their products. In 1855, however, the railroad bridge over Pipe Creek collapsed, plunging a freight train into the water. The Frankton railroad station remains a landmark. Frankton is now a thriving agricultural community. Most of the population commutes to work in the General Motors plant in Anderson.

FREDERICKSBURG, Town; Pop. 155; Washington County, S Indiana; Zip Code 47120; 21 mi. SW of Salem on the Blue River in a lumbering and agricultural area. Fredericksburg was first settled in 1805 along an ancient buffalo trace. Salt licks can still be found in the vicinity. The Lick Creek Friends Church (1815) was one of the first Quaker churches in the area. Annually, the town hosts the Olde Blue River Festival, a popular local event.

FREELANDVILLE, Town; Pop. 720; Knox County; S Indiana; Zip Code 47535; 20 mi. N of Vincennes in an agricultural and lumbering area. Freelandville is a producer of chickens, fertilizer, seed corn, crushed rock, and lime.

FREETOWN, Town; Pop. 450; Jackson County; S Indiana; Zip Code 47235; 10 mi. NW of Brownstown in an agricultural area noted for feed grains and livestock. It is a trade center for pet food, seeds, and fertilizer.

FREMONT, Town; Pop. 1,407; Steuben County; NE Indiana; Zip Code 46737; 45 mi. N of Fort Wayne. The first name given the area was Willow Prairie. In 1835, the name was changed to Brockville and, in 1851, it became Fremont. Incorporation was in 1867. An agricultural community, its manufactures include a lumber mill, automotive parts, plastics, and baking. Nearby is the 53-acre Walter's Lake, which has recreational facilities.

FRENCH LICK, Town; Pop. 2,087; Orange County; S Indiana; Zip Code 47432; 45 mi. WNW of New Albany. Founded in 1811, its name was derived from an animal salt lick within the confines of the pioneer settlement, which had a French trading post. The town is a popular resort, its appeal based on the French Lick-Sheraton Hotel (formerly French Lick Springs Hotel) and its medicinal springs. Thomas Taggart, former U.S. senator, was one of the many owners of the rambling hotel. It was built in 1840 by Dr. William A. Bowels, who realized the commercial value of the mineral-laden springs. Just north of the hotel are the three artesian springs: Pluto, Proserpine, and Bowles, which are enclosed in a marble and tile bathhouse. Golfing, tennis, horseback riding, and trap shooting are offered on the 1,700-acre grounds. Once a gambling casino, the hotel was frequently visited by wealthy Eastern families, including the Vanderbilts, Morgans, and Whitneys.

French Lick is located in a region rich in natural resources. Supporting industries include bituminous coal mining, quarrying, lumbering, and fruit farming.

FULTON, Town; Pop. 371; Fulton County; N Indiana; Zip Code 46931; 15 mi. NNE of Logansport in an agricultural area. South of Fulton is Fletcher Lake, a popular resort.

FULTON, County; Pop. 16,984; N Indiana; area 367 sq. mi.; drained by the Tippecanoe River. The county was organized in February 1836 and named for Robert Fulton, inventor of the steamboat. Four months later, Rochester was selected as the county seat. The land of the county is level to undulating, and is dotted with numerous lakes. Lake Manitou has been dammed to encompass 775 acres. The county is primarily agricultural in character (truck, poultry,

Dictionary of Places

livestock, soybeans), with minor manufacturing carried on at Rochester and Akron. The primary industry is the production of men's apparel.

GALENA, Town; Pop. 350; Floyd County; SE Indiana; approximately 10 mi. NW of Louisville, Kentucky. Located at an altitude of 840 ft., Galena was once a popular Indian camping and hunting ground. Numerous streams and salt springs were located along the ancient buffalo trail. Galena was platted in 1836 and has many fine century-old homes. The town had hopes of becoming a great city because of its location on the Paoli Turnpike, Indiana's first toll road (1840). The New Albany-Paoli Toll House, used until 1913, still stands just east of town. Livestock and some truck farming are the mainstay of Galena's economy.

GALVESTON, Town; Pop. 1,609; Cass County; N central Indiana; Zip Code 46932; 8 mi. NW of Kokomo in an agricultural area based on livestock farming and feed grains. There is also a cheese-making plant in town.

GARRETT, City; Pop. 5,349; DeKalb County; NE Indiana; Zip Code 46738; 20 mi. N of Fort Wayne. Garrett was once a division point for the Baltimore & Ohio Railroad. It is now primarily a farming community and shipping point for livestock, grain, and soybeans. The railroad shops manufacture air hoses and lubricators.

GARY, City; Pop. 116,646; Lake County; extreme NW Indiana; Zip Code 46401; at the south end of Lake Michigan; 25 mi. SE of Chicago, Illinois. The second largest city in Indiana, Gary was founded in 1906 in a previously desolate, uninhabited region of the Indiana dune country. The tract had been purchased by the U.S. Steel Corporation in 1905, which intended to found a city centered between the iron regions of the Northwest and the coal mines of the East and Northeast.

Named for Judge Elbert H. Gary, the city was practically born overnight. The steel mill site was elevated 15 ft. by pumping material from Lake Michigan through pipes and spreading it over the surrounding swamplands. A whole river was diverted to a new location, and three railroad rights-of-way were repositioned. Early inhabitants were mostly rugged steel workers who lived in shacks spread out along a single street surrounded by white sand dunes.

The Gary Land Company took over the camp and platted the new city. U.S. Steel bought an adjacent 7,000 acres of land and zoned it according to city regulations. A water system was laid, streets and sidewalks were paved, and electrical facilities were provided. To soften the bleak atmosphere, an ambitious landscaping project ensued, which resulted in tree-lined streets and Marquette Park, a landscaped tract of land along the shores of Lake Michigan. The park was subsequently dedicated to the Jesuit missionary Pere Jacques Marquette.

Gary has become the hub of the Calumet industrial district. Together with Hammond, Burns Harbor, East Chicago, and Whiting, it mushroomed into one of the nation's most important steel- producing areas. Although U.S. Steel is the leading steel producer, subsidiary industries have developed and flourished. These include Republic Steel, Standard Steel Spring Company, and Pittsburgh Screw and Bolt Corporation. Eighty percent of the nation's industrial output is produced in the Calumet district. Other smaller industries produce cement, chemicals, automobile accessories, clothing, and metal products. Gary's steel works boast ingots with an 8,000,000 net ton capacity, coke plants, 12 blast furnaces, 50 open-hearth furnaces, and rolling, rail, plate, wheel, and axle mills. Unfortunately, industrial pollution has taken its toll in Gary. The Grand Calumet and Little Calumet rivers, both of which have port facilities, are heavily polluted. A thick, orange mist--a product of chemical and industrial wastes from the steel mills--can be seen frequently over the city.

Recreational facilities can be found at various Lake Michigan beaches and at South Gleason Park, an 18-hole golf course in the city.

GAS CITY, City; Pop. 6,296; Grant County; E central Indiana; Zip Code 46933; 5 mi. SSE of Marion. Gas City owes its existence to the natural gas boom of 1887, which affected many of the settlements in E central Indiana. Busi-

Dictionary of Places

ness boomed until 1891, when the gas supply was exhausted. A relic of the gas boom, and still the leading industry in town, is the Owens-Illinois Glass Company plant. Other manufactures include barrels and concrete products. Agriculture plays an important role in the town's economy. Large numbers of dairy, livestock, grain, and poultry farms border the town. Recreational facilities can be found at nearby Lake Galacia, a 17-acre lake especially popular for ice- fishing.

GASTON, Town; Pop. 979; Delaware County; E central Indiana; Zip Code 47342; 12 mi. NNW of Muncie in an agricultural area. There is a cannery in town.

GENE STRATTON PORTER STATE MEMORIAL, Noble County; NE Indiana; near Rome City. The estate in Wildflower Woods was the last Indiana home of Hoosier Authoress Gene Stratton Porter, who wrote such noted books as *A Girl of the Limberlost* and *Freckles* in the early 1900s. The estate is maintained by the Indiana Department of Conservation. The red cedar log house was named "Limberlost Cabin" for Porter's earlier home at Geneva *(q.v.)*.

GENEVA, Town; Pop. 1,280; Zip Code 46740; Adams County; E Indiana; 35 mi. NE of Muncie. Geneva was the home for Gene Stratton Porter from 1886 to 1913. The famous authoress wrote novels including *A Girl of the Limberlost,* which was inspired by the Limberlost Swamp (now drained), and *Freckles* while living there. The 14-room cabin is preserved as a state memorial in town.

Geneva is an agricultural community with farming generally concentrated on feed grains and livestock. Just north of town is a large Amish colony. Recreational facilities can be found at nearby Rainbow Lake and the Wabash Valley Golf Club. (*See* also Limberlost State Memorial.)
  ●HISTORICAL PLACES... (See Hist. Places Sect for details.)
  Porter, Gene Stratton, Cabin (Limberlost Cabin).

GENTRYVILLE, Town; Pop. 277; Spencer County; SW Indiana; Zip Code 47537; 32 mi. ENE of Evansville. The town was named for James Gentry, an early merchant who employed young Abraham Lincoln. In 1830, Lincoln and his father moved from Gentryville to Illinois. Lincoln was once an overnight guest in the Col. William Jones Home (1834), preserved intact.

Farming is the mainstay of Gentryville's economy. Soybeans, corn, wheat, and tobacco are the leading agricultural products.

GEORGE ROGERS CLARK NATIONAL HISTORIC PARK AND MEMORIAL, Knox County; S Indiana; at Vincennes. The memorial, which is circular in form, 90 ft. in diameter, and 82 ft. high, commemorates the winning of the Old Northwest and the achievements of George Rogers Clark in the American Revolution. The park also contains the first capital of Indiana Territory (1800-13). The Clark Memorial consists of 16 Doric columns, each 39 ft. high and more than 6 ft. in diameter. The interior contains a bronze statue of Clark, and seven murals by Ezra Winter depicting scenes in the history of the Northwest Territory.

GEORGETOWN, Town; Pop. 2,092; Floyd County; S Indiana; Zip Code 47122; 8 mi. W of New Albany in an agricultural region with predominant beech-maple forest that is ideal for cattle grazing. Just east of town is Georgetown Reservoir, a nine-acre lake that offers public fishing. The town is a manufacturing center for metal detectors for the lumber and veneer industry, and has a meat-processing plant.

GIBSON, County; Pop. 30,444; SW Indiana; area 498 sq. mi.; bounded on the W by the Wabash River and on the N by the White River. It is drained by the Patoka and Black rivers and Pigeon Creek. Gibson County was formed in April 1813 and named for Gen. John Gibson, secretary of the territory from 1801 to 1816. Princeton has been the county seat since the county was formed. Gibson County is known for its cantaloupe, watermelon, peaches, and potatoes. There are also numerous bituminous coal mines and oil and natural gas wells.

GLENDALE STATE FISH AND WILDLIFE AREA, Daviess County; SW Indiana; 12 mi. SE of Washington in a scenic, hilly area. Water recreation is available on a 1,400-

Dictionary of Places

acre lake which has a maximum depth of 40 feet. There are excellent facilities for camping, boating, fishing, and hunting.

GLENWOOD, Town; Pop. 285; on the border of Rush and Fayette counties, E Indiana; Zip Code 47343; 8 mi. W of Connersville. It is located in an agricultural area given over to livestock and feed grains.

GOLDSMITH, Village; Pop. est. 235; Tipton County; central Indiana; Zip Code 46045; 6 mi. W of Tipton in an agricultural area noted for livestock and feed grains. The town is a trade center for poultry feeds.

GOODLANDS, Town; Pop. 1,033; Newton County; NW Indiana; Zip Code 47948; 32 mi. NW of Lafayette in an agricultural and dairying area. There is some stone quarrying nearby. The town is a manufacturing center for electric coils and transformers, coil assemblies, dry-mix and liquid fertilizer, and feeds.

GOSHEN, City; Pop. 23,797; seat of Elkhart Count; N Indiana; Zip Code 46526; on the Elkhart River, 24 mi. ESE of South Bend. Goshen is an agricultural community with Mennonite and Amish influences. The city was settled around 1830 and incorporated in 1868. Goshen College, a Mennonite institution, evolved from the Elkhart Academy in 1894. It became a four-year, coeducational college in 1909.

Goshen is the principal trading center for the Mennonites of Elkhart County. Manufactures include steel products, hydraulic presses, batteries, wood products, radios, phonographs, rubber products, and refrigerators. Recreational facilities can be found at nearby Fish and Wolf lakes.

GOSPORT, Town; Pop. 764; Owen County; SW central Indiana; Zip Code 47433; on the West Fork of the White River, 40 mi. SW of Indianapolis. Gosport was platted in 1829 on the site of the "Ten O'Clock Line," an imaginary boundary established in 1809 by a land cession treaty between William Henry Harrison and the Indians at Fort Wayne. The boundary was so-called because the Indians insisted that it be drawn where the sun cast its shadow at 10 A.M.

Gosport began as a leading shipping point for the flatboat trade on the White River. With the decline of the river trade, the importance of Gosport waned. The city retains a residential character and is a center for agricultural and cement products. Gosport contains Indiana's only remaining brick train barn and depot, built in the 1850s.

GRABILL, Town; Pop. 751; Allen County; NE Indiana; Zip Code 46741; 13 mi. NE of Fort Wayne in an agricultural area noted for cattle, calves, truck crops, and soybeans. Nearby is Cedarville Lake, which is a popular local recreational site.

GRANDVIEW, Town; Pop. 761; Spencer County; SW Indiana; Zip Code 47615; on the Ohio River; 33 mi. E of Evansville. The town is named for its picturesque location atop a bluff overlooking the river. The view is unobstructed for five miles in either direction. Grandview is in an agricultural area noted for livestock, soybeans, corn, and tobacco.

GRANGER, Town; Pop. 125; St. Joseph County; NW Indiana; Zip Code 46530; 10 mi. NE of South Bend in an industrial and agricultural area noted for livestock and feed grains. The town is a manufacturing suburb of South Bend producing trailers, motor homes, septic tanks, pre-cast dry wells, steel dies, rafters, trusses, silk-screen products, and specialty machinery.

GRANT, County; Pop. 83,955; E Indiana; area 421 sq. mi.; drained by the Mississinewa River. Grant County was organized in April 1831 and named for Capt. Samuel Grant and Moses Grant, both of whom were killed in an Indian battle in 1789. Marion is the county seat.

The county is both agricultural and industrial in character. It played a large role in the natural gas boom in 1887 because of its location within the Trenton natural gas field. Leading industries produce automobile parts, cathode ray tubes, lighting and wiring equipment, glass containers, iron castings, paperboard, tablets, and envelopes.

Dictionary of Places

GREENCASTLE, City; Pop. 8,984; seat of Putnam County; W central Indiana; Zip Code 46135, near the Eel River; 40 mi. WSW of Indianapolis. The town was laid out 1822. It grew up around De Pauw University (1837), a four-year nonsectarian institution which includes a college of liberal arts and a school of music. On campus is the restored First Methodist Church of Indiana, which was built in Charlestown in 1807.

Greencastle is a center for livestock, lumber, cement, and crushed rock. Among some of the larger industries is an International Business Machine plant. Recreational facilities can be found at the city park and at nearby Mansfield, Cataract, and Edgewood lakes. The area is attractive to visitors because of its ever-changing scenery of wooded hills, limestone bluffs, prairies, and rolling farmlands.

GREENDALE, Town; Pop. 3,881; Dearborn County; SE Indiana; Zip Code 47025; near the Ohio River; just N of Lawrenceburg. Greendale's only major industry is whiskey distilling. The aroma of the fermenting mash permeates the town. The first whiskey still was built in 1809. The industry shut down during Prohibition, but after 15 years of inactivity, the equipment was bought, reactivated, and modernized. The industry has grown to become Greendale's major economic asset. Visitors are treated to a tour of either the James Walsh & Company Distillery or the Joseph E. Seagram plant.

GREENE, County; Pop. 26,894; SW Indiana; area 549 sq. mi.; drained by the White River and Indian, Doans, Plummer, Richland, and Beech creeks. The county was formed in February 1821 and was named for Gen. Nathaniel Greene, a hero of the American Revolution. Bloomfield is the county seat (1821). Bituminous coal mining is a leading activity, along with agriculture and fruit farming.

GREENE-SULLIVAN STATE FOREST, Green and Sullivan counties; SW Indiana; 7 mi. S of Dugger. The forest encompasses 4,692 acres of bluestem prairie and oak-hickory forest, and has excellent facilities for camping, picnicking, hiking, boating, swimming, and horseback riding.

The 1,000 acre lake has a ten-mile shoreline and a maximum depth of 15 feet.

GREENFIELD, City; Pop. 11,657; seat of Hancock County; central Indiana; Zip Code 46140; 21 mi. E of Indianapolis. The city is the birthplace of James Whitcomb Riley, the famous Hoosier poet. Brandywine Creek, along whose banks the city was settled in 1828, inspired many of his poems. "Old Swimmin' Hole," "Little Orphan Annie," and the "The Raggedy Man" are among the many poems Riley wrote in the Riley Homestead (1850), now a museum. James Whitcomb Riley Memorial Park, at the eastern edge of town, preserves the "old swimming hole." Also in the park is the County Log Jail, which still contains the original cell, and houses many pioneer artifacts. A statue of the poet stands in front of the courthouse.

Greenfield is in a noted agricultural area (livestock, grain, vegetables), and is a shipping point for tomatoes. Manufactures include underwear and canned goods. Nearby is the Eli Lilly Company Biological Laboratories, which keeps experimental animals used in pharmaceutical research.

Recreational facilities are found at the nearby Sugar Creek Park.

GREENSBORO, Town; Pop. 204; Henry County; E central Indiana; Zip Code 47344; 6 mi. SW of New Castle in an agricultural region noted for feed grains and livestock.

GREENSBURG, City; Pop. 9,286; seat of Decatur County; SE central Indiana; Zip Code 47240; 45 mi. SSE of Indianapolis. The city was founded by Col. Thomas Hendricks. Of note is the Courthouse Tower Tree, an aspen which grows out of the concrete block roof of the county courthouse 110 ft. above the ground. Carl G. Fisher, founder of the Indianapolis Speedway, and developer of Miami Beach, Florida, was born in Greensburg in 1874. The city is on the 9-mile excursion route of the 1936 Baldwin steam locomotive sponsored by the Indiana Railway Museum.

Greenburg is in an agricultural area noted for tobacco, and is at the southern edge of the Trenton oil and natural

Dictionary of Places

gas field. Manufactures include food products, wire fences, hardware, and brooms.

GREENBURG RESERVOIR STATE FISHING AREA, on the Greensburg Reservoir; Decatur County; SE central Indiana; adjacent to Greensburg. The state lands cover 36 acres and have facilities for boat launching and fishing.

GREENS FORK, Town; Pop. 416; Wayne County; E Indiana; Zip Code 47345; on a fork of the Whitewater River, 9 mi. NW of Richmond in an area noted for cattle, hogs, oats, soybeans, wheat, and corn.

GREENTOWN, Town; Pop. 2,172; Howard County, central Indiana; Zip Code 46936; 9 mi. E of Kokomo. Founded in 1848, the settlement was named for Chief Green, a Miami Indian. Greentown grew up along Wildcat Creek and developed into a farming community. The Greentown Glass Museum has a vast collection of glassware recovered from the Indiana Tumbler and Goblet Company, which was destroyed by fire in 1903. The glassware has become a nationwide collector's item.

GREENVILLE, Town; Pop. 508; Floyd County; S Indiana; Zip Code 47124; 11 mi. NW of New Albany. Settled in 1807 and platted in 1816, Greenville is Floyd County's second oldest town. It began as a stagecoach stop, and later grew up along the old Paoli Turnpike. Its location, in a region of white-oak timber, aided Greenville's expansion as a manufacturing center for barrels, wine kegs, and wood clocks. The principal activities now are livestock and grain farming.

GREENWOOD, Town; Pop. 26,265; Johnson County; central Indiana; Zip Code 46142; 12 mi. S of Indianapolis. It is a manufacturing and agricultural shipping point for household appliances, canned goods, automobile parts, and livestock remedies. South of town is the Presbyterian Westminster Village.

GRIFFIN, Town; Pop. 171; Posey County; SW Indiana; Zip Code 47616; 25 mi. NW of Evansville in an agricultural area noted for livestock, soybeans, wheat, and corn. Oil deposits are nearby. Big Bayou and Black River provide recreational facilities.

GRIFFITH, Town; Pop. 17,916; Lake County; NW Indiana; Zip Code 46319; 8 mi. SW of Gary. Settled in 1891, it was incorporated in 1904. It is a commercial center for castings, paper products, and photographic supplies.

GROUSELAND, Knox County; S Indiana; in Vincennes. It was the home of William Henry Harrison, governor of Indiana Territory (1800-12). In 1801, Harrison purchased 300 acres of cleared land, and built the spacious house during 1803 and 1804. Surrounded by a grove of walnut trees, Grouseland was the first brick building in Vincennes. The stone for the foundation was brought from the nearby Wabash River. Some of the original floors remain.

After 1812, Grouseland passed into other hands, and was once used a storage place for grain. In 1909, the building was saved from destruction by the Francis Vigo Chapter of the Daughters of the American Revolution, which continues to maintain it. Of note is the Council Chamber, or parlor, in which Harrison signed treaties with the Shawnee Indians.

HAGERSTOWN, Town; Pop. 1,835; Wayne County; E Indiana; Zip Code 47346; on the Whitewater River, 16 mi. WNW of Richmond. An agricultural trading center, it is also a manufacturer of machinery, piston rings, and fertilizer.

HAMILTON, Town; Pop. 684; NE Indiana; Zip Code 46742; 34 mi. NNE of Fort Wayne. The town was founded in 1836 as Enterprise. Located on Hamilton Lake, the site was originally chosen for its hydropower potential. A water-driven mill and a sawmill constitute the major industries. Lake Hamilton is a popular tourist spot, providing good fishing and swimming. Spring Hills Golf Course is located there.

HAMILTON, County; Pop. 54,532; N central Indiana; area 401 sq. mi.; drained by the White River. The topography is generally level and the soils are fertile, making the county a leading agricultural producer of feed grains and livestock. Hamilton County was organized in April 1823 and was named for the patriot and statesman Alexander Hamilton. Noblesville is the county seat. North of the county seat is Strawtown, the approximate location of the earliest crossroad trail in central Indiana, and also the site of the Indian mounds of the White River. Hamilton County's leading industry is the manufacture of rubber products.

HAMLET, Town; Pop. 789; Starke County; NW Indiana; Zip Code 46532; 27 mi. SW of South Bend. Hamlet was platted in 1863 and named for its founder, John Hamlet. It grew up at the junction of the Pennsylvania and New York Central railroads and is a shipping point for farm produce. The town has an 18-hole golf course.

HAMMOND, City; Pop. 84,236; Lake County; NW Indiana; Zip Code 46320; just W of Gary. Hammond is the oldest city of the Calumet industrial complex. It was originally named Hohman for its first settler, Ernest Hohman, a Prussian tailor who escaped the cholera epidemic of 1851 in Chicago and settled in the sand dunes and swamps of the area. He then built the Hohman Inn, the site of which is now occupied by the American Steel Foundries. George Hammond, a Detroit butcher, later located his slaughterhouse across from the inn. From 1869 onward, his business thrived; at one time, he employed up to 1,500 workers. Much of the meat was shipped to Europe, and Hammond perfected the method of shipping beef in refrigerated railroad cars. Hammond died on 1886 and his business was bought for $6,000,000.

In 1882 the first railroads came to the town. As a result, it was incorporated as a city in 1884. The real economic boom came at the turn of the century, when the steel industry began to establish plants there and in other Calumet area cities. Hammond has become the commercial center for the area, and today is Indiana's sixth largest city. Diversified manufactures include cold-rolled steel, castings, dairy products, tile roofing, railway supplies, corn syrup, car wheels, forgings, candy, chains, books, petroleum products, urgical instruments, clothing, and soap.

Hammond is a city of many firsts. It was the home of the nation's first professional football team and the inventor of the first automatic potato digger. Alvah Roebuck, the co-founder of Sears & Roebuck, was from Hammond.

There are many city parks, among them Lake Front, Dowling, Riverside, and Wolf Lake. Most visitors tend to prefer the natural beauty of nearby Indiana Dunes State Park, a rugged wilderness of sand dunes, swamps, and lakeshore.

HANNA, Town; Pop. 500; La Porte County; N Indiana; Zip Code 47126; 10 mi. S of La Porte in an industrial and farming area. The town is a manufacturer of agricultural chemicals, fertilizers, and feeds.

HANCOCK, County; Pop. 35,096; E central Indiana; area 305 sq. mi.; drained by the Big Blue River and Sugar and Brandywine creeks. The county was formed in March 1828 and named for John Hancock, a signer of the Declaration of Independence. Greenfield has been the seat of government since the county's inception. The land is level and the soils fertile and ideally suited to the cultivation of feed grains and the raising of hogs and cattle. There is some manufacturing and canning at Greenfield and Fortville.

HANOVER, Town; Pop. 3,610; Jefferson County; SE Indiana; Zip Code 47243; 5 mi. WSW of Madison. The town is the seat of the Hanover College (1827), Indiana's oldest private four-year college. The campus sits atop a bluff overlooking the Ohio River, but the buildings were destroyed by a tornado that struck Hanover in 1974. The town is a farming community and an agricultural center for feed grains and livestock. To the east is the largest privately-owned power plant in the world.

HARDINSBURG, Town; Pop. 322; Washington County; S Indiana; Zip Code 47125; 28 mi. WNW of New Albany in an agricultural region noted for livestock and feed grains. Hardinsburg's only industry is the Schmidt Cabinet Company.

HARDY LAKE STATE RECREATION AREA, Scott County; S Indiana; 10 mi. NE of Austin. Hardy Lake covers

Dictionary of Places

1,902 acres and has facilities for hiking, picnicking, fishing, camping, boat launching, hunting, and swimming.

HARLAN, Town; Pop. 500; Allen County; NE Indiana; Zip Code 46743; 16 mi. NE of Fort Wayne in an agricultural area noted for livestock, corn, and other feed grains. Industries produce pre- hung doors, custom-built cabinets, plastics, and wood products.

HARMONIE STATE RECREATION AREA, Posey County; S Indiana; near New Harmony; on the Wabash River. The state lands cover 3,192 acres of elm, ash, and southern floodplain forest and have water recreation on the river. Other facilities include campgrounds and picnic areas.

HARRISON, County; Pop. 20,423; S Indiana; area 479 sq. mi.; bordered on the S by the Ohio River and drained by the Ohio and Blue rivers and Indian Creek. The county was organized in December 1808 and named for William Henry Harrison.

Rich in history, Harrison County is one of the oldest in the state. Corydon is the county seat and contains the state's first capitol building. The topography is diversified. Much of the land is broken by hills, woods, and streams. The Knobs, a series of wooded ridges, border the eastern section of the county. The whole area is rich in natural resources, and lumber milling, limestone quarrying, and natural gas extraction supplement the county's basic agricultural economy. Tobacco is a leading commodity.

Several large caves and underground streams are located in Harrison County. Among the most noted cave systems are the Squire Boone Caverns, which were explored by Daniel Boone's brother.

HARRISON-CRAWFORD STATE FOREST, Harrison County; S Indiana; 10 mi. SW of Corydon. The state lands cover 22,489 acres of southern floodplain forest. A popular tourist area, it is noted for its fine hills and valleys spread out along the Ohio River. Recreational facilities include campgrounds, hiking trails along the rocky bluffs and ledges, picnicking areas, boating and fishing areas, and horseback riding trails.

HARTFORD CITY, City; Pop. 6,960; seat for Blackford County; E Indiana; Zip Code 47348; 18 mi. N of Muncie. Settled in 1832 and platted in 1839, the city was named for Hart's Ford, a crossing at Lick Creek which was the property of David Hart. Hartford City is an agricultural and manufacturing (glass, school supplies, hardware) community. Its location in a region rich in natural resources (fertile soil, natural gas, petroleum) has made the city a leading trade center. The first two gas wells in Blackford County were located there. Recreational facilities are at nearby Lake Mohee and Lake Placid. There is also a golf course two miles east of town.

HARTSVILLE, Town; Pop. 391; Bartholomew County; S central Indiana; Zip Code 47244; 12 mi. ENE of Columbus in an agricultural area noted for livestock and feed grains. It was the original home of Hartsville College (1850), which was destroyed by fire in 1898. A park marks the site.

HAUBSTADT, Town; Pop. 1,455; Gibson County; SW Indiana; Zip Code 47539; 17 mi. N of Evansville in an area noted for cantaloupe, watermelon, peaches, sweet potatoes, and feed grains.

HAZELTON, Town; Pop. 357; Gibson County; SW Indiana; Zip Code 47540; on the White River; 9 mi. N of Princeton. The town was founded in 1807 by Jarvis Hazelton, a local hunter. Located in the midst of the cantaloupe belt of the Midwest, Hazelton is a leading shipping point for the melons. There is also a tomato cannery in the town, which is also known as Hazelton.

HEBRON, Town; Pop. 3,183; Porter County; NW Indiana; Zip Code 46341; 13 mi. SW of Valparaiso in an agricultural area noted for livestock and feed grains.

HELMER, Village; Pop. 110; Stueben County; NE Indiana; Zip Code 46744; 16 mi. SW of Angola. Helmer is near Pokagon State Park *(q.v.),* a popular summer and winter playground. Manufactures include feeds, seeds, insecticides, and fertilizers.

HELMSBURG, Town; Pop. 180; Brown County; S Indiana; Zip Code 47435; 6 mi. NW of Nashville in a scenic section

Dictionary of Places

of the Hoosier Hills. Industries include the production of lumber and household and industrial brooms and mops.

HELTONVILLE, Town; Pop. 400; Lawrence County; S Indiana; Zip Code 47436; 8 mi. NE of Bedford in an agricultural and limestone quarrying area. The town is a trade center for limestone products, cabinets, and lumber.

HEMLOCK, Town; Pop. 125; Howard County; central Indiana; Zip Code 46937; 9 mi. SE of Kokomo in a farming and dairying region. The town is a farm trade center for grains and fertilizers.

HENDRICKS, County; Pop. 53,974; central Indiana; area 417 sq. mi.; drained by the Eel and Whitelick rivers and Mill Creek. The land surface is rolling, and the extremely fertile soils are conducive to agriculture and stock raising. Hendricks County was formed in December 1823 and named for William Hendricks, then governor of Indiana. Danville was selected as the county seat.

HENRY, County; Pop. 52,603; E Indiana; area 400 sq. mi.; drained by the Blue River and Fall Creek. The county was formed in June 1822 and named for Patrick Henry, patriot and orator during the American Revolution. Newcastle is the county seat.

The topography is gently undulating, with a large percentage of the land given over to stock-raising and feedgrain cultivation. It is also an industrial leader; major manufactures include automobile parts, piston rings, castings, steel, canned goods, vinyl folding doors, and brake linings. Henry County was the setting for the novel *Rain Tree County*.

HENRYVILLE, Town; Pop. 600; Clark County SE Indiana; Zip Code 47126; 14 mi. N of Jeffersonville in a timber and farming area. Henryville is a manufacturer of furniture parts and hardwood lumber products.

HIGHLAND, Town; Pop. 23,696; Lake County; NW Indiana; Zip Code 46322; 7 mi. SW of Gary. A Dutch settlement, it was founded in 1850 in the midst of a truck-farming region. Little commercial activity is evident, and most of the population is employed in the Calumet district cities of Gary and Hammond.

HILLSBORO, Town; Pop. 499; Fountain County; W Indiana; Zip Code 47949; 15 mi. WNW of Crawfordsville. Rough countryside and infertile clay soils have made farming unfavorable, but the town has used the clay, which is of excellent quality, for the manufacture of tile and bricks. Bituminous coal mining is the only other major industry.

HINDOSTAN FALLS STATE FISHING AREA, Martin County; S Indiana; 6 mi. S of Loogootee. The area covers 134 acres and has facilities for fishing, camping, and boat launching. The falls are located on the White River and contain the scenic bluffs of Beaver Bend.

HOAGLAND, Town; Pop. 500; Allen County; NE Indiana; Zip Code 46745; 12 mi. SE of Fort Wayne in an agricultural and dairying area. The town is a trade center for sheet-metal products, grains, seeds, fertilizers, twine, and planting products.

HOBART, City; Pop. 21,822; Lake County; NW Indiana; Zip Code 46342; 7 mi. SE of Gary. The city was platted in 1849 and named for a brother of its founder, George Eavleo. Hobart was incorporated in 1921. The city is a trading center for clay products and packed meat. Clay pits are nearby. The Indian Ridge Lake Country Club is located 1 mi. S of the city.

HOLLAND, Town; Pop. 675; Dubois County; SW Indiana; Zip Code 47541; 36 mi. NE of Evansville. Located in the Wabash Lowland, the surrounding fertile soils have aided its development as an agricultural center (soybeans, corn). In 1969, a large Dutch windmill was built in the American Legion Memorial Park. Recreational facilities can be found at Holland Lake No. 1 and Holland Lake No. 2, both at the N edge of town.

HOLTON, Town; Pop. 451; Ripley County; S Indiana; Zip Code 47023; 7 mi. W of Versailles and Versailles State Park *(q.v.).* The Jefferson Proving Grounds are just N of town.

Dictionary of Places

Holton is a producer of liquid-mix fertilizers, grain bins, and sawmill products.

HOME CORNER, Village; Pop 900; Grant County NE central Indiana; Zip Code 46952; a suburb of Marion. Home Corner, like many of the cities of central Indiana, grew up during the natural gas boom of 1887. It is a quiet farming community in an area noted for livestock and feed grains.

HOOSIER NATIONAL FOREST, S Indiana; covering 172,000 acres, it affords some of the most breathtaking scenery in the state, particularly in the spring and autumn. Within the forest are several recreation areas, including Buzzard Roost Overlook, German Ridge, Saddle Lake, and Hardin Ridge. An area called the Pioneer Mothers' Memorial Forest has been set aside near Paoli for ecological studies of its virgin timbers. Much of the surface is hilly and encompasses the Crawford and Norman uplands, which are divided NW to SE by the Mitchell Plain. The sandy soils arecovered by dense stands of climax forest which include beech, maple, oak, and hickory. Much commercial lumbering is carried on in the towns of Paoli, West Baden Springs, Nashville, and Bedford. Squirrel, turkey, deer, grouse, and fox hunting are popular. Recreational facilities provide camping, picnicking, hiking, boating, fishing, and swimming. Hoosier National Forest also encompasses Brown County State Park and Monroe Dam and Reservoir *(q.v.)*.

HOPE, Town; Pop. 2,171; Bartholomew County; S central Indiana; Zip Code 47246; 39 mi. SSE of Indianapolis. The town was founded in 1830 by Moravians, members of a religious sect from Bohemia. The Moravian church, built in 1874, has been preserved, and stands near the original cemetery with its unusual horizontal tombstones. Hope is an agricultural center for truck and fruit farming, and has a lumber mill. A popular local recreational spot is Shaefer's Beach, 3 mi. SE of town.

HOVEY LAKE, Posey County; SE Indiana; 10 mi. S of Mount Vernon, in the Hovey Lake State Fish and Game Area. The lake has a maximum depth of only 4 ft. but covers 1,400 acres, making it the largest lake south of Indianapolis. Great numbers of cypress stands surround the shoreline, and the encompassing area is a natural bird sanctuary for herons, cormorants, and wild ducks.

HOVEY LAKE STATE FISH AND GAME AREA, Posey County; SW Indiana; 10 mi. S of Mount Vernon. The state lands encompass 4,400 acres of woods and water, and have excellent facilities for fishing, picnicking, camping, and hunting. In the area are large stands of virgin oak, cottonwood, maple, wild pecan, red birch, and cypress. It is a bird sanctuary and flyway for herons, wild ducks, and cormorants.

HOWARD, County; Pop. 83,198; N central Indiana; area 293 sq. mi.; drained by the Wildcat River and its tributaries. The county was organized in May 1844 and named for Tilghman A. Howard, noted Indiana statesman of the 1800s. It is an agricultural county given over to corn, oats, soybeans, and other feed grains, as well as to stock raising. Kokomo, the county seat, is also the leading manufacturer. Industries include the manufacture of automobile radios and transmissions, magazine printing, and food processing.

HOWE, Town; Pop. 650; Lagrange County; NE Indiana; Zip Code 46746; 6 mi. N of Lagrange in an agricultural area noted for livestock and feed grains. Howe is a manufacturer of travel equipment, mobile homes, feeds, seeds, fertilizers, metal stampings, and dairy products.

HUDSON, Town; Pop. 438; Stueben County; NE Indiana; Zip Code 46747; 32 mi. N of Fort Wayne in a potato and onion-growing area.

HUNTERTOWN, Town; Pop. 1,330; Allen County; NE Indiana; Zip Code 46748; 10 mi. N of Fort Wayne in an agricultural and dairying region. The town is a manufacturer of lumber, feed, custom electrical and electronic control panels and systems, and winding equipment parts.

HUNTINGBURG, City; Pop. 5,242; Dubois County; SW Indiana; Zip Code 47542; 40 mi. NE of Evansville. Founded in the 1840s by German immigrants, the town's economy is based on the clay deposits of the area, which are among the

Dictionary of Places

finest in the U.S. The Uhl Pottery Works is noted for its 60-gallon clay jars which weigh 400 lbs. Other manufactures in Huntingburg include electronic equipment, furniture, and wood products. The Peter Morgan Greenhouses have taken prizes at the National Flower Show for the American Beauty rose. Recreational facilities are at nearby Huntingburg Lake and the Huntingburg Country Club. Every Labor Day, the Huntingburg Airport is the scene of a spectacular air show.

HUNTINGTON, City; Pop. 16,389; seat of Huntington County; NE central Indiana; Zip Code 46750; on the Little River, 24 mi. SW of Fort Wayne. Originally called Wepecheange ("place of flints"), the town was renamed in 1831 for Samuel Huntington, a member of the first Continental Congress. Numerous treaties with the Indians were signed there. Francis La Fontaine, a Miami Indian chief, is buried at the Mount Calvary Cemetery north of Huntington; his house (1833) has been reconstructed. Huntington was also the home of John R. Kissinger, a soldier who submitted to the yellow fever tests conducted by Dr. Walter Reed in 1900. He contracted the disease and never fully recovered.

The Little River was an important waterway for the Maumee- Wabash Portage. Buildings constructed over the river have been preserved as unique landmarks. The Huntington Reservoir, a 900- acre man-made lake, is located within the Little Turtle State Recreation Area. The reservoir was developed by Indiana and the U.S. Army Corps of Engineers.

Huntington is a manufacturing and farm trade center. Products include rubber goods, furniture, cranes, radios, phonographs, machinery, furnaces, paint, and disinfectants. There are also some limestone quarries. *Our Sunday Visitor*, the Roman Catholic newspaper with the largest circulation in the U.S. is published there, as are the Catholic magazines *Living Light* and *Priest Magazine*. The city is the seat of Huntington College (1897), a liberal arts institution.

HUNTINGTON, County; Pop. 34,970; NE central Indiana; area 369 sq. mi.; drained by the Wabash, Salamonie, and Little rivers and by Langlois Creek. The county was formed in December 1834 and named for Samuel Huntington, a Connecticut delegate to the Continental Congress and a signer of the Declaration of Independence. Huntington is the county seat.

The soils are fertile and ideally suited for growing fruit, grains, and soybeans, and for raising stock. Diversified manufacturing supplements of the economy; leading industries produce electronic components, canned goods, dairy products, brake linings, and fabricated metals. There is also some limestone quarrying and lumbering.

The 900-acre Huntington Reservoir and a large section of the Salamonie Reservoir lie within the Huntington County. Both were jointly developed for recreational and water supply purposes by Indiana and the U.S. Army Corps of Engineers.

HUNTSVILLE, Town; Pop. 300; Madison County; E central Indiana; 7 mi. from Anderson. The town was founded in 1830 and named for Eliazer Hunt. The first Madison County fair was held in Huntsville in 1839, but because of poor attendance and lack of interest, the fair headquarters were moved to Anderson. There are some small businesses, but Huntsville remains essentially an agricultural community (livestock, feed grains).

HYMERA, Town; Pop. 771; Sullivan County; SW Indiana; Zip Code 47855; 21 mi. SSE of Terra Haute. The town was platted in 1870 after the discovery of rich bituminous coal deposits. It was originally named Pittsburgh. When it was discovered that there was already a Pittsburgh, Indiana, the town was renamed High Mary, after the postmaster's tall daughter. This name was later shortened to Hymera. Coal mining is still the leading industry, followed by grain and livestock farming. Nearby is Shakamak State Park *(q.v)*, a popular tourist attraction.

IDAVILLE, Town; Pop. 600; White County; NW Indiana; Zip Code 47950; 5 mi. E of Monticello in an agricultural area noted for livestock and feed grains. The town is a manufacturing center for pallets, furniture, tank car culverts, and feeds.

Dictionary of Places

INDIANA DUNES STATE PARK, south end of Lake Michigan in Lake County, Indiana. Comprising 2,182 acres, the park was created in 1925. It is a magnificent blend of shifting sand, pearly beaches, and luxuriant, almost tropical forest. Some of the dunes are "dead," or non-shifting, whereas others are "live" and shifting, such as the giant dune, Mount Tom, which reaches a height of 192 feet. Binding plants, such as grasses and vines, keep many of the dunes from migrating. The Big Blowout, a semi-circular dune which looks like an explosion crater, was actually formed by wind erosion.

The Indiana Dunes National Lakeshore was established in 1972. It surrounds the state park, which has remained a separate entity.

INDIANA TERRITORY STATE MEMORIAL, Knox County; S Indiana; at Vincennes. It includes the first capital of the Indiana Territory (1800), and a reconstruction of Elihu Stout's print shop, home of the first newspaper in the territory. The memorial is located in Harrison Park across from Vincennes University. The old capitol, restored in 1919, consists of a simple, two-storied frame building with a stoop porch and small paned windows. Original furniture is placed throughout, including the oddly-shaped walnut desk upon which were signed the laws for the Indiana Territory. The first territorial legislature met there in 1805.

INDIANAPOLIS. *See article on page 344.*
   ●HISTORICAL PLACES... (See Hist. Places Sect for details.)

Allison Mansion; Athenaeum (Das Deutsche Haus); Ayres, L.S. Annex Warehouse; Benton House; Christ Church Cathedral; City Market; Crown Hill Cemetery; Harrison, Benjamin, House; Indiana State Museum; Indianapolis Union Railroad Station; Lockerbie Square Historic District; Michigan Road Tollhouse; Military Park; Morris Butler House; Old Pathology Building; Propylaeum, The (John W. Schmidt House); Riley, James Whitcomb, House; State Soldiers and Sailors Monument; U.S. Courthouse and Post Office; Woodruff Place.

INGALLS, Town; Pop. 889; Madison County; E central Indiana; Zip Code 46048; 24 mi. NE of Indianapolis. The town was founded in 1893 and named for M.E. Ingalls, president of the Big Four Railroad Company. Essentially a farming community (livestock, feed grains), Ingalls benefitted--on a lesser scale than many of the Madison County towns--from the natural gas boom of 1887. As a direct result of the boom, however, a glass factory and zinc works were established there. Ingalls incorporated in 1896, but never achieved the economic status that its founders had envisioned.

IRELAND, Town; Pop. 340; Dubois County; S Indiana; Zip Code 47545; 4 mi. NW of Jasper in an agricultural and timbering region. The town is a trade center for logs, sample cases, cabinets, vanities, and poultry.

IROQUOIS RIVER, in Indiana, flows generally NE to SW for 50 mi. across the NW corner of the state to empty into the Illinois River.

JACKSON, County; Pop. 33,187; S Indiana; area 520 sq. mi.; drained by the East Fork of the White River and tributaries of the Muscatatuck River. The county was organized in 1816 and named in honor of Gen. Andrew Jackson, hero of the Battle of New Orleans. Brownstown is the county seat.

Jackson County is one of the most scenic counties in Indiana. A range of hills passes through it from NE to SW. The NW corner contains another set of hills, or knobs. Breathtaking panoramas can be viewed along Skyline Drive in the Jackson-Washington State Forest. The intervening bottomlands occupy half of the county and are extremely fertile. Grain, livestock, and poultry are the leading agricultural products. Diversified manufacturing (automobile parts, shoes, shirts, plastic products) is evident in the larger towns.

JACKSON-WASHINGTON STATE PARK, Jackson and Washington counties; S Indiana; just S of Brownstown. The forest consists of a north and south unit and encompasses an area totaling 15,181 acres. There are excellent facilities

Dictionary of Places

for hiking, picnicking, camping, fishing, hunting, and horseback riding. The forested hills and valleys within the area are unexcelled for beauty. Knob Lake, covering 10 acres, has been stocked with fish.

JAMES, LAKE, Stueben County; NE Indiana; near Agola. Located within the boundaries of Pokagon State Park *(q.v.)*, Lake James covers 900 acres and has a maximum depth of 94 ft. It is Indiana's third largest natural lake. It is picturesquely surrounded by low hills and woods, and has been a popular lake for sailing and swimming by enthusiasts from Indiana, Michigan, and Illinois.

JAMESTOWN, Town; Pop. 764; Boone County; central Indiana; Zip Code 46147; 17 mi. SE of Crawfordsville in an agricultural area noted for livestock and feed grains. Once a busy stagecoach stop, Jamestown is now a quiet farming community with a lumber mill.

JASONVILLE, City; Pop. 2,200; Greene County, SW Indiana; Zip Code 47438; 24 mi. SSE of Terre Haute in an agricultural area noted for grain and fruit. The city also has coal mines nearby. Manufactures include rubber goods, electronics, and cold-storage lockers. Recreational facilities are at nearby Lake Lenape and Shakamak State Park *(q.v.)*.

JASPER, City; Pop. 10,030; seat of Dubois County; SW Indiana; Zip Code 47546; on the Patoka River; 45 mi. NE of Evansville. Jasper was settled in 1828, largely by German immigrants. Until World War II, German was the primary language of the townspeople. Colloquial speech, known as "Jasper Dutch," is still prevalent. The city is a farming (strawberries, grain) and manufacturing (desks, canned goods, wood products, pianos, gloves) center. Many of the buildings date from the late 1800s and exhibit a unique German stepped-gable architecture. A fine example is the Gramelspacher-Gutzweiler House (1849). Southeast of town is Emlow's Mill (1866), built to replace the mill to which Abraham Lincoln brought his grain.

The Jasper Summer Theater presents popular Broadway plays every June, July, and August. Other recreational facilities are at Beaver Dam Lake, Jasper Country Club, and the Jasper Municipal Golf Course.

JASPER, County; Pop. 20,429; NW Indiana; area 562 sq. mi.; bounded on the N by the Kankakee River and drained by the Iroquois River. The county was formed in 1838 and named for Sgt. Jasper from South Carolina. The original seat was at Parish Grove, selected because it was near the center of population and because it was one of the few high dry spots in the region. The honor was ceded to Rensselaer in 1839, and it remains the county seat. Much of the history of the county is vague because two fires (1843, 1864) almost totally destroyed the records for that period.

The county's main economic activities are agriculture and stock raising, with almost no industry except lumber milling.

JASPER-PULASKI FISH AND WILDLIFE AREA, Jasper and Pulaski counties. N Indiana; 6 mi. N of Medaryville. The state lands cover 7,585 acres and have facilities for hiking, picnicking, camping, and hunting. The game-breeding station is noted for its pheasant. A bird sanctuary offers refuge for thousands of waterfowl in spring and fall.

JAY, County; Pop. 23,575; E Indiana; area 386 sq. mi.; bounded on the E by Ohio and drained by the Salamonie River. The county was organized in March 1836 and named for John Jay, patriot and statesman. Portland is the county seat.

Originally, Jay County was a leading producer of hardwood timber. After the forests were depleted, agriculture (livestock, grain, poultry, soybeans, truck) became dominant in the economy. Diversified manufacturing is carried out in the larger towns such as Portland and Dunkirk. Leading industries produce glassware, canned and processed foods, work clothes, and automobile parts.

JEFFERSON, County; Pop. 27,006; SE Indiana; area 366 sq. mi.; bounded partly on the S by the Ohio River and drained by Big Creek. The county was formed in February 1811 and named for Pres. Thomas Jefferson. Madison is the county seat.

Dictionary of Places

A notable feature of Jefferson County is its varied topography. The western area is gently rolling, the center is a wooded plateau, and the southern and eastern region is traversed by the Ohio River, and consists of a series of uninterrupted hills and valleys which are interspersed with high bluffs and deep ravines.

Wheat and corn are grown on the fertile alluvial soils. Fruit and tobacco--successfully introduced in the late 1800s-- have become two of the county's leading exports. Limestone quarrying and some manufacturing supplement the agricultural economy.

Jefferson County encompasses Clifty Falls State Park *(q.v.)*, a 1,200 acre park which offers a striking view of the Ohio River. The county hosts the annual Madison Regatta and Governor's Cup Race, a hydroplane spectacular which is held on the Ohio River during the Fourth of July weekend.

JEFFERSONVILLE, City; Pop. 21,841; seat of Clark County; SE Indiana; Zip Code 47130; just E of New Albany, on the Ohio River. The city was platted in 1802 by William Henry Harrison, who named it for Thomas Jefferson, the original planner.

The Howard Shipyards, once the city's major industry, were active from 1834 to 1931. The famous "Robert E. Lee" steamboat was rebuilt there in 1870 after a race with the "Natchez" from New Orleans to St. Louis. Some of the first large boats to ply the Yukon River during the gold rush of 1898 were built at the shipyards.

Jefferson was severely damaged in 1937 by a flood that inundated 95 percent of the city. The city is now a manufacturing community. Products include wood items, steel products, kitchen cabinets, snack foods, and machinery. American Commercial Barge Line Inc., one of the world's largest barge construction companies, has a terminal there. The city's largest employer, however, is the United States Census Bureau.

Every year Jeffersonville sponsors the Steamboat Festival on the riverfront. On the Ohio River is the John Fitzger-

ald Kennedy Memorial Bridge, which connects the city with Louisville, Kentucky.
> •HISTORICAL PLACES... (See Hist. Places Sect for details.)

Howard Home.

JENNINGS, County; Pop. 19,454; SE Indiana; area 377 sq. mi.; drained by Vernon, Graham, and Sand creeks. The county was organized in February 1817 and named for Jonathan Jennings, first state governor of Indiana. Vernon was selected as the county seat shortly thereafter.

Jennings County is located in a bituminous coal, limestone, and agricultural (livestock, feed grains, tobacco) area. Some manufacturing is carried out in Vernon. Fabricated metal production is the main industry.

JOHNSON, County; Pop. 61,138; central Indiana; area 315 sq. mi.; drained by the West Fork and tributaries of the East Fork of the White River. The county was organized in May 1823 and named for John Johnson, one of the first judges on the Indiana Supreme Court. Franklin is the county seat.

The land surface is level and covered with glacial drift. It has been called the greatest corn-producing county in the world, although other feed grains and vegetables are grown in great abundance. Manufacturing is diversified and generally centered in Franklin, Greenwood, and Edinburg. The major industries produce automobile parts, processed food, and plastics.

JONESBORO, Town; Pop. 2,073; Grant County; E central Indiana; Zip Code 46938; on the Mississinewa River; 6 mi. S of Marion. Jonesboro was named for Obadiah Jones, one of its founders, who platted the town in 1837. Jonesboro is a farming and manufacturing trade center for feed, electric wire, and cable.

JONESVILLE, Town; Pop. 221; Bartholomew County; S central Indiana; Zip Code 46938; 10 S of Columbus in an agricultural area dedicated to cattle, poultry, and feed-grain farming.

Dictionary of Places

JUDSON, Town; Pop. 61; Parke County; W Indiana; Zip Code 47856; 28 mi. NNE of Terre Haute in an agricultural and coal- mining region.

JUG ROCK, Martin County, S Indiana; in Jug Rock Park, 5 mi. N of Shoals. Jug Rock, a natural stone pillar, is 60 ft. high and 15 ft. in diameter. Resembling a huge jug, it is formed of variegated rock strata in which hikers and picnickers have carved their initials. Also within the park is the Pinnacle, another stone formation.

KANKAKEE RIVER, rises near South Bend, Indiana, and flows SW into Illinois. The Kankakee is approximately 135 mi. long and drains a major portion of Indiana's cornbelt. It is dredged along almost its total length to provide drainage for the flat terrain. The Iroquois River is its major tributary. The Kankakee daily carries 1,300,000,000 gallons of water out of Indiana.

KANKAKEE STATE RECREATION AREA, Starke County, NW Indiana; west of Knox. The recreation area, which encompasses 2,200 acres of state land, centers on the Kankakee River and is noted for its fishing and wildlife refuge. Recreational facilities include a primitive campground and fishing, boating, and picnic areas.

KEMPTON, Town; Pop. 362; Tipton County; central Indiana; Zip Code 46049; 14 mi. SSE of Kokomo in an agricultural area noted for cash grains and vegetables.

KENDALLVILLE, City; Pop. 7,773; Nobel County; NE Indiana; Zip Code 46755; on the Elkhart River, 27 mi. NNW of Fort Wayne. The city, founded in 1833 by David Bundle, who named it after Postmaster General Amos Kendall. It was platted by William Mitchell in 1847, and incorporated in 1863. Bundle established a prosperous tavern in the area, which is still standing on Gold Street.

    The settlement grew slowly until the coming of the railroad in 1857. Progress followed, and two family-operated industries became world suppliers: McCray Refrigerators, and Flint & Walling windmills. Kendallville became the state's leading shipping point for onions, and it is also a center for livestock, dairy products, and soybeans.

Manufactures include refrigerators, pumps, brushes, and artificial bait, and Kendallville is also the home of Kraft Foods, producer of marshmallows and caramels.

The Mulholland Museum contains pioneer relics and Indian artifacts. Recreational facilities are at nearby Bixler, Cree, Round, and Wible lakes.

KENNARD, Town; Pop. 382; Henry County; E central Indiana; Zip Code 47351; 8 mi. W of New Castle in an agricultural area noted for livestock and feed grains.

KENTLAND, Town; Pop. 1,798; seat of Newton County; NW Indiana; Zip Code 47951; 38 mi. NW of Lafayette. Kentland was settled in 1860 and is the birthplace of George Ade, famous Hoosier author, humorist, and playwright. His home stands opposite the county courthouse. The town is basically a farming community and has a large whole-mild cheese-making plant.

KEWANNA, Town; Pop. 542; Fulton County; N Indiana; Zip Code 46939; 20 mi. N of Logansport in an agricultural region noted for livestock and feed grains. Bruce Lake is nearby.

KIMMEL, Town; Pop. 350; Wells County; NE Indiana; Zip Code 46759; 12 mi. S of Bluffton in an agricultural and dairying area. The town is a trade center for grain, feeds, seed, fertilizer, popcorn, and hybrid seed corn.

KINGMAN, Town; Pop. 561; Fountain County; W Indiana; Zip Code 47952; 21 mi. WSW of Crawfordsville in a region of fertile soils ideally suited for farming and cattle grazing. There is some bituminous coal mining.

KINGSBURY, Town; Pop. 258; La Porte County; NW Indiana; Zip Code 46343; 6 mi. S of La Porte. The town is a shipping point for grain, onions, and peppermint.

KINGSBURY STATE FISH AND WILDLIFE AREA, La Porte County; NW Indiana; 5 mi. S of La Porte. It covers 4,498 acres and has facilities for hiking, picnicking, fishing, camping, boating, and hunting.

Dictionary of Places

KINGSFORD HEIGHTS, Village; Pop. 1,486; La Porte County; NW Indiana; Zip Code 46346; 10 mi. S of La Porte in a livestock and feed grain area.

KIRKLIN, Town; Pop. 707; Clinton County; central Indiana; Zip Code 46050; near Sugar Creek; 10 mi. SE of Frankfort. Kirklin was founded in 1832 on the Michigan Road, which is now the Main Street of town. Nathan Kirklin, for whom the town was named, built a thriving tavern after the first settlers arrived. Today, farming is predominant, and the fertile soils are ideally suited for feed grains (corn, oats, soybeans), and livestock.

KNIGHTSTOWN, Town; Pop. 2,048; Henry County; E central Indiana; Zip Code 46148; on the Big Blue River, 34 mi. E of Indianapolis. Knightstown was founded in 1825 and named for Jonathan Knight, the government engineer in charge of construction of the National Road through the town. Platted in 1827, Knightstown is an agricultural and manufacturing center for the area. Agriculture produced includes corn, soybeans, hay, cattle, and hogs, and manufactures include automotive accessories and knitwear. It is the site of the Indiana Soldiers' and Sailors' Children's Home, which offers vocational training. Fort Montgomery is a resort two mi. N of town.

KNIGHTSVILLE, Town; Pop. 740; Clay County; W Indiana; Zip Code 47857; just NE of Brazil in an agricultural area noted for feed grains and livestock. There is some bituminous coal mining.

KNOBS, THE Floyd County; S Indiana; near New Albany. The Knobs are a range of hills that rise 200 ft. above sea level and are covered with dense woods. The scenery is unsurpassed anywhere in the state. The ancient hills have been worn down by stream erosion over the centuries until they have become rounded or "knobby."

KNOX, City; Pop. 3,705; seat of Starke County; NW Indiana; Zip Code 46534; on the Yellow River, 33 mi. SW of South Bend. Basically a farming community. Knox has a large population of Scandinavian, Slavic, and Italian immigrants who raise mint and onions. Knox has become a leading shipping center for their produce. Manufacturing (electrical appliances, clothing) is also important.

Nearby is Bass Lake, Indiana's largest lake. The Lightning Dude Ranch is a popular resort which offers rodeos, trail rides, and horse shows.

KNOX, County; Pop. 41,546; SW Indiana; area 515 sq. mi.; bounded on the W by the Wabash River, the E by the West Fork of the White River, and the S by the White River. It is drained by the Deshee River and Maria Creek. Knox County is known as the "Mother of Indiana Counties," having been surveyed before the territorial government was established. The county was officially organized on June 30, 1790, by Winthrop Sargent, secretary of the Northwest Territory. It was named for Gen. Henry Knox, the first secretary of war of the U.S. Vincennes, the only county seat, attracts thousands of visitors to its multitude of historic shrines (George Rogers Clark Memorial; the first territorial capitol; Grouseland; Elihu Stout's print shop).

Knox County encompasses some of the richest land in Indiana. It is famous for the "Decker" cantaloupe and is a center for the production of livestock, fruit, feed grains, and coal. Principal industries produce wire springs, structural steel, glass, and glass products.

KOKOMO, City; Pop. 44,962; seat of Howard County, central Indiana; Zip Code 46901; on Wildcat Creek; 50 mi. N of Indianapolis. Kokomo was platted in 1844 and named for Chief Kokomo, a renowned Miami Indian leader. A monument to him is situated in the Pioneer Cemetery.

As did many other cities in central Indiana, Kokomo experienced rapid growth during the natural gas boom of 1887. Businesses such as glass factories, steel works, and furnace factories were erected. Perhaps Kokomo's greatest claim to fame came in 1893, when the Hoosier inventor Elwood Haynes (1857-1925) tested the first clutch-driven, electric-ignition automobile. He ran it successfully on Pumpkin Vine Pike. Haynes' home has been restored and is now a public museum which houses memorabilia of his life, including early Haynes automobiles.

Dictionary of Places

Today, Kokomo is a thriving industrial city. Both General Motors and Chrysler have plants there, and numerous other businesses produce tools, ceramics, cutlery, canned goods, clothing, playground equipment, and cosmetics. A branch of Indiana University opened there in 1965.

Highland Park on Deffenbaugh Street has two superlative exhibits. "Old Ben," a taxidermically preserved steer, is reported to have weighed 4,470 lbs. and was 16 ft. 8 in. long and 6 ft. 4 in. high. The hollow stump of a sycamore tree, 59 ft in circumference, has held 12 people and a telephone booth comfortably. Kokomo is the site of the Greentown Glass Museum, noted for its "chocolate ware" and "holly amber" glass, last manufactured in 1903. The Howard County Historical Museum has a collection of Lincoln, Indian, and Civil War artifacts. Recreational facilities are at the two city golf courses and Kokomo Reservoir No. 2, 4 + mi. E of the city.

●HISTORICAL PLACES... (See Hist. Places Sect for details.)

Sieberling Mansion.

KOSCIUSKO, County; Pop. 48,127; N Indiana; area 540 sq. mi.; drained by the Tippecanoe and Eel Rivers and by Turkey Creek. The county was formed in June 1837 and was named for Gen. Thaddeus Kosciusko, a Polish soldier, patriot, and aide-de-camp to Gen. George Washington. Warsaw is the county seat.

One of the state's largest counties, Kosciusko is also in the center of Indiana's lake region. More than 100 sparkling lakes afford a summer playground to thousands of visitors who come there annually to enjoy swimming, boating, and fishing.

Kosciusko is an agricultural county. It is a center for livestock, poultry, truck, dairy products, soybeans, and timber. Diversified manufacturing produces automobile parts, boats, mobile homes, iron castings, movie screens, and books.

KOUTS, Town; Pop. 1,603; Porter County; NW Indiana; Zip Code 46347; 11 mi. S of Valparaiso in an agricultural region noted for livestock and feed grains.

LACONIA, Town; Pop. 75; Harrison County; S Indiana; Zip Code 47135; 23 mi. SW of New Albany. The town is a farming community in an area noted for cattle and hogs. Of note is the Kintner-Withers Plantation House (1837), built in Classic Revival style and containing a large private collection of Civil War antiques.

LA CROSSE, Town; Pop.677; La Porte County; NW Indiana; Zip Code 46348; 30 mi. SE of Gary in a region noted for livestock and feed grains.

LADOGA, Town; Pop. 1,124; Montgomery County; W central Indiana; Zip Code 47954; on Raccoon Creek; 11 mi. SSE of Crawfordsville. Ladoga was the seat of Central Normal College which, on May 19, 1878, was virtually "kidnapped" and taken to Danville, 22 mi. away. The town is now a quiet farming community and a trade center for livestock, soybeans, and corn.

LAFAYETTE, City; Pop. 43,764; seat of Tippecanoe County; W central Indiana; Zip Code 47901; on the Wabash River; 60 mi. NW of Indianapolis. Lafayette was founded and named in 1825 by William Digby for the Marquis de LaFayette, who served as a general under George Washington in the American Revolution.

For many years, Lafayette was a leading river port. Produce was brought in by wagons from the surrounding area and, in turn, was shipped to other markets via steamboats on the Wabash River or the canal boats of the Wabash and Erie Canal. Modern Lafayette is the manufacturing center of Tippecanoe County, with agriculture and coal mining, along with the production of rubber, paper, gears, tools, drugs, soap, safes, plumbing supplies, and automotive products.

Historical sites abound in and around Lafayette. Fort Ouiatenon, 4 mi. NE of the city, was built by the French in 1717 to guard the Maumee-Wabash route and to establish a fur trading post with the Indians. It was the first guarded post established by the white man in Indiana. The fort was destroyed in 1791, but a blockhouse replica marks the site. The Tippecanoe Battlefield, 7 mi. N of Lafayette, is preserved in memory of those soldiers who died in the battle

Dictionary of Places

fought between Tenskwatawa, the Shawnee Prophet, and Gen. William Henry Harrison in 1811 (*see* Tippecanoe Battlefield State Memorial). Prophet's Town, established in 1808 by Tecumseh, Tenskwatawa's brother, was located 3 mi. downstream on the Tippecanoe River. The Tippecanoe County Historical Museum (1852) has relics of the battle, as well as pioneer artifacts from Fort Ouiatenon and the local countryside.

West Lafayette, sister city to Lafayette, is the seat of Purdue University (1869), one of the first land-grant colleges. Recreational facilities can be found at the city's Columbian Park, which includes a zoo, and at nearby Hoon and Marsh Lakes.

●HISTORICAL PLACES... (See Hist. Places Sect for details.)
Fowler, Moses, House; Tippecanoe County Courthouse; Fort Ouiatenon; Indiana State Soldiers Home Historic District; Tippecanoe Battlefield.

LA FONTAINE, Town; Pop. 909; Wabash County; NE central Indiana; Zip Code 469490; near the Mississinewa River; 8 mi. NNW of Marion in an area noted for livestock and feed grains.

LAGRANGE, Town; Pop. 2,382; seat of Lagrange County; NE Indiana; Zip Code 46761; on the Pigeon River; 28 mi. E of Elkhart. The original settlement was founded in 1835, platted in 1836, and named for the Marquis de LaFayette's residence near Paris, France.

Lagrange became the county seat in 1844 and developed into a leading dairying center surrounded by fertile farmland. There are several poultry hatcheries in town. Some of the many small lakes in the area are remnants of previously drained swamplands. The Mongo Reservoir and Royer Lake have been developed into recreational sites, and the Pigeon River State Fish and Game Area is a popular sportsman's attraction.

LAGRANGE, County; Pop. 20,890; NE Indiana; area 381 sq. mi.; bounded N by Michigan and drained by the Pigeon and Little Elkhart rivers. The county was organized in April 1832 and the town of Lagrange became the county seat in

1844. Both were named for the home of the Marquis de La-Fayette near Paris, France.

Lagrange is basically an agricultural county (dairying, soybeans, feed grains, stock raising, poultry). One of the largest Amish settlements in the U.S. is located in the western part of the county between Topeka and Shipshewana.

LAGRO, Town; Pop. 496; Wabash County; NE central Indiana; Zip Code 46941; on the Wabash River; 5 mi. ENE of Wabash. The town was named for Les Gros, an Indian chief. It developed during the canal boat era, and the bed of the Wabash and Erie Canal can still be seen running along Main Street.

Lagro is a center for rock-wood products. The Salamonie River State Forest is 3 mi. from town. It encompasses the Lost Bridge State Recreation Area (Salamonie Reservoir), which contains a 2,855-acre lake noted for its beaches and fishing.

LAKE, County; Pop. 546,253; NW Indiana; area 513 sq. mi.; bounded on the N by Lake Michigan (for which it is named), W by Illinois, and S by the Kankakee River. The county is traversed by the Grand Calumet and Little Calumet rivers. Lake County was formed in February 1837 and Crown Point was made the county seat.

Prior to 1899, the whole northern tier of Lake County was a desolate wasteland of sand dunes, marshes, and scattered farms. With the construction of the U.S. Steel Company mill at Gary in 1905, however, Lake County mushroomed into the leading industrial county of the state. The Calumet district, "American's Ruhr Valley," embraces the cities of Gary-Hammond-Whiting-East Chicago, and is one of the world's greatest industrial centers. It is a leading producer of steel, oil, petrochemicals, cement, soap, and related products.

Southward is a farm belt where the soils were reclaimed from the mosquito and muskrat-infested Kankakee Marshes. The fertile bottomlands now yield wheat, corn, oats, vegetables, and soybeans. Livestock and horses are prominent features of the county's diversified economy.

Dictionary of Places

Lake County has, for a long period of time, been an anomaly to the Hoosier state. It is more often than not identified with its sister counties in northern Illinois. Proposals to deed Lake County to Chicago have been presented to numerous legislative sessions.

LAKETON, Town; Pop. 500; Wabash County; N Indiana; Zip Code 46943; 12 mi. N of Wabash in an agricultural area noted for livestock and feed grains. The town is a manufacturing center for rubber and plastic molds and petroleum products.

LAKE VILLAGE, Town; Pop. est 650; Newton County; N Indiana; Zip Code 46349; 26 mi. N of Kentland in an agricultural area noted for livestock and feed grains.

LAKEVILLE, Town; Pop. 655; St. Joseph County; N Indiana; Zip Code 46536; 11 mi. S of South Bend. Lakeville was named for the group of nearby lakes, and has become a popular summer resort and trading center. Pleasant and Riddle lakes provide good fishing and boating facilities.

LANESVILLE, Town; Pop. 512; Harrison County; S Indiana; Zip Code 47136; 10 mi. WSW of New Albany. The town was settled in 1792 and platted in 1817. It was named for Gen. Lane, a government surveyor and early settler in the area. It developed originally as a stagecoach stop between Corydon and New Albany, and is now a trading center for livestock and feed grain.

J.F.D. LANIER STATE MEMORIAL, Madison, Jefferson County; S Indiana. The stately mansion was built in 1844 for James F.D. Lanier, a banker and financier whose loans helped Indiana avert bankruptcy during the late 19th century. The house was designed by the famous architect Francis Costigan; it contains the original furnishings.

LAOTTO, Town; Pop. 300; Noble County; N Indiana; Zip Code 46763; 13 mi. N of Fort Wayne in an agricultural and dairying area. Laotto is a manufacturing center for truck equipment, fertilizer, LP gas tank trailer, tools, dies, and molds.

Encyclopedia of Indiana

LAPAZ, Town; Pop. 562; Marshall County; N Indiana; Zip Code 46537; 16 mi. S of South Bend in an agricultural area noted for livestock and feed grains. It is also known as La Paz.

LAPEL, Town; Pop.1,742; Madison County; E central Indiana; Zip Code 46051; 26 mi. NE of Indianapolis. Platted by David Conrad in 1876, it was named for its shape, which resembled a coat lapel. The town is basically an agricultural community, but contains the Brockway Glass Company, which was founded during the natural gas boom of 1887. The company employs almost 550 people. Small businesses thrive in town. The limestone quarry, which is geologically part of an ancient reef, has yielded many fine fossil samples.

LA PORTE, City; Pop. 21,507; seat of La Porte County; NW Indiana; Zip Code 46350; on Pine Lake; 33 mi. E of Gary. The city was founded in 1830 at the time the Michigan Road was built. It was named La Porte (French for "door" or "gate") because of its location at the point where Indiana's original forests met the open prairie. La Porte became a trading center between central and southern Indiana, the Indiana lake region, Illinois, and Michigan.

Diversity is evident in La Porte's manufactures, which include farm implements, rubber products, radiators, furniture, metal doors, baby carriages, and automobile equipment. One of the finest historical museums in Indiana is located in the basement of the county courthouse. A pioneer log cabin, which contains pioneer relics, including an 1833 Kentucky squirrel rifle, is in the museum. Other displays include the Edward Vail collection of native birds and a coin collection. Winter recreation is available at Ski Valley, 5 mi. W of town.

LA PORTE, County, Pop. 105,342; N Indiana; area 607 sq. mi.; bounded on the NW by Lake Michigan, and S by the Kankakee River. The county was organized in January 1832. The city of La Porte has been the seat since the county was formed.

Dictionary of Places

Fruit growing is a big business in La Porte County. Small lakes are interspersed with rolling hills covered with orchards and vineyards. Much of the rest of the county is farmland drained from the Kankakee Marshes and ideally suited to feed grains.

La Porte County is also a leading manufacturing center. Its main industries produce farm and industrial machinery, railroad cars, truck trailers, furniture, fabricated metals, appliances, and electronic equipment.

•HISTORICAL PLACES... (See Hist. Places Sect for details.)
Michigan City Lighthouse.

LARWILL, Town; Pop. 219; Whitley County; NE Indiana; 26 mi. WNW of Fort Wayne in an agricultural area noted for livestock and feed grains. Larwill, Robinson, and Troy Cedar lakes are popular resort spots.

LASALLE FISH AND WILDLIFE AREA, Newton County N Indiana; near Lake Village. The wildlife area covers 3,551 acres and has a 500 acre lake with facilities for water recreation. There are also a campground, picnic area, and boat-launching ramp.

LAUREL, Town; Pop. 544; Franklin County; SE Indiana; Zip Code 47024; 10 mi. SSE of Connersville in an agricultural area noted for livestock and feed grains. The town was founded in 1836 by James Conwell, who named it for Laurel, Delaware. Historical buildings can be seen throughout the town, including the one-cell stone jail and the Methodist Church (1846). Nearby is an old remnant of the Whitewater Canal, which now contains a feeder dam. At the north edge of town and rising 150 ft. above is Laurel Hill, a prehistoric Indian mound. The view from its summit has been described as "one of the loveliest in Indiana."

LAWRENCE, City; Pop. 26,763; Marion County; central Indiana; Zip Code 46226; on the West Fork of the White River, just NE of Indianapolis. Lawrence is a quiet residential community; most of its inhabitants are employed in Indianapolis.

LAWRENCE, County; Pop. 38,038; S Indiana; area 459 sq. mi.; drained by the East Fork of the White River and by Salt Creek. The county was formed in March 1818 and named for Capt. James Lawrence. Bedford became the county seat in 1825.

Out of Lawrence County has come some of the finest building limestone in the world. The quarries at Bedford and Oolitic have been the main suppliers. Other industrial products include cement and nonferrous castings. Fruit and grain are the leading agricultural products.

LAWRENCEBURG, City; Pop. 4,375; seat of Dearborn County; SE i Zip Code 47025; 50 mi. S of Richmond. Lawrenceburg was founded in 1801 by Capt. Samuel Vance and became a prosperous Ohio River port. Gambler's Row, an early vice district, was known from Pittsburgh to New Orleans. A flood destroyed much of the city in 1937, leaving 6,000 people homeless. Industries began to flourish after the flood, and today Lawrenceburg has some of the nation's largest distilleries. Other manufactures include feed, machinery, lumber, shoes, and pharmaceuticals.

LEAVENWORTH, Town; Pop. 320; Crawford County; S Indiana; Zip Code 47137; near the Ohio River; 29 mi. W of New Albany. The town was founded in 1818 on the banks of the Ohio River, but a flood in 1937 swept most of it away. The new town, dedicated on Dec. 15, 1938, was located atop a bluff overlooking the river. Remnants of the old site can still be seem. Leavenworth remains a farming community in an area noted for feed grains and livestock.

LEBANON, City; Pop. 12,059; seat of Boone County; central Indiana; Zip Code 46052; 25 mi. NW of Indianapolis. Lebanon was founded in 1832 and named for the surrounding forest, the trees of which were likened to the Biblical cedars of Lebanon. Agriculture (corn, soybeans, tomatoes) and manufacturing (farm equipment, tools, bus chassis', artificial Christmas trees, concrete products, chemicals, filtration equipment, business forms) are the mainstays of the economy.

Dictionary of Places

Of particular note is the county courthouse, dedicated July 4, 1912, which is built of granite and Bedford limestone. The eight huge pillars at the north and south entrances are the largest one-piece limestone columns in the world. Each column is 3 stories high and weighs 50 tons. Lebanon was the home of Samuel M. Ralston (1857-1925), an Indiana governor and U.S. Senator.

Cool Lake Park and golf course are 7 mi. N of town.

LEESBURG, Town; Pop. 584; Kosciusko County; n Indiana; Zip Code 46538; 31 mi. SE of South Bend in an agricultural area noted for livestock and feed grains. James and Tippecanoe lakes and Indian Hills Golf Course provide recreational facilities for the surrounding area.

LETTERS FORD, Town; Pop. 250; Fulton County; n Indiana; Zip Code 46945; 11 mi. NW of Rochester in an agricultural area noted for feed grains and livestock. Letters Ford has a gravel and a sand pit and a fertilizer plant.

LEO, Town; Pop. 600; Allen County; NE Indiana; Zip Code 46765; 11 mi. NE of Fort Wayne in an agricultural and dairying area. Leo is a manufacturing center for bulletin boards, steel, and garage and patio doors.

LEWISVILLE, Town; Pop. 437; Henry County; E Indiana; Zip Code 47352; near Flatrock Creek; 9 mi. S of New Castle in an agricultural area noted for livestock and feed grains.

LEXINGTON, Town; Pop. 350; Scott County; S Indiana; Zip Code 47138; 10 mi. SE of Scottsburg in a lumber and farming area. Lexington is a manufacturing center for tools, dies, jigs, and wood products.

LIBERTY, Town; Pop. 2,051; seat of Union County; E Indiana; Zip Code 47353; 13 mi. S of Richmond. A quiet farming community, it dates back to 1822. The town is a shipping center for livestock, dairy products, paint, and agricultural implements. Liberty was once a stop on the Underground Railway, the "freedom train" for runaway slaves. Gen. Ambrose Burnside, a Civil War leader credited with originating the "sideburns" hairstyle, was born there.

Nearby is Whitewater State Park, which is dedicated to those men who served in World War II.

LIBERTY MILLS, Town; Pop. 300; Wabash County; N Indiana; Zip Code 46946; 18 mi. N of Wabash in an agricultural and dairying area. Wabash is a trade center for grain and feeds and is a manufacturer of screens and knives.

LIGONIER, City; Pop. 3,443; Nobel County; NE Indiana; Zip Code 46767; on the Elkhart River; 37 mi. SE of South Bend. It is a peaceful farming and trade center whose products include dairy items, furniture, refrigerators, work clothes, bedding, and flour. Nearby Diamond Lake is a popular recreational area.

LIMBERLOST STATE MEMORIAL, Geneva; Adams County; E Indiana. The memorial contains the original two-story 14-room "Limberlost Cabin" designed and occupied from 1893 to 1913 by Gene Stratton Porter, Indiana's most famous authoress. At the log cabin, which is surrounded by lattice work, she began writing her best-known novels, *Freckles* and *A Girl of the Limberlost.* Limberlost Swamp, which inspired her books, has since been drained.

LINCOLN BOYHOOD NATIONAL MEMORIAL, Spencer County; S Indiana; just S of Lincoln City. The memorial is dedicated to Abraham Lincoln and his mother, Nancy Hanks Lincoln. Established in 1932, it encompasses 1,731 acres of wooded hills and forests of which Lincoln State Park is also a part. In this area Lincoln spent his boyhood years from the ages 7 to 21 before moving to Illinois.

The memorial contains the site of the family's log cabin and grave of Lincoln's mother, who died of the "milk-sick" in 1818. (The "milk-sick" was an epidemic caused by cows eating white snake-root, which poisoned their milk.) Included at the site are Abraham Lincoln Hall, which houses a chapel; Nancy Hanks Lincoln Hall; a museum; and a Living Historical Farm. The visitor's center is a wrap-around structure that winds behind the sculptured panels of the memorial halls.

LINCOLN HERITAGE TRAIL, a three-state network of highways in Kentucky, Indiana, and Illinois that traces the migration route of Abraham Lincoln from his birthplace in Kentucky to his final resting place in Illinois. Along the entire route are restored shrines and numerous memorials and markers depicting events in the president's life. The Indiana sector includes the Lincoln Boyhood National Memorial Park, Lincoln Pioneer Village, and Lincoln State Park.

LINCOLN STATE PARK, Spencer County; S Indiana; just S of Lincoln City. The park, one of Indiana's tributes to Abraham Lincoln, encompasses 1,173 acres of beautiful, natural woodlands. It was established in 1932; an additional 114 acres were dedicated in 1963. There is a large artificial lake which offers excellent swimming and fishing. A modern campground, picnic area, and observation tower are also situated there.

LINDEN, Town; Pop. 718; Montgomery County; W Indiana; Zip Code 47955; 17 mi. S of Lafayette in an agricultural area noted for livestock and feed grains.

LINTON, City; Pop. 5,814; Greene County; SW Indiana; Zip Code 47441; 32 mi. SSE of Terre Haute. Located in one of Indiana's richest coal fields. Linton began in the 1830s as a mining town with a varied ethnic population. The earliest German and English populations intermingled with Scots. Poles, Hungarians, and French. Near Linton, a 6-ft. lacquered coal marker designates the nation's center of population in 1930.

Good fishing facilities can be found at nearby Downing, Stephen's and Wampler lakes, and at the Linton Conservation Ponds.

LITTLE YORK, Town; Pop. 155; Washington County; S Indiana; 31 mi. NW of New Albany in an agricultural region noted for livestock and feed grains. Several Amish farms are in the vicinity.

LIZTON, Town; Pop. 410; Hendricks County; central Indiana; Zip Code 46149; 22 mi. WNW of Indianapolis. The 1851 settlement was located in a swampy lowland which has since been drained and converted to fertile farmland. Corn, hogs, and cattle figure prominently in Lizton's economy.

LOGANSPORT, City; Pop.16,812; seat of Cass County; N central Indiana; Zip Code 46947; at the confluence of Eel and Wabash rivers. 36 mi. NE of Lafayette. In 1828, land in the vicinity of the present city was purchased from the Potawatomi and Miami Indians by the U.S. government. Logansport sprang up almost overnight as stores were erected to serve the Indians. The settlement was dedicated the same year and named for James Logan, a nephew of Tecumseh, who was killed fighting for the U.S. in the War of 1812. Logansport flourished as a leading trade center for more than 100 years, and by 1860 was reputed to be one of the Midwest's most prominent railroad centers.

Modern Logansport is an industrial city. Batteries, missile components, cement, dishes, radiators, and fishing tackle are a few of the city's diversified manufactures. Nearby is the Logansport State Hospital for the mentally ill.

The Cass County Historical Museum contains pioneer objects and Civil War memorabilia. The ancestral home of the Miami Indians, known as "Olde Towne," is 6 mi. E of the city. France Park, 4 mi. W of town, provides camping and recreational facilities. Twin Hills Lake is also a popular recreational site.

LOST RIVER, S Indiana; rises near Orleans and flows generally NE to SW across Orange County to empty into the White River in Martin County. The river is a "disappearing stream"--that is, in various places along its course it disappears into the surrounding limestone bedrock, which is everywhere traversed by cave systems and sinkholes. The entire Lost River system occupies 352 sq. mi. in sections of Washington, Orange, Lawrence and Martin counties.

The first 15 mi. of the river's course appears like that of a normal stream. Its middle course is marked by sudden disappearances into, and reappearances from, underground caverns. At Tolliver Swallowhole, the river at times takes trees, mud and parts of farmer's fields underground with it. The stream is also a habitat for blind fish and crayfish.

LONG BEACH, Town; Pop. 2,044; La Porte County; NW Indiana; on Lake Michigan; 4 mi. NE of Michigan City.

Dictionary of Places

Long Beach caters mainly to the tourists who annually visit the sand dune country surrounding the town. The region is known as the summer playground of Indiana.

LOOGOOTEE, City; Pop. 2,884; Martin County; SW Indiana; Zip Code 47553; near the East Fork of the White River; 50 mi. S of Bloomington. Founded in 1853 by Thomas Gootee, and incorporated in 1903, the city is located in a ruggedly beautiful section of Indiana, rich in natural resources. Fertile farmlands, contributing such crops as corn and soybeans, stands of timber, bituminous coal deposits, and oil and natural gas pockets all contribute to Loogootee's prosperity. The main manufactures include clothing, veneer, and tile products.

LOSANTVILLE, Town; Pop. 253; Randolph County; central Indiana; Zip Code 47354; 20 mi. SE of Winchester. The town is a manufacturer of tools, dies, special machinery, casket shells, and farm supplies.

LOST BRIDGE STATE RECREATION AREA, near Lagro, Wabash County; NE central Indiana. Lost Bridge comprises 12,000 acres of woods and water in the Salamonie River State Forest. Salamonie Lake is the main attraction. It covers 2,855 acres and offers excellent camping, swimming, fishing, and boating. Bridle paths and nature trails have been blazed through the surrounding forest.

LOWELL, Town; Pop. 6,430; Lake County; NW Indiana; Zip Code 46356; 22 mi. S of Gary. Lowell was founded in 1849 on the Kankakee marshes. Fertile farmlands have made it a commercial center for dairy products and nursery stock. The leading manufacture is brushes. The Crown Point-Lowell Race Course was popular in the early 1900s. George Ade, noted Hoosier humorist, once said of it: "The race course runs through the center of town, and the speed maniacs from the city help make life more interesting and uncertain in the sylvan retreat."

LYDICK, Village; Pop. 650; St. Joseph County; N Indiana; 7 mi. WNW of South Bend in an agricultural area noted for livestock and feed grains.

LYNN, Town; Pop. 1,183; Randolph County; E Indiana; Zip Code 47355; 16 mi. N of Richmond. A quiet livestock and farming center, it was founded in 1847. Rugged beauty surrounds the town; to the E is the highest point in Indiana, rising to 1,240 ft.

LYNNVILLE, Town; Pop. 640; Warrick County; SW Indiana; Zip Code 47619; 22 mi. NE of Evansville in an area noted for livestock and feed grains. Lynnville Park is a popular resort and visitor's attraction.

LYONS, Town; Pop. 753; Greene County, SW Indiana; Zip Code 47443, 32 mi. NE of Vincennes in an agricultural area noted for livestock and feed grains. Mining of bituminous coal is a major activity. An annual handicraft and agricultural fair is held in September.

MACY, Town; Pop. 218; Miami County; N Indiana; Zip Code 46951; 15 mi. N of Peru in an agricultural area noted for livestock and feed grains. Macy is a manufacturing center for farm post-buildings and lumber products.

MADISON, City; Pop. 12,006; seat of Jefferson County; SE Indiana; Zip Code 47250; on the Ohio River 40 mi. NNE of New Albany. The area around Madison was first settled in 1805, and the city was founded four years later. Advantageously situated on the banks of the Ohio River, it quickly mushroomed into a leading river port.

Madison is one of Indiana's oldest and most beautiful cities. Many pre-Civil War homes have been preserved along the riverfront and the many narrow sidestreets. Among the finest examples of the 19th century architecture are the Paul House (1808), oldest brick building in Madison; the Schofield Mansion (1817); the James F.D. Lanier Home (1844), an elaborate building complete with a cupola, a portico with 30-ft. pillars, and a three-story spiral staircase; and the Shrewsbury House (1846). On the west edge of town is the 1835 railroad which climbs 400 ft. in one mile, the steepest non-cog railroad in the world. A non-profit organization, Historic Madison, Inc., was founded in 1960 for the purpose of preserving the old homes and landmarks in and around the city.

Dictionary of Places

Madison is a leading tobacco market and a manufacturer of wood products and packed meats. The river is still important. Heavily laden barges carry oil, steel, coal, iron, sulphur and other commodities. The Delta Queen, one of the last remaining passenger-carrying stern-wheelers, makes a regular stop at Madison. The annual Governor's Cup hydroplane race is held there annually on the Ohio River. Entertainers Frank Sinatra, Dean Martin, and Shirley MacLaine caused much excitement in 1958, when the motion picture *Some Came Running* was filmed in the city.

Nearby is Clifty Falls State Park *(q.v.)*, one of the most scenic tourist attractions in Indiana. Hanover College, now at Hanover, was temporarily located at Madison in 1844. The campus consists of 400 wooded acres overlooking the Ohio River Valley.

●HISTORICAL PLACES... (See Hist. Places Sect for details.)

Jefferson County Jail; Madison Historic District.

MADISON, County; Pop. 138,451; E central Indiana; area 453 sq. mi.; drained by the West Fork of the White River and by Pipe, Kilbuck, Fall, Duck and Lick creeks. The county was formed in July 1823 and named for James Madison, fourth president of the U.S. Anderson is the county seat.

Madison county began to develop with the building of the Central Canal, which connected with the Wabash and Erie Calal. After the canal-building boom ended, the entire county declined until the the arrival of the railroads in 1851. Business increased after trade and transportation routes were improved, and natural gas was discovered on a farm near Alexandria in 1887. The subsequent industrial boom was unequalled in the history of the county. Many factories sprang up almost overnight. First were the glass factories, attracted by the cheap source fuel, in almost every town in the county. Even after the gas supply was depleted, the industrial momentum continued.

Madison today is one of the leading industrial counties in the state. Major industries produce electrical wire assemblies, headlights, fabricated metals, canned goods, packaged meats, processed food, glass products, ceramic tile, insulation, and industrial machinery. Agriculture (hogs, cattle, corn, tomatoes, soybeans, poultry,) is also important. There is some oil refining and limestone quarrying. The county contains Mounds State Park *(q.v.)*, which contains the mounds and relics of an ancient Indian culture.

MARION, City; Pop. 32,618; seat of Grant County; E central Indiana; Zip Code 46952; on the Mississinewa River; 30 mi. NNW of Muncie. Marion was laid out in 1831 and named for Gen. Francis Marion, a cavalry officer in the American Revolution. The Battle of Mississinewa (1812) was fought 4 mi. NW of town on the Francis Slocum Trail. Marion remained a peaceful farming community until 1887, when natural gas was discovered beneath the city. As in other E central Indiana towns, industry mushroomed with the discovery, and Marion became known as the "Queen City of the gas belt." Glass factories, paper mills, iron works, and rolling mills sprang up almost overnight.

Marion has maintained the momentum ever since. It is a leading southern Indiana industrial center. Its diversified manufactures include trucks, glass, paper, oil-well machinery, radios, railroad equipment, furniture, and food products.

Marion College (1920), a liberal arts and sciences school, is located there. The average enrollment is 700 students. Matter Park, 3 + mi. N of town, has the Octogenarian Museum, which contains a fine display of pioneer relics and Indian artifacts.

MARION, County Pop. 792,299; central Indiana; area 392 sq. mi.; drained by the West Fork of the White River and Eagle Fall and Buck creeks. The county's topography is diversified, ranging from a nearly level plain to rolling hills, The County was created in December 1821 and named for Gen. Francis Marion, a calvary officer in the American Rev

Dictionary of Places

olution. Indianapolis, already the state capital, was selected as the county seat.

Marion County is an important commercial, market, and manufacturing area. Farming (wheat, corn truck, soybeans) and stock raising (cattle, hogs) go hand in hand with heavy industry. Major manufacturers include automobile parts, aircraft parts, television receivers, telephones, electronic components, packaged meats, processed foods, metal work, industrial machinery, drugs, and chemical products.

MARKLE, Town; Pop. 1,208; on the border of Huntington and Wells counties.; NE central Indiana; Zip Code 46770; on the Wabash River; 20 mi. W of Fort Wayne. Originally called Tracy, the town of Markle was established in 1852, its moniker being the maiden name of Samuel Morse's wife. It is the location of a sizable agricultural industry, producing such products as corn, wheat, oats, beans, rye, tomatoes, strawberries, cherries, apples peaches and pears. The town's manufactures include metal products, moulding, and boat building; its biggest production is lime, and several large kilns operate in the area. Building stone is also a large industry, with much of it being quarried and shipped to some of the larger cities throughout the country.

MARKLEVILLE, Town; Pop. 412; Madison County; E central Indiana; Zip Code 46056; 32 mi. ENE of Indianapolis. The town was platted in 1852 by John Markle, for whom it was named. Near the town in 1824, nine Indians were murdered by white men. Fearful of a revenge attack, the settlers tried, found guilty, and hanged the white men. It was the first case in the U.S. in which a white man was executed for killing an Indian. Markleville is an agricultural community and center for livestock and feed grains.

It is also a trade center for tools, dies, and extruded aluminum products.

MARSHALL, Town; Pop. 379; Parke County; W Indiana; Zip Code 47859; 30 mi. NNE of Terre Haute, in an agricultural area noted for livestock and feed grains. There are also some bituminous coal mines.

Encyclopedia of Indiana

●HISTORICAL PLACES... (See Hist. Places Sect for details.)
Lusk Home and Mill Site.

MARSHALL, County; Pop. 34,986; N Indiana; area 392 sq. mi.; drained by the Yellow and Tippecanoe rivers. The surface of the land is composed of glacial till. Numerous lakes are located within the county, among them Maxinkuckee, which is one of the most beautiful lakes in the state. Much swampland has been drained; the fertile soils are excellent for the cultivation of corn, wheat, oats, mint, hay. Marshall County was formed in April 1836 and named for John Marshall, chief justice, of the U.S. Supreme Court. Plymouth is the county seat. The county is a leading producer of mobile homes and boats.

MARTIN, County; Pop. 10,969; SW Indiana; area 345 sq. mi.; drained by Lost River and the East Fork of the White River. The county is very picturesque, its many steep hills having been eroded and sculptured into strange, natural stone formations. The region is generally unsuitable for cultivation. The White River bottomlands, however, have been given over to hay, corn, and wheat. Bituminous coal, natural gas, oil, and timber supplement the economy. Gypsum and clay products are manufactured at Shoals and Loogootee. The county was formed in 1820 and named for Maj. John T. Martin of Kentucky. Shoals is the county seat. The Pinnacle, Hindostan Falls, Jug Rock, and McBrides's Bluff are all scenic natural features of the county.

MARTIN STATE FOREST, Martin County; S Indiana; 2 mi. E of Shoals. The forest covers 6,000 acres and has a 15-acre lake with a maximum depth of 15 ft. The lake is available for public fishing, boating, and swimming. There are also facilities for camping, picnicking, and hiking. The forest, located in scenic hill country, contains thousands of pine trees that were planted by the State of Indiana. Within the forest is a 100-ft. high firetower. It is also a trade center for tools, dies, and extruded aluminum products.

Dictionary of Places

MEDARYVILLE, Town; Pop. 689; Pulaski County; NW Indiana; Zip Code 47957; on Big Monon Creek, 45 mi. N of Lafayette. Medaryville is a commercial trade center for tile, bricks, and cheese, and is located in an area noted for cattle and hogs. The Jasper-Pulaski Fish and Game Area is 5 mi. NW of town.

MEDORA, Town; Pop. 805; Jackson County; S Indiana; Zip Code 47260; 18 mi. E of Bedford in an agricultural noted for livestock and feed grains. East of town is the longest covered bridge in Indiana, built in 1875 and measuring 434 ft.

MELLOTT, Town; Pop. 222; Fountain County; W Indiana; Zip Code 47958; 17 mi. NW of Crawfordsville in an agricultural area noted for livestock and feed grains.

MENTONE, Town; Pop. 912; Kosciusko County; N Indiana; Zip Code 46539; 12 mi. SW of Warsaw in an agricultural and dairying area. The town is a manufacturing center for hospital equipment, ice-vending equipment, woodworking machinery, farm products, grains, and metal machining products.

MEROM, Town; Pop. 257; Sullivan County; SW Indiana; Zip Code 47861; on the Wabash River, 26 mi. N of Vincennes in a fertile agricultural region (feed grains, livestock). The town was once a popular Chautauqua site, attracting 50,000 people annually. Noted speakers included William Jennings Bryan and "Billy" Sunday. To the north are Indian mounds and village sites, but they are obscured because of extensive cultivation. Numerous skeletons and artifacts dating back to the Stone Age have been unearthed.

Of note is the former Merom Institute (1859), now a conference center, which has one of the county's tallest wooden spiral staircases.

MERRILLVILLE, Town; Pop. 27,257; Lake County; NW Indiana; Zip Code 46410; 30 mi. SE of Chicago, and adjacent to Crown Point in an agricultural and tourism area. The area was originally populated by the Potawatomi Indians, who often congregated at McGwinn's Village, an In dian camp and site of a major burial ground. In 1834, Jeremiah Wiggins staked his claim, covering all of McGwinn's Village, and began farming, with the area being known as Wiggin's Point. The Old Sauk Trail passed by his farm, and after a tavern/hotel was built, the area became a popular stop-off point for stagecoach wagons heading west. After his death in 1838, it was renamed Centerville. In 1837 two brothers, Dudley and William Merrill, settled there, and in 1848, the name Merrillville was established by the C & O Railroad for the crossroads community.

Along with the early Indian village, the town was once the crossroads of 16 Indian trails. A historical marker denotes the location of the Great Sauk Trail.

Merrillville is an important trade and manufacturing center. Industries include ornamental iron works, plastic and steel fabricating, corrugated box machinery, and drapery manufacturing; there also is some agricultural production.

MEXICO, Town; Pop. 800; Miami County; N Indiana; Zip Code 46958; 5 mi. NW of Peru in an agricultural noted for livestock and feed grains. Manufacturing includes grain milling and the production compasses for cars, boats, and airplanes. Mexico was once an important stagecoach stop between Indianapolis and Michigan City.

MILLHOUSEN, Town; Pop. 151; Decatur County; SE central Indiana; Zip Code 47261; 29 mi. SE of Shelbyville in an agricultural region (livestock, feed grains).

MILLTOWN, Town; Pop. 917; on the boundary of Crawford and Harrison counties; S Indiana; Zip Code 47145; on the Blue River; 25 mi. WNW of New Albany. The economy is based on the quarrying and processing of limestone. The quarrying is done in underground mines, and the resulting huge caverns are popular attractions for rock and fossil collectors.

MILROY, Town; Pop. 696; Rush County; central Indiana; Zip Code 46156; 8 mi. S of Rushville in a manufacturing and farming area. Milroy produces trim stampings, plastic

Dictionary of Places

products, stone and cement products, school supplies, canned goods, and agricultural products.

MILTON, Town; Pop. 634; Wayne County; E Indiana; Zip Code 47357; on the Whitewater River, 14 mi. W of Richmond in an agricultural area (livestock, feed grains).

MISHAWAKA, City; Pop. 42,608; St. Joseph County; N Indiana; Zip Code 46544; on the St. Joseph River, just E of South Bend. Mishawaka was founded in 1832 and named for the daughter of Chief Elkhart of the Shawnee, who lived in the vicinity before 1800. Mishawaka is mainly an industrial suburb of South Bend. Its diversified manufactures include clothing, furniture, rubber goods, industrial machinery, bedding, trucks, and food products. An ethnic community of Flemish-Dutch citizens resides in the southwestern part of the city. Most of the 6,000 Belgians arrived there after World War I. They work in the city and in South Bend and are noted for their meticulously-kept vegetable and flower gardens.

Mishawaka is the seat of Bethel College, a four-year fully- accredited liberal arts college with an average enrollment of 500 students. The Mishawaka Children's Museum contains outstanding exhibits of Alaska, pioneer life, and science. The St. Joseph River and Merrifield Park offer excellent recreational facilities.

●HISTORICAL PLACES... (See Hist. Places Sect for details.)

Bieger House.

MISSISSINEWA DAM AND RESERVOIR, Miami County; E central Indiana; 7 mi. SE of Peru. The facility was developed jointly by the State of Indiana and the U.S. Army Corps of Engineers. It encompasses the 3,210-acre Mississinewa Lake with 59 mi. of shoreline and two state recreation areas: Miami and Red Bridge. The land area totals 14,000 acres and includes facilities for camping, swimming, fishing, picnicking, hunting, and boating. Four boat launching ramps are situated around the lake.

MISSISSINEWA RIVER, rises in Darke County, Ohio, and flows W into Indiana, NW past Marion, and empties into the Wabash River at Peru. Approximately 100 mi. long, the river is dammed 7 mi. SW of Peru to form 3,210-acre Mississinewa Lake, a popular recreational facility.

MITCHELL, City; Pop. 4,669; Lawrence County; S Indiana; Zip Code 47446; 9 mi. S of Bedford. Mitchell was a community as early as 1813, but it was not until the 1850s, when the Monon Railroad extended its services to Lawrence County, that the city was platted. The Baltimore and Ohio Railroad followed in 1856, at which time Mitchell began to flourish as an important manufacturing and shipping center for limestone, agricultural products, cement, clothing, and lime. The company CBW (formerly Carpenter Bodyworks), manufacturer of school buses, is the city's largest employer. The area has also become known as a center for antique shops.

Mitchell was the childhood home of Virgil "Gus" Grissom, the American astronaut who died at Cape Canaveral in 1967. A memorial to him has been erected at nearby Spring Mill State Park *(q.v.)*. A persimmon festival is annually held in town, in conjunction with a candlelight tour of the authentic pioneer village in the state park.

MODOC, Town; Pop. 218; Randolph County; E Indiana; Zip Code 47358; 16 mi. SE of Muncie in an agricultural area (livestock, feed grains).

MONON, Town; Pop. 1,585; White County; NW central Indiana; Zip Code 47959; on Little Monon Creek; 29 mi. WNW of Logansport. The town was incorporated in 1879 and named for the stream which flows through town. "Monon" is derived from the Indian word *monon* ("swift running water"). The town became the division point for Monon Railroad, which took its name from the town. Monon is an important shipping and manufacturing center for corn, oats, soybeans, and crushed stone. The Monon Corporation, one of the largest manufacturers of tractor-trailers, is located here, and another local company, PFT, manufactures metal fabrication.

MONROE, County; Pop. 84,849; S central Indiana; area 386 sq. mi.; drained by the West Fork of the White River, and by Salt Beanblossom and Clear creeks. The county was

Dictionary of Places

formed in April 1818 and named in honor of James Monroe, fifth president of the U.S. Bloomington is the county seat and home of Indiana University (1824). The economy is based on farming, stock raising, dairying, limestone quarrying, and some manufacturing. Leading industries produce electronic components, television receivers, and processed food.

The Monroe Reservoir, largest body of water in Indiana (10,750 acres), is located wholly within the county.

MONROE, Town; Pop. 788; Adams County; E Indiana; Zip Code 46772; 25 mi. SSE of Fort Wayne in an agricultural area noted for livestock and feed grains. Monroe is a manufacturer of rat and mouse bait, mobile homes, fertilizer, and sprinkler systems.

MONROE CITY, Town; Pop. 538; Knox County; SW Indiana; Zip Code 47557; 10 mi. SE of Vincennes in an agricultural area noted for feed grains livestock. Bituminous coal are nearby.

MONROE DAM AND RESERVOIR, Monroe County; S Indiana; 6 mi. S of Bloomington. The reservoir was jointly established by the state of Indiana and the U.S Army Corps of Engineers. The central focus is 10,750-acre Lake Monroe. The Monroe facility, Paynetown State Recreation Area, and Fairfax State Recreation Area, together comprise 22,500 acres of recreational lands. Boat ramps are situated around the lake, which has excellent fishing and swimming. Other facilities include a modern campground and picnic sites.

MONROEVILLE, Town; Pop. 1,232; Allen County NE Indiana; Zip Code 46773; 16 mi. ESE of Fort Wayne near the Ohio border. It is an agricultural community noted for livestock and feed grains.

MONROVIA, Town; Pop. 600; Morgan County; central Indiana;; Zip Code 46157; on the Tippecanoe River; 38 mi. SSW of South Bend in an agricultural area (livestock, feed grains).

MONTEREY, Town; Pop. 230; Pulaski County; NW Indiana; Zip Code 46960; on the Tippecanoe River; 38 mi. SSW of South Bend in an agricultural area (livestock, feed grains).

MONTEZUMA, Town; Pop. 1,134; Parke County, W Indiana; Zip Code 47862; on the Wabash River; 22 mi. N of Terre Haute. A large Indian village once occupied the site. The area remained uninhabited by white men until Samuel Hill built his two-story log cabin there in 1821. Montezuma, named for the Aztec emperor of Mexico, grew up around Sam Hill's cabin. The town remained quiet until 1848, when the Wabash and Erie Canal was complete. Montezuma was platted the following year, flourished for a while as a river and canal port, but declined when the canal project was abandoned in the 1860s.

Today, Montezuma is a peaceful farming community which also depends heavily upon coal mining, fishing, and the manufacture of clay products. The town participates in the annual autumn Parke County Covered Bridge Festival, the proceeds of which go toward preservation of the county's 36 covered bridges. Reeder Park on the Wabash River is a popular picnicking site.

MONTGOMERY, County; Pop. 33,930; W central Indiana; area 507 sq. mi.; drained by Sugar and Raccoon creeks. The county was formed in March 1823 and named for Gen. Richard Montgomery. Crawfordsville is the county seat. The land is composed of some of the most fertile soils in the state. Aside from its great agricultural and livestock resources, Montgomery County also has a vast supply of shale deposits and is a leader in the manufacture of bricks. Other industries include book printing and the production of fabricated metals.

MONTGOMERY, Town; Pop. 351; Daviess County, SW Indiana; Zip Code 47558; 26 mi. E of Vincennes in an agricultural (livestock, feed grains) area. There are several bituminous coal mines in the vicinity. Montgomery was built up around St. Peter's Church (1818) in hopes that it would eventually become the site of a great Catholic university. Plans were abandoned when construction of the University of Notre Dame began at South Bend in 1842. Ruritan Park contains a recreational facility, including a 26-

acre lake.

MONTICELLO, City; Pop. 5,237; seat of White County; NW central Indiana; Zip Code 47960; on the Tippecanoe River; 21 mi. W of Logansport. The city was founded in 1834 on a high bluff overlooking the river. Its location between Freeman and Shafer lakes has rendered it a popular vacation spot. Fishing, boating, and swimming are excellent on all waters, and it is said that "Noah unloading the original pair of black bass into the Tippecanoe River at this point."

Monticello is also an important manufacturing center. It has a thread mill, a printing plant, and a hydroelectric power station. Products include flour, packed meat, and furniture. Of note is the suspension bridge, Indiana's largest, which spans a section of Shafer Lake. Indiana Beach, "Indiana's Atlantic City," is on the lakes and includes three beaches, ski shows, dancing, horseback riding, excursion boat rides, and an amusement park.

MONTPELIER, Town; Pop. 1,880; Blackford County; E Indiana; Zip Code 47359; on the Salamonie River; 27 mi. NNE of Muncie. The town was platted on 1836 by Abel Baldwin, who named it for the capital of Vermont, his home state. Incorporation came one year later. Nearby, Francois Godfroy, a Frenchman, had operated a trading post for the Miami Indians. The Godfroy Reserve, part of his landholdings, can be seen in NE Blackford County. The area is noted for dairy farms, livestock, soy beans, and feed grains. Montpelier, like many other E central Indiana towns, benefitted from the natural gas boom of 1887. Manufacturing products, directly related to the gas discovery, include crude oil, chemical supplies, and glass.

MOORELAND, Town; Pop. 465; Henry County; E Indiana; Zip Code 47360; 8 mi. NE of New Castle. It was named for Philip Moore, an early settler. The main business in town is a grain elevator. The vicinity is noted for livestock and feed grains.

MOORES HILL, Town; Pop. 649; Dearborn County; SE Indiana; Zip Code 47032; 12 mi. W of Aurora. Located at the altitude of 917 ft., Moores Hill is on the highest point in Dearborn County. A Methodist college was built there in 1854, but it burned down in 1915. The college was removed to Evansville in 1919, and was subsequently renamed. Moores Hill remains a quiet agricultural community.

MOORESVILLE, Town; Pop. 5,541; Morgan County; central Indiana; Zip Code 46158; on the Whitelick River; 16 mi. SW of Indianapolis. The town, founded in 1824 by Samuel Moore, and incorporated in 1838, became a noted agricultural center for dairy products, livestock, fruit, grain, and flour. Its manufactures include burial vaults, tile, wood products, laboratory equipment, machine shops, sand and gravel, and engine bearings. Mooresville was the home of Paul Kadley, a Hoosier artist who designed the official state flag. The original flag can be seen at the Children's Museum in Indianapolis.

Nearby is the Goethe Link Observatory, subsidized by Indiana University. During the summer months, the observatory is a popular visitor's attraction because of its weekly lectures and viewings. The Kendrick Memorial Hospital and Center for Hip and Knee Surgery is located here and is an internationally known teaching hospital.

MORGAN, County; Pop. 44,176 central Indiana; area 40 sq. mi.; drained by the West Fork and White River, Whitelick River and Camp Creek. The county was organized in February 1822 and named for Gen Daniel Morgan. Martinsville has been the seat since the county's inception.

Morgan County is in a rich agricultural area (hogs, grain, fruit, poultry), and there is manufacturing in Martinsville and Mooresville (food processing, lumbering, brick, tile). The Grassy Fork Fish Hatchery, largest producer of goldfish in the world, is located at Martinsville.

MORGAN-MONROE STATE FOREST, Morgan and Monroe counties; S Indiana; 8 mi. S of Martinsville. The state lands encompass 25,000 acres of primarily beech-maple forest and have facilities for camping, picnicking, hiking, boating, fishing, and riding. There are 6 artificial

Dictionary of Places

lakes in the park, with water recreation available on a 20-acre lake.

In 1929, a forest fire annihilated much of the virgin stands of walnut, oak, hickory, and maple. Successful reforestation has helped to reclaim much of the land since that time. Cascade Park, within the confines of the forest, has scenic cliffs, deep ravines, and small waterfalls.

MORGANTOWN, Town; Pop. 978; Morgan County; central Indiana; Zip Code 46160; near Camp Creek; 28 mi. S of Indianapolis. Morgantown is a farming community and a manufacturer of furniture.

MORNINGSIDE, Village; Pop. 1,700; Delaware County; E central Indiana, near Muncie in an agricultural area (cattle, hogs, pigs, feed grains). The village is in the midst of the Trenton oil and natural gas field.

MOROCCO, Town; Pop. 1,044; Newton County; NW Indiana; Zip Code 47963; 48 mi. S of Hammond. The town was once known as Beaver Prairie because its streams and Beaver Lake teemed with beaver. Willow Slough is a remnant of Beaver Lake, which once encompassed 10,000 acres. The lake was drained and the resulting fertile soils were planted in grain and soybeans. Willow Slough has been designated a State Fish and Game Area, and nearby J.C. Murphy Lake (1,700 acres) has excellent camping, swimming, and fishing facilities.

MORRISTOWN; Town; Pop. 980; Shelby County; central Indiana; Zip Code 46161; on the Big Blue River; 26 mi. ESE of Indianapolis. For years, Morristown's only industry was a canned goods plant. With a readily available supply of natural gas in more recent years, however, Morristown has managed to boost its economy by bringing in three new industries. Located there are the International Packing Company, a producer of rubber goods, Indiana's Steel Products, a manufacturer of leaf springs for heavy trucks; and the Nabisco soybean processing plant. As a result, new banks, schools, and subdivisions have been built.

Of note is the Kopper Kettle Restaurant (1923), which was originally a grain elevator (1849). The elevator became obsolete in 1958 when the Junction Railroad, which served the town, was abandoned. Recreational facilities can be found at nearby Gordon's Lake.

MOUNDS STATE PARK, N of Anderson. The 254-acre state park, situated on a bluff overlooking the White River, contains an enigmatic cluster of earthworks believed to have been constructed by prehistoric moundbuilders belonging to a branch of the Hopewell Culture of Woodland Indians, who lived in this area from 500 BC to 500 AD. Among the several mounds, the largest measures 1,200 ft. around and is 9 ft. high. The park provides numerous hiking trails and bridle paths, as well as playgrounds and limited camping facilities.

MOUNT AYR, Town; Pop. 151; Newton County; NW Indiana; Zip Code 47964; 7 mi. W of Rensselaer in an agricultural area noted for livestock and feed grains.

MOUNT SUMMIT, Town; Pop. 238; Henry County; E Indiana; Zip Code 47361; 13 mi. S of Muncie. Mount Summit, at 1,088 ft. altitude, was named for its location at one of the "loftier" elevations in Henry County. The town is a farming community (livestock, feed grains).

MOUNT VERNON, City; Pop. 7,217; seat of Posey County; SW Indiana; Zip Code 47620; on the Ohio River; 18 mi. W of Evansville. The city was founded in 1805 by Andrew McFadden and was known as McFadden's Landing until 1816. Indiana's southern most city, Mount Vernon is an important agricultural trade center for the surrounding area. Products include flour, corn, canned goods, and cheese.

Reminders of the river boat era can be seen in several early buildings. The courthouse dates from 1876. On the courthouse square is the Soldiers and Sailors Monument (1908), designed by Hoosier architect Rudolph Schwartz. South of town is the Hovey Lake State Game Preserve, noted for its variety of wildlife and the stands of bald cy-

press that grow in the shallow water of Lake Hovey.
●HISTORICAL PLACES... (See Hist. Places Sect for details.)
Mann Site.

MUNCIE, City; Pop. 71,035; Clinton County; central Indiana; Zip Code 46058; on the West Fork of the White River; 50 mi. NE of Indianapolis. White settlers first came to the area in 1818, after the local Indians ceded their lands to the U.S. in the Treaty of St. Mary's. A 672-acre tract was bought and platted as Munseytown in 1827. The name was derived from the Munsee tribe of the Delaware Indians which had previously occupied the site. Munseytown was changed to Muncie in 1845, was incorporated as a town in 1847, and as a city in 1865.

In 1887, Muncie was part of the great natural gas boom that affected many towns in central Indiana. Wells were drilled, natural gas was struck, and the seemingly endless supply brought in speculators and industries almost overnight. Glass works, iron mills, and pulp and rubber factories, all which depended on the fossil fuel, boomed; thousands of workers poured into the newly- formed manufacturing city. The lure of fabulous job offers brought in so many new people that housing projects could not keep up with the pace. As a result, ramshackle shanties were erected by the newcomers in Avondale, the only unplatted section within the city limits. "Shedtown" remained for years until the shacks were replaced by modern cottages.

Reports ran rampant that the gas supply was inexhaustible. Fires at the wells were kept burning night and day, but the gas supply dwindled in 1890. Some of the industries left the city, but the groundwork for an industrial city had been laid, and most of the businesses remained. They found other means to power their equipment and, by the 1970s, more than 100 plants were located in Muncie. Notable among them are the Ball Brothers plant, which manufactures glass canning jars; Warner Gear Division; Delco Battery; a Chevrolet plant; Indiana Steel and Wire Company; and a Westinghouse Electric transformer plant. Other manufactures include electric equipment, castings, cutlery, furniture, bedding, sporting goods, and dairy products.

In 1924, Muncie became the national focus of attention when two sociologists, Robert and Helen Merrell Lynd, conducted a research study on the psychological and sociological trends of the city. Their findings were published in two well-known books *Middletown* (1929) and *Middletown in Transition* (1937). Their study was aimed at reflecting the life in an average American city.

Muncie is the seat of Ball State University (1918), a four-year, fully-accredited teacher's college which was almost wholly subsidized by funds donated by the Ball brothers. The 538-acre campus contains the Ball State Gallery, Emens Auditorium, Christy Woods (arboretum and gardens), and a 5-telescope planetarium and observatory. Average enrollment is 17,500 students.

Muncie contains a replica of the statue "Appeal to the Great Spirit," designed by Cyrus Dallin. The original stands in front of Boston's Museum of Fine Arts. The statue is a life-size image of an Indian on his pony, and it is located on the original campsite of the Munsee tribe.

Excellent recreational facilities can be found at McCullough and Heekin parks, and at Prairie Creek Reservoir (1,125 acres), 6 mi. SE of the city. Muncie also has two golf courses. Annual events include the Delaware County Fair and the National and Hoosier Cup hydroplane and speedboat races on the Prairie Creek Reservoir.

MUNSTER, Town; Pop. 19,949; Lake County; extreme NW Indiana; Zip Code 46321; on the Illinois border; 4 mi. S of Hammond. Located in an agricultural area noted for livestock and feed grains. Munster is a shipping point for garden produce and nursery stock.

MUSCATATUCK STATE PARK, Jennings County; S Indiana; 1 mi. from North Vernon. The park covers 205 acres and contains the ruins of Vinegar Mill (1830s). The park offers rugged scenery and is a popular rendezvous for hikers and nature lovers. Fishing is available on adjacent Muscatatuck River; the Muscatatuck Fish Management

Dictionary of Places

Headquarters are within the park. There are also areas for camping and picnicking.

NAPOLEON, Town; Pop. 238; Ripley County; E central Indiana; Zip Code 47034; 12 mi. NW of Versailles in a farming and lumbering area. The town is noted for crushed stone and stone products, lumber, portable farm buildings, feeders, and casket hardware.

NAPPANEE, City; Pop. 5,510; Elkhart County; N Indiana; Zip Code 46550; 21 mi. SE of South Bend in an agricultural area noted for mint, onions, and grain. The town was platted in 1874 along the tracks of the Baltimore & Ohio Railroad. It has become a railroad shipping center for furniture (its principal industrial product), canned goods, and flour. A large Amish farming population resides in and around Nappanee; their horse-drawn carriages are a common sight in town.

NASHVILLE, Town; Pop. 873; seat of Brown County; central Indiana; Zip Code 47448; 40 mi. S of Indianapolis. Turn-of-the-century homes are located everywhere in Nashville, which is nestled among wooded hills. Some of the most beautiful scenery in the Midwest can be found there and, as a result, the town has become a haven for painters, photographers, and tourists. Log cabins built in the 19th century have been restored and turned into studios for members of the famous Brown County Artists' Colony. The Brown County Art Gallery has a fine display of Hoosier art.

Next to the county courthouse is an old log jail (1837) with walls 5 ft. thick. The jail contains an excellent collection of Indian artifacts. Nashville is a tourist attraction in every season. In the spring, visitors come to view the scenery enhanced by blooming redbud and dogwood trees. Autumn foliage brings others who come to buy berries, nuts, maple syrup, and apple butter. Nearby are Brown County State Park and the Hoosier National and Yellowood State forests, all of which have excellent recreational facilities.

●HISTORICAL PLACES... (See Hist. Places Sect for details.)
Steele, Theodore Clement, House and Studio.

NEW ALBANY, City; Pop. 36,322; seat of Floyd County; S Indiana; Zip Code 47150; on the Ohio River, opposite Louisville, Kentucky. New Albany was founded in 1813 on an 86.5 acre tract nestled at the foot of the Knobstone Escarpment. From its inception, the city depended upon the river for its prosperity, and flourished as a port-of-call for ferries operating between Indiana and Kentucky and steamboats running from Pittsburgh to New Orleans. Seven shipyards operated between 1830 and 1860, and such famous steamboats as the "Eclipse" and the "Robert E. Lee" were built there.

After the prosperous riverboat era, New Albany continued to grow as a commercial center. Until 1887, it was a leader in glass manufacturing, but the natural gas boom removed the industry to the eastern part of the state. Climatic conditions and natural resources favored the location of a hardwood veneer plant in New Albany. Today, the city is one of the largest plywood manufacturing centers in the U.S. Other principal manufactures are furniture, prefabricated houses, machine tools, clothing, fertilizer, and automobile parts.

Many of the historic buildings of the riverboat era have been preserved. Notable examples are the 27-room Culbertson Mansion (1868), with its cantilever staircase; Sloan House (1853), which resembles a riverboat; and the Scribner House (1814), home of the first settlers in New Albany. Many scenic parks line the riverfront, and the view from the Knobs is breathtaking.

North of the city is Indiana University Southeast (1941), a branch of Indiana University at Bloomington. Annual events include the 4-H Fair in July and the Harvest Homecoming in October. New Albany was selected as an All-American City in 1969.

●HISTORICAL PLACES... (See Hist. Places Sect for details.)
Culbertson Mansion.

NEW AUGUSTA, Town; Pop. 225; Marion County; central Indiana; Zip Code 46268; 11 mi. N of Indianapolis in an agricultural area. The town is a trade center for shade trees,

Dictionary of Places

plants, fertilizers, and various industrial products.

NEWBERRY, Town; Pop. 207; Greene County; SW Indiana; Zip Code 47449; on the West Fork of the White River.; 32 mi. ENE of Vincennes in an area noted for feed grains, livestock, and bituminous coal mining.

NEWBURGH, Town; Pop. 2,880; Warrick County; SW Indiana; Zip Code 47630; on the Ohio River; 9 mi. E of Evansville. Settled in 1803 by John Sprinkle (an early name of the area was Sprinklesburgh), the town flourished as a river port, and its industry included coal mines, mills, and tobacco factories. The town's name came into being after the Indiana Legislature combined two of the area's settlements--Sprinklesburgh and Mt. Prospect--to create Newburgh in 1837. Originally incorporated in 1849, it was dissolved in 1851, then reincorporated in 1852. In July of 1862, during the Civil War, Newburgh was raided and then captured by Adam Johnson and thirty-two Confederate soldiers.

The modern economy is based on manufacturing (aluminum) and agriculture (tobacco, flour, corn, soybeans). On the riverfront can be seen the old Ohio Dam 47 and the locks.

- HISTORICAL PLACES... (See Hist. Places Sect for details.)

Roberts-Morton House.

NEW CARLISLE, Town; Pop. 1,446; St. Joseph County; Zip Code 46552; N Indiana; 12 mi. W of South Bend in an agricultural area of livestock and feed grains. Of note is the Augustine Homestead built in 1834 by carpenter Henry Brown. Its squared logs are believed to have been hauled from distant sawmills. The house is built in Greek Revival style.

NEW CASTLE, City; Pop. 17,753; seat of Henry County; E Indiana; Zip Code 47362; on the Big Blue River; 18 mi. S of Muncie. The city was founded in 1820 and platted in 1836. A monument to Wilbur Wright, a propeller mounted on a stone base, is near New Castle, outside of which the pioneer aviator once lived. The city was an early pioneer automobile manufacturing center, producing such classic cars as the Maxwell, Lawter, and Universal.

New Castle is a trade and distribution center for livestock, grain, and poultry. Manufactures include automobile parts, machinery, steel products, furniture, and clothing. New Castle is the seat of the Henry County Historical Museum (1870), which has a fine display of pioneer, Civil War, and Wilbur Wright memorabilia. Recreational facilities can be found at Henry County Memorial and Baker parks.

NEW CHICAGO, Town; Pop. 2,066; Lake County NW Indiana; Zip Code 46342; just SE of Gary in an agricultural area noted for livestock and feed grains. New Chicago is located on the old council grounds of the Potawatomi Indians. It is best known for the electric buggy, invented there by the U.S. Electric Carriage Company.

NEW HARMONY, Town; Pop. 846; Posey County; SW Indiana; Zip Code 47631; on the Wabash River; 22 mi. WNW of Evansville. Originally known as Harmonie, the town was founded in 1814 by members of the Rappite Society for the purpose of establishing a colony based on communal living. The Rappites, a religious group under the leadership of George Rapp, had emigrated from Wurttemberg, Germany, to Pennsylvania before settling along the Wabash River. They cleared 25,000 acres of forest and swampland and converted it into farms. Their town of 200 homes and 2 churches became the showplace for the surrounding countryside. The Rappites sold the town in 1825 to Robert Owen, a Welsh philanthropist and social reformer who renamed the settlement New Harmony. Owen intended to establish a society of social and economic equality based on a system of universal education. The program failed, however, because of his frequent absences and the rivalries among his followers.

New Harmony developed into one of the first scientific centers in the U.S. Sir Charles Lyell, the noted Scottish geologist, and James Audubon, the ornithologist, visited there. The Laboratory Building, built by David Dale Owen, the first U.S. geologist, became the headquarters for the U.S.

Dictionary of Places

Geological Survey. Much scientific research was carried on there between 1824 and 1856.

The Workingmen's Institute, Library, and Museum (1838) is still in use today. It was founded by William Maclure, who was a pioneer in establishing traveling libraries.

For the past century, New Harmony has remained a farm trading center for the surrounding countryside, but the town thrives well on the tourists, who are attracted by the many historic landmarks. A state memorial commission was established in 1935 to restore the sturdy Rappite buildings. Notable examples are the Rappite Community House (1816); the Old Rappite Fort Granary, built as a defense against "marauding neighbors"; the Rapp-Maclure Mansion (1814); the Colonial Dames Harmonist Museum House, a restored Rappite family dwelling; and the Barrett-Gate House (1814), the oldest house in New Harmony. The city's beauty is further enhanced by thousands of "gate trees" that were imported from China and Korea in 1825. The round-topped trees have long sprays of yellow flowers which bloom in June and shed their blossoms in a golden rain. The Rappite Cemetery, a 3- acre tract, contains the unmarked graves of 230 Rappites.

The Restored Labryinth, made of boxwood hedges, has only one exit leading to the Temple, a summer house. The Roofless Church, erected in memory of New Harmony settlers, is a rectangular structure enclosed by brick walls, but without a roof. In the center of the church is a large bronze sculpture, "Descent of the Holy Spirit," by Jacques Lipschitz. Paul Tillich Park contains the remains of the world-famous theologian, and is a noted visitor's attraction.

●HISTORICAL PLACES... (See Hist. Places Sect for details.)

New Harmoy Historic District.

NEW HAVEN, Town; Pop. 9,320; Allen County; NE Indiana; Zip Code 46774; on the Maumee River; 6 mi. E of Fort Wayne. The town was named for New Haven, Connecticut, and owes its existence to the Wabash and Erie Canal. A suburb of Fort Wayne, its manufactures include showcases, cement vaults, and wood products. The Havenhurst Golf Course is NE of town.

NEW MARKET, Town; Pop. 614; Montgomery County; W central Indiana; Zip Code 47965; 6 mi. S of Crawfordsville in an agricultural area (feed grains, livestock).

NEW MIDDLETOWN, Town; Pop. 82; Harrison County; S Indiana; Zip Code 47605; 15 mi. SW of New Albany in an agricultural area (feed grains, livestock).

NEW PALESTINE, Town; Pop. 671; Hancock County; central Indiana; Zip Code 46163; on Sugar Creek; 15 mi. ESE of Indianapolis in an agricultural area (feed grains, cattle, horses, hogs, sheep).

NEW PARIS, Town; Pop. 1,080; Elkhart County; N Indiana; Zip Code 46553; 6 mi. S of Goshen. The town produces popcorn, publications, sheet metal, feed and dairy products, cabinets, recreational vehicles, plastic-laminated products, sporting equipment, and specialized welded products.

NEWPOINT, Town; Pop. 296; Decatur County; SE central Indiana; Zip Code 47263; 29 mi. ESE of Shelbyville. Newpoint began as a limestone quarrying center, but its economy declined after the industry was moved to Bloomington and Bedford. Today, farming constitutes the main source of income.

NEWPORT, Town; Pop. 627; seat of Vermillion County; W Indiana; Zip Code 47966; near the confluence of the Little Vermillion and Wabash rivers, 30 mi. N of Terre Haute. The Newport courthouse burned down twice (1844 and 1866), but all the county records were saved. Cannel coal mining is an important activity, and the area around Newport is noted for its fruit orchards and Shetland ponies.

NEW RICHMOND, Town; Pop. 312; Montgomery County; W central Indiana; Zip Code 47967; 18 mi. SSW of Lafayette in an agricultural area (livestock, feed grains). The inexhaustible supply of shale around the town has provided a base for the manufacture of bricks and tile.

NEW ROSS, Town; Pop. 318; Montgomery County; W central Indiana; Zip Code 47968; near Raccoon Creek; 12 mi.

Dictionary of Places

ESE of Crawfordsville in agricultural area (livestock and feed grains.)

NEW SALISBURY, Town; Pop. 350; Harrison County; S Indiana; Zip Code 47161; 17 mi. NW of Louisville, Kentucky, in a lumbering and agricultural area. The town is a manufacturing center for dog and cat foods, furniture, cabinets, and agricultural products.

NEWTON, County; Pop. 11,606; NW Indiana; area 413 sq. mi.; bounded on the W by Illinois and on the N by the Kankakee River. It is drained by the Kankakee and Iroquois rivers. The last county to be organized in Indiana, it was formed in December 1859 and named for Sgt. John Newton. Kentland is the county seat.

Newton County is very fertile and a leading producer of grain and seeds, which are shipped to nearby markets. Manufacturing (electronic and appliance parts, cheese, cosmetics) is carried out in the larger towns. A fine road-building limestone is quarried near Kentland. The quarry is unique because its strata stand on edge rather than lying horizontally, apparently the result of volcanic upheaval. George Ade, famous turn-of-the- century author, humorist, and playwright, made his home in Newton County.

NEWTON, Town; Pop. 243; Fountain County; W Indiana; Zip Code 47969; 18 mi. NW of Crawfordsville in an agricultural area (feed grains and livestock).

NOBLE, County; Pop. 31,382; NE Indiana; area 412 sq. mi.; drained by the Elkhart River. The county was formed in 1836 and named for Noah Noble, governor of Indiana (1831-37). Albion is the county seat. The county was part of the Underground Railroad that aided runaway slaves on their northward flight to freedom.

Numerous small lakes have made Nobel County a popular resort area. Chain O'Lakes State Park *(q.v.)* is probably the most popular attraction. Agriculture (livestock, poultry, fruit, grain, soybeans, truck) and manufacturing (food processing, refrigeration, machinery, electrical wire assemblies, iron castings, plastic products, candy) aid the county's prosperity.

Encyclopedia of Indiana

NOBLESVILLE, City; Pop. 17,655; Hamilton County; central Indiana; Zip Code 46060; 15 mi. N of Indianapolis. Originally inhabited by the Delaware Indians who were forced to migrate west, the area was founded in 1823 by William Connor. It was incorporated in 1851 and named for Senator James Noble. It took a few years for the population to build up, but by 1869 there was a growth of industry, including flour mills, a woolen factory, a saw mill, wagon and carriage makers, furniture makers, and blacksmithing.

By the start of World War I, the population had grown to 6,000, and some of the business firms in the area included the Union Sanitary Manufacturing Company, the Carbon Company, the Strawboard Company, and the Noblesville Milling Company.

In 1925 there was nationwide interest in the trial of D. C. Stephenson, a former Indiana leader of the Ku Klux Klan, who was accused of the murder of Madge Oberholtzer, and tried at the Hamilton County Circuit Courthouse in Noblesville. In November of that year, Stephenson was convicted of second degree murder and sentenced to life imprisonment.

Today, Noblesville is an agricultural center, producing corn, wheat, and soybeans. The city's manufactures include machinery, automotive parts and supplies, electrical goods, farm- product raw materials, and processed foods.

OAKLAND CITY, City; Pop. 2,810; Gibson County; SW Indiana; Zip Code 47560; 28 mi. NNE of Evansville. The town's economy is dependent upon coal mining and agriculture (cantaloupe, peaches, sweet potatoes, corn, soybeans). The town is the seat of Oakland City College (1885), a Baptist liberal arts institution which has an average enrollment of 550 students.

OAKTOWN, Town; Pop. 655; Knox County; SW Indiana; Zip Code 47561; 14 mi. NNE of Vincennes. It is a shipping center for melons, peaches, apples, and sweet potatoes. There is a fruit packing plant in town, and oil and natural gas wells are in the vicinity.

Dictionary of Places

ODON, Town; Pop. 1,475; Daviess County; SW Indiana; Zip Code 47562; 31 ENE of Vincennes in an agricultural area (livestock and feed grains.)

OGDEN DUNES, Town; Pop. 1,499; Porter County; NW Indiana; on Lake Michigan just E of Gary. In the early 1900s, the dunes were the home of "Diana of the Dunes," a famous female hermit also known as "Dunehilda." Reputedly the daughter of a wealthy physician, Diana lived off the meager wages she earned by selling her homemade wild berry wine. She lived alone for many years studying the plants and animals of the dunes.

Ogden Dunes was founded in 1925 and laid out along 432 acres of dune county. It has always been a residential and resort town, and no commercial enterprises have been allowed there. Remnants of a 1927 Olympic-size ski jump can be seen. Excellent boating, fishing, swimming, and golfing facilities are in and around the town.

OHIO, County; Pop. 4,289; SE Indiana; area 87 sq. mi.; bounded on the E by Kentucky and drained by the Ohio River and Laughery Creek. Organized in January 1844, the county was named for the Ohio River. Rising Sun is the county seat.

Agriculture is the mainstay of the economy. The river valley soils are fertile and conducive to truck and tobacco farming and livestock raising. The rest of the county is very rugged and picturesque, broken by several ranges of heavily forested hills.

OHIO RIVER, 981 mi. long, formed by the confluence of the Allegheny and Monongahela rivers at Pittsburgh, Pennsylvania. In Indiana, the river forms the state's southern boundary and has long been an important means of commerce. It was discovered by La Salle in 1669 and became a major navigation center for settlers heading west and south. Improvement of navigability came with the opening of the Wabash and Erie Canal in 1827.

Chief tributaries of the Ohio River are the Muskingum, Scioto, Kanawaka, Miami, Wabash, Big Sandy, Tennessee,

Green and Cumberland rivers. The total watershed encompasses 200,000 square miles.

The Indiana topography around the Ohio is particularly rugged and beautiful. High, wooded bluffs border both banks, and between the north bank and Bloomington lies a vast limestone belt broken by numerous disappearing streams, mineral springs, caves, and sinkholes. The Ohio River is an important part of the extensive Mississippi River system of inland waterways. The original Ohio River Navigation Project, which was completed in 1929, increased traffic from 20,000,000 tons to 89,000,000 annually.

The U.S. Army Corps of Engineers has established flood control projects all over Indiana, but mainly in the Ohio River Basin. The program deals with the problems of flood control, water supply, water quality, navigation, hydroelectric power, floodplain planning, recreation, and fish and wildlife development.

OLDENBURG, Town; Pop. 715; Franklin County; SE Indiana; Zip Code 47036; ESE of Shelbyville. Oldenburg was founded in 1837 by German immigrants who worked in the town's once prosperous brick factories. Today, Oldenburg is a quiet farming community. In town is the Sisters of St. Francis Convent and Academy (1851), which operates more than 70 mission schools. A Franciscan monastery and seminary is next to the Church of the Holy Family. The Shrine of the Sorrowful Mother (1871), 1 mi. E of the town, resembles the wayside chapels in the Bavarian Alps. A fragment of a rock from Calvary, another from the temple ruins at Baalbek, and a third from the Roman Colosseum are contained within the shrine.

ONWARD, Town; Pop. 63; Cass County; S Indiana; Zip Code 46967; 10 mi. ESE of Logansport in an agricultural area (livestock and feed grain).

OOLITIC, Town; Pop. 1,424; Lawrence County; S Indiana; Zip Code 47451; on Salt Creek; 4 mi. NNW of Bedford. The town was named for the oolitic (fish-egg) texture of the limestone found in the quarries that surround it. Many of the buildings are composed of the limestone, which was

Dictionary of Places

mined up to the peak year of 1924. Since then the industry has declined, and the town's economy is now largely based on agriculture.

ORANGE, County; Pop. 16,968; S Indiana; 405 area sq. mi.; drained by the Lick, Lost, and Patoka rivers. The county was organized in February 1816 and named for Orange County, North Carolina, from which many of the early settlers came. Paoli is the county seat.

Orange County is rugged, hilly, and unsuitable for most farming. Fruit growing, dairying, and stock raising are profitable activities. The greatest resources of the county, however, are its world-famous mineral waters. Health spas such as French Lick and West Baden attract thousands of visitors yearly. "Pluto Water" from Pluto Spring at French Lick is sent all over the world. There is some industry at Paoli, including the manufacture of television receivers, radios, and furniture.

ORESTES, Town; Pop. 458; Madison County; E central Indiana; Zip Code 46063; 7 mi. E of Elwood. Originally called Lowry's Station, the town began as a railroad switch stop, with a grain elevator constituting the only business. The natural gas boom of 1887 brought some industry to Orestes, but the town declined with the gas supply. Orestes was almost totally destroyed in 1922 when a tornado struck without warning.

Today, Orestes is a sleepy farming community. The Madison County Historical Society dedicated a memorial plaque to a 300- year old oak tree in town on May 6, 1973. The tree was once a landmark for a Delaware Indian Trail and for Orestes.

ORLAND, Town; Pop. 361; Stueben County; NE Indiana; Zip Code 46776; near the Michigan border; 55 mi. E of South Bend in an agricultural area (cattle, hogs, feed grains). Nearby is the 90-year old Collins School, a restored memorial to early education in which 19th-century school books and desks are on display.

ORLEANS, Town; Pop. 2,083; Orange County; S Indiana; Zip Code 47452; near Lost River; 14 mi. S of Bedford.

Founded in 1815, the town was named for New Orleans, Louisiana, and is the oldest town in the county. Orleans is a dairy center and has a large creamery. There are also several large fruit orchards. Orleans is the home of the annual spring Dogwood Festival and has been called the "Dogwood Capital of the Indiana." Of note is the grave of Ann Todd Teagarden, aunt to Abraham Lincoln's wife.

OSCEOLA, Town; Pop. 1,999; St. Joseph County; N Indiana; Zip Code 46561; on the St. Joseph River; 10 mi. E of South Bend in a resort and agricultural area (livestock and feed grains).

OSGOOD, Town; Pop. 1,688; Ripley County; SE Indiana; Zip Code 47037; 18 mi. SE of Greensburg. A farm trading center for the surrounding area, the town is also a manufacturer of wood and cement products, polo balls, and condensed milk. Limestone quarries are nearby.

OSSIAN, Town; Pop. 2,428; Wells County; E Indiana; Zip Code 46777; on Longlois Creek; 14 mi. S of Fort Wayne in an agricultural area (cattle, hogs, feed grains).

OTTERBEIN, Town; Pop. 1,291; Benton County; W Indiana; Zip Code 47970; 13 mi. WNW of Lafayette. Originally called Pond Grove, Dr. John K. Thompson built the first house in the area, and Otterbein was platted in 1872 by John Levering and his wife. The town was named for William Otterbein Brown, its first postmaster.

Otterbein's agricultural products are corn, soybeans, wheat and oats, and its manufactures include crafts, trusses, machinery, and racing cars.

OTWELL, Town; Pop. 550; Pike County; S Indiana; Zip Code 47564; 12 mi. E of Petersburg in a lumbering and farming area. The town has an agricultural feed plant.

OUBACHE STATE RECREATION AREA, Wells County; E Indiana; 6 mi. E of Bluffton. Formerly known as the Wells County State Game Farm, it encompasses 1,037 acres of woods and has a small lake for fishing and boating. There are also camping, picnicking, and hiking facilities, as well as a wildlife exhibit and a lookout and fire tower.

Dictionary of Places

OWEN, County; Pop. 12,163; SW Indiana; area 390 sq. mi.; drained by the West Fork of the White River and Mill Creek. The county was organized in January 1819 and named for Col. Abraham Owen, who was a casualty of the Battle of Tippecanoe (1811). Spencer is the county seat.

The topography of the Owen County is rolling to hilly, and the heavy forest cover forms the basis of the leading lumbering industry. It is both an agricultural (grain, fruit, livestock) and manufacturing center. Industries include cement production, food processing, and the production of drugs, and typewriter ribbons. The county has a large limestone and bituminous coal output. Although the coal has been greatly depleted, its quality has been described as Indiana's best, with only a 15 percent ash content.

Prehistoric artifacts and Indian burial mounds are evident throughout the county. Points of interest are Cataract Falls on the Eel River and McCormick's Creek State Park *(q.v.).*

OWEN-PUTNAM STATE FOREST, Owen County; S Indiana; 10 mi. NW of Spencer. The forest encompasses 6,235 acres of primarily beech and maple forest and has recreational facilities for hiking, picnicking, hunting, and horseback riding.

OWENSVILLE, Town; Pop. 1,053; Gibson County; SW Indiana; Zip Code 47565; 22 mi. NNW of Evansville. Owensville was settled in 1817 and incorporated in 1881. It is a flourishing farm trade and mining center in an area rich in natural resources. Some of the most fertile soils in the state surround Owensville. Orchards, truck, livestock, and grain farms are numerous, and densely wooded areas provide lumber for the town's mills. Coal mines and oil and gas wells are nearby.

OXFORD, Town; Pop. 1,273; Benton County; W Indiana; Zip Code 47971; 21 mi. W of Lafayette in an agricultural area (soybeans, livestock). Oxford was the birthplace and home of the famous race horse, Dan Patch. The horse was born in December 1896 on a manure pile behind Kelly's Livery Stable. Dan Messner, his owner and an Oxford storekeeper, was at first disappointed in Dan Patch's appearance. Under the careful training of John Wattles, however, he became a fine pacer with great stride and grace. At age four, Dan Patch won his maiden race at Boswell by one-eighth of a mile. After that, he never lost a race. Dan Patch toured the country, changed hands many times, and was admired the world over. At his death in 1916, he earned $2,000,000 for his owners.

PALMYRA, Town; Pop. 621; Harrison County; S Indiana; Zip Code 47164; 18 mi. WNW of New Albany. Palmyra was founded in 1810 as a farming community.

PAOLI, Town; Pop. 3,542; seat of Orange County; S Indiana; Zip Code 47454; on the Lick River; 22 mi. S of Bedford. Paoli was settled in 1807 and developed into a regional trade and manufacturing center. Products include furniture, wood items, canned goods, timber, dairy items, and chairs. The courthouse (1850) is a masterpiece of Greek Revival architecture; 6 fluted Doric columns accent the portico, and a cupola with a four-faced clock surmounts the roof. NW of town is a bubbling mineral spring formed where Lost River emerges from its underground limestone channel and continues above ground. Lost River Acres is a popular resort along the river. Nearby Spring Valley, Tucker, and Walton lakes provide other recreational activities.

PARAGON, Town; Pop. 515; Morgan County; central Indiana; Zip Code 46166; near the West Fork of the White River; 16 mi. N of Bloomington in an agricultural (livestock, feed grains) and lumbering area. Nearby is Tumbling Waters Cave, a small natural cavern formerly known as Porter's Cave, which has an underground stream and a 35-ft. waterfall. The cane and stream canyon are popular with hikers and tourists.

PARKE, County; Pop. 14,600; area 451 sq. mi.; bounded on the W by the Wabash River and drained by Sugar and Raccoon creeks. The county was established in 1821 and named for Benjamin Parke, first territorial delegate to the U.S. Congress. The county seat, Rockville, is a leading manufacturing center.

Dictionary of Places

Parke County is generally rolling, wooded, and traversed by creeks and streams that have cut gorges and canyons in many areas, making it one of the most scenic areas in the Midwest.

The county is noted for its many covered bridges, which were built between 1856 and 1921. The bridges, built when timber was cheaper than iron, were covered to preserve the wood. Although many counties also have covered bridges, Parke County carried out an extensive program to preserve them. Of the original 52 bridges, 36 remain. An annual Covered Bridge Festival is sponsored in conjunction with autumn activities and maple fairs.

Parke County is noted for feed grains and livestock and includes bituminous coal-mining areas. Timber, clay and gravel pits, mineral springs, and fisheries are important to the county's economy. Leading manufacturing centers are Rockville and Montezuma. Within Parke County are Turkey Run and Raccoon Lake state parks *(q.q.v.)*.

PARKER CITY, Town; Pop. 1,323; Randolph County; E Indiana; Zip Code 47368; 9 mi. E of Muncie in an agricultural area (livestock and feed grains).

PATOKA, Town; Pop. 704; Gibson County; SW Indiana; Zip Code 47566; on the Patoka River; 19 mi. S of Vincennes. The town was settled in 1789 and platted in 1813. Its name was derived from Indian words meaning "logs on the bottoms," that described the Patoka River.

The low hills surrounding the town has given it an air of serenity. Patoka began as a center for distilleries, sawmills, and gristmills, but has become the center for the SW Indiana fruit and vegetable growing district. Feed grains are also an important commodity. Of note are the two 19th-century covered bridges, which are 163 ft. and 150 ft. long, respectively. Long Pond, 3 miles W, provides recreational facilities.

PATOKA STATE FISH AND WILDLIFE AREA, Pike County; S Indiana; just S of Winclow. The area covers 7,000 acres and has a 300-acre lake which is available for fishing and boating. There are also a campground, picnic area, and hiking trails.

PATRIOT, Town; Pop. 190; Switzerland County; SE Indiana; Zip Code 47038; on the Ohio River; 24 mi. SW of Cincinnati, Ohio. Patriot was an active river port until a disastrous flood inundated the town in 1937. Patriot never fully recovered and is a quiet community for retired farmers and river men. Several 19th-century homes overlook the river.

PAYNETOWN STATE RECREATION AREA, Monroe County; S central Indiana; 6 mi. S of Bloomington. It is one of two recreational units located on the Monroe Dam and Reservoir, the whole of which encompasses 22,500 acres. Facilities include swimming, picnicking, boating, camping, fishing, and hunting.

PEKIN, Town; Pop. 912; Washington County; S Indiana; Zip Code 47165; 7 mi. SE of Salem in an agricultural area (livestock and feed grains). The main industry in Pekin produces plastics. There are also livestock feed mills and a newspaper plant. Pekin has the longest tradition in the U.S. of celebrating the Fourth of July. The annual celebration, begun in 1830, features a parade which is famous throughout the state.

PENCE, Town; Pop. 100; Warren County; N Indiana; Zip Code 47973; 19 mi. NW of Williamsport in an agricultural and dairying area. Pence is a trade center for fertilizer, seed, and feeds.

PENDLETON, Town; Pop. 2,309; Madison County; E central Indiana; Zip Code 46064; 27 mi. NE of Indianapolis. Called "Cradle of Madison County." Pendleton was originally settled by colonists from Ohio. The town was platted in 1823 by Thomas Pendleton, for whom it is named. Shortly thereafter, it became the first seat of Madison County, a position it relinquished to Anderson in 1827.

Pendleton is a center for agriculture (livestock, grains, dairy products) and manufacturing (clothing, canned goods, metal products). Nearby Falls Park, a scenic spot with a natural pool just below the waterfall, was closed to swim-

Dictionary of Places

mers because of heavy pollution in recent times. Many well-kept century-old buildings are a source of pride to the citizens of Pendleton. Among them, the Methodist Episcopal Church (1823) dates back to the original settlers. The Pendleton Town Hall, a long-time landmark, was destroyed in an accidental explosion in 1936.

PENNVILLE, Town; Pop. 637; Jay County; NE Indiana; Zip Code 47369; on the Salamonie River, 24 mi. NNE of Muncie. In March of 1836, two Quaker men, Jeremiah Smith and Samuel Grisell, founded what would eventually become Pennville, which was named in honor of William Penn. Before that name was finally settled on, however, the area had three previous names--New Lisbon, Camden, and Penn.

An agricultural town, its crops include wheat, corn, soybeans, and tomatoes, as well as feed, grain and livestock. Manufactures include deli-foods, country crafts, and wood pallets. A memorial tablet to Eliza Harris, a runaway slave who was depicted in *Uncle Tom's Cabin,* is north of town.

PERRY, City; Pop. 19,075; S Indiana; area 384 sq. mi.; bounded S and partially E by the Ohio River, which forms the border with Kentucky. It is drained by the Anderson River, a tributary of the Ohio. The county was formed in 1814 and named for Commodore Oliver H. Perry. Cannelton was designated the county seat. Agriculture plays a leading part in Perry County's economy, as do lumbering and sandstone quarrying. Leading manufacturers include radio and television tubes and furniture.

PERRYSVILLE, Town; Pop. 443; Vermillion County; W Indiana; Zip Code 47974; on the Wabash River, 40 mi. N of Terre Haute in an agricultural area (livestock and feed grains). Cannel coal mines are nearby.

PERU, City; Pop. 12,843; seat of Miami County; N central Indiana; Zip Code 46970; on the Wabash River; 15 mi. E of Logansport. Peru was founded in 1826 on the site of a Miami Indian village. Southeast of the city is the old trad ing post of Francois Godfrey, the second richest Indian in America in his time.

Peru has sometimes been referred to as the "Circus City of the World." In 1883, Ben Wallace bought a defunct traveling show and set up a professional circus. From that time on, the Wallace Circus Farm was the winter headquarters of many of America's great traveling circuses. Each year, Peru stages a week-long festival, complete with a 3-ring circus, to commemorate those days. In 1969, the city finished roofing its remodeled lumber yard to accommodate a performing arena half as large as a football field. Pioneer, circus, and Indian relics are displayed in the Miami County Historical and Puterbaugh museums. The songwriter Cole Porter was born in Peru in 1893; his home is 7 mi. southeast of town.

Agriculturally, the area produces corn, grains, dairy, hogs, and tomatoes. Peru's manufactures include electrical switches, steam boilers, bunk beds, high alloy castings and tubings, heating components, furniture, commercial offset printing, party favors, clothes hampers, and automotive parts, among several others.

Points of interest in the city include the Grissom Air Force Base, and the Circus Hall of Fame.

PETERSBURG, City; Pop. 2,449; seat of Pike County; SW Indiana; Zip Code 47567; near the White River; 19 mi. SE of Vincennes. Petersburg was founded in 1817 at a fording place on the White River. It developed during the days of the Wabash and Erie Canal; the passenger depot (now Wyatt Seed Company) and a section of the old canal can still be seen. Several 19th-century buildings have been restored. Of note is the 12-room Proffit-Morgan House. Petersburg is a shipping center for coal, oil, timber, flour, and concrete blocks. NE of town is the R.E.A. power plant with its two 300-ft. smokestacks.

PIERCETON, Town; Pop. 1,030; Kosciusko County; N Indiana; Zip Code 46562; 30 mi. WNW of Fort Wayne in an agricultural area (livestock, poultry, feed grains). There is a

Dictionary of Places

lumber mill in town. Nearby Robinson Lake provides recreational facilities.

PIGEON RIVER, NE Indiana and S Michigan, rises in Indiana in NE Stueben County and flows SW, NW and W to widen into several small lakes. Also known as Pigeon Creek, it reaches a reservoir in N Lagrange County, where it runs through Pigeon River State Fish and Wildlife Area and then flows NW into Michigan. The river returns SW into Indiana to the St. Joseph River just N of Bristol, having covered a distance of approximately 65 miles.

PIGEON RIVER STATE FISH AND WILDLIFE AREA, Lagrange County; NE Indiana; near Mongo. Its 10,535 acres have facilities for water recreation in a 150-acre lake and the adjacent Pigeon River. There are also facilities available for hiking, picnicking, camping, and hunting. It is a favorite spot for trout fishermen, mushroom hunters, and bird watchers.

PIGEON ROOST STATE MEMORIAL, Scott County; S Indiana; near Underwood. It commemorates the pioneers who were slain there by the Shawnee Indians in 1812. The attack has been ascribed to resentment over the Battle of Tippecanoe (1811) and the excitement of the War of 1812. A 44-ft. limestone shaft marks the spot.

PIKE, City; Pop. 12,281; SW Indiana; area 335 sq. mi.; bounded on the N by the White River and its East Ford and drained by the Patoka River. The county was formed on February 1, 1817 and named for Gen. Z.M. Pike, who fell at the capture of York in April 1813. Petersburg is the county seat.

Pike County lies in the heart of Indiana's coal-mining country and is almost wholly underlain by fine workable veins of bituminous coal, 4 to 9 ft. thick. Oil wells, clay pits, and fine stands of timber abound, and agriculture is also important. Leading crops are feed grains and tobacco. Manufactures include concrete blocks, wood products, and flour.

PIKE STATE FOREST, Pike County; S Indiana; 6 mi. E of Winslow. The forest encompasses 2,898 acres of land and has facilities for hiking, picnicking, fishing, camping, hunting, and horseback riding.

PINE VILLAGE, Town; Pop. 134; Warren County, W Indiana; Zip Code 47975; on Big Pine Creek; 20 mi. W of Lafayette in an agricultural area (livestock and feed grains).

PINNACLE, THE, natural stone formation resembling a pillar, in Jug Rock Park, S Indiana; 5 mi. N of Shoals. The Pinnacle is formed of variegated rock strata and is a favorite attraction to visitors in the park. Jog Rock *(q.v.)* for which the park is named, is also located there.

PITTSBORO, Town; Pop.815; Hendricks County; central Indiana; Zip Code 46167; 18 mi. NW of Indianapolis in an agricultural area (livestock and feed grains).

PLAINFIELD, Town; Pop. 10,433; Hendricks County; central Indiana; Zip Code 46168; on the Whitelick River; 14 mi. WSW of Indianapolis in an agricultural area (livestock, feed grains, dairy products). The town contains the Indiana Boy's School (1867) for the reform and education of juvenile delinquents. Two unusual monuments are on the grounds. One, a statue carved by a 15-year old inmate from a block of Bedford limestone, represents Whittier's "Barefoot Boy." The other is a monument to the memory of Thomas Pain Westendorf, a school official and composer of the song "I'll Take You Home Again Kathleen."

Recreational facilities are provided at nearby Pay Lake.

PLAINVILLE, Town; Pop. 444; Daviess County; SW Indiana; Zip Code 47568; 11 mi. N of Washington in an agricultural area (feed grains, livestock). Plainville is a trade center for feeds and grains.

PLEASANT LAKE, Town; Pop. 600; Stueben County; NE Indiana; Zip Code 46779; 4 mi. S of Angola in a resort and farming area. Manufactures include concrete blocks and septic tanks.

PLYMOUTH, City; Pop. 8,303; seat of Marshall County; N Indiana; Zip Code 46563; on the Yellow River, 24 mi. S of South Bend. Founded in 1834, Plymouth occupies the site

Dictionary of Places

of a former Potawatomi Indian village. Between Pretty and Twin lakes is the Chief Menominee Monument, which honors the Potawatomi leader who unsuccessfully fought the removal of his tribe to the West. U.S. soldiers surrounded the Indians on Myers Lake in 1836, and marched them across the prairies in the summer's heat. Many died along the way, and the trek is remembered as the "Trail of Death."

Plymouth is a shipping and agricultural trading center for the surrounding area. Manufactures include grinding machines, automobile parts, stokers, batteries, and emery products. The Marshall County Historical Society and Museum has interesting local pioneer artifacts. Centennial Park and Camper's Roost provide camping and recreational facilities.
- HISTORICAL PLACES... (See Hist. Places Sect for details.)
Marshall County Jail.

POKAGON STATE PARK, Stueben County; NE Indiana; 6 mi. N of Angola. Known as Indiana's year-round playground, this 1,175 acres park on the shore of beautiful Lake James offers a vast variety of activities for the sports enthusiast. It was named for the Potawatomi Indian chief, Simon Pokagon, who was educated at the University of Notre Dame and Oberlin College. The park is located at an altitude of 1,000 ft., one of the highest points in the state. Facilities include a saddle barn, bicycle rentals, and archery range, a bathing beach, picnic grounds, and campgrounds.

Water-skiing and sailing are popular summer pastimes and, in the winter, Pokagon's 1,700-ft. double-lane toboggan slide attracts thousands of enthusiasts.

The charming Potawatomi Inn sits on a ridge overlooking the lake and offers dining and accommodations all year.

POLAND, Town; Pop. 200; Clay County; central Indiana; Zip Code 47868; 16 mi. SE of Brazil in an agricultural and farming area. Manufactures include crates, pallets and knock-down boxes.

PONETO, Town; Pop. 236; Wells County; E Indiana; Zip Code 46781; 7 mi. SSW of Bluffton in an agricultural area (livestock and feed grains).

PORTAGE, City; Pop. 29,060; Porter County; NW Indiana; Zip Code 46368; 9 mi. E of Gary. Originally located in a sparsely settled farming area, Portage was incorporated as a town in 1958, and as a city in 1969. Its borders include Midwest Steel, Burns Ditch, and part of Bethlehem Steel. In 1966, a federal grant was made available for the construction of the state's only deep-water harbor on Lake Michigan, known as the Port of Indiana.

Portage has continued to grow as a major steel-producing industrial complex. Midwest Steel, which began operations there in 1957, produces cold steel rolled products. Boat-launching facilities are located where the Little Calumet and Illinois rivers empty into Lake Michigan. Woodland Park provides picnicking, swimming, ice skating, tennis, and a nature area.

PORTER, Town; Pop. 3,118; Porter County NW Indiana; Zip Code 46304; near Lake Michigan; 13 mi. E of Gary. Porter was once a thriving rail and brick manufacturing center. The brickyards are gone, however; most of the population is employed in Gary's steelworks. The Sander Wood Engraving Company, last of its kind, does wood block engraving for books, magazines, and catalogs.

Nearby is the Augsburg Svenska Skola (Augsburg Swedish School) built in 1880. It is, in fact, not a school at all, but a white shingled church with a seating capacity of only 7. The cemetery behind it covers an Indian mound. Porter Park is 1.5 mi. S of town.

PORTER, City; Pop. 87,114; NW Indiana; area 425 sq. mi.; bounded on the N by Lake Michigan, and S by the Kankakee River. It is drained by the Little Calumet and Grand Calumet rivers.

The county was organized by the U.S. Navy. Valparaiso is the county seat. It is well-known for its huge stretches of wild, sparsely populated dunelands bordering Lake Michigan. Indiana Dunes State Park attracts thousands of visitors

Dictionary of Places

on hot summer weekends. The dunelands' unique flora and fauna comprise a natural outdoor laboratory for the serious or amateur biology student.

The rest of the county is rich farmland, conducive to the raising of corn, soybeans, and dairy cattle. Industrially, it was one of the fastest growing areas in Indiana. Steel, nonferrous castings, bearings, and magnets are among the leading manufactures.

●HISTORICAL PLACES... (See Hist. Places Sect for details.)

Bailly, Joseph, Homestead.

PORTLAND, City; Pop. 6,483; seat of Jay County; E Indiana; Zip Code 47371; on the Salamonie River; 28 mi. NE of Muncie. Once an important lumber-milling town, it has gradually become an agricultural center (livestock, dairying, soybeans, grain). Manufactures include work clothes, canned goods, silos, brooms, and dairy equipment. Portland is the birthplace of Hoosier automobile inventor Elwood Haynes; the site is marked at High and Commerce streets. Hickory Grove Lake, 8 mi. S of town, is a popular resort.

POSEY, County; Pop. 21,740; sw Indiana; area 412 sq. mi.; bounded W by the Wabash River, and S by the Ohio River, and drained by Big Creek. The county was formed in November 1814 and named for Thomas Posey, the last governor of Indiana Territory. The county seat is at Mount Vernon.

The surface of the land is level to gently rolling and ideally suited for the growing of feed grains, vegetables, and fruit. Posey County is especially noted for its watermelon and cantaloupe. Mount Vernon and New Harmony have some industry (machinery, tanks, stoves, cigars, and food products).

POSEYVILLE, Town; Pop. 1,089; Posey County; SW Indiana; Zip Code 47633; 18 mi. NW of Evansville in an agricultural area (cattle, calves, hogs, soybeans, wheat, corn). Poseyville has a poultry hatchery and a meat-packing plant.

PRINCETON, City; Pop. 8,127; seat of Gibson County; SW Indiana; Zip Code 47570; 27 mi. N of Evansville. The city was founded in 1814 and named for Capt. William Prince, later a representative in the U.S. Congress. The courthouse was built in 1884 and many other fine 19th-century buildings remain.

Princeton has become an important oil, coal, and agricultural center. Diversity of manufactures--among them oil-well supplies, paint brushes, electric clocks, and food products--reflect Princetons's economic prosperity. Railroad repair shops are in the city, and bituminous coal mines are nearby. King's Mine, 450 ft. deep, is Indiana's deepest coal mine shaft. Lafayette Park and South Side Park provide recreational activities.

PULASKI, County; Pop. 12,534; NW Indiana; area 433 sq. mi.; drained by Big Monon Creek and the Tippecanoe River. The county was formed in 1835 and named for Casimir Pulaski, a Polish officer who was killed in the American Revolution. The county seat is at Winamac.

The county's soil ranges from clay to loam and is considered among the best in the state for the cultivation of corn and soybeans. One of the world's largest game farms (5,200 acres) and Tippecanoe River State Park are located in Pulaski County.

PUTNAM, County; Pop. 26,932; W central Indiana; area 49 sq. mi.; drained by the Eel River and Raccoon and Mill creeks. The county was organized in April 1822 and named for Gen. Israel Putnam of the American Revolution. The county seat is Greencastle.

Agriculture and stone quarrying are the mainstay of the economy, but there is some manufacturing at Greencastle. Richard Lieber State Park, encompassing 1,500-acre Cataract Lake, is located in the southern section of Putnam County.

RACCOON LAKE STATE RECREATION AREA, Parke County; W central Indiana; 7 mi. E of Rockville. The 3,938-acre recreation area provides access to the Mansfield Flood Control Reservoir, which is operated in cooperation with the U.S. Army of Corps Engineers. Five boat-launching ramps are situated around the lake, and the area pro-

Dictionary of Places

vides excellent boating, swimming, and fishing. There is also a campground and a picnic area.

RAMSEY, Town; Pop. 700; Harrison County; S Indiana; Zip Code 47166; 11 mi. NW of Corydon in a lumbering and farming area. Ramsey is a trade center for chicks, feeds, dog food, and popcorn.

RANDOLPH, County; Pop. 28,915; E Indiana; area 457 sq. mi.; bounded on the E by Ohio and drained by the Mississinewa and Whitewater rivers and the West Fork of the White River. The county was formed in August 1818 and named for its sister county in North Carolina. The county seat is at Winchester.

Randolph County is in a rich agricultural area noted for livestock, feed grains, and poultry. There is also some stone quarrying and manufacturing at Union City and Winchester, including the production of glass containers, castings, foods, and truck bodies.

RED BRIDGE STATE RECREATION AREA, Miami County; E central Indiana; 7 mi. SE of Peru. It is one of two units located on the Mississinewa Dam and Reservoir. The facilities encompass a total of 14,000 acres and include the 3,300-acre Mississinewa Lake, which was developed jointly by the state of Indiana and the U.S. Army Corps of Engineers. Recreational facilities include campgrounds, picnic areas, a swimming beach, and boat ramps.

RED KEY, Town; Pop. 1,383; Jay County; E Indiana; Zip Code 47373; 18 mi. NE of Muncie in an agricultural area (livestock and feed grains). Red Key has a canning food plant and lumber mill.

REELSVILLE, Village; Pop. 155; Putnam County; S Indiana; Zip Code 46171; 10 mi. SW of Greencastle in a stone quarrying and lumbering region. The local stone quarry produces crushed stone and agricultural lime.

REMINGTON, Town; Pop. 1,247; St. Joseph County; NW Indiana; Zip Code 47977; 12 mi. S of Rensselaer in an agricultural area (livestock and feed grains). Remington is a manufacturer of fertilizers, soy protein concentrates, and other food products, metal alloys, and lumber.

RENSSELAER, City; Pop. 5,045; seat of Jasper County; NW Indiana; Zip Code 47978; on the Iroquois River; 45 mi. S of Gary. The city was established in 1837 and named after James Van Rensselaer, merchant and founder of the town. Rensselaer was incorporated in 1897.

The town is a prosperous trading center for agricultural products, especially flour and dairying items. Saint Joseph's College (1889) is located there; its oldest building, Drexel Hall, was once an Indian mission school. The college is a fully- accredited four-year liberal arts institution. The Halleck Student Center is named for Congressman Charles Halleck, a Rensselaer resident. In the city, Milroy Park contains a statue of Gen. Robert Milroy, a Civil War hero and member of the 1850 Indiana constitutional convention.

●HISTORICAL PLACES... (See Hist. Places Sect for details.)
St. Joseph's Indian Normal School.

REYNOLDS, Town; Pop. 528; White County; NW central Indiana; Zip Code 47980; 24 mi. N of Lafayette in an agricultural area (livestock and feed grains).

RICHARD LIEBER STATE PARK, Owen County; W Indiana; 15 mi. S of Greencastle. The 8,283-acre park provides access to Cataract Lake, which covers 1,500 acres and offers excellent swimming, boating, and water-skiing. The adjacent lands are all part of Cagles Mill Flood Control Reservoir. Federal authorities control the lake level.

RICHLAND, Town; Pop. 600; Spencer County; S Indiana; Zip Code 47634; 10 mi. NW of Rockport in a scenic part of the "Hoosier Hills." Richland is a trade center for agricultural products, chemicals, and automobile-body masking supplies.

RICHMOND, City; Pop. 38,705; seat of Wayne County; E Indiana; Zip Code 47374; on the East Fork of the Whitewater River; 65 mi. E of Indianapolis. Richmond was founded in 1806 by soldiers who once served under George Rogers Clark. Initially, it was the fertile soils that attracted

Dictionary of Places

settlers to the area, and the village expanded rapidly. Richmond became a town in 1816, the year of Indiana's statehood. The Quaker community in 1847 founded the Friends' Boarding School which, in 1859, became known as Earlham College. A four-year liberal arts school, Earlham College has an enrollment of about 1,100 students annually. On campus, the Joseph Moore Museum houses a fine display of birds and mammals in their native habitat.

William Foulke, Indiana political reformer and supporter of women's suffrage, once lived in Richmond and became editor of the local newspaper. At the turn of the century, he established a precedent by hiring the city's first female stenographer.

Modern Richmond is a leading industrial community. Diversity of manufactures reflect its economic prosperity. Among many of the products manufactured there are machine tools, farm implements, automobile parts, phonograph records, lawn mowers, school buses, moving stairs, aircraft parts, clothing, pianos, refrigerators, and plastics. Richmond also has one of the largest rose-growing industries in the world. Hill Greenhouses produces roses, chrysanthemums, and grafted rose plants. The concern was founded by E. Gurney Gill (1847-1935), who was noted for his introduction of such new roses as the Richmond Rose, a beautiful hybrid produced in 1905.

The Wayne County Historical Museum is housed in the former Hicksite Friends' Meeting House, built in 1864. It has a reconstructed pioneer kitchen, general store, apothecary shop, and cobbler shop. Many historic relics are on display, including an Egyptian mummy. Three outside buildings are encompassed by the museum: the county's first log school house; an agricultural building with pioneer farm implements; and a pole barn with early farm machinery.

Glen Miller Park features rose gardens, a golf course, a zoo, summer bandstand concerts, and an archery range. "Madonna of the Trails," a monument to pioneer women, is located in the park. Other recreational facilities can be found at Clear Creek Park and the 177-acre Middlefork Reservoir.

●HISTORICAL PLACES... (See Hist. Places Sect for details.)
Old Richmond Historic District; Starr Historic District.

RIDGEVILLE, Town; Pop. 808; Randolph County; E Indiana; Zip Code 47380; on the Mississinewa River; 20 ENE of Muncie in an agricultural area (livestock and feed grains). There is some stone quarrying. The town was settled in 1817 and incorporated in 1868.

RIPLEY, County; Pop. 21,138; SE Indiana; area 442 sq. mi.; drained in April 1818 and named for Gen. E. W. Ripley, an officer in the War of 1812. The county seat is at Versailles.

Ripley County is noted for feed grains, corn, tobacco, dairying, and livestock. The leading industries produce furniture and caskets. Versailles State Park, Indiana's second largest, is located in the county.

RISING SUN, Town; Pop. 2,311; seat of Ohio County; SE Indiana; 47040; on the Ohio River, 22 mi. SW of Cincinnati, Ohio. Rising sum was platted in 1814, and for many years flourished as a major river port. Several old buildings remain along Front Street as relics of the riverboat era. The Ohio County Courthouse (1845) is the oldest courthouse in Indiana and is still in use today. The Speakman House (1846) is built on an Indian mound and was originally a stopover on the Underground Railway. The Ohio County Historical Society operates a museum, which includes in its displays "Hoosier Boy," the record-holding speedboat of the early 1900s.

Rising Sun is a shipping point for livestock, truck, tobacco, flour, dairy products, and furniture. Arnold's Creek Embayment and Island Branch provide recreational facilities.

ROACHDALE, Town; Pop. 902; Putnam County; W central Indiana; Zip Code 46172; 35 WNW of Indianapolis in an agricultural area (dairy products, grain, soybeans).

ROANN, Town; Pop. 447; Wabash County; NE central Indiana; Zip Code 46974; on the Eel River; 14 mi. NNE of Peru. Originally called Village of Squirrel Creek, the area

Dictionary of Places

was founded in 1835 by John Anderson and his family, and incorporated in 1853. There is a rather whimsical story concerning how the town was named. According to one source, Ann Beckner Brower was crossing the Eel River in a small boat. A storm was approaching, causing alarm to those waiting on the shore who began shouting, "Row, Ann, row, Ann"--and it occurred to someone present that the new town might be called Roann. The story is authenticated by her obituary to be true.

Situated in an agricultural area, production include corn, soybeans, hogs, livestock, feedgrains, and dairy.

ROANOKE, Town; Pop. 1,018; Huntington County; NE central Indiana; Zip Code 46783; on the Little River; 16 mi. SW of Fort Wayne. The town was founded in 1861 and was perhaps best known for the Roanoke Classical Seminary, which was considered "the last word in culture by Hoosier." Eventually, the school was moved to North Manchester and became Manchester College.

The Home of Kilsoquah, granddaughter of the Miami Indian chief Little Turtle, is at the SE edge of town. At the time of her death in 1915, she was the only full-blooded Indian in Huntington County. Roanoke is a center for grain and dairy products and a manufacturer of electric coils.

ROCHESTER, City; Pop. 5,969; seat of Fulton County; N Indiana; Zip Code 46975; near Lake Manitou; 24 mi. NNE of Logansport. Rochester was founded in 1831 as an Indian trading post. Four years earlier, a gristmill had been constructed there by the U.S. government to grind corn for the Potawatomi under the terms of an 1826 treaty.

Indian legends state that Lake Manitou was the home of the "Great Spirit Manitou" who, if angered, swallowed up canoes and their passengers. Stories about monsters which occasionally surface are still told today. Several popular resorts and a golf course are located along the shores of the lake. Rochester is also a trading center for soybeans and grain, and is a manufacturer of cement products, canned goods, and dairy products.

ROCKPORT, City; Pop. 2,315; Spencer County Seat; SW Indiana; on the Ohio River; 29 mi. ESE of Evansville. Rockport is picturesquely situated on high bluffs overlooking the river. According to tradition, the family of revivalist preacher James Langford occupied a cave in the bluffs for one winter season. Subsequently, the site was settled by Daniel Grass in 1807. Abraham Lincoln settled 16 mi. north of town in 1816 and remained there for 14 years. The Lincoln Pioneer Village in the city park contains restored pioneer cabins. The entire village was designed by artist and sculptor George Honig and constructed during the Great Depression. In addition to the reproduction of Lincoln's cabin, the village includes a museum, law office, church, blockhouse, and pioneer farm implements. The Crooks-Anderson House (1859) on Walnut Street is one of the only 6 octagonal houses remaining in Indiana.

Rockport is in area rich in natural resources. Oil and natural gas wells are nearby, and the city is a manufacturing center for bricks, tiles, concrete, buttons, and flour. Recreational facilities are at Lake Alda, an artificial reservoir.

ROCKVILLE, Town; Pop. 2,706; seat of Parke County; W Indiana; Zip Code 47872; 23 mi. NNE of Terre Haute. Rockville was settled in 1823 and incorporated in 1854. It is mainly a farming community, but is also involved in bituminous coal mining and lumber milling. Covered bridges stand in Rockville's town square and on the golf course, the only one in the world with that distinction. Billie Creek Village is a reconstructed turn-of-the- century community, complete with a one-room school house, country store, weaver's shop, barn, livery stable, governor's house, and log cabin.

The annual Parke County Maple Fair is held in Rockville in March when the "sap's a' runnin'," and the Parke County Covered Bridge Festival is held in the city every October. Recreational facilities can be found at nearby Raccoon Lake State Recreation Area and at Turkey Run State Park.

Dictionary of Places

ROLLING PRAIRIE, Town; Pop. 700; La Porte County, NW Indiana; Zip Code 46371; 7 mi. NE of La Porte in a resort and farming area noted for feed grains and livestock. Three Indian trails crossed the site of the present town, among them the famous Sauk Trail.

Rolling Prairie was founded in the early 1830s by Ezekiah Provolot and has thrived ever since as a farming community. The La Porte County Farm Bureau Co-op Association is located there; it deals in feed, seeds, and grain. Manufactures include copper wire, tools, dies, and axle assemblies for mobile homes and utility trailers. Recreational facilities can be found at nearby Hog, Rolling Timbers, and Saugany lakes.

ROME CITY, Village; Pop. 1,138; Noble County; NE Indiana; Zip Code 46784; on Sylvan Lake; 7 mi. NW of Kendallville. The site was settled in 1837 primarily as a base camp for French and Irish workers, who built a dam across a tributary of the Elkhart River, creating Sylvan Lake. Rome City was platted in 1839 is a resort community. Several springs in and near the village have medicinal properties, but they have not been fully exploited.
- HISTORICAL PLACES... (See Hist. Places Sect for details.)
    Porter, Gene Stratton, Cabin (The Cabin in Wildflower Woods).

ROSEDALE, Town; Pop. 783; Parke County; W Indiana; Zip Code 47874; near Raccoon Creek; 14 mi. NNE of Terre Haute in an agricultural area (livestock and feed grains) and coal-mining region.

ROSELAND, Town; Pop. 706; St. Joseph County; N Indiana; a N suburb of South Bend in an agricultural area (livestock and feed grains, peppermint).

ROSSVILLE, Town; Pop. 1,175; Clinton County; central Indiana; Zip Code 46065; on a fork of Wildcat Creek; 16 mi. E of Lafayette in an agricultural area (feed grains, livestock).

ROYAL CENTER, Town; Pop. 859; Cass County; N central Indiana; Zip Code 46978; 11 mi. NW of Logansport in an agricultural area (livestock and feed grains) and lumbering area. There is a canned food plant in town.

RUSH, County; Pop. 20,352; E central Indiana; area 490 sq. mi.; drained by the Big Blue River and Flatrock Creek. The county was organized in December 1821 and named for Dr. Benjamin Rush, famous early American physician. The county seat is at Rushville. The soils are especially fertile and suited for feed grains, corn, apples, and livestock. The area specializes in importing and breeding Jersey cattle. The leading industry produces furniture.

RUSHVILLE, City; Pop. 5,533; seat of Rush County; E central Indiana; Zip Code 46173; on Flatrock Creek, 40 mi. ESE of Indianapolis. The city was founded in 1822 and named for Dr. Benjamin Rush, noted physician, philanthropist, and signer of the Declaration of Independence. Rushville is centrally located in a rich farming area noted for corn and hogs. Manufacturing plays a leading part in the city's economy; products include lumber, furniture, machinery, flour, packed meat, canned goods, and gloves.

Wendell Wilkie, presidential candidate, lived there and was the owner of 7 farms. The Wendell Wilkie Grave and Memorial is in Rushville's East Hill Cemetery. The many historical sites in Rushville include the century-old blacksmith shop across from the courthouse. The Hackleman Log Cabin in Memorial Park was the birthplace of Gen. Pleasant A. Hackleman, a Civil War hero. Of note is the Rush County Historical Museum, which houses one of the finest collections of North America artifacts in the country. The museum's stable annex houses a pioneer vehicle exhibit.

The Werline and Halbieb Horse Auction is held in Rushville every week, and is the largest such auction in the U.S. Annual events include the Rush County Fair and the Festival of Arts and Crafts. Recreational facilities are available at nearby Wofal Lake.

- HISTORICAL PLACES... (See Hist. Places Sect for details.)

Melodeon Hall.

RUSSELLVILLE, Town; Pop. 336; Putnam County; W central Indiana; Zip Code 46175; 36 mi. NE of Terre Haute in

Dictionary of Places

an agricultural area (livestock, feed grains, poultry).

SAINT ANTHONY, Town; Pop. 290; Dubois County; S Indiana; Zip Code 47575; 10 mi. S of Jasper in a lumbering and agricultural area noted for feed grains and livestock. The town is a trade center for corrugated boxes, hospital equipment, furniture, fertilizer, and poultry feeders.

SAINT BERNICE, Town; Pop. 900; Vermillion County; W Indiana; Zip Code 47875; 18 mi. SW of Newport. Saint Bernice is a trade center and manufacturer of sportswear, rainwear, and fertilizer.

SAINT JOE, Town; Pop. 452; De Kalb County; NE Indiana; Zip Code 46785; on the St. Joseph River; 21 mi. NE of Fort Wayne in an agricultural area (feed grains, pickles, flour).

SAINT JOHN, Town; Pop. 4,921; Lake County; NW Indiana; Zip Code 46373; 12 mi. SW of Gary. A small community of Roman Catholic farmers, it was named after John Houck, the town's first German settler and builder of NW Indiana's first Roman Catholic church (1842). Saint John is noted for its horse farms, which have increased steadily in importance since the 1960s. Every summer weekend, horse shows are held in Saint John and nearby Dyer. It has been said that the area around the town has more riding horses than anywhere else in the country.

SAINT JOSEPH, County; Pop. 245,045; N Indiana; area 466 sq. mi.; bounded on the N by Michigan and drained by the St. Joseph, Yellow, and Kankakee rivers. The county was formed in 1830 and named for the St. Joseph River. South Bend is the county seat. The county was the first area of Indiana to be seen by a European, when Pere Marquette visited the region in 1675.

Saint Joseph County is rich in fruit orchards, mint farms, and grain fields. Diversified manufacturing is prevalent in the large cities; the leading industrial products are automobiles, automobile parts, aircraft parts, industrial machinery, rubber and plastic products, food and missiles.

SAINT JOSEPH RIVER, rises in Hillsdale, S Michigan,

and flows NW and then generally W and SW past Elkhart and South Bend. It empties into Lake Michigan. The Elkhart River and Pigeon Creek are its major tributaries.

SAINT MARY'S RIVER, rises in Auglaize County, Ohio, and flows about 100 mi. NW past Saint Mary's, Medon, Rockford, and Wilshire, Ohio, into Indiana. In Indiana, it passes Decatur and Fort Wayne, where it joins the Saint Joseph River to form the Maumee. The river was a key point in the development of the Wabash and Erie Canal system. (1832-70).

SAINT MEINRAD, Village; Pop. 850; Spencer County; SW Indiana; Zip Code 47577; on the Anderson River; 15 mi. N of Tell City. The village is a community of German Roman Catholics, most of whom are employed by the Benedictine Saint Meinrad Archabbey. The abbey and seminary, which are the focus of the village, were founded in 1857 by two Benedictine monks from the Archabbey of Einsiedein, Switzerland.

The Archabbey is totally self-sufficient. Members of the order engage in a variety of agricultural and industrial activities, including carpentry, coal mining, and rock quarrying. The seminary is the second largest in the U.S. The Abbey Press was founded in 1876, when a small printing press and some type were purchased; it publishes on a wide variety of subjects. Recently, an abbey chicken coop was converted into a modern plaster-casting and metal finishing studio. Visitors to Saint Meinrad are immediately impressed with the beauty of the village and the hospitality of its inhabitants.

The Archabbey is 100 years old; its Romanesque church and towers are an impressive sight. There are 13 altars within the church; the one in the crypt is of gold. Rock gardens were built in 1936 to enhance the terrain's natural shale outcroppings. The surrounding countryside is given over to the monastery vineyards, which provide the monks with their own wine. NE of Saint Meinrad is the Monte Cassino Chapel (1868), a popular shrine for the backwoods Roman Catholic families. Pilgrimages from the abbey to the shrine are held each May and October.

Dictionary of Places

SAINT PAUL, Town; Pop. 1,032; on the border of Decatur and Shelby counties; SE central Indiana; Zip Code 47272; 11 mi. SE of Shelbyville in an agricultural area (livestock and feed grains).

SALAMONIA, Town; Pop. 381; Jay County; E Indiana; on the Salamonie River; 30 mi. ENE of Muncie in an agricultural area (livestock and feed grains, poultry).

SALAMONIE RIVER, E and NE central Indiana; rises near Salamonia in E Jay County and flows about 82 mi. NW past Portland and Mount Pelier to the Wabash River opposite Lagro. The river is dammed in Wabash and Huntington counties to form the Salamonie Reservoir, a joint recreational project developed by the state of Indiana and the U.S. Army Corps of Engineer.

SALAMONIE RIVER STATE FOREST, Wabash County; N Indiana; 14 mi. SE of Lagro. The northern and southern recreational units-- Salamonie Forest State Recreation Area and Lost Bridge State Recreational Area *(q.v.),* respectively--are encompassed within the states forest's boundaries. Open all year, the Salamonie State Forest provides water recreation on the adjacent Salamonie River and Salamonie Reservoir. There are also facilities for camping, picnicking, hunting, and horseback riding.

SALEM, City; Pop. 5,619; seat of Washington County; S central Indiana; Zip Code 47167; on the Blue River; 27 mi. SE of Bedford. Salem was founded in 1814, and incorporated in June of 1868. The name was chosen by Mrs. William Lindley, in honor of her hometown in North Carolina. The city's growth was severely hampered by the cholera epidemic of 1833, which virtually depopulated the town.

Agriculturally, Salem produces corn, hay, soybeans, wheat, oats, tobacco, timber, cattle, dairy, hogs, sheep, and horses. Its manufactures include office furniture, wood products, powdered metallurgy parts, plastic molding, concrete products, clothes, rock wool, and lumber.

Salem was the birthplace of John Hay (1838-1905), the statesman, author, and private secretary to Abraham Lincoln from 1861 to 1865. Hay House, which has been restored, was originally built in 1824 to house the Salem Grammar School. The school building soon became too small, and was sold in 1831 by Hay's father, who was one of the county's pioneer physicians. The house was declared a National Historic Site in 1971. To the rear of Hay House is the Steven Memorial Museum (1970), which is built of native bricks taken from old local buildings. The Historical Society of Washington County is located there. The county courthouse dates back to 1886.

Southwest of Salem is Beck's Mill, built in 1808. Recreational facilities can be found at Elk Creek and Salinda lakes and at the Western Hills Golf Course. Two impounding reservoirs, Lake Salinda and Lake John Hay, provide adequate supplies of water to the city and have given the area a new source of recreational activities.

●HISTORICAL PLACES... (See Hist. Places Sect for details.)

Hay-Morrison House.

SANBORN, Town; Pop. 528; Knox County; SW Indiana; Zip Code 47578; 24 mi. NE of Vincennes in an agricultural and bituminous coal-mining area.

SAN PIERRE, Town; Pop. 300; Starke County; S Indiana; Zip Code 46374; 21 mi. SW of Knox in an agricultural area noted for livestock and feed grains. San Pierre is a manufacturer of fertilizer and feeds and has a printing and a die-stamping plant.

SANTA CLAUS, Town, Pop. 927; Spencer County; SW Indiana; Zip Code 47579; 38 mi. ENE of Evansville. The village, founded in 1846, receives mail addressed to Santa Claus and has the only post office in the U.S. with this name. The post office is situated next to Santa Claus Land, one of the largest amusement parks in the country. It covers 45 acres and includes Santa's headquarters, toyland, and a petting zoo.

SARATOGA, Town; Pop. 266; Randolph County; E Indiana; Zip Code 47382; 25 mi. E of Muncie in a limestone quarrying and agricultural area noted for livestock and feed

Dictionary of Places

grains.

SCALES LAKE STATE BEACH AND STATE PARK, Warrick County; S Indiana; near Booneville. Less well-known than other Indiana state parks, Scales Lake offers camping, boating, fishing, and swimming. Also located there is the Scales Lake Fish Hatchery.

SCHERERVILLE, Town; Pop. 19,926 County; NW Indiana; Zip Code 46375; 10 mi. SW of Gary. Originally a crossroads for several Indian trails, Schererville later became a stopping place for wagon trains going West. The town was named for Nicholas Sherer, its founder. His house on Wilhelm Street has been restored. The town is a quiet residential community, and much of the population is employed in the Gary steel works. Recreational facilities include an amusement park, a golf course, a stock-car race track, and a riding school.

SCHNEIDER, Town; Pop. 310; Lake County NW Indiana; Zip Code 46376; near the Kankakee River; 29 mi. S of Gary in an agricultural and resort area.

SCOTT, County; Pop. 17,144; SE Indiana; area 193 sq. mi.; bounded on the N by the Muscatatuck River and drained by its tributaries. The county was organized in January 1820 and named for Gen. Charles Scott, an officer in the American Revolution. The county seat is at Scottsburg.

Although it is the state's fourth smallest county, its topography is diversified, ranging from hills to tablelands and bottomlands. An abundance of bottomlands provide large areas planted in grain, tobacco, and truck. Livestock and poultry are also noted in the region. The main industry is canning.

SCOTTSBURG, Town; Pop. 5,334; seat of Scott County; SE Indiana; Zip Code 47170; 28 mi. N of New Albany. The town was platted in 1871 as the new county seat, replacing Lexington. It is picturesquely situated in a wide valley surrounded by tumbled, wooded hills known as The Knobs. The economy is based on agriculture (grain, truck, poultry) and manufacturing (canned goods, work clothes, lumber). Limestone quarries are nearby. Raintree Lake Park resort is

4 mi. W of town.

SEELYVILLE, Town; Pop. 1,090; Vigo County; W Indiana; Zip Code 47878; 8 mi. ENE of Terre Haute. Seelyville began as a prosperous coal mining town, but mining has since declined. Farming is now the main activity.

SELLERSBURG, Town; Pop. 5,745; Clark County; SE Indiana; Zip Code 47172; near Silver Creek, 8 mi. NNE of New Albany in an agricultural area noted for livestock and feed grains. Sellersburg is mainly a residential suburb of New Albany. Manufactures include special machines, asphalt paving material, kitchen cabinets, and cement products.

SELMA, Town; Pop. 800; Delaware County; E Indiana; Zip Code 47383; 6 mi. E of Muncie in an agricultural area noted for feed grains and livestock.

SELMIER STATE FOREST, Jennings County; S Indiana; 7 mi. NE of North Vernon. The forest covers 352 acres and has facilities for hiking, fishing, and hunting.

SEYMOUR, City; Pop. 15,576; Jackson County; S Indiana; Zip Code 47274; 17 mi. S of Columbus in an agricultural area noted for livestock and dairy products. The world's first train robbery occurred at Seymour on the night of Oct. 6, 1866. The Reno Gang of Jackson County took over an Ohio & Mississippi train and escaped with $15,000.

Seymour is a modern manufacturing center whose diverse products include appliances, furniture, canned goods, flour, fertilizer, cheese, drugs, printers' supplies, and lumber. The H. Vance Swope Memorial Art Gallery has a fine collection of original paintings. A stone marker stands 1 mile N of Seymour on the site of the first blockhouse built in defense against attacking Indians. Recreational facilities can be found at nearby Cypress and Labline Bed lakes.

SHADES STATE PARK, near Waveland, Montgomery County, W central Indiana. Natural beauty is reflected in the dense stands of virgin woods and deep ravines of the

Dictionary of Places

2,948-acre park. Sugar Creek abounds in game fish, and the park offers camping, picnicking, hiking, and boating. Shades is the site of the annual Sugar Creek Canoe Race.

SHAFER RESERVOIR, White County; NW Indiana; at Monticello. Shafer Reservoir, also known as Shafer Lake, was created in 1923 by the Norway Dam, which reaches 1,200 ft. across the Tippecanoe River. Lake Freeman forms a south unit, and together the two bodies of water furnish hydroelectric power and recreational facilities for hundreds of surrounding communities. The E shore of Shafer Reservoir is the site of Indiana State Beach.

SAKAMAK STATE PARK, near Jasonville, Greene County; SW Indiana. The 1,000-acre park was established in 1929 and named for a local stream known to the Indians as Shakamak ("river of the long fish"). Shakamak Lake, within the park, offers swimming, boating, and fishing. The park is heavily wooded, and some parts of it contain reclaimed strip mines. The park has a wildlife exhibit.

SHARPSVILLE, Town; Pop. 769; Tipton County; central Indiana; Zip Code 46068; 8 mi. SSE of Kokomo in an agricultural area noted for livestock and feed grains. The town is a manufacturing center for fiberglass boats, pedal boats, specialty wire, lumber, chemicals, and metal farm structures.

SHELBURN, Town; Pop. 1,147; Sullivan County; SW Indiana; Zip Code 47879; 21 mi. S of Terre Haute. The town was founded in 1818 in a region noted for a variety of natural resources (coal, oil, timber, fertile soils). Its real growth did not begin until 1868, when the district's first of 12 bituminous coal mines was opened. The town became incorporated in 1872 as a direct result of the mining industry's prosperity.

Agriculture, along with coal mining and lumber milling, plays an important role in Shelburn's present economic picture. Grain, livestock, and poultry farms are plentiful, and dairy products are shipped to local marketing centers.

Near Shelburn is Morrison Creek, site of the May 13, 1815, massacre by Potawatomi Indians of Lt. John Morrison and four of his soldiers. The incident was the last encounter between the white man and the Indian in the region.

SHELBY, County; Pop. 37,797; central Indiana; area 409 sq. mi.; drained by the Big Blue River and Flatrock and Sugar creeks. Shelby County was part of a huge territory known as the New Purchase, which was ceded by the Delaware Indians to the U.S. on Oct. 3, 1818. The county was officially established in 1821 and named for Isaac Shelby, twice governor of Kentucky and a resident of Indiana. The town of Shelbyville is the county seat. The county encompasses a rich farming region noted for corn, hay, grain, stock raising, and dairying,

SHELBYVILLE, City; Pop. 15,336; seat of Shelby County; central Indiana; Zip Code 46176; on the Big Blue River, 27 mi. SE of Indianapolis. The city was platted in 1822 and named for Isaac Shelby, officer of the American Revolution and the Indian wars, and the first governor of Kentucky. Shelbyville's location--in the middle of Indiana's richest corn, livestock, and dairy belt-- has aided its growth as a leading trade and manufacturing center. Manufactures include furniture, paper products, fiberglass, stoves, lawn mowers, automobile parts, clothing, dairy products, and canned goods.

Shelbyville was the home of author Charles Major (1856-1913) and Thomas A. Hendricks (1819-1885), vice-president of the U.S. and governor of Indiana. A stone marker outside the city commemorates the building of the first railroad in Indiana. The track was 1.5 mi. long and had wooded rails and horse-drawn carts. Today, the Penn Central Railroad serves Shelbyville.

The Shelby County Historical Society maintains the Bear of Blue River Trail, a 15 mi. nature walk along the Blue River. The trail passes over Hog Back Ridge, an ancient Indian burial ground.

SHERIDAN, Town; Pop. 2,046; Hamilton County; central Indiana; Zip Code 46069; 25 mi. N of Indianapolis in an agricultural area (feed grains, livestock, dairy products). Sheridan is a commercial trade center for cement products,

Dictionary of Places

canned goods, condensed milk, flour, chemicals, and packed meats.

SHIPSHEWANA, Town; Pop. 524; Lagrange County; NE Indiana; Zip Code 46565; 20 mi. E of Elkhart in a farming area that includes one of the largest Amish communities in the U.S. Their closed horse-drawn buggies can be seen in and around town. Nearby is Lake Shipshewana, a popular resort. Near the lake is a 12-ft. stone memorial that marks the grave of Chief Shipshewana, a Potawatomi leader.

SHIRLEY, Town; Pop. 817; on the border of Hancock and Henry counties; E central Indiana; Zip Code 47384; 32 mi. ENE of Indianapolis in an agricultural area (livestock and feed grains).

SHOALS, Town; Pop. 853; seat of Martin County, SW Indiana; Zip Code 47581; on the East Fork of the White River; 21 mi. E of Washington. The town was founded in 1816 and was named for its

location at a shallow ford, or shoals, in the river. The area is very picturesque; high hills and woodlands interspersed with caves and cliffs surround the town. Jug Rock and The Pinnacle *(q.q.v.),* eroded rock formations, are out 276 ft. above the White River near Shoals. According to legend, an Indian silver treasure remains hidden in the caves around McBride's Bluff.

The townspeople are engaged in lumber milling and furniture and button production. Farming and fishing supplement their income. Near the town is the U.S. Gypsum Company plant, which employs a large portion of the population in its underground mines.

Beautiful Hindostan Falls, Martin State Forest, and Trinity Springs, all popular tourist attractions, are situated near Shoals.

SILVER LAKE, Pop. 528; Kosciusko County; N Indiana; 40 mi. W of Fort Wayne. Silver Lake is basically a resort town surrounded by lakes, but is also a shipping point for vegetables.

SOMERVILLE, Town; Pop. 223; Gibson County; SW Indiana; Zip Code 47583; 23 mi. NNE of Evansville in an agricultural and bituminous coal-mining area.

SOUTH BEND, City; Pop. 105,511; seat of St. Joseph County, N Indiana; Zip Code 46600; on the St. Joseph River, 75 mi. ESE of Chicago, Illinois. The area around the present city was first visited by Europeans in 1675, when Pere Marquette explored the region from N Illinois to the shores of Lake Michigan. Four years later, Robert Cavelier sieur de La Salle, the French explorer, made a portage between the St. Joseph and Kankakee rivers, opening a new passage between the St. Lawrence Basin and the Mississippi River. He later succeeded in obtaining a treaty of alliance between the Miami and Illinois Indians, signed under the Council Oak which lies in South Bend's Highland Cemetery.

In 1820, the American Fur Company appointed agents to establish fur-trading posts throughout the Northwest Territory. Two of them, Alexis Coquillard from Detroit and Pierre F. Navarre from Monroe, established a post on the St. Joseph River for those who traded with the Indians in N Indiana and S Michigan. The post became known as Big St. Joseph Station. Settlers, however, called it "The Bend," or "South Bend," for a meander in the river. The latter name was finally adopted in 1830. South Bend was platted in 1831, and its designation as seat of newly- formed St. Joseph County followed shortly thereafter. Incorporation to town status came in 1835 and to city status in 1865.

The city's growth was slow until 1925, when Henry and Clement Studebaker opened a blacksmith and wagon shop there. The business was the foundation for the Studebaker Brothers Manufacturing Company (1852), which was for many years the mainstay of the city's economy. South Bend remains a diversified industrial center, whose manufactures include automobile accessories, aircraft and parts, industrial and farm machinery, foundry products, ranges, sewing machines, paint, paper, clothing, textiles, watches, toys, asphalt insulation, beer, and sporting goods.

The city is the seat of Indiana University-South Bend

Dictionary of Places

campus (1933) and two Roman Catholic universities are located in the nearby suburb of Notre Dame: the University of Notre Dame (1842) and St. Mary's College (1843). Leeper Park, in the city contains Pierre Navarre's original log cabin. The Northern Indiana Historical Society Museum is housed in the former St. Joseph Courthouse (1855) and contains more than 15,000 historical artifacts reflecting the life and times of pioneer Indiana. Entertainment and recreational facilities can be found at Storyland Zoo, at the 160-acre Rum Village Park, and at Potawatomi Park with its conservatory and indoor swimming pool.

●HISTORICAL PLACES... (See Hist. Places Sect for details.)
Old Courthouse (Second St. Joseph County Courthouse); Oliver, Joseph D., House (Copshaholm); Tippecanoe Place (Studebaker House).

SOUTH MILFORD, Town; Pop. 200; Lagrange County; N Indiana; Zip Code 46785; 15 mi. SE of Lagrange in an agricultural and dairying area. The town is a manufacturing center for insulated wire products, hardwood lumber, and electronic wire products.

SOUTHPORT, Town; Pop. 1,969; Marion County; central Indiana; Zip Code 46227; 9 mi. S of Indianapolis in an industrial and agricultural area. Southport is a quiet residential suburb of Indianapolis.

SOUTH WHITLEY, Town; Pop. 1,482; Whitley County, NE Indiana; Zip Code 46787; on the Eel River; 25 mi. W of Fort Wayne in an agricultural area noted for livestock and feed grains. It is a shipping point for railroad equipment and grain.

SPEEDWAY, Town; Pop. 13,092; Marion County; central Indiana; Zip Code 46224; just W of Indianapolis. The town was laid out in 1912 and incorporated in 1926. It is the home of the Indianapolis Speedway, which stages the Indianapolis "500" race every Memorial Day. More than 250,000 fans annually arrive to see some of the greatest race-car drivers in the world compete for top honors. A museum at the track has an exhibit of race cars which date back to 1909. The rear-view mirror, the balloon tire, and ethyl gasoline are a few of the many innovations inaugurated at the track. The speedway itself embraces 433 acres, has a 2.5 mi. long rectangular track, and has a grandstand with a seating capacity of 234,000. Most of the residents of Speedway are employed by factories in town. Manufactures include storage batteries, steel castings, and electrical goods. In 1970, Speedway was one of 4 small communities that chose to remain independent of the expanded metropolitan government of Indianapolis, known as Uni-Gov.

SPENCER, Town; Pop. 2,609; seat of Owen County; SW central Indiana; Zip Code 47460, on the West Fork of the White River, 45 mi. SW of Indianapolis. The town was settled in 1815 and named for Capt. Spier Spencer, killed at the Battle of Tippecanoe (1811). Several distinguished citizens--including the Hoosier poets William Vaugh Moody and William Herschell--made their homes in Spencer. It was also the home of Ban Johnson, one of the founders of the American Baseball League, and of Samuel Ralston, a former governor of Indiana.

Spencer is a farming community (corn, fruit, livestock) and manufacturer of food products, drugs, and typewriter ribbons. Bituminous coal mining and limestone quarrying are carried out on a lesser scale. Many of the town's older buildings are constructed of St. Genevieve limestone, which characteristically turns whiter with age.

Recreational facilities can be found at nearby McCormick's Creek State Park *(q.v.)* and at Shady Lake.

SPENCER, County; Pop. 17,134; SW Indiana;; area 396 sq. mi.; bounded on the S by the Ohio River and drained by the Anderson River and Little Pigeon Creek. The county was formed in February 1818 and named for Capt. Spier Spencer, who was killed at the Battle of Tippecanoe (1811). The county seat is Rockport.

The area is noted for livestock, feed grains, and poultry, and is also a center for manufacturing. Leading industries produce bricks, tile, concrete blocks, buttons, flour, and lumber. The Lincoln Boyhood National Memorial and Lin-

Dictionary of Places

coln State Park *(q.q.v.)* are located within the county.
- HISTORICAL PLACES... (See Hist. Places Sect for details.)

Brown-Kercheval House.

SPENCERVILLE, Town; Pop. 340; DeKalb County; NE Indiana; Zip Code 46788; 12 mi. S of Auburn in an agricultural area noted for livestock and feed grains. Spencerville is a trade center for swimming pool parts, boats, petroleum equipment, and livestock and poultry equipment.

SPICELAND, Town; Pop. 757; Henry County; E central Indiana; Zip Code 47385; 8 mi. SSW of New Castle. The town was settled in 1828 by Quakers who farmed the fertile surrounding soils. Today, the main occupation is still farming. Spiceland Academy (1834), now a high school, includes the noted historian Charles A. Beard among its alumni.

SPRING MILL STATE PARK, Lawrence County; S Indiana; just E of Mitchell. Spring Mill, one of the best-loved parks in Indiana, contains an authentic restoration of an early pioneer village and an 1816 gristmill with an overshot waterwheel. Col. Richard Lieber (1869-1944), a former state conservation officer who was responsible for the preservation of the village, said of it: "You come down from the top of the hill 200 feet and you go back 100 years." The mill grinds corn for visitors who come to the park year round. The village includes many of the original residences and the hat shop, post office, boot shop, and apothecary. A visitor's center to commemorate Virgil "Gus" Grissom, the U.S. astronaut who was killed in a launched fire at Cape Canaveral in 1967, has been erected in the park.

The park consists of 1,139 acres of hills, woods, and caves. Virgin woodlands covering 100 acres contain some of the largest specimens of white oak and tulip known in the area. There are many small caverns within the park, most of which can be explored on foot. Of special note are the Donaldson and Twin caves, which have unusual limestone formation, underground streams with blind fish, and daily boat excursions. Also featured at the park is the annual candlelight tour of the pioneer village, which takes place in September in conjunction with the Mitchell persimmon festival. Park activities including hiking, swimming, horseback riding, camping, and boating.

SPRINGPORT, Town; Pop. 194; Henry County; E Indiana; Zip Code 47386; 10 mi. S of Muncie, in an agricultural area (feed grains and livestock).

SPRING VALLEY STATE FISH AND WILDLIFE AREA, Orange County; N Indiana; 8 mi. SE of French Lick in a scenic wooded and hilly region. Water recreation is available on a 127-acre lake which has a maximum depth of 37.5 feet. There are also facilities for camping and picnicking. The game area encompasses 1,165 acres of land.

SPURGEON, Town; Pop. 149; Pike County; SW Indiana; Zip Code 47584; 26 mi. NE of Evansville in an area noted for agriculture, oil-wells, and bituminous coal mines.

SQUIRE BOONE CAVERNS, natural limestone caves near Corydon; Harrison County; S Indiana. The caverns were discovered in 1790 by Squire Boone, a brother of Daniel Boone, while he was on a hunting trip. On one occasion, he was attacked by Indians and hid in the caves. He returned there many times and, at the mouth of the caverns, built a gristmill which was powered by an underground stream. Boone died in 1815 and was buried in the cave. His grave was later desecrated, and his remains were removed to a secret place in Kentucky.

The caverns became privately owned in 1973. They contain many examples of cave formations, among them the world's largest known rimstone formation. (Rimstone, or travertine, as it is most commonly called, is formed by water running over rock-pool ledges, evaporating, and leaving a drapery-like deposit.) Cave onyx, stalagtites, stalagmites, cave pearls, and a waterfall are found within the caverns. An artificial exit has been blasted out of the solid rock.

STAR CITY, Town; Pop. 500; Pulaski County; N Indiana; Zip Code 46985; 7 mi. SE of Winamac in an agricultural

Dictionary of Places

and dairying area. The town is a manufacturing center for farm supplies, millwork, and concrete blocks.

STARKE, County; Pop. 19,280; NW Indiana; area 310 sq. mi.; bordered on the NW by the Kankakee River and drained by the Yellow River and tributaries of the Kankakee River. The county was organized in 1844 and named for Gen. John Starke, a war hero. Knox is the county seat.

Starke County is situated in a rich agricultural area especially noted for its mint and onions. There is some manufacturing at Knox. Koontz Lake, in the NE corner of the county, is famous for its excellent fishing.

STARVE HOLLOW STATE FOREST, Jackson County; S Indiana; 3 mi. SE of Vallonia. Starve Hollow encompasses 270 acres, including a 170-acre lake. Recreational facilities include picnicking, fishing, camping, boating, and swimming.

STAUNTON, Town; Pop. 592; Clay County; W Indiana; Zip Code 47881; 12 mi. E of Terre Haute in an agricultural area noted for livestock and feed grains and some bituminous coal mining.

STUEBEN, County; Pop. 20,159; NE Indiana; area 309 sq. mi.; bounded on the N by Michigan and E by Ohio, and drained by Pigeon Creek.

The county was organized in February 1832 and named for Baron Stueben, who joined the U.S. army during the American Revolution. The county seat is Angola.

Stueben County contains numerous Indian mounds and burial grounds, indicating settlement of the region by Indian tribes over the centuries. In addition to being a rich farming, timber, and dairying area, the county is also a popular resort spot with numerous lakes. The N central area encompasses Pokagon State Park *(q.v.)*, with beautiful Lake James.

STILESVILLE, Town; Pop. 298; Hendricks County; central Indiana; Zip Code 46180; on Mill Creek; 27 mi. WSW of Indianapolis in fertile agricultural area ideally suited for oats, wheat, soybeans, and feed corn.

STINESVILLE, Town; Pop. 204; Monroe County; S central Indiana; Zip Code 47464; 11 mi. NW of Bloomington in an agricultural area (livestock and feed grains).

SULLIVAN, City; Pop. 4,663; seat of Sullivan County; SW Indiana; Zip Code 47882; near Busseron Creek; 25 mi. S of Terre Haute. The city was platted in 1842 and named for Gen. Daniel Sullivan, an Army courier. Sullivan prospered as a coal-mining and agricultural trade center. In 1925, it was the scene for one of the state's worst mining disasters. A gas explosion at the City Coal Mine buried 55 miners under tons of rubble. Deadly after-damp impeded rescue operations, and it took 2 days to reach the men. Only 4 of the 55 survived.

Sullivan was the home of William H. Hayes, movie czar and postmaster general of the U.S., who was in charge of the "Hayes Office," a 1930s censorship board.

Sullivan is a modern manufacturing city whose diverse products include machine-shop tools, cheese, fertilizer, and lumber. Oil and gas wells are nearby, and coal mining continues to be an important aspect of the city's economy.

Two popular local resort areas are at nearby Lake Paradise and Sullivan County Park.

SULLIVAN, County; Pop. 19,889; SW Indiana; area 457 sq. mi.; bounded on the W by the Wabash River and drained by Busseron and Maria creeks. The county was formed in January 1817 and named for Gen. Daniel Sullivan, who was killed by Indians while carrying dispatches for George Rogers Clark. The county seat is at Sullivan. The county is located in a rich coal, oil, and natural gas area. Agriculture (grain, fruit, livestock, poultry, dairy products) is also prevalent, and there is diversified manufacturing in Sullivan and Farmersburg.

SULPHUR SPRINGS, Town; Pop. 257; Henry County; E central Indiana; Z 47388; 7 mi. NNW of New Castle in an agricultural area (livestock and feed grains).

Dictionary of Places

SUMMITVILLE, Town; Pop. 1,010; Madison County; E central Indiana; Zip Code 46070; 15 mi. S of Marion. Summitville was incorporated as a town in 1881. It is basically a farming community (chiefly feed grains, livestock), but has a canned foods plant. The largest drain tile business in the country was at one time located there.

SUNMAN, Town; Pop. 623; Ripley County; SE Indiana; Zip Code 47041; 23 mi. ESE of Greensburg in an agricultural area (feed grains, livestock). Resort facilities can be found at nearby Bar- K Lake.

SWAYZEE, Town; Pop. 1,059; Grant County; E central Indiana; Zip Code 46986; 9 mi. WSW of Marion in an agricultural area (livestock and feed grains). There is a canned foods plant in town.

SWEETSER, Town; Pop. 924; Grant County; central Indiana; Zip Code 46987; 6 mi. W of Marion in an agricultural and dairying region. Sweetser is a trade center for ready-mix concrete, liquid and dry fertilizers, and tomatoes.

SWITZ CITY, Town; Pop. 257; Greene County; SW Indiana; Zip Code 47465; 35 mi. NE of Vincennes in an agricultural area (livestock and feed grains). Many of the inhabitants are employed in the nearby bituminous coal mines.

SWITZERLAND, County; Pop. 6,306; SE Indiana; area 221 sq. mi.; bounded on the E and S by the Ohio River. The county was organized in October 1814 and named for the European country of Switzerland. The county seat is at Vevay.

Rivers and creeks have formed large alluvial bottomlands which are ideal for the cultivation of feed grains, tobacco, and vegetables. The major industry is the manufacture of shoes.

SYLVAN LAKE, Noble County; NE Indiana; just E of Rome City. The 1,200-acre artificial lake was built in 1827 as a feeder for the proposed Michigan and Erie Canal. The canal was never completed, and today the lake serves as

Rome City's principal tourist attraction. The south shore is the site of the Gene Stratton Porter State Memorial *(q.v.)*

SYRACUSE, Town; Pop. 1,546; Kosciusko County, N Indiana; Zip Code 46567; on Lake Wawasee, 32 mi. SE of South Bend. Surrounded by lakes, it is basically a resort community. There is also a cedar chest business in town, which employs a large number of residents. Lake Wawasee, named for Chief Wawasee, has 21 mi. of shoreline and is the largest natural lake in Indiana. The Wawasee Fish Hatchery is at the SE corner of the lake. Syracuse also has two municipal golf courses.

T.C. STEELE STATE MEMORIAL, memorial to the famous Indiana artist, Theodore Clement Steele; near Belmont, Brown County; S central Indiana. The memorial includes the painter's home and studio, which are situated on a 211-acre tract. Steele was the originator of the Brown County Art Colony.

TELL CITY, City; Pop. 8,088; Perry County; S Indiana; Zip Code 47586; on the Ohio River; 45 mi. W of Evansville. The city was founded in 1857 by a colony of Swiss immigrants who named it for William Tell, their legendary hero. Old World craftsmanship has contributed to Tell City's renown as a leading furniture maker. Other manufactures include electronic equipment, electric motors, woolen textiles, river barges, and pleasure craft. There are also an oil refinery, distillery, coal mines, and packing plants. The Tell City Chair Company (1865) manufactured the "Jackie Kennedy" ballroom chairs ordered in 1962 for the White House by the former First Lady. Byrd's Echo Lake, 3 mi. E of Tell City, is a popular resort.

TENNYSON, Town; Pop. 267; Warrick County; SW Indiana; Zip Code 47637; 27 mi. ENE of Evansville in an agricultural and bituminous coal-mining area.

TERRE HAUTE, City; Pop. 57,483; seat of Vigo County; W Indiana; Zip Code 47808; on a plateau above the Wabash River. The city was founded in 1816 on the border between the former French colonial provinces of Canada and Louisiana. It was named Terre Haute ("high land") by the French,

Dictionary of Places

who governed the area until 1763. Fort Harrison was built in 1811 by the Americans three mi. to the N, and in 1818, the town was designated the county seat. Terre Haute was officially incorporated as a town in 1832, and as a city in 1853.

During the early 1800s, Terre Haute was an important point on the National Road and the Wabash and Erie Canal. New factories were established along the canal, including a flour mill, foundry, brewery, candle factory, and blast furnace. Before long, the city was known as the "Pittsburgh of the West." After the decline of the canal in the 1860s, the railroads continued the economic expansion of the city. Large-scale mining of nearby vast bituminous coal deposits added new sources of fuel. Much of the coal was later mined to supply World War I demands. The coal- mining business increased steadily, although several miners strikes caused periodic declines.

Terre Haute was the birthplace of Paul Dreiser, the composer of Indiana's state song "On the Banks of the Wabash"; of his brother, the novelist Theodore Dreiser; and of Eugene V. Debs, socialist leader and founder of the American Railway Union. Max Ehrmann, who wrote the poem *Desiderata*, was a lifelong resident, and Ida Husted Harper, a journalist, suffragist, and biographer of Susan B. Anthony, began her career in Terre Haute in 1872 by writing regular columns for the local newspaper, residing in the city from 1871 to 1890.

Terre Haute is a leading industrial, mining and railroad center. Manufactures are diverse, including brick, tile, glass, coke by-products, steel, paper, clothing, pharmaceuticals, liquor, and food products. In 1984, the first compact disc produced in America was made in Terre Haute. Disaster struck Terre Haute in 1963 when an explosion at the Home Packing Company killed 17 people and injured 50 more. Two more explosions followed within a month, causing more injuries and damages. Leaking gas was said to be the cause, and city residents sarcastically began to refer to Terre Haute as "Boomtown, U.S.A."

Of cultural interest are the Sheldon-Swope Art Gallery, which features European, American, Oriental, and African works of art; the Historical Museum of Wabash Valley, housed in an 1868 Italianate mansion; and the Early Wheels Museum, which has a collection of antique and classic automobiles.

Terre Haute is the seat of Indiana State University (1865), a four-year, fully-accredited school with an enrollment of 13,000 students. The university also has a School of Graduate Studies and the Turman Gallery of Fine Arts. Nearby are St. Mary-of-the- Woods College (1840) for women, and Rose Polytechnic Institute (1874), the first private and independent engineering school west of the Alleghenies. Of note is the J.W. Davis Company, the largest greenhouse in the world, with 35 acres cultivated under glass.

Many recreational and resort spots can be found in and around Terre Haute. They include Deming Park, 160 acres in town; Raccoon Lake State Recreation Area; Fowler Park; Hartman; North, South, and Walton lakes; the Rea Park Golf Course; and Indiana State University Stadium Golf Course.

●HISTORICAL PLACES... (See Hist. Places Sect for details.)

Condit House; Debs, Eugene V., House; Dresser, Paul, Birthplace; Sage-Robinson-Nagel House; State Bank of Indiana, Branch of (Memorial Hall).

THORNTOWN, Town; Pop. 1,506; Boone County; central Indiana; Zip Code 46071; on Sugar Creek; 18 mi. ENE of Crawfordsville. On the site of an 18th-century Indian village, called Keewaskee ("place of thorns"), the town was an early trading post and Jesuit mission. From 1818 until the Indians were removed in 1828, Thorntown was an Indian Reservation. The land tract was sold in 1829 to Cornelius Westfall, who platted the present town. Modern Thorntown is a trade center for livestock and feed grains, and has poultry hatcheries and a livestock serum plant.

TIPPECANOE, Town; Pop. 350; Marshall County; N Indiana; Zip Code 46570; 18 mi. SE of Plymouth. The town is

Dictionary of Places

a manufacturing center for mill equipment, iron castings, plastic parts, tools, dies, metal siding, building components, scout hats, and pallets.

TIPPECANOE, County; Pop. 109,378; W central Indiana; area 500 sq. mi.; crossed by the Wabash River and drained by the Tippecanoe River and Wildcat Creek. The county was organized in March 1826 and named for the Tippecanoe River. It was in Tippecanoe County that Gen. William Henry Harrison defeated the Indians led by Tenskwatawa, the Shawnee Prophet and brother of Tecumseh, in 1811. The county seat is at Lafayette.

Although most of its surface is level, sections of Tippecanoe County along the Wabash River are broken into rugged hills ranging from 50 to 200 ft. in height. Agriculture, coal mining, and manufacturing are the mainstays of the economy. Diversified manufacturing includes the production of aluminum extrusions, prefabricated homes, automotive gears, and fabricated metals.

TIPPECANOE BATTLEFIELD STATE MEMORIAL, Battle Ground; Tippecanoe County; W central Indiana; 7 mi. N of Lafayette. The memorial marks the site of the Battle of Tippecanoe, Nov. 7, 1811, in which soldiers of the 4th Regiment under the leadership of Gen. William Henry Harrison, were victorious over Indian forces led by Tenskwatawa, the Shawnee Prophet. Tenskwatawa, who was Tecumseh's brother, led 700 warriors into battle in an attempt to win back Indian lands and drive the white settlers south of the Ohio River. The Indian losses were reportedly greater than those of Harrison's men, 37 of whom were killed, 29 fatally wounded, and 150 others wounded. A 100-ft. shaft marks the site, and smaller stones indicate where officers fell. The soldiers were buried in a mass grave.

TIPPECANOE RIVER, Indiana; rises in NW Whitley County; flows 166 mi. NW to W past Monterey and then SW to the Wabash River, of which it is a major tributary. The river was the site of the 1811 Battle of Tippecanoe (at Battle Ground) in which Gen. William Henry Harrison defeated the Indians led by Tenskwatawa, The Shawnee Prophet.

The Tippecanoe River is the site of Indiana's largest hydroelectric power plant, the Oakdale Plant, which has a producing capacity for 11,000 kilowatts. Tippecanoe River State Park is located near Winamac in Pulaski County.

TIPPECANOE RIVER STATE PARK, Pulaski Count; NW Indiana; just N of Winamac. The park, which encompasses 2,761 acres of land, stretches for 8 mi. along the Tippecanoe River. The scenic woods have winding roads and hiking trails, and there are facilities for group camps and family camping. There are also areas for swimming, fishing, and picnicking.

TIPTON, City; Pop. 4,751; seat of Tipton County; central Indiana; Zip Code 46072; on Cicero Creek; 15 mi. SSE of Kokomo. Originally known as Canton, the city was platted in 1845 and named after John Tipton. Immigrants began settling here in the 1830's, coming from such countries as Sweden, Germany, Scotland, Ireland, England, and France. Agriculturally, its products include corn, soybeans, wheat, and tomatoes. Manufactures include machinery, furniture, piston rings, canned goods, cigars, chemicals, and brooms. Library Park contains a memorial erected to celebrate the state's 100th anniversary. A museum containing pioneer relics is located in the county courthouse.

TIPTON, County; Pop. 16,650; central Indiana; area 261 sq. mi.; drained by Cicero, Turkey, and Wildcat creeks. The county was organized in May 1844 and named for Gen. John Tipton, a U.S. senator (1832-39). The city of Tipton (formerly Canton) is the county seat.

Much of the county, which is level, was once covered by water, but the many marshlands have been drained and turned over to farming. The extremely fertile soils produce vegetables and grains of all kinds. Food canning is the leading industry.

TIPTON TILL PLAIN, vast glacial morainic deposit covering central Indiana. During the Pleistocene Epoch, glaciers covered most of Indiana and laid down what came to be known as the Tipton Till Plain. The ice, at times 2,000 ft. thick, leveled the entire area. The glacial subsoil of the

Dictionary of Places

plain is many feet deep and composed of finely ground rock flour, clay, sand, and gravel. The area has been traditionally noted for its fine farm and pasture lands.

TOPEKA, Town; Pop. 912; Lagrange County; NE Indiana; Zip Code 46571; 24 mi. ESE of Elkhart in an agricultural area (cattle, sheep, poultry, feed grains). Emma Lake and the L.C.C. Association Golf Course offer recreational facilities.

TRAFALGAR, Town; Pop. 531; Johnson County; central Indiana; Zip Code 46181; 25 mi. S of Indianapolis in an area noted for some of the best corn production in the world.

TRAIL CREEK, Town; Pop. 2,463; La Porte County NE Indiana; just E of Michigan City in the sand dune region of the state. The area is noted for fruit orchards specializing in apples, cherries, pears, cider, honey, and grapes.

TRI-COUNTY FISH AND WILDLIFE AREA, Kosciusko County; N Indiana; 2 mi. NE of North Webster in a gently rolling area of prairie lands. Its 3,437 acres include a 500-acre lake which has excellent fishing and boating.

TRINITY SPRINGS, Martin County; S Indiana; about 8 mi. N of Loogootee. The springs, together with nearby Indian Springs, were popular health and recreation spas in the early 20th century.

Eleven hotels, a dance hall, bowling alley, swimming pool, and restaurant were part of the facilities. Today, only crumbling buildings remain, and the springs are overgrown by brush.

TROY, Town; Pop. 465; Perry County; S Indiana; Zip Code 47588; at the confluence of the Ohio and Anderson rivers, 3 mi. NNW of Tell City. Troy was one of the first settlements downstream from the falls of the Ohio. Many of the early houses were built of sandstone quarried from the hill around which the town is situated. Early settlers from Virginia turned Troy into an important river shipping point, and it was the county seat until 1818.

Above the Ohio River on a bluff is the "Christ of the Ohio," a statue erected by Dr. James, a Tell City physician, to inspire riverboat travelers. Today, Troy is a quiet farming community. Many of the residents are employed at the nearby bituminous coal mines.

TURKEY RUN STATE PARK, Parke County; W Indiana; near Marshall. The park derives its name from the thousands of wild turkeys that once sought shelter in the area. Turkey Run is 2,181 acres of rugged gorges, steep canyons, glens, bathing beaches, and waterfalls. Formed by the erosive action of Sugar Creek, a tributary of the Wabash River, the park is a haven for thousands of tourists who visit it annually. Sugar Creek abounds in black bass, crappie, and rock bass. Miles of foot trails lead through virgin forest of black walnut, oak, and poplar. There is a new campground and the remodeled Turkey Run Inn.

TWIN CAVES, Spring Mill State Park *(q.v.),* Lawrence County; S Indiana; near Mitchell. Twin Caves are part of a vast system of limestone caverns which traverse the park and are available for exploration. The caves are unique in that they contain a small lake; boat rides are frequently taken into them. The boats usually go in for 475 ft., but Upper Twin Cave has been explored by this means for 4,674 ft. Both have typical cave animals and limestone formations.

ULEN, Town; Pop. 50; Boone County.; central Indiana; just N of Lebanon in an agricultural area (livestock and feed grains).

UNION, County; Pop. 6,582; E Indiana; area 168 sq. mi.; bounded on the E by the Ohio and drained by the East Fork of the Whitewater River. The county, organized in February 1821, derived its name from the hope that it would harmonize difficulties existing in relation to Wayne and Fayette counties, which border it N and W, respectively. Liberty is the county seat.

The eastern part of the county is level and composed of deep fertile soils. Farming in the region produces quality corn, wheat, hay, and tobacco. There is also livestock and

Dictionary of Places

hog raising on the less fertile areas. The western part has an abundance of limestone gills which produce high-quality building stone. There are also several bituminous coal mines and sand and gravel pits. There is manufacturing at Uniontown, Sturgis, and Morganfield. Whitewater State Park *(q.v.)* is located nearby.

UNION CITY, City; Pop. 3,612; Randolph County; E Indiana; Zip Code 47390; 30 mi. E of Muncie. Union City straddles the state line between Indiana and Ohio, although three-fourths of it is in Indiana. It also sits astride the Quaker Trace, a favorite route for runaway slaves which linked Richmond and Fort Wayne. The trace was also the first road through Randolph County.

Union City is a manufacturing center for bus bodies, automobile parts, furniture, luggage, canned goods, and dairy equipment. It is also a shipping point for agricultural products and livestock. It contains a memorial to the Greenville Treaty Line (1784).

UNIONDALE, Town; Pop. 289; Wells County; E Indiana; Zip Code 46791; 19 mi. SSW of Fort Wayne in an agricultural area (livestock and feed grains).

UNION MILLS, Town; Pop. 600; La Porte County; N Indiana; Zip Code 46382; 11 mi. S of La Porte in an agricultural area noted for feed grains and livestock. Union Mills has a cluster of 11 Indian mounds from which have been excavated human skeletons, clay pipes, hatchets, and other artifacts. The artifacts are on display in local museums. The town is otherwise a quiet farming community with a farm cooperative that stocks grains, fencing, coal, farm supplies, and fertilizer.

UNIVERSAL, Town; Pop. 392; Vermillion County; W Indiana; Zip Code 47884; 12 mi. NNW of Terre Haute in an agricultural area noted for livestock and feed grains. Bituminous coal mining is an important activity.

UPLAND, Town; Pop. 3,295; Grant County; E central Indiana; Zip Code 46989; 11 mi. ESE of Marion. Upland was platted in 1867 in conjunction with the coming of the railroads. It thrived for a time as a sawmill center, but with the natural gas boom of 1887, Upland mushroomed into a self-sufficient manufacturing center (window glass, gloves, canned goods, lumber).

Upland is the seat of Taylor University (1893), a United Brethren coeducational college of liberal arts. Of note is the Ayres Memorial Library.

Recreational facilities can be found at nearby Kilgore and Pine Lakes.

URBANA, Town; Pop. 350; Wabash County; N Indiana; Zip Code 46990; 7 mi. N of Wabash in an agricultural area noted for feed grains and livestock. Urbana is a manufacturer of farm equipments, metal stampings, seed sowers and spreaders, and poultry equipment.

VALLONIA, Town; Pop. 500; Jackson County; S Indiana; Zip Code 47281; 4 mi. SW of Brownstown in an agricultural and timbering area. Vallonia is a trade center for lumber and feeds. It was founded in 1812 on the site of Fort Vallonia, a French outpost. The location was once considered for the state capitol.

VALPARAISO, City; Pop. 24,414; seat of Porter County; NW Indiana; Zip Code 46383; 18 mi. ESE of Gary. The site of Valparaiso was originally purchased from the Potawatomi Indians by the U.S. government in 1832. The first white settlers arrived in 1834. Valparaiso became the county seat in 1837 and obtained city status in 1865. It is popularly known as "Valpo" in the vicinity.

The city has become a major industrial and manufacturing center, and the majority of Valparaiso residents are employed in local industries. Major enterprises include Coca-Cola, Owens- Corning Fiberglass Corporation, and McGill Manufacturing Company. Principal manufactures include bakelite products, magnets, ball bearings, electric lamp guards, automobile parts, refined metals, fiberglass tanks, steel rollers, and automatic sprinkler systems.

Higher educational opportunities are plentiful in Valparaiso. Located there is Valparaiso University (1859), originally owned by citizens of the city and by the Methodist

Dictionary of Places

Church. It was purchased in 1925 by the newly-formed Lutheran University Association, and has since remained under Lutheran administration. The university is a fully-accredited, four-year college offering 57 fields of study. Average enrollment is 4,000 students. Of note is the Chapel of the Resurrection (1956), the world's largest college chapel, with a seating capacity of 3,000. Architecturally, the chapel resembles the Church of the Nativity in Bethlehem, Israel. The Brandt Campanile, 140 ft. high, plays morning and evening hymns and marks the class hours. Also in Valparaiso is the Valparaiso Technical Institute (1874), known nationally for its excellent electronics and communications programs.

Porter Memorial Hospital and Porter County Municipal Airport serve the surrounding area. Recreational facilities can be found at nearby Indiana Dunes State Park *(q.v.)*.

Valparaiso is situated on the Valparaiso Glacial Moraine, and is surrounded by rolling hills and glacial lakes that provide unlimited recreational facilities. The Porter County Historical Society Museum, in the County Building, has pioneer relics and dresses from the Lincoln inaugural ball.

Annual events include the Porter County Fair, which features agricultural displays.

VAN BUREN, Town; Pop. 934; Grant County; E central Indiana; Zip Code 46991; 11 mi. ENE of Marion in an agricultural area (livestock and feed grains).

VANDERBURGH, County; Pop. 168,772; SW Indiana; area 241 sq. mi.; bounded on the S by the Ohio River and drained by Pigeon Creek. The county was organized in February 1818 and named for Capt. Henry Vanderburgh of the American Revolution. Evansville is the county seat.

Farming and manufacturing go hand in hand in Vanderburgh County. Fertile soils are used for the cultivation of winter wheat, soybeans, and corn. Hog raising is also a leading activity. The county is a major manufacturing and market center for refrigerators, meat, flour, beer, fabricated metals, construction machinery, air conditioners, and pharmaceuticals.

Prehistoric Indians lived in the area, and their artifacts can be found throughout the county. Angel Mounds, near Evansville, is the site of an ancient city of Mound Builders from the Mississippian culture.

VERMILLION, County; Pop. 16,793; W Indiana; area 263 sq. mi.; bounded on the W by Illinois, E by the Wabash River, and drained by the Vermillion River. The county was formed in January 1824 and named for the Vermillion River. Newport has been the county seat since it was organized.

Vermillion is sometimes called the "Shoe String County" because of its long, narrow shape, averaging only 6 mi. in width. The land surface is high and generally level, except near the streams. Seams of cannel (block) coal underlie the land. The beds average 5 to 7 ft. in thickness and are interstratified with fine-quality fire clay. Coal mining is a major activity. Feed grains and fruit are grown on the bottomlands, and there is some manufacturing at Cayuga and Clinton.

VERNON, Town; Pop. 370; seat of Jennings County; SE Indiana; Zip Code 47282; on Vernon Creek; 20 mi. NW of Madison. The provisions of the land grant of 1815 included a clause which stipulated that Vernon remain the county seat forever.

During the Civil War, 400 men gathered in Vernon to ward off Confederate Gen. John Hunt Morgan and his 2,200 cavalrymen. It was the only town in Indiana not conquered by Morgan's Raiders.

The North American House, across from the courthouse, contains the Jennings County Historical Society Museum. The house, built in the 1820s, was a former stagecoach stop and inn. The Milhouse Home is the birthplace of former Pres. Richard Nixon's mother. Vernon remains a quiet farming community given over to livestock raising and feed grains. Wipporwill Lake provides recreational facilities.

VERSAILLES, Town; Pop. 1,791; seat of Ripley County; SE Indiana; Zip Code 47042; 40 mi. SE of Shelbyville. The town, founded in 1818, has always served as a farm center.

Dictionary of Places

The Ripley County Historical Museum has many Civil War relics. Outside the city is Versailles State Park, second largest in the state; its 176-ft. covered bridge was built in 1885.

VEVAY, Town; Pop. 1,393; seat of Switzerland County; SE Indiana; Zip Code 47043; on the Ohio River; 15 mi. E of Madison. The town was founded in 1801 by a group of Swiss immigrants who settled there to establish vineyards. The resultant wine industry became nationally famous, but eventually gave way to agriculture. Today the town is a center for dairy products, flour, grain, livestock, vegetables, and tobacco.

Vevay was the birthplace of Edward Eggleston, the 19th- century author, who is best known for his novel *Hoosier Schoolmaster* (1871). His home stands near the courthouse.

The Switzerland County Historical Society Museum contains riverboat artifacts and memorabilia of the life of Edward Eggleston. Vevay was the setting for the 1975 television movie, *A Girl Named Sooner,* starring Lee Remick.
   ●HISTORICAL PLACES... (See Hist. Places Sect for details.)
   Eggleston, Edward and George Cary, House.

VIGO, County; Pop. 114,528; W Indiana; area 415 sq. mi.; bounded on the W by Illinois, and drained by the Wabash River and Honey Creek. The county was formed in January 1818 and named for Col. Francis Vigo, an Italian merchant who came to Vincennes in 1777. Terre Haute is the county seat.

The land surface throughout the county is level and unbroken, and most of it is underlain with bituminous coal seams. The coal has been mined since the 1800s and the county is still a leader in its production. The soils are especially good for raising wheat, and stock-raising is prominent in all sections of Vigo County. There is diversified manufacturing at Terre Haute; leading industries produce foods, plastic film, chemicals, drugs, fabricated metals, castings, and extrusions. There are also printing and publishing firms.

VINCENNES, City; Pop. 19,859; seat of Knox County; SW Indiana; Zip Code 47591; on the east bank of the Wabash River; 55 mi. S of Terre Haute. Vincennes is the oldest city in Indiana and the third oldest in the territorial expanse known as the Northwest Territory. The first permanent white settlement was the French mission-fort built in 1732 by Francois Morgan de Vincennes, for whom the town is named. It was established on the Buffalo Trace, an old trail beaten out by thousands of buffalo as they forded streams there. The land around the early settlement was parceled off by lots, and deeds were sold to anyone who wished to settle there.

Vincennes was ceded to Great Britain in 1763 by the Treaty of Paris and continued a peaceful pastoral existence under British control until February 1779, when the fort, then known as Sackville, was captured by Virginia troops under the leadership of George Rogers Clark. Upon surrender, the state of Virginia claimed all the lands northwest of the Ohio River, and Illinois County was organized. Virginia was unable to govern this huge expanse of land, and ceded it to the U.S. in 1784. The Northwest Territory consequently was organized in 1787, and on March 5, 1791, 5,000 acres were given by Congress to all the inhabitants of Vincennes for use as pasture land.

The year 1800 saw the formation of Indiana Territory. Vincennes became the first territorial capital and began to take on a new character. Until then, Vincennes had been a rough-and- tumble prairie town with little law and order, but with the arrival of influential government officials, lawyers, and other professionals, it began to take on a more distinguished air.

The capitol buildings, a two-story frame house, was erected in 1800. It has been restored and commemorated as a state memorial (*see* Territorial Capitol State Memorial). Vincennes remained the territorial seat of government until 1813, when the capital was removed to Corydon.

Historical landmarks are profuse in Vincennes. The Old Cathedral (1826) and the adjoining Old French Cemetery are noted landmarks, as are the William Henry Harrison

Dictionary of Places

mansion of Grouseland (1803) *(q.v.)*, the first mansion in Indiana; the George Rogers Clark National Historic Park, a 20-acre plaza at the site of Fort Sackville; and the Old State Bank (1836), now an art gallery with exhibits of the Northwest Territory.

Vincennes depends heavily on the tourist trade, but is also a leading rail-shipping and manufacturing center. It is noted for its peach and apple orchards, and its truck farming and dairy complexes. The Tip-Top Creamery is the second largest creamery in Indiana. Manufactures include structural steel, glass, ice, boxes, canned vegetables, paper products, and flour. Power is supplied to many of the industries by coal mined at the Standard Coal Company; 1,500,000 tons of coal are produced annually in and around Vincennes.

The town is the seat of Vincennes University (8101), which was the first land-grant college of the Northwest Territory and

the oldest junior college in the U.S.; Sigma Pi fraternity was organized here, and Indian youths from neighboring tribes were given free education. On campus is the Territorial Capitol, the Dunseth Planetarium and Museum, and the Maurice Thompson Birthplace (1842). Thompson was the author of *Alice of Old Vincennes,* a popular novel. The replica frame building of the first newspaper printing shop is here; Elihu Stout, the publisher, issued the *Indiana Gazette* in 1804.

Kimmell Park, a favorite local camp and fishing site, is located 1.25 mi. NW of Vincennes. The Trailblazer Railroad offers tourists a historic sightseeing tour of the city.

●HISTORICAL PLACES... (See Hist. Places Sect for details.)

George Rogers Clark National Historical Park; Harrison, William Henry, Home (Grouseland); Old State Bank; Territorial Capital of Former Indiana Territory; Vincennes Historic District.

VIRGIL I. GRISSOM STATE MEMORIAL, Spring Mill State Park *(q.v.)*, Lawrence County; S Indiana; near Mitchell. The Indiana memorial was dedicated on July 21

(Apollo Day), 1971, and serves as the visitor's center for the park. It is dedicated to Virgil "Gus" Grissom, the Hoosier astronaut who was killed in a fire on Jan. 27, 1967. The building houses a display of America's space age achievements, including the original space capsule in which Grissom and John Young made their 81,000-mi. Gemini flight on March 23, 1965. Memorabilia of Grissom's life are placed throughout the building. Some of the exhibits are on loan from the Smithsonian Institution and will be rotated periodically as new material becomes available. Within the memorial, the Universe Room includes a 6-ft. diameter illuminated globe of the Earth in bas relief.

WABASH, City; Pop. 12,127; seat of Wabash County; NE central Indiana; Zip Code 46992; on the Wabash River; 40 mi. WSW of Fort Wayne. The territory surrounding the city site became available for white settlement with the signing of the Treaty of Paradise Springs in October 1826. A bronze plaque on a boulder near the courthouse in Wabash marks the treaty site. The city was founded in 1835 at a former gathering place for Indians known as Oubache ("water over white stones"). It was located on the Wabash and Erie Canal, which was completed from Ohio, through Wabash, to Evansville in 1853. The canal, however, was soon to be overshadowed by the railroads. Wabash was the first electrically lighted city in the world. Four electric arc "Brush Lights," invented by Charles F. Brush, were installed on the courthouse tower and tested at twilight on March 31, 1880.

Wabash is an agricultural and manufacturing center noted for electronic equipment, furniture, automobile parts, asbestos, clothing, baking powder, lime, and rubber products. Livestock and dairy farming are also important.

The Wabash County Historical Museum houses pioneer artifacts. Of note are the Honeywell Auditorium and the Honeywell Gardens, resplendent with flowers and landscaped shrubbery. Nearby are several excellent recreational spots, among them the Frances Slocum State Recreation Area, Salamonie River State Forest, Salamonie Dam and Reservoir, and the Mississinewa Dam and Reservoir *(q.v.)*.

Dictionary of Places

WABASH, County; Pop. 35,553; NE central Indiana; area 398 sq. mi.; drained by the Wabash, Eel, Salamonie, and Mississinewa rivers. The county was organized in March 1825 and named for the Wabash River. The city of Wabash is the county seat.

The land surface is level to gently rolling, and a large part of the county is covered by river bottomlands which are extremely fertile and conducive to growing soybeans, wheat, and corn. The drier sections are turned over to pasture for horses, cattle, hogs, and sheep. Wabash County is distinguished for its horse markets and is a leader in horse breeding. Manufacturing is an important port of the county's economy, especially the production of furniture, store fixtures, wood products, electronic equipment, and rubber goods.

The Mississinewa Dam and Reservoir, dedicated in 1969, is located almost entirely in Wabash County.

WABASH AND ERIE CANAL, a federal waterways project begun in 1832. The canal stretched for 468 mi. from Evansville, Indiana, to Toledo, Ohio--380 mi. in Indiana alone. It was one of the worst financial disasters in transportation history. The longest canal in the U.S., it failed through mismanagement, floods, and the coming of the railroads, and cost Indiana $25,000,000.

Only two boats ever traveled the entire route from Lake Erie to the Ohio River. Descendants of early canal workers, most of whom were Irish, still live along the canal route in Indiana. Remnants of the bed and old canal locks can be seen in many places.

WABASH LOWLAND, physiographic region of SW Indiana, the northern two-thirds of which is covered with glacial drift. The Wabash Lowland is also an alluvial plain through which the Wabash River and its tributaries meander to the Ohio River. Alluvial and glacial deposits are everywhere underlaid with limestones, shales, and thin coals, which in many places are mined.

WABASH RIVER, rises in Grand Lake, Ohio, enters Indiana in Jay County, and flows W and SW past Logansport and Lafayette. It then turns S and SW past Terre Haute and Vincennes, forming 200 mi. of the Indiana-Illinois border, and finally flows into the Ohio River at the SW corner of Indiana. In all, the Wabash is 475 mi. long and drains two-thirds of the state. Its principal tributary is the White River.

WAKARUSA, Town; Pop. 1,667; Elkhart County N Indiana; Zip Code 46573; 10 mi. S of Elkhart in an agricultural area noted for feed grains and livestock. Wakarusa is a manufacturing center for ladders, dairy products, concrete vaults, truck caps, travel trailers, polyurethane foam, farm supplies, and camping equipment.

WALDRON, Town; Pop. 700; Shelby County; central Indiana; Zip Code 46182; 8 mi. SE of Shelbyville in an agricultural area noted for feed grains and livestock. Waldron is a manufacturing center for wire enameling dies, dune buggies, boats, and fiberglass products.

WALKERTON, Town; Pop. 2,061; St. Joseph County; N central Indiana; Zip Code 46574; 19 mi. SW of South Bend. The first settlement was made by Christian Fulmer in 1835. Platted around 1856, the town was incorporated in 1876, and named after James H. Walker, who planned and built a railway line from Plymouth to La Porte.

Walkerton is a shipping point for peppermint, onions, corn, soybeans, and feed grains. The area is one of the largest mint- growing centers in the U.S., its peaty soils being conducive to the cultivation of the crop. Recreational facilities can be found at nearby Indiana Dunes State Park *(q.v.)*.

WALLACE, Town; Pop. 89; Fountain County; W Indiana; Zip Code 47988; 14 mi. WSW of Crawfordsville in an area noted for feed grains, livestock, and bituminous coal mining.

WALTON, Town; Pop. 1,053; Cass County; N central Indiana; Zip Code 46994; 10 mi. SE of Logansport in an agricultural area (feed grains and livestock).

WANATAH, Town; Pop. 852; La Porte County; N Indiana; Zip Code 46390; 20 mi. SW of La Porte in an agricultural

Dictionary of Places

and manufacturing area. Wanatah is a trade center for conveyors, aluminum products, lumber, and building supplies. It was settled in 1865 and thrived briefly as a railroad hub. The name comes from an Indian phrase meaning "knee-deep-in-mud", referring to Hog Creek, which to this day periodically overflows its banks.

WARREN, County; Pop. 8,705; W Indiana; area 368 sq. mi.; bounded on the W by Illinois and on the SE by the Wabash River.

The county was formed in March 1827, and was named for Gen. Joseph Warren who served in the American Revolution. The county seat is at Williamsport.

The surface ranges from level to hilly, and the NW corner is covered by fertile, black loam soils which yield large crops of corn, oats, hay, and soybeans. Lumber milling is still prevalent, although many of the well-wooded hills have been depleted of trees. The manufacture of cellophane is the county's chief industry.

WARREN, Town; Pop. 1,185; Huntington County; NE central Indiana; Zip Code 46792; on the Salamonie River; 14 mi. SSE of Huntington. The town was founded in 1833 by Samuel Jones, and originally called Jonesboro; it was incorporated in 1879. Between 1890 and 1910, there was substantial growth due to an oil boom within the area.

Warren is located midway between the Huntington and Salamonie reservoirs, which are dam projects developed jointly by the State of Indiana and the U.S. Army Corps of Engineers. Both are popular recreational spots. The town is a center for poultry, livestock, soybeans, grain, dairy products, and canned tomatoes.

Its manufactures include packaging and corrugated boxes.

WARRICK, County; Pop. 29,972; SW Indiana; area 391 sq. mi.; bounded on the S by the Ohio River and drained by Pigeon and Little Pigeon creeks.

The county was formed in March 1813, and was named for Capt. Jacob Warrick, who was a casualty of the Battle of Tippecanoe in 1811. The county seat is at Boonville. The old Wabash and Erie Canal traversed the NW part of Warrick County, and the canal bed can still be seen in several places.

Coal is the county's chief resource, and coal-mining is its principal industry. The rich bottomlands produce large crops of corn, fruit, and vegetables. Several upland sections yield good quality tobacco.

WARSAW, City; Pop. 10,968; seat of Kosciusko County; N Indiana; Zip Code 46580; on the Tippecanoe River; 40 mi. WNW of Fort Wayne. Warsaw, founded in 1836, is in the center of Indiana's lake region, and is a popular resort city. Over 100 lakes are in the vicinity, including those in the Chain O' Lakes State Park *(q.v.).* Warsaw is a leading manufacturing center, whose diverse products include automobile and aircraft equipment, castings, furniture, vacuum cleaners, and cut glass. There is also a lumber mill. Recreational facilities include the Rozella Golf Course.

WASHINGTON, City; Pop. 10,838; seat of Daviess County; SW Indiana; Zip Code 47501; 19 mi. E of Vincennes. The city had its beginnings in 1805 when Fort Flora was erected on the site to protect the white population from Indian attacks. It possesses many century-old buildings. Amish farmers, with their horse-drawn buggies and austere garb, are often seen on the streets on their way to market. A large colony of Amish is located in Daviess County. Washington is a leading manufacturing center for wood products, clothing, flour, canned goods, toys, railroad supplies, and electric signs. The fertile soils in the vicinity yield feed grains and fruit. Oil and gas wells are nearby. Recreational facilities can be found at Dogwood Lake in the Glendale Fish and Wildlife Area, and at the Washington Country Club.

WASHINGTON, County; Pop. 19,278; S Indiana; area 516 sq. mi.; bounded on the N by the Muscatatuck River and the East Fork of the White River. It is drained by the Blue and Lost rivers and by Twin Creek. Washington County was organized in 1813, and Salem became the county seat the following year. The county is rich in natural resources and is a noted grain producing, lumbering, and stone quarrying

Dictionary of Places

center. Major industries include cabinet making and furniture manufacturing.

WATERLOO, Town; Pop. 2,040; DeKalb County; NE Indiana; Zip Code 46793; on Cedar Creek; and 26 mi. NNE of Fort Wayne in an agricultural area noted for livestock and feed grains, especially soybeans. Commodities such as canned goods, wood products, and flour are shipped to other communities in NE Indiana.

WAVELAND, Town; Pop. 474; Montgomery County; W Indiana; Zip Code 47989; 34 mi. SW of Lafayette in an agricultural area noted for livestock and feed grains. Shades State Park *(q.v.)* lies north of the town.

WAWAKA, Town; Pop. 300; Noble County; N Indiana; Zip Code 46794; 4 mi. N of Albion, in an agricultural and dairying region. Wawaka is a manufacturing center for camper and truck caps, sit- down bath units, and reinforced plastics.

WAWASEE LAKE, N Indiana; at Syracuse. The lake, largest in Indiana, is 4 mi. long and is a important tourist attraction. The Wawasee State Fish Hatchery and Fishing Area are located here. The lake covers an area of 3,060 acres, and is noted for its excellent fishing. Some of the fish have been stocked from the hatchery, which is the oldest in the state. Its ponds are fed by the artificial Papakeechee Lake. Lake Wawasee derives its name from an Indian chief, also called Old Flat Belly.

WAYNE, County; Pop. 79,109; E Indiana; area 405 sq. mi.; bounded on the E by the Ohio; and drained by the Whitewater River, as well as its East Fork and other tributaries.

The county was organized in November 1810, and was named in honor of Gen. "Mad Anthony" Wayne. Richmond is the county seat. Wayne County was a center for abolitionist movements even before the Civil War, and became an important stopover on the Underground Railroad which took runaway slaves to freedom in the North and Canada.

In early days the National Road, which crosses through Wayne County, was a pioneer gateway for emigrants traveling to Indiana and the great West. Wayne is mainly a farming county, and its rich soils yield feed grains, flowers, and apples. It is famous for poultry, livestock, and horses, and contains some large animal farms. Wayne County has diversified manufacturing; leading products include piston rings, agricultural machinery, fabricated metals, insulated wire, bus and truck bodies, and missile parts.

WAYNETOWN, Town; Pop. 911; Montgomery County; W Indiana; Zip Code 47990; 10 mi. WNW of Crawfordsville. Waynetown is a leading manufacturer of tile and brick, a result of its location in an excellent fire clay area. There are also lumber, feed, and mills in town.

WEED PATCH HILL, (elevation 1,085 ft.), Brown County; S Indiana; in Brown County State Park. The scenic beauty that surrounds Weed Patch Hill made it a popular visitor's attraction long before the state park was opened in 1929. At its summit is a 100-ft. watch tower. The entire region was formed by melt-waters from the Illinois Glacier, which stopped just north of the Bean Blossom Overlook. The resultant streams carved valleys in the uplands, leaving a system of ridges (of which Weed Patch Hill is a part), that have been called the "Little Smokies". There are three mineral springs near the summit and the remnants of two old bear wallows. The hill was named by a group of Kentucky hunters who found rank weeks growing on the top.

WELLS, County; Pop. 23,821; E Indiana; area 368 sq. mi.; drained by the Wabash and Salamonie rivers, and by Longlois Creek. The county was formed in February 1837, and was named after Capt. William H. Wells, who was killed by Indians in 1812 while attempting to escort the garrison of Fort Dearborn (in what is now Chicago, Illinois) to Fort Wayne. Bluffton is the county seat.

Wells County is located in a rich agricultural area noted for livestock, dairy products, soybeans, and feed grains. There is also some limestone quarrying. Manufacturing is prevalent in the larger towns, and industries include canning, food processing, and the production of motors.

Dictionary of Places

The 1,00-acre Ouabache State Recreation Area is located in Wells County, as also are the peat bogs immortalized by Gene Stratton Porter in her novel *A Girl of the Limberlost*.

WEST BADEN SPRINGS, Town; Pop. 675; Orange County S Indiana; Zip Code 47469; on the Lost River and 22 mi. SSW of Bedford. West Baden is picturesquely located in the wooded hills of southern Indiana. It grew up to become an important resort town as a direct consequence of its location near seven medicinal springs. Long before the coming of the white men, the Indians had declared it a neutral area designed for hunting the wild animals which came to lick the minerals deposited by the springs on nearby rocks.

The West Baden Springs Hotel, "eighth wonder of the world", was built in 1901 and thrived as a fashionable resort until the Great Depression of the 1930s. Its casinos were sometimes frequented by the Chicago gangster Al Capone. The hotel contains 708 rooms, the world's widest unsupported dome (208 ft.), and a mosaic tile floor in the atrium. The floor has since been damaged by settling. The hotel is now the headquarters for the Northwood Institute, a coeducational liberal arts and vocational college.

●HISTORICAL PLACES... (See Hist. Places Sect for details.)
West Baden Springs Hotel (Northwood Institute of Indiana).

WEST COLLEGE CORNER, Town; Pop. 686; Union County; E Indiana; 17 mi. S of Richmond. It is the sister town of College Corner, Ohio across the state line.

WEST HARRISON, Town; Pop. 395; Dearborn County; SE Indiana; on the Whitewater River; and 32 mi. SSE of Connersville. West Harrison was founded in 1813. Many Indian mounds are found in the vicinity.

WESTFIELD, Town; Pop. 3,304; Hamilton County, central Indiana; Zip Code 46074; 19 mi. N of Indianapolis in an agricultural area noted for livestock and feed grains. There are many gravel pits nearby. Westfield was founded in 1834 by Quakers and was a stop on the Underground Railroad, the secret network by which slaves from the southern states escaped northward to gain their freedom before the Civil War.

WEST LAFAYETTE, City; Pop. 25,907; Tippecanoe County; W central Indiana; Zip Code 57906; on the Wabash River opposite Lafayette. West Lafayette was incorporated in 1924 and is the home of Purdue University (1869), one of the first land grant colleges. The school was named after John Purdue, its first benefactor, and is a leading technical college with an enrollment of 25,000 students. It has excellent agricultural and engineering programs. Outside of the city is the State Soldiers' Home, and Tecumseh Trail Rest Park, which is on the site of a famous Indian trail.

WEST LEBANON, Town; Pop. 760; Warren County; W Indiana; Zip Code 47991; 29 mi. WSW of Lafayette; Originally called Lebanon, the area was platted in 1830 and incorporated in 1869. The Wabash Railroad was built there in 1855, and as the town subsequently grew, it was renamed West Lebanon. Agriculturally, the area produces corn, soybeans, wheat, oats, hay, poultry, cattle, hogs, and sheep.

WESTPORT, Town; Pop. 1,478; Decatur County; SE central Indiana; Zip Code 47283; 27 mi. SSE of Shelbyville in an agricultural area noted for livestock and feed grains.

WEST TERRE HAUTE, City; Pop. 2,495; Vigo County; W Indiana; Zip Code 46885; just W of Terre Haute. West Terre Haute was incorporated as a city in 1933. The city is a manufacturing center for steel products, lumber products, and commercial printing.

WESTVILLE, Town; Pop. 5,255; La Porte County; NW Indiana; 10 mi. WSW of La Porte in an agricultural area noted for livestock, feed grains, and horses. Westville is situated on the old Sauk Trail. Located within the town are Beatty Memorial Hospital for the mentally ill, and Purdue-North Central campus. Recreational facilities can be found at Red Rock Ranch (horseback riding), and at Cedar Lake, just north of town. A historical marker records a stop of President Lincoln's funeral train.

WHEATFIELD, Town; Pop. 621; Jasper County; NW Indiana; Zip Code 46392; 32 mi. SSE of Gary in an agricultural

Dictionary of Places

area noted for livestock and feed grains.

WHEATLAND, Town; Pop. 439; Knox County; SW Indiana; Zip Code 47597; 11 mi. E of Vincennes in an agricultural area noted for feed grains and livestock. Wheatland is a leading shipping center for the surrounding fruit growing area. Recreational facilities can be found at nearby Thompson Bed Lake.

WHETZEL TRACE, a wilderness road through central Indiana terminating at Waverly, a former pioneer village located 19 mi. S of Indianapolis. The trace, cut through 60 mi. of wilderness by Jacob Whetzel in the early 1800s, became the route for the majority of early settlers entering central Indiana.

WHITE, County; Pop. 20,995; NW central Indiana; area 497 sq. mi.; bounded on the E by the Tippecanoe River (which also drains it), and by Big Monon and Little Monon creeks. The county was organized in April 1834, and was named after Col. Isaac White, who died in the Battle of Tippecanoe in 1811. Monticello is the county seat. The land surface is almost wholly covered by rich, loamy soils which yield abundant crops of corn, oats, wheat, and soybeans. Manufactures include dairy and food products, furniture, bricks, electrical wire assemblies, and TV cabinets.

WHITELAND, Town; Pop. 2,446; Johnson County; central Indiana; Zip Code 46184; 16 mi. SSE of Indianapolis in an agricultural area noted for feed grains and livestock.

WHITE RIVER, principal tributary of the Wabash River. The White River is formed by the confluence of the East Fork and West Fork Rivers. The West Fork rises in Randolph County, E Indiana; the East Fork is formed by the confluences of tributaries near Columbus, Indiana. The East and West Fork rivers merge to the White River in their journey S and SW. The U.S. Army Corps of Engineers has three flood control reservoirs in the White River Basins: Cagles Mill on Mill Creek, Mansfield on Raccoon Creek, and Monroe on Salt Creek.

WHITESTOWN, Town; Pop. 476; Boone County; central Indiana; Zip Code 46075; 15 mi. NW of Indianapolis in an agricultural area noted for feed grains and livestock.

WHITEWATER CANAL STATE MEMORIAL, Franklin County; E central Indiana; 2 mi. W of Metamora. The Whitewater Canal, part of an ambitious government waterways project, was built between 1836 and 1845. It cost Indiana $1,165,000 to build a total length of 76 mi. of canal between Hagerstown, Indiana, and Elizabethtown, Ohio. Along the way were seven feeder dams and 56 canal locks, with a total fall of 490 feet. As with other canal projects in the area at this time, the Whitewater Canal suffered great financial losses due to mismanagement, floods, and the coming of the railroads.

The Whitewater Valley area was an early crossroads for pioneer settlements in Indiana, which followed centuries of Indian occupation as evidenced by the Indian mounds found throughout the valley. The Whitewater Canal Memorial preserves a 14-mi. segment of the canal, extending from the Laurel Feeder Dam to Brookville. An operating gristmill at Metamora houses a museum which overlooks the sluiceway, and the canal boat "Valley Belle" provides rides through the Milville Lock and the shed aqueduct.

WHITEWATER RIVER, in Indiana and Ohio, formed by the headstreams N of Connersville, Indiana. It flows generally in a S and SE direction past Brookville and on to the Great Miami River in Hamilton, Ohio. The total length is 70 mi. Along its course are remnants of the old Whitewater Canal *(q.v.)*, which has been preserved for 14 mi. near Metamora.

WHITEWATER STATE PARK, Union County; S central Indiana; 2 mi. S of Liberty. The park covers 1,515 acres of woods and water. It is dedicated to those men and women who served in World War II. A 200-acre lake provides boating, fishing, and swimming. Other recreational facilities include a modern campground and a riding stable.

WHITING, City; Pop. 5,155; Lake County NW Indiana; Zip Code 46394; on Lake Michigan near Chicago, Illinois.

Dictionary of Places

Whiting was founded in 1885, and for many years remained a predominantly German settlement. It incorporated in 1903, but remained economically stagnant until 1934 when the Carbide and Carbon Chemicals Corporation built its plant right across from that of Standard Oil, the town's only enterprise at the time. Today, Whiting remains an industrial community, part of the vast Calumet district which includes Gary, Hammond, and East Chicago. Large chemical plants and oil refineries can be seen for miles.

Of note is the Memorial Community House (1938), built with funds contributed by John D. Rockefeller and Standard Oil. Recreational facilities can be found at Whiting Park on Lake Michigan. The park offers tennis, picnicking, and fishing.

WHITLEY, County; Pop. 23,395; NE Indiana; area 336 sq. mi.; drained by the Blue and Eel rivers. The first white settlers

arrived in the early 1820s to find a fertile land of woods and lakes, inhabited mainly by Miami and Potawatomi Indians. The land was ceded to the white settlers by treaties with the Indians.

For many years, lumbering was the county's main source of occupation, but as the timber was exhausted, agriculture began to predominate. Livestock, grain, truck, poultry, and soybeans are the main products. Manufacturing is prevalent in Columbia City, the county seat, and South Whitley. The leading industries make electrical wire assemblies and electronic components.

WILBUR WRIGHT STATE MEMORIAL, Henry County; E central Indiana; 2 mi. N of Milville. The memorial marks the site of the birthplace of Wilbur Wright (Aug. 16, 1867) co-inventor, with his brother Orville, of the airplane. The farmhouse was destroyed by fire in 1884. The monument is in the shape of a propeller mounted on a stone base.

WILBUR WRIGHT STATE RECREATION AREA, Henry County; E central Indiana; 2 mi. N of New Castle and near the Wilbur Wright birthplace *(q.v.).* Covering 850 acres, the recreation area provides water sports on the adjacent stream and has facilities for camping, picnicking, and hiking.

WILKINSON, Town; Pop. 446; Hancock County central Indiana; Zip Code 46186; 31 mi. ENE of Indianapolis in an agricultural area noted for livestock and feed grains.

WILLIAMS DAM STATE FISHING AREA, Lawrence County; S Indiana; 10 mi. SW of Bedford in a scenic hilly and wooded area. Its 21 acres of land are a prime location for fishing on the adjacent White River, as well as camping and boating.

WILLIAMSPORT, Town; Pop. 1,798; seat of Warren County; W Indiana; Zip Code 47993; on the Wabash River; and 24 mi. WSW of Lafayette. The town was settled in 1829, and was named after Gen. William Henry Harrison, who owned the land on and around the present site. A spur of the Erie Canal was built to the town, bringing business to local merchants. In 1856, the Wabash Railroad arrived, and consequently diverted traffic from the river and canal. The town boasts a lumber mill and poultry hatchery. Near the business district, the waters of Fall Creek drop over a 75 ft. sandstone ledge to form the Williamsport Falls.

WILLOW SLOUGH STATE RECREATION AREA, Newton County; NW Indiana; 4 mi. NW of Morocco. The recreation area centers on the 1,500-acre Willow Slough, which has a maximum depth of 8 ft. The entire state land area covers 9,280 acres and has an abundance of woods, water, and wildlife. There is open hunting during the fall season, at which time the lake is closed to water recreation. Recreational facilities include a campground, picnic area, boat rental, beach and licensed fishing.

WINAMAC, Town; Pop. 2,262; seat of Pulaski County; NW Indiana; Zip Code 46996; on the Tippecanoe River; and 45 mi. NNE of Lafayette. Winamac was founded in 1835 and was named for Chief Winamac, a Potawatomi Indian who made a stand against white soldiers in the Battle of Tippecanoe. The site of the present town was once a Miami village, but the land was later ceded to the Potawatomis.

Dictionary of Places

Winamac is a trade center for livestock, poultry, grain, and soybeans, and manufactures canned goods, clothing, and lumber. The Tippecanoe River flows through the town, with the Tippecanoe River State Park *(q.v.)* on its northern bank. Five mi. SW of town is the Moss Creek Country Club.

WINCHESTER, City; Pop. 5,095; seat of Randolph County; E Indiana; Zip Code 47394; on the West Fork of the White River; and 20 mi. E of Muncie. Winchester was founded in 1812 and has become a leading grain and livestock shipping center for the area. Manufactures include glass, machine-shop products, furniture, and gloves. Northwest of the city are the Fudge Indian Mounds, which were excavated in 1931 and found to be contemporaneous with the Adena culture of AD 400-800. Artifacts include skeletons, copper bracelets, and spear points.

Recreational facilities can be found at nearby Mont Longnecker Lake. The city is also the site of the Winchester Speedway, "The World's Fastest Half Mile High Bank Asphalt Track."

WINDFALL, Town; Pop. 779; Tipton County, central Indiana; Zip Code 46076; 12 mi. SE of Kokomo in an agricultural area noted for livestock and feed grains.

WINGATE, Town; Pop. 275; Montgomery County; W Indiana; Zip Code 47994; 14 mi. NW of Crawfordsville an agricultural area noted for livestock and feed grains.

WINONA LAKE, Town; Pop. 4,053; Kosciusko County; N Indiana; Zip Code 46590; on Winona Lake, just SE of Warsaw. The town holds an annual Chautauqua Bible conference and is the scene of many summer religious activates. Evangelist Billy Sunday and singer Homer Rodehever were among the town's noted citizens. The Billy Sunday Tabernacle, with a seating capacity of 7,500 people, was built by the evangelist.

WINSLOW, Town; Pop. 875; Pike County; SW Indiana; Zip Code 47598; on the Patoka River, and 26 mi. SE of Vincennes in an agricultural and coal mining region.

WOLCOTT, Town; Pop. 886; White County; NW central Indiana; Zip Code 47995; 26 mi. W of Logansport in an agricultural area noted for livestock and feed grains. The town is a manufacturing center for tile and bricks.

WOLCOTTVILLE, Town; Pop. 879; on the Noble and La Grange county lines; NE Indiana; Zip Code 46795; 34 mi. NNW of Fort Wayne in a lake resort and agricultural area noted for feed grains and livestock. Wolcottville was settled in the early 1800s and grew up around a gristmill, sawmill, tan yard, and distillery. Chain O'Lakes State Park *(q.v.)* is nearby.

WOLF LAKE, Town; Pop. 400; Noble County; N Indiana; Zip Code 46796; 7 mi. S of Albion in an agricultural and dairying area. The town is a manufacturing and trade center for pallets, lumber, wood products, tubular heaters for the refrigeration industry, automobile parts, and tires.

WOODBURN, Town; Pop. 1,321; Allen County; NE Indiana; Zip Code 46797; 17 mi. E of Fort Wayne in an agricultural and dairying area. The town is a manufacturing center for tires, crushed stone, agricultural lime, light production machinery, wire drawing dies, and petroleum products.

WORTHINGTON, Town; Pop. 1,473; Greene County SW Indiana; Zip Code 47471; on the West Fork of the White River and 33 mi. SE of Terre Haute. The town owes its existence to the Wabash and Erie Canal, but declined after the canal project was abandoned. Worthington is an agricultural area noted for feed grains and livestock.

WYANDOTTE, Town; Pop. 50; Crawford County; SE Indiana; Zip Code 47179; 12 mi. W of Corydon. Wyandotte became known for its two large limestone caverns: Little and Big Wyandotte. Big Wyandotte Cave is the second largest cave in the U.S. and was named for the Wyandotte Indians, who used it for shelter and for the mining of alabaster deposits. There are 23 mi. of explored passageways in Big Wyandotte Cave, but Little Wyandotte, although an entity in itself, is believed to be an extension of the larger cave. Big Wyandotte has five levels and the largest underground room of any cavern in the world. Its circumference reaches one-quarter mile and it has a height of 200 ft.

Scientists feel that the cave was used by Indians as far back as 7000 BC, primarily for shelter. During the War of 1812, it was used as a source of saltpeper, which was used in the manufacture of gunpowder. A new entrance was found in 1850, and visitors began flocking to it in order to view its varied formations, which included stalagmites, stalagtites, helictites, gypsum flowers, and epsom salt crystals. Both Little and Big Wyandotte caves are dry, maintain a year-round temperature of 52F, and have been modernized with electric lighting by the Indiana Department of Natural Resources, which purchased the caves and surrounding forest lands in 1966.

YELLOWOOD STATE PARK, Brown County; S Indiana; just N of Belmont. Yellowood State Forest encompasses 22,451 acres of forest, and is located in one of the most scenic parts of Indiana. Fall colors bring thousands of visitors to the area, which is also a favorite with artists. Excellent facilities for camping, hiking, picnicking, fishing, and hunting are available. There is a 135-acre lake which is used for water recreation.

YEOMAN, Town; Pop. 145; Carroll County; NW central Indiana; Zip Code 47997; 20 mi. NNE of Lafayette, near Freeman Lake, in an agricultural area noted for livestock and feed grains.

YORKTOWN, Town; Pop. 4,106; Delaware County; E central Indiana; Zip Code 46077; on the West Fork of the White River and 6 mi. W of Muncie in an agricultural area noted for livestock and feed grains.

ZIONSVILLE, Town; Pop. 5,281; Boone County; central Indiana; Zip Code 46077; on small Eagle Creek, and 14 mi. NNW of Indianapolis. Zionsville is a farming community in a rich dairy and livestock area. Its main business enterprise is the manufacturing of pharmaceuticals. At the Lion Club Memorial is a stone marker which indicates where Abraham Lincoln spoke from the back of a train platform on Feb. 11, 1861 on a stop enroute to his inauguration.

INDIANAPOLIS

City; Marion County Seat; Pop. 741,952; Zip Code 461+; Lat. 39-46-06 N; 085-48-19W.

Created out of swamp and forest on the banks of the White River in 1821, Indianapolis has become a major regional trade and manufacturing center. Centrally located within the state, it became the 11th largest city in the United States when it boldly adopted a metropolitan form of government in the 1970s.

Indianapolis is a city of contrasts. It has given the United States one president and three vice-presidents; the bank robber, John Dillinger; the conservative John Birch Society; liberal author, Kurt Vonnegut, Jr.; the Indianapolis Symphony Orchestra; and basketball star Oscar "Big O" Robertson. It boasts a magnificent Museum of Art. The city contains a Carmelite monastery and the Indiana Women's Prison. Once the headquarters for most major labor unions, it also was once controlled by the Ku Klux Klan. A city of fierce political fighting, Indianapolis is flat and landlocked, wealthy, somewhat bland and provincial, and considered a nice place to raise a family. The city spent the first decades of the 20th century tending to itself, opening its gates once a year to welcome visitors to the greatest spectacle in car racing, the annual Indianapolis 500.

About 1960, a decision was made to change the city's image and bring it forth from its shell. In the next decade, the dramatically changed skyline of the downtown area was rimmed with an interstate belt that attracted shopping centers and motels and hurried the exodus of its residents to the suburbs. Professional sports were introduced, conventions were held, magnificent structures for cultivating the arts and culture were constructed, and the long-standing policy of disdaining dollars from the federal government was reversed.

History The city's location on both banks of the West Fork of the White River was chosen as the site for the state's capital because of its central position--despite the fact that in the early 19th century, the land was covered with forest and supported only about a dozen settlers who traded with the Indians. The seat of government was moved to Indianapolis in 1824 from Corydon, a few miles north of the Ohio River. When the legislature met in Indianapolis for the first time the following year, there were 600 settlers. As cities go, Indianapolis is a youngster--but an active one. The swamps and diseases that rose to plague the early settlers were conquered; the forests were leveled and farms were created. Indianapolis got its name by simply adding the Greek word for city (polis) to the name of the state. In 1836, Indianapolis was incorporated as a town and, in 1847, it became a city.

The city plan. Alexander Ralston, a gentle Scot who had helped an imaginative Frenchman, Pierre Charles L'Enfant, to plan Washington, D.C., was commissioned to lay out Indianapolis. He employed a simplified Washington plan, creating a circle with four diagonal streets emanating from it, and then using a grid system of nine north-south and nine east-west streets. He had the foresight to make the streets wide boulevards; Washington Street, the main east-west street, was made 30 feet wider than the others in anticipation of the National Road reaching the city.

At the center of the city circle was a little knoll which Ralston circled with an 80-foot wide street. This hill is still the center of the city, from which the downtown area fans out in four directions. The original plans called for a governor's mansion to occupy the knoll, but the chief executives' wives objected to the lack of privacy. For awhile, it was a park, and then was fenced off for grazing cows. It wasn't until 1901, when the Soldiers and Sailors Monument was completed, that the heart of Indianapolis received its permanent character. The monument, an ornate structure with fountains and statuary, including a statue of Miss Liberty atop a 284-foot shaft, is the focal point of the city. Intermittently criticized by visiting journalists for its ostentation, Monument Circle nonetheless is revered by its citizens. It is the site of parades and rallies, streakers and evangelists. During the Christmas season the monument is adorned with colored lights and turned into the world's largest Christmas tree.

Indianapolis

Economic growth. The founding legislators envisioned the White River as the source of the city's growth as a trade center, but the river has never been navigable. It was the railroad that most influenced the growth of the city into a major trade and manufacturing center. Water power was introduced in 1839 when the canal--part of a statewide network of canals that never was completed--was built. Woolen, grist, and paper mills then sprang up. By 1860, more than 100 manufacturing firms were located in Indianapolis, most of them owned by a group of wealthy, close-knit families--a situation that continued until after World War II, when many of the industries merged with the nation's major corporations. A ready access to coal and the proximity of farmers accelerated the city's growth.

THE CONTEMPORARY CITY

Environment. Indianapolis enjoys moderate temperatures, with a winter average of 31 F and a summer average of 73 F. The mean annual precipitation is 39 inches.

Residents who do not drive automobiles--and there are not many--rely on the Metro Bus System, which was purchased by the city from private investors in 1974 after the operation was threatened to be abandoned because of financial difficulties. Efforts were then made to upgrade the system and attract riders, but it likely will take a major gasoline shortage to make it truly effective.

Demography. The city's population had climbed to roughly 850,000 by the mid-1970s. The census showed that 82.7 percent of the population was white, 17 percent was black, and the small remainder was of other races. Of those professing religious affililation, more than 70 percent were Protestant, 20 percent were Roman Catholic, and the rest were adherents to Judaism and other religions or sects.

Ethnic groups. The old ethnic neighborhoods, which retained their identity through the Great Depression and World War II, began breaking up when postwar affluence gave the children and grandchildren of immigrants an opportunity to move into homes far removed from those of their parents. Early Italians settled on the Southside near the produce markets, where they sold fresh fruits and vegetables to the city's grocers. Many Italians still maintain stalls in the City Market, an ancient structure located across Market Street from the City-County Building, the towering glass structure that houses local government offices. The Market, with its colorful and aromatic displays of shiny fruit, bread and meats, cheese and fish, fresh flowers and spices, long ago would have been torn down had it not been for a covenant that mandated the city to maintain it. One of the city's treasures, it underwent major renovation in the mid- 1970s, sponsored by Lilly Endowment, Inc.

German influence was especially strong in Indianapolis, bringing industriousness to the city and a penchant for culture, athletic fitness, and making money. Anti-German feelings ran so high during World War I, however, that teaching German in the schools was abandoned, Das Deutsche Haus was renamed the Athenaeum, the Turnverein became the Indianapolis Athletic Club, and the Maennerchor was renamed the Academy of Music. By the 1970s, there were nearly 20 German groups in Indianapolis; 11 members of the Federation of German Societies operated German Park, and the Indianapolis Saenger-Chor gave annual spring and fall concerts.

The Irish came to the city in great numbers. They were assimilated, as were many of the Eastern European immigrants who settled on the industrial Westside. Estonians, Latvians, and Syrians, however, have diligently tried to hold on to their customs. There is a Hispano-American Center and the Brittania Club is active. The International Center coordinates international cultural services in the city.

The Northside. The Northside always has been home to the wealthy. Indeed, North Meridian Street, north of 38th Street, long has been considered one of the finest residential streets in America. An avenue of large brick mansions set well back from the street, it has given testimony to the wealth that produced them half a century ago. Residents have managed to maintain the beauty of the street and were instrumental in inducing the state to relocate the Governor's Mansion four blocks north of its location in the 4300 block of North Meridian Street.

Indianapolis

A nice view of what Indianapolis looked like when Booth Tarkington was describing "the Establishment" at the turn of the 20th century may be found along a half-mile stretch of North Delaware Street, one mile north of the downtown district. The three-story home of Benjamin Harrison, who served as president of the United States from 1889 to 1893, is preserved as a National Historic Landmark. The Propylaeum, an ornate Victorian mansion nearby, has been the home of one of the oldest women's cultural clubs in the city since 1923. Meredith Nicholson's Georgian home is a few houses south of 16th Street. Still a private residence, it was lighted during the holidays as "The House of a Thousand Candles" in honor of his popular novel of that name. "The Little Wedding Cake House," built as a wedding present in 1873, was rescued and restored by Eli Lilly and given to the Indianapolis Episcopal Diocese. The small, white house with a rich array of gingerbread was renamed Kemper House for the first Episcopal bishop in Indiana.

Lockerbie Square. In the 1970s Indianapolis was making an effort to renovate a nearby area called Lockerbie Square. Its principal attraction was the home of the famed Hoosier poet James Whitcomb Riley, the dapper bon vivant whose poetry was so loved that 35,000 mourners passed by his bier when he died in 1916. The Victorian home is a National Historic Landmark.

Urban transition. Noted as a city of homeowners, Indianapolis has not developed any particular architectural style, but thousands of one-story ranch homes--many fronted with Indiana limestone--were erected following World War II. The city's growth all but destroyed the ornate residences that once fanned north from Monument Circle. Northsiders were able to move farther north to avoid encroaching slums. The old neighborhoods of middle-class housing became rapidly occupied by poor blacks who, in turn, continued to move north in an ever-widening fan. Left behind was a familiar American phenomenon of a growing wasteland of abandoned and boarded up frame houses standing among hundreds of vacant lots.

Indianapolis' growth has not been impeded by suburban communities. As the city moved outward, it absorbed small communities such as Irvington, once the home of Butler

University and an intellectual center, and Woodruff Place, an attractive walled community about one mile east of the downtown area. Woodruff Place, which is the creation of James O. Woodruff, a native of New York, is more than 100 years old. It features gracious two- and three-story homes overlooking grassy esplanades adorned with statuary. It was the setting for Booth Tarkington's *The Maganificent Ambersons*. Because it is in the National Register of Historic Landmarks, homeowners in Woodruff Place are allowed to receive federal assistance in restoring their properties.

Architecture. Indianapolis has a few architectural treasures. The Central Library is considered one of the finest examples of Doric architecture in the world. An unusual Tudor Gothic structure is the Scottish Rite Cathedral. Christ Church Cathedral, the city's oldest, is a gray stone gem on Monument Circle whose neat little lawn is the site of a Strawberry Festival each June. St. John's Catholic Church, once the Cathedral for the Indianapolis Roman Catholic Archdiocese, has been restored to serve the visiting conventioners at the new Indiana Convention-Exposition Center across Capitol Avenue.

Indianapolis treasures its few open spaces downtown, principally University Square, which is part of a five-block showcase area. At one end is the beautiful Federal Courts Building, at the other is the Central Library. Also in the stretch is the World War Memorial, a massive monument to the victims of World War I; both the state and international Headquarters of the American Legion; and a paved block with an obelisk set in a fountain, which is part of the War Memorial. The Scottish Rite Cathedral faces the paved square on one side, and the Federal Building is situated on the opposite side.

Renovation of the downtown area. Government led the way in the rebirth of the downtown area. Recent structures have included the City-County Building, a new Marion County Jail, the Education Center, the Post Office, the State Office Building, a convention center, and Market Square Arena, a 17,500-seat sports arena.   The business community has also invested in the rebuilding of the downtown district. A glittering array of glass structures of clear, blue, and gold hues, one of the most spectacular being the Indi-

Indianapolis

ana National Bank tower of 37 stories, have been erected. Next to a large mall, Merchants National Bank erected a complex that included a 535-room Regency Hyatt Hotel. The old Union Station, considered the finest example of Romanesque Revival architecture in the United States, was converted into a collection of shops, pubs, and restaurants in a Victorian setting.

There is hardly a block in the downtown area that has not undergone some major change since the 1950s. The city, however, continued to struggle with its image as a somewhat staid town. In recent years, a state law banning the sale of alcohol on Sundays was amended to allow establishments earning $100,000 a year in food sales to sell liquor on Sundays in hopes that the change, along with the sports arena, convention center, and new hotels, would turn the city's image around and put some pedestrian traffic on the streets after office hours.

ECONOMY

Indianapolis is economically healthy. In a recent study by the Council of Municipal Performance, Indianapolis rated high among cities in the United States with the healthiest economies. In cities of 500,000 or more population, it boasted one of the highest median per capita family incomes above the national average. The economic boom has been dramatic; personal income in the Indianapolis metropolitan area (Indianapolis and seven contiguous counties) by 1973 doubled that of 1963--according to the U.S. Department of Commerce. In 1950, 8.3 percent of all employees were in the service industries, and by 1973, the percentage had jumped to 14.1 percent. Government workers comprised 9.7 percent of the work force in 1950; they were 16.3 percent in 1973. In the same period manufacturing dropped from 33.5 percent of the work force to 28.4 percent.

Manufacturers. Indianapolis primarily is a trade and manufacturing center. More than 1,100 firms in the eight-county metropolitan area manufacture more than 1,200 products. The main ones are pharmaceuticals, transportation equipment, communication and electronic equipment, and rubber and paper products.

The largest and most prestigious manufacturing firm in Indianapolis is Eli Lilly & Co., whose 25,000 employees (7,500 of whom work in Indianapolis) produce a major amount of the world's pharmaceuticals. By the 1970s the firm was undergoing a $150,000,000 expansion program. Lilly Endowment, established by the Lilly Family, had assets of $1,003,500,000, making it the second largest foundation in the nation. The endowment remains a major source of many of the cultural, educational, and health improvements in the city.

Indianapolis produces automobile parts and truck engines and bodies in huge amounts. At one time, it was the major producer of automobiles in the United States, turning out as many as 65 different cars. Although Indianpolis' reign in the auto industry has ended, it still is proud of the quality cars once produced, including the Stutz, Duesenberg, and Marmon.

Trade and transport. The city is a major trade center of corn and grain. At one time, Indianapolis liked to call itself the "Crossroads of the World," a title it still can defend. Seven interstate highways funnel into Indianapolis. Another nine federal highways bring traffic to the city. In addition to an interstate belt (I-465) that rings the fringe of the city, Indianapolis recently completed an inner loop circling the downtown area.

Indianapolis is a leading truck, rail, and airline center. Weir Cook Municipal Airport is located on the western edge of the city. It has undergone steady expansion since the 1950s.

Research. More than 7,500 scientists and engineers are engaged in research both in industry and at universities. In recent years, Indianpolis has been able to lure scientists with three new organizations: the Indianapolis Center of Advanced Research at Indiana University-Purdue University at Indianapolis, the Holcomb Research Institute at Butler University that deals with the biological sciences, and the Regenstrief Institute for Health Care, operated by the Indiana University School of Medicine.

Indianapolis

Financial services. Indianapolis is a large insurance center. One of the most unusual insurance headquarters is located in three 11-story glass buildings shaped like modern pyramids in College Park, a development unveiled by College Park Life Insurance Company in 1972. The city has many banking institutions, several of which have more than $1,000,000,000 on deposit. Banks and savings and loan associations also operate a number of branch offices.

Labor unions. Socialist leader Eugene V. Debs spent a great deal of time in Indianapolis in his efforts to lead the first industry-wide union, the American Railway Union, in its battle with railroad management in the 1890s. The Socialist Party of America, on March 6, 1900, nominated Debs as its presidential candidate in Indianapolis--site of the party's first convention.

Most of the country's labor unions are now located in Washington, D.C., near the seat of power. Many of them moved there from Indianapolis, including the Carpenters, Teamsters, Laundry Workers, Stonecutters, Bookbinders, and Bricklayers unions. John L. Lewis established the United Mine Workers Union in Indianapolis, and the city was home at one time for Samuel Gompers and William Green, both of whom became presidents of the American Federation of Labor. Big Bill Hutchenson of the Carpenters Union and Dan Tobin of the Teamsters also lived in Indianapolis.

(Please see Chronology Section for more recent events.)

•HISTORICAL PLACES... (See Hist. Places Sect for details.)

Allison Mansion; Athenaeum (Das Deutsche Haus); Ayres, L.S., Annex Warehouse; Benton House; Christ Church Cathedral; City Market; Crown Hill Cemetery; Harrison, Benjamin, House; Indiana State Museum; Indianapolis Union Railroad Station; Lockerbie Square Historic District; Michigan Road Tollhouse; Military Park; Morris-Butler House; Old Pathology Building; Propylaeum, The (John W. Schmidt House); Riley, James Whitcomb, House; State Soldiers and Sailors Monument; U.S. Courthouse and Post Office; Woodruff Place.

Pictorial Scenes

The Indiana State Capitol in Indianapolis

Encyclopedia of Indiana

Indianapolis International Airport

Indianpolis Skyline

Pictorial Scenes

Atop the Salamonie Dam in Jay County

The "Indy 500"

Billie Creek Village, Rockville

Lower Hamer House in Spring Mill State Park

Pictorial Scenes

Saint Meinrad's Benedictine Monastery

Aerial view of Salem

Soldiers and Sailors Monument in Indianapolis

Pictorial Scenes

A 100-foot shaft erected erected in memory of the slain soldiers of the Battle of Tippecanoe

Encyclopedia of Indiana

The 1816 grist mill in Spring Mill State Park

Tipton County Courthouse, Tipton

Pictorial Scenes

The Delta Queen, at Madison

Encyclopedia of Indiana

Limberlost State Memorial

Visitor's center of the Lincoln Memorial at Lincoln City

Pictorial Scenes

Athletic and Convocation Center, Notre Dame University

The main library, Notre Dame University

Encyclopedia of Indiana

Squire Boone Caverns near Corydon

Pictorial Scenes

Cool ravines along Sugar Creek in Shades State Park

The Potawatomi Inn, Pokagon State Park

The toboggan slide in Pokagon State Park

Pictorial Scenes

The mecca covered bridge (1873), in Parke County

Barge traffic on the Ohio River

Turkey Run State Park

Pictorial Scenes

The Roofless Church, New Harmony

The Cannelton Locks on the Ohio River

Twin Caves in Spring Mill State Park

Prehistoric Indian mounds near Vicennes

Pictorial Scenes

Rural setting in agricultural Wells County

Memorial Center of Purdue University in West Lafayette

Encyclopedia of Indiana

Metamora and Whitewater Canal

Drifting sands, Indiana Dunes State Park

Pictorial Scenes

The Culbertson Mansion (1868), one of the many historic buildings of New Albany's riverboat era.

Guide to Historical Places

DESIGNATIONS OF HISTORICAL PLACES

Frequently the designations **NHL, HABS, HAER,** and/or **G** follow the ownership and accessibility. These are explained as follows:

NHL — *National Historical Landmark* is a building, structure, site, district, or object declared eligible for recognition as a property of national significance by the Secretary of the Interior under the provisions of the Historic Sites Act of 1935. These properties are not administered by the National Park Service.

HABS — A *Historic American Buildings Survey* designation indicates that documentation by photographs, measured drawings, and/or data sheets has been made as evidence of a building's architectual or historical significance. The Historic American Buildings Survey is conducted by the National Park Service in cooperation with the American Institute of Architects and the Library of Congress where the records are deposited. A HABS designation is included in the description of historic districts when at least one property has been documented by the Historic American Buildings Survey.

HAER — A *Historic American Engineering Record* designation means that the property has been recognized and recorded as an important example of American engineering. The Historic American Engineering Record is conducted by the National Park Service in cooperation with the American Society of Civil Engineers. Records are kept at the Library of Congress.

G — A *Grant* designation means that the property has received a National Park Service grant-in-aid under the National Historic Preservation Act of 1966.

Historical Places

ADAMS COUNTY

Geneva. **PORTER, GENE STRATTON, CABIN (LIMBERLOST CABIN),** 200 E. 6th St., 1895. Log and frame construction, shingling (upper story); 2 1/2 stories, T-shaped, gabled and gambrel roof sections, unhewn log ground floors, polygonal solarium on side, full-width porch; interior paneling. Home from 1895 to 1914 of Gene Stratton Porter, popular author of novels and nature studies. Cabin and natural environment provided setting for many of her works. *State.*

ALLEN COUNTY

Fort Wayne. **FORT WAYNE CITY HALL,** 308 E. Berry St., 1892–1893, Wing and Mamurim, architects. Sandstone, 2 1/2 stories, modified rectangle, hipped roof sections, high interior chimneys, polygonal and square corner towers with checkerboard ornamentation, coped gabled wall dormers with end turrets, alternating smooth and rock-faced banding over whole building, round arched entrances and some windows; interior altered. Distinctive local variation of Richardsonian Romanesque style, with pronounced variety of texture. *Municipal.*

Fort Wayne. **JOHNNY APPLESEED MEMORIAL PARK,** Swanson Blvd. at Parnell Ave. along Old Feeder Canal, 19th C.. Park including grave of John Chapman ("Johnny Appleseed"), the legendary itinerant nurseryman who spent his last 20 years in this area and planted one of his largest orchards. *County.*

BROWN COUNTY

Nashville vicinity. **STEELE, THEODORE CLEMENT, HOUSE AND STUDIO,** SW of Nashville off IN 46, 20th C.. Frame house, 1-story split-level rambler. Frame studio, 1 1/2 stories, rectangular, gambrel roof, N wall almost entirely of large windows. Theodore Clement Steele (1847–1926) was well known Indiana artist credited with establishing Brown County Art Colony and noted for his works of Indiana countryside and his portraits of state residents. *State.*

CLARK COUNTY

Borden. **BORDEN INSTITUTE,** West St., 1884–1885. Brick, 2 stories, modified rectangle, gabled roof, pedimented gable ends, paired brackets on cornice, side tower with mansard roof and dormers, windows in recessed panels, stone lintels and sills; 2nd-floor auditorium. Italianate and Second Empire elements. House institute founded by William Wesley Borden, geologist and member of silver-mining firm with Marshall Field. *Municipal.*

Clarksville vicinity. **OLD CLARKSVILLE SITE,** 1783. Site of the first town in what became the Northwest Territory; named after George Rogers Clark, conqueror of the Northwest, who lived here from 1803 to 1809; land granted to the force that served with Clark during the Revolutionary War. Unexcavated. *Multiple public/private.*

Historical Places

Jeffersonville. **HOWARD HOME,** 1101 E. Market St., 1890, Drach and Thomas, architects. Brick, 3 stories, irregular shape, gabled roof with conical tower on W and prominent interior chimneys, round arched entrance, leaded and stained glass windows. Richardsonian Romanesque. Built as home for Edmunds J. Howard. Adapted for museum use, 1954. Houses full-scale and hull models of river boats made by Howard's building firm (1834–1941), which pioneered in river craft design. *Private.*

DEARBORN COUNTY

Aurora. **HILLFOREST (FOREST HILL),** 213 5th St., 1852–1856. Frame, flush siding; 2 stories, modified rectangle, flat roof, large central circular belvedere, wide modillion cornice, semicircular center entrance bay surrounded by 2-tier porch with slender columns; full-width 1st-floor porch, floor-length 1st-floor windows, 2nd-floor bracketed window entablatures, round arched windows in bay, side bays and porches, quoins; interior murals; landscaped estate, stone front wall; restored Italianate elements. Fine villa overlooking river, built for Thomas Gaff, Scottish-born industrialist and businessman. Museum. *Private:* HABS.

Aurora vicinity. **VERAESTAU,** 1 mi. S of Aurora on IN 56, 1810. Frame, clapboarding, and brick; 1–2-story sections, U-shaped, gabled and hipped roof sections; hipped roof 1-story original brick section; gabled 1838 Greek Revival main block with paired interior end chimneys, center entrance with transom and side lights, Doric portico with paired pillars, simple entablature, and floor-length windows with bracketed entablatures; major 1913 addition with alterations to earlier block; 1937 brick addition; 1937 Georgian Revival carriage house. Greek Revival and Georgian Revival elements. House overlooking Ohio River, expanded and altered; built for Jesse L. Holman, earlyarea lawyer, state supreme court justice; birthplace of his son William Steele Holman, U.S. congressman; later home of Edith Hamilton, author on ancient Greece, and Alice Hamilton, first woman on Harvard medical faculty. *Private.*

DECATUR COUNTY

Greensburg. **DECATUR COUNTY COURTHOUSE,** Courthouse Sq., 1854–1860, Edwin May, architect. Brick, rock-faced stucco; 2 stories, modified rectangle, gabled and flat roof sections, broad interior chimneys; corner towers, one crenelated and one with a pyramidal roof and aspen trees growing out of tower roof since c. 1870; center gabled pavilions flanked by smaller towers, round arched openings with label molds, buttresses; interior alterations; stucco added 1903. Fine example of Romanesque Revival style. Courthouse was subject in one of William Allen White's famous editorials on "What's the Matter with Kansas?" in the *Emporia Gazette. County:* HABS.

DEKALB COUNTY

Auburn vicinity. **CORNELL, WILLIAM, HOMESTEAD,** SW of Auburn off IN 627, c. 1863. Brick, 2 1/2 stories, T-shaped, gabled roof with octagonal cupola, 1 interior chimney, "gingerbread" work at roof lines, 3-bay front porch, round and segmental and round arched windows. High Victorian Italianate. Possibly used as station on the Underground Railroad. *Private.*

Historical Places

FAYETTE COUNTY

Connersville. **CANAL HOUSE,** 111 E. 4th St., 1842. Brick, painted; 2 stories, rectangular, gabled roof, Doric portico supporting pediment and wide entablature; restoration underway. Greek Revival. Built by the Whitewater Valley Canal Co. and used as headquarters until 1853. *Public/private.*

FLOYD COUNTY

New Albany. **CULBERTSON MANSION,** 914 E. Main St., 1868. Brick, stone trim; 2 1/2 stories, irregular form, mansard roof, semicircular front bay, bracketed modillion cornice, roof balustrade, segmental pedimented dormers, cast iron railings on top of porches, arcaded front porch with coupled columns, round arched windows; elaborate interior includes painted ceiling in ballroom and parquet floors; c. 1883 library addition. Second Empire. Built for W. S. Culbertson, who made a fortune during the Civil War on scarce cotton. Museum. *Private.*

FRANKLIN COUNTY

Brookville. **FRANKLIN COUNTY SEMINARY,** 412 5th St., 1828-1830. Brick, 2 stories, rectangular, gabled roof, 2 interior end chimneys, center entrance, regular fenestration. Numerous alterations include early-20th C. removal of the central cupola and addition of a 3-room rear section and front entrance porch. Federal. Established as one of 63 county seminaries mandated by the state's 1816 state constitution. Opened as a secondary school in 1831, closed by 1851 state constitution. One of 6 county seminaries remaining in state. *County.*

Metamora. **WHITEWATER CANAL HISTORIC DISTRICT,** From Laurel Feeder Dam to Brookville, 1836–1846. District including 15-mi. stretch of canal, mill, feeder dam, lock remains, restored lock, and reconstructed aqueduct. Section of original 76-mi. state canal project with 7 feeder dams, 56 locks, total fall of 490'. Developed as transport route into interior of state, connecting with Ohio River, and as source of hydraulic power for numerous mills; flood damage and construction of railroad led to early abandonment for transport. In response to canal's bankruptcy, state adopted new constitution forbidding bonded indebtedness. *State.*

HARRISON COUNTY

Corydon. **CORYDON HISTORIC DISTRICT,** 19th C.. Town planned in 1808 by Harvey Heth in a grid plan centered around a public square; became county seat the same year. Served as territorial capital of Indiana, 1813–1825; first state capital when Indiana became state on Dec. 11, 1816. Several buildings dating from the town's period as capital remain. *Multiple public/private:* HABS.

HOWARD COUNTY

Kokomo. **SIEBERLING MANSION,** 1200 W. Sycamore St., 1889–1891, Arthur LaBelle, architect. Brick, stone; 2 1/2 stories, modified rectangle, gable-on-hip roof sections, high paneled interior brick chimneys, dormers, semicircular rock-faced stone entrance tower with 3rd-floor arcade and bell-cast roof; wraparound porch with brick columns, Romanesque capitals, and ornate entablature; 2nd-floor windows with carved fans beneath stone arches;

Historical Places

side bay, porches; ornate interior with variety of woodwork and latticework, murals, and many types of glass; carriage house. Richardsonian Romanesque and Queen Anne elements. Bold mansion built for Monroe Seiberling, industrialist who founded plate glass and rubber companies. Museum. *State:* HABS.

JASPER COUNTY

Rensselaer vicinity. **ST. JOSEPH'S INDIAN NORMAL SCHOOL**, St. Joseph's College campus off U.S. 231, 1888. Brick, stone 1st floor; 3 1/2 stories, hollow square, high hipped roof, gabled entrance vestibule with fanlight, segmental arched windows, belt courses, center gable; remodeled, 1937; bell tower removed. Eclectic. Built as one of 2 Indian boarding schools in state, operated by Bureau of Catholic Indian Missions; later adapted for use as dormitory for St. Joseph's College. *Private.*

JEFFERSON COUNTY

Madison. **JEFFERSON COUNTY JAIL**, Courthouse Sq., 1848–1850. Ashlar, brick, partially stuccoed; 2 stories, T-shaped, gabled roof, interior end chimneys, pedimented end gable; front center recessed entrance with side lights, entablature, and pilasters; kitchen wing added 1859. Greek Revival. Brick forepart of structure contains sheriff's house; ashlar rear houses, 2-tiered block of cells surrounded by open-vaulted space. *County:* HABS.

Madison. **MADISON HISTORIC DISTRICT**, 19th C.. Ohio River town featuring many early- and mid-19th C. buildings, including Federal, Greek Revival, and Second Empire buildings, and numerous Italianate structures. Detached residences and many 3-story commercial structures included. Town inc. 1823; grew rapidly during 19th C., serving as cultural and commercial center for surrounding territory; major pork-packing center in world in late-19th C. Many streets of buildings preserved due to later decline of town's prosperity. *Multiple public/private:* HABS.

KNOX COUNTY

Vincennes. **GEORGE ROGERS CLARK NATIONAL HISTORICAL PARK,** 2nd St., S of U.S. 50, Late-18th and early-19th C.. Park containing memorial commemorating George Rogers Clark's Revolutionary activities which helped secure the Old Northwest for the U.S. Site of Fort Sackville, captured from the British by Clark's troops after a surprise winter attack, Feb. 23–25, 1779. *Federal/NPS.*

Vincennes. **HARRISON, WILLIAM HENRY, HOME (GROUSELAND)** , 3 W. Scott St., 1803–1804. Brick, painted; 2 1/2 stories, rectangular, hipped roof, interior end chimneys, gabled dormers; front and side entrances, each with 1-story porch; restored 1949, additions removed. Georgian elements. Home, c. 1804–1812, of William Henry Harrison, then territorial governor of IN, and later 9th U.S. President; Harrison met the Indian leader Tecumseh here and in 1811 launched the campaign that climaxed in the Battle of Tippecanoe (see also Tippecanoe Battlefield, IN). *Private:* NHL; HABS.

Vincennes. **OLD STATE BANK,** N. 2nd St., 1838, John Moore, builder. Brick, scored stucco front; 2 stories rectangular temple-form, gabled roof with pedimented tetrastyle Doric portico, dentil cornice around entire building, central cupola; steel bank vault inside. Greek Revival. Only bank W of Alleghenies to survive the 1837 panic. *Private.*

Vincennes. **TERRITORIAL CAPITOL OF FORMER INDIANA TERRITORY,** Bounded by Harrison, 1st, Scott, and Park Sts., Early-19th C.. Frame, clapboarding; 2 stories, rectangular, gabled roof, 1 interior end chimney, 1-story shed roof front porch; moved several times. Headquarters of IN territorial governor; housed sessions of general assembly during first 13 years following creation of territory in 1800. *State.*

Vincennes. **VINCENNES HISTORIC DISTRICT,** 18th–20th C.. Site of Indian settlement, 3 fort sites, old French town reflecting French architectural influence, Indiana Territorial Capital Memorial (see also Territorial Capital of Former Indiana Territory, IN), early college buildings, commercial buildings, and residential area represent several phases of Indiana history. Captured for U.S. by George Rogers Clark in 1779 and became part of Northwest Territory; territorial capital under Gov. William Henry Harrison (see also Grouseland, IN); 19th C. commercial and cultural center. *Multiple public/private.*

LAKE COUNTY

Crown Point. **LAKE COUNTY COURTHOUSE,** Public Sq., 1878, John C. Cochran, architect. Brick, stone trim; 2 stories over high basement, modified rectangle, gabled roof, bracketed cornice, large central and smaller end towers, pedimented center and end pavilions, round arched windows with stone surrounds, quoins; 1907 wing additions in similar style; 1928 end sections. Italianate elements. On the courthouse steps in 1909, Louis Chevrolet received the winner's cup for one of the early major auto races in the U.S. *County.*

LA PORTE COUNTY

Michigan City. **MICHIGAN CITY LIGHTHOUSE,** Washington Park, 1858. Stone, brick, clapboarded upper story; 2 1/2 stories, rectangular, gabled roof, interior chimney, low off-center octagonal light tower; center pedimented gable with 1st-story semielliptical Ionic entrance porch with balustraded deck flanked and surmounted by Palladian frame windows; modillion cornice; extensively altered and remodeled, 1904; oil storage and tool sheds. Georgian Revival additions. Replaced first lighthouse (1837) built to guide lake transportation; moved inland and used as keeper's quarters in 1940; remodeled for use as museum. *Municipal.*

MADISON COUNTY

Anderson vicinity. **MOUNDS STATE PARK,** 3 mi. E of Anderson on IN 32, Middle Woodland (300 B.C.–500 A.D.). Eight Middle Woodland burial mounds and geometric earthwork enclosures. Excavated. *State.*

MARION COUNTY

Indianapolis. **ALLISON MANSION,** 3200 Cold Spring Rd., 1911–1914, H. Bass, architect. Reinforced concrete, brick veneer, stone trim; 2 1/2 stories, modified rectangle, hipped roof, interior chimneys, off-center columned hipped porch, balustraded corner patio; luxurious interior features carved mahogany woodwork, marble mantels, parquet floors; leather, silk, and velour wall coverings; originally contained conservatory with pipe organ, aviary with stained glass roof, and heated swimming pool. Prairie Style with eclectic interiors. Built for James Allison who manufactured first efficient automobile headlight, designed and developed motor launch enginesadapted to airplanes, and co-founded Indianapolis Motor Speedway. *Private:* HABS.

Indianapolis. **ATHENAEUM (DAS DEUTSCHE HAUS)**, 401 E. Michigan St., 1893–1894, Vonnegut and Bohn, architects. Brick, 3 stories, U-shaped, hipped and gabled roof sections, alternating stone and brick 1st-floor coursing; several towers, elaborate entrance ensembles with stone trim, composite round arched and rectangular windows, oculi, interior courtyard or "sommergarten" with bandstand; major 1897–1898 extension by same architects. Eclectic. Large recreation and social club in German community, which had expanded greatly with new immigration in 1880's and 1890's. *Private.*

Indianapolis. **AYRES, L. S., ANNEX WAREHOUSE (14–22 ELLIOTT'S BLOCK)**, Maryland St., 1875. Brick, 3 stories, rectangular, flat roof, large sheet-metal cornice, cast iron 1st-floor arcade, 2nd-floor round arched and 3rd-floor segmental arched windows with stone surrounds, full-height pilasters between bays. High Victorian Italianate. Representative well-maintained commercial building of era. *Private:* HABS.

Indianapolis. **BENTON HOUSE**, 312 S. Downey Ave., 1873. Brick, 1 1/2 stories, irregular shape, modified rectangle, mansard roof, dormers, mansarded corner entrance tower, cornice with paired brackets, bracketed window hoods, segmental and round arched windows. Second Empire. Museum. *Public/private:* HABS.

Indianapolis. **CHRIST CHURCH CATHEDRAL,** 131 Monument Circle, 1857, William Tinsley, architect. Rock-faced limestone, 1 1/2 stories, Latin cross shape, intersecting gabled roofs, buttressed front corner tower with octagonal spire; tall lancet arched windows, some with trefoil cusping. Gothic Revival. *Private:* HABS.

Indianapolis. **CITY MARKET,** 222 E. Market St., 1886, D. A. Bohlen and Son, architects. Brick, 1 story, rectangular, gabled and flat roof sections; front center gabled section with 2 tiers of round arched windows, center entrance, and 2 front slightly projecting corner towers; flanking flat wings, nave with side aisles plan; interior open space spanned by lightweight iron trusses supported by cast iron columns, side stalls. Under restoration. *Municipal:* HABS; HAER.

Indianapolis. **CROWN HILL CEMETERY,** Boulevard Pl., W 32nd St., and Northwestern Ave., 19th–20th C.. 374-acre cemetery founded 1863 with late-19th C. landscaping and High Victorian chapel, gates, and office building, the work of architects Adolf Scherrer and Diedrich A. Bohlen. Includes graves of many noted persons, including Benjamin Harrison. *Private:* HABS.

Indianapolis. **HARRISON, BENJAMIN, HOUSE,** 1204 N. Delaware St., 1874–1875. Brick, 2 1/2 stories, modified rectangle, hipped roof, Ionic columned porch on 2 sides, pedimented 2nd-floor windows, wide bracketed entablature with alternating windows and brick panels; contains original furnishings. Italianate.

Historical Places

Home of Benjamin Harrison, President and U.S. senator, who accepted Republican Presidential nomination here in 1888. *Private:* NHL.

Indianapolis. **INDIANA STATE MUSEUM,** 202 N. Alabama St., 1909–1910, Rubush and Hunter, architects. Brick, stone facing; 4 stories, rectangular, mansard-type roof behind paneled parapet, end pavilions with broad 2-story Doric pilasters on 2nd floor with aedicules between; center block with 3 pedimented 1st-floor entrances, engaged 2-story Doric columns on 2nd and 3rd floors, denticulated cornice; interior features central rotunda with glass dome, elaborate marble inlay and coloration, and murals. Neo-Classical Revival. Museum. *State.*

Indianapolis. **INDIANAPOLIS UNION RAILROAD STATION,** 39 Jackson Pl., 1886–1888, Thomas Rodd, architect. Brick, 3 stories, square, intersecting gabled and hipped roof sections; projecting corner and center pavilions, each articulated by turrets; N center main entrance with 3 doors surmounted by a wide marquee; N and S large center rose windows, each set in carved arches forming the ends of the interior waiting room barrel vault; projecting tall corner bell and clock tower with recessed panels and turrets. Brick interpretation of Richardsonian Romanesque. Built on site of first Union Station in the U.S. *Private:* HABS.

Indianapolis. **LOCKERBIE SQUARE HISTORIC DISTRICT,** Mid-19th–20th C.. Residential area on fringe of business district, with about 80 structures, many of them 2-story brick or frame houses with Italianate elements. Typical of largely middle-class urban residential area of the period, with original brick sidewalks; some restoration. *Multiple public/private:* HABS.

Indianapolis. **MICHIGAN ROAD TOLLHOUSE,** 4702 Michigan Rd., NW., c. 1850. Frame, clapboarding; 2 stories, L-shaped, gabled and hipped roof sections, 2 interior chimneys, brick and stone foundation; portion removed when road widened; 2nd story added, 1882. Used as tollhouse on the Michigan Road which connected the Ohio River with Lake Michigan in the early-19th C.; also included store and post office. Museum. *Private.*

Indianapolis. **MILITARY PARK,** Bounded by West, New York, and Blackford Sts. and the canal, 19th C.. Park containing pavilion and shelter house. Created from tract of land given by federal government for use as state capitol complex; first state fair held here, 1852; military camp during Civil War; presently recreational area. *State.*

Indianapolis. **MORRIS-BUTLER HOUSE,** 1204 N. Park Ave., 1864. Brick, 2 1/2 stories, irregular shape, mansard roof, center mansarded tower with round arched entrance, off-center porch and pavilion with grouped round and segmental arched windows; side bay; ornate interior; reconstructed rear kitchen and fence. Second Empire. Fully-furnished house of the period, built for local banker and businessman; attributed to Diedrich A. Bohlen, local architect. Museum. *Private:* HABS.

Indianapolis. **OLD PATHOLOGY BUILDING,** 3000 W. Washington St. (Central State Hospital), 1895. Brick, 2 stories, modified rectangle, hipped roof, interior chimneys, polygonal center entrance pavilion with 2 side entrances, rear amphitheater; stone lintels, sills, belt courses; original equipment and library. Eclectic. State's first medical center and medical educational facility, built as Pathological Department of the Central Indiana Hospital for the Insane. Museum. *State.*

Historical Places

Indianapolis. **PROPYLAEUM, THE (JOHN W. SCHMIDT HOUSE)**, 1410 N. Delaware St., 1890–1891. Brick, stone trim; 2 1/2 stories, irregular shape, hipped and gabled roof sections, ornamented frieze, interior chimneys, pedimented dormers, gabled entrance pavilion with round arched entrance and short clustered Romanesque columns, porch with circular corner platform; stone belt courses, window trim; porte-cochere; ornate interior; iron fence, 2 1/2-story brick carriage house. Eclectic. Built for brewer John W. Schmidt; served the Propylaeum, women's social and cultural club, since 1923. *Private.*

Indianapolis. **RILEY, JAMES WHITCOMB, HOUSE,** 528 Lockerbie St., c. 1850. Brick, 2 1/2 stories, modified rectangle, hipped roof sections with deck, 2 interior end chimneys with corbeling, bracketed cornice with alternating windows and panels in frieze, ornate side porch, segmental and round arched windows with label molds. Italianate. Home of James Whitcomb Riley, "Hoosier poet" remembered for poems and speeches in American vernacular and on genre subjects. Museum. *Private:* NHL.

Indianapolis. **STATE SOLDIERS AND SAILORS MONUMENT,** Monument Circle, 1888–1901, Bruno Schmitz, architect. Center city monument, 285'-high ashlar structure with coursed rusticated base, square tapering shaft, and observation room topped by figure of Victory. Designed by Berlin architect Bruno Schmitz after international competition; features numerous sculptural groups by George Brewster and Rudolph Schwartz, portraying historical and allegorical figures; interior elevator and iron stairway. Beaux-Arts Classical. *State:* HABS.

Indianapolis. **U.S. COURTHOUSE AND POST OFFICE,** 46 E. Ohio St., 1905, John Hall Rankin and Thomas W. Kellogg, architects. Limestone, 4 stories, extended U shape, flat roof with stone balustrade, heavy cornices, bays defined by engaged Ionic columns on raised stone balustraded terrace, 2 main entrances accented by pairs of heroic statues by John Massey Rhinde. Ornate interior is representative of opulent early-20th C. public architecture. Neo-Classical Revival. *Federal/GSA.*

Indianapolis. **WOODRUFF PLACE,** Roughly bounded by 1700–2000 E. Michigan and E. 10th Sts., Late-19th–20th C.. "Residential park" district of 3 broad streets and a single cross street, with center esplanades, fountains, statuary, urns, variegated planting, and restored original lighting fixtures. Composed of detached residences with Georgian Revival and other laten19th C. styles, with stained glass windows common and often 3rd-floor ballrooms. Developed 1872 as coherent exclusive community with minimum lot sizes and house prices. Model for setting in Booth Tarkington's 1919 Pulitzer Prize-winning novel, *The Magnificent Ambersons. Multiple private/municipal:* HABS.

MARSHALL COUNTY

Plymouth. **MARSHALL COUNTY JAIL,** 601 N. Center St., 1879, J. C. Johnson, architect. Brick and stone sections, 2 1/2 stories with tower, rectangular, hipped roof with gabled dormers, cupola on stone section, 3 interior chimneys; decorative stonework, brick corbel table, porch on SE. High Victorian Italianate and Second Empire elements. Served as county jail and sheriff's residence nearly 100 years. *County:* HABS.

Historical Places

MONROE COUNTY

Bloomington vicinity. **STOUT, DANIEL, HOUSE,** NW of Bloomington off IN 46, on Maple Grove Rd., 1828, Daniel Stout, builder. Fieldstone, 2 stories, L-shaped, gabled roof, rear wing (1943); skillfully crafted poplar doors, mitred framework, and interior mantels and wainscoting. Federal. Oldest house in county; built by Daniel Stout, who served under Gen. William Henry Harrison. *Private.*

NOBLE COUNTY

Rome City vicinity. **PORTER, GENE STRATTON, CABIN (THE CABIN IN WILDFLOWER WOODS),** SE of Rome City off IN 9, 1914, Gene Stratton Porter, designer. Log construction, 2 stories, rectangular, gabled and flat roof sections, open porches surround one wing on both floors; interior includes built-in furniture. Designed by Porter after swamp near her previous cabin was drained (see also Gene Stratton Cabin (Limberlost Cabin), IN). Here, until 1920, she produced several novels and nature works, and one motion picture. *State.*

ORANGE COUNTY

West Baden. **WEST BADEN SPRINGS HOTEL (NORTHWOOD INSTITUTE OF INDIANA),** W of IN 56, 1901–1902, Harrison Albright, architect; Oliver J. Westcott, engineer. Brick, 6 stories; 16-sided ring of guest rooms surrounding domed circular atrium 195' in diameter; plain exterior with projecting towers and attached wings; atrium features elaborate mosaic floor, iron balconies, large tiled firplace, and steel and glass dome supported on huge Ionic columns. Elaborate decorations added after 1917, most of which, along with Moorish exterior elements, removedafter 1932 when building became a Jesuit seminary. Dome an engineering triumph; climax to 19th C. experimentation in use of metal and glass; may have been largest of its type in the world when constructed. Popular early-20th C. resort; housed business college since 1967. *Private:* HAER; HABS.

PARKE COUNTY

Marshall. **LUSK HOME AND MILL SITE,** Off IN 47 in Turkey Run State Park, 1826–1846. Dwelling and mill complex including 2-story brick Federal home; site of 2 1/2-story frame mill of which the mill race and footing notches in stone remain; a Burr arch truss covered bridge, 121' long; and the site of related structures such as the pork-packing house, granary, store, and tavern. House and mill built by Salmon Lusk, Jr.; illustrates the various types of construction, architecture, commercial and industrial principle common to the area. Mill and other buildings destroyed by freshet, 1847. *State.*

PORTER COUNTY

Porter vicinity. **BAILLY, JOSEPH, HOMESTEAD,** W of Porter on U.S. 20 in Indiana Dunes National Lakeshore, 1822. Log house (c. 1834), enlarged and altered until c. 1900, and log storehouse. Remnants of trading post est. 1822 by Joseph Bailly, independent French-Canadian fur trader who was probably first settler in northwestern IN; near trails from Detroit and Fort Wayne (see also Fort Wayne, MI) to Fort Dearborn, post developed as stopping place and social center for Indian and white travelers. *Federal/NPS.*

Historical Places

POSEY COUNTY

Mt. Vernon vicinity. **MANN SITE,** Middle Woodland–Middle Mississippian. Several earthwork enclosures, 4 large ceremonial mounds, and at least 5 burial mounds mark the site of one of the most intensive Middle Woodland occupations in E North America. Other minor components at the site include Paleo-Indian and Middle Mississippian materials. Unexcavated. *Multiple private; not accessible to the public.*

New Harmony. **NEW HARMONY HISTORIC DISTRICT,** Main St. between Granary and Church Sts., 19th C.. District containing about 35 restored buildings, mostly of brick, associated with both Rappite and Owenite communal experiments. Founded and built as self-sufficient community, Harmony, in 1815 by the Rappites, German religious refugees led by George Rapp; purchased and renamed New Harmony in 1825 by Robert Owen, British industrialist, social critic, and Utopian. Community dissension led Owenite experiment to fail by 1826, but town was responsible for many scientific, educational, and social innovations over course of 19th C. *Multiple public/private:* NHL; HABS.

RUSH COUNTY

Rushville. **MELODEON HALL,** 210 N. Morgan St., Late-19th C.. Brick, 2 stories, rectangular, flat roof with overhanging bracketed cornice, tall round arched windows; modern shopfronts on 1st floor, hall on 2nd floor. Typical of Victorian commercial building. County cultural, social, and civic center for over 50 years. *Multiple private; not accessible to the public.*

SPENCER COUNTY

Lincoln City. **LINCOLN BOYHOOD NATIONAL MEMORIAL**, IN 162, 1816. Cabin site and grave of Abraham Lincoln's mother, Nancy Hanks Lincoln, on site of Lincoln farm. Lincoln's boyhood home, 1816–1830. *Federal/NPS/non-federal.*

Rockport. **BROWN-KERCHEVAL HOUSE**, 314 S. 2nd St., 1853–1854. Frame, 2 1/2 stories, rectangular with 1-story wing, gabled roof with front center intersecting gabled section, 4 interior chimneys, columned front porch (1908) with balustraded flat roof; hand-made nails and original window sash containing hand-blown glass; enlarged 1880 and 1908; several outbuildings. Gothic Revival elements. Samuel Gibson Brown, important community landowner, bought the house and finished its construction; later residence of Samuel E. Kercheval, owner and editor of the *Rockport Republican Journal* and state legislator. *Private.*

ST. JOSEPH COUNTY

Mishawaka. **BIEGER HOUSE**, 317 Lincolnway E., 1903–1909. Rusticated limestone, 2 1/2 stories, irregular shape, hipped red tile roof with 2 interior chimneys and arched dormers, 2-story Corinthian porch flanked by 1-story porch wings, elaborate wood cornice. Martin V. Bieger was founder and first president of frontier boot making company which developed into one of Nation's largest rubber footwear operations, Ball Band, now part of the Uniroyal industrial complex. *Private; not accessible to the public.*

South Bend. **OLD COURTHOUSE (SECOND ST. JOSEPH COUNTY COURTHOUSE)**, 112 S. Lafayette Blvd., 1855, John M. Van Osdel, architect. Stone, 2 stories, rectangular temple-form, low gabled roof, ornate clockfaced octagonal tower with segmental arched louvers, 2-story pedimented hexastyle portico with modified papyrus capitals, center entrance with round arched window above, side windows set in recessed panels; moved, 1896, interior altered. Greek Revival and Italianate elements. Museum. *County:* HABS.

South Bend. **OLIVER, JOSEPH D., HOUSE (COPSHAHOLM),** 808 W. Washington Ave., 1895-1896, Lamb and Rich, architects; 1938, Walter Johnson, architect (interior remodeling). Stone, 3 stories with 1-story projections, irregular shape, gabled and hipped roofs, several interior chimneys, NE tower, pillared porch around tower and front, attached pergola, carriage house. Queen Anne. Home of Joseph D. Oliver, creator of financial expansion (1880-1920's) of industry which produced Oliver plows patented by his father; also played a significant role in American immigration history. Mansion representative of life enjoyed by the early-20th C. nouveau riche. Named after Scottish village from which the Oliver family came. *Private.*

South Bend. **TIPPECANOE PLACE (STUDEBAKER HOUSE),** 620 W. Washington Ave., 1885-1886, Henry Ives Cobb, architect. Random coursed fieldstone, 3 stories, irregular mass with numerous projections, intersecting gabled roofs with dormers, 6 interior chimneys, contrasting dressed limestone trim. Richardsonian Romanesque. Home of Clement Studebaker, president of Studebaker Co., one of the first U.S. major automotive corporations. *Municipal.*

SWITZERLAND COUNTY

Vevay. **EGGLESTON, EDWARD AND GEORGE CARY, HOUSE,** 306 W. Main St., 1837. Brick, painted; 2 stories, L-shaped, gabled roof, substantially altered. Home of Edward Eggleston, one of America's earliest literary realists. Surrounding countryside provided material for his best known works, including *The Hoosier Schoolmaster* and *Roxby*. *Private.*

TIPPECANOE COUNTY

Lafayette. **FOWLER, MOSES, HOUSE,** Corner of 10th and South Sts., 1851–1852, Moses Fowler, designer. Brick, stuccoed; 2 1/2 stories, modified T shape, gabled roof, gabled wall dormers, interior chimney with clustered pots, off-center entrance, wrap-around porch with polygonal columns and flattened arches, center cross gable, ornate pierced bargeboards, bay windows with tracery and pointed arched windows, label molds; interior with Gothic detailings; additions, 1916; landscaped grounds. Early Gothic Revival. Designed by local businessman Moses Fowler; was among most ornate houses in region when constructed and among finer houses of this style in state. Museum. *County.*

Lafayette. **TIPPECANOE COUNTY COURTHOUSE,** Public Sq., 1881. Ashlar, 3 stories over high basement, modified rectangle, hipped roof sections, interior chimneys with ornate caps, central tower with attenuated dome, coursed 1st-floor rustication, array of 2nd-floor Corinthian columns, center pedimented tetrastyle pavilions, corner towers with dormers, round arched windows with tracery; ornate interior with original elevator and iron cage; alterations. Eclectic. Exuberant local

Historical Places

courthouse, including sculptural groups with George Rogers Clark, George Washington, and Tecumseh. *County.*

Lafayette vicinity. **FORT OUIATENON,** 1717. Site of trading post and fort established by the French to protect their fur trading interests with the Indians. Later occupied by the British until burned by Americans (1791) during frontier border disputes. Investigated by the Indiana Historical Society and Indiana University, 1968, 1969, 1970. *Private.*

Lafayette vicinity. **INDIANA STATE SOLDIERS HOME HISTORIC DISTRICT,** N of Lafayette off IN 43, 1895. Complex includes 4 original buildings—the post exchange, commandant's house, library, and administration building. Construction of the home for Civil War veterans represented an unprecedented major state effort toward humanitarian activities. *State.*

Lafayette vicinity. **TIPPECANOE BATTLEFIELD,** 7 mi. NE of Lafayette on IN 225, 1811. Memorial shaft and small stone markers designate site where Gen. William Henry Harrison defeated Shawnee chief Tecumseh (Nov. 7, 1811), destroying Indian attempt at consolidated resistance to white settlement of W territories. Battle also precipitated War of 1812, as Americans believed Great Britain encouraged Indian raids. Victory exploited in Harrison's Presidential campaign slogan "Tippecanoe and Tyler too," 1840. *State:* NHL.

VANDERBURGH COUNTY

Evansville. **EVANSVILLE POST OFFICE,** 100 block N.W. 2nd St., 1876–1879, Alfred B. Mullett, architect. Rock-faced limestone, 2 1/2 stories, T-shaped, high hipped roof sections, interior chimneys, dormers, center 1st-floor arcade of pointed arches on squat columns, large center wall dormer with pointed arched window and coping with crockets, dark stone belt courses and alternating voussoirs, pointed arched and segmental pointed arched windows, side oriel. High Victorian Gothic. Bold, polychrome former post office by Treasury Architect Alfred B. Mullett. *Federal/GSA; not accessible to the public.*

Evansville. **FORMER VANDERBURGH COUNTY SHERIFF'S RESIDENCE,** 4th St. between Vine and Court Sts., 1891. Stone, 2 1/2 stories, modified L shape, gabled roof sections, central circular 4-story tower, balustraded porch with Tudor arches; crenelated stepped gable ends, tower, and roofline; turrets. Romantic Eclectic. Sheriff and his family lived here until 1969. *County; not accessible to the public.*

Evansville. **OLD VANDERBURGH COUNTY COURTHOUSE,** Entire block bounded by Vine, 4th, Court, and 5th Sts., 1888–1891, Henry Wolters, architect. Stone, 3 stories, Greek cross shape, hipped roof sections; central dome on round base with projecting Ionic sections dividing those with round arched openings, volutes over columned sections, clockfaces over windows and beneath segmental pediments, open cupola surmounting dome; projecting bowed corner bays, elaborate classical elements include swag and wreath reliefs, fancy Ionic columns and pilasters, circular windows inside scrollwork, and denticulated cornices supporting roof balustrades. Beaux-Arts Classicism and Neo-Classical Revival. County seat for Evansville and Vanderburgh County for 78 years. *County.*

Historical Places

Evansville. **REITZ, JOHN AUGUSTUS, HOUSE,** 224 S.E. 1st St., 1872. Brick, painted; 3 stories, L-shaped, mansard roof with gabled dormers and cast iron cresting; dark wood quoins, bracketing, and window frames. Second Empire. Home of John Augustus Reitz, a leading philanthropist in the town. *Private.*

Evansville. **WILLARD LIBRARY,** 21 1st Ave., 1883–1884, James Reid, architect. Brick, 2 stories, modified rectangle, hipped roof sections, large square exterior end chimney, ornate cornice with paired brackets, corner gabled entrance tower, 1st-floor row of pointed arched windows; stone banding, alternating voussoirs, and window surrounds; interior cast iron columns. High Victorian Gothic. Designed by architect who moved in 1880's to CA where he had a major firm. *Private.*

Evansville vicinity. **ANGEL MOUNDS,** 8 mi. SE of Evansville, Angel Mounds State Memorial, 1400–1600. Mississippian temple mound site consisting of 12 conical and truncated pyramidal mounds, and an extensive associated village. Comprehensive excavations by the Indiana Historical Society have uncovered numerous rectangular houses, temples, a central plaza and a surrounding earthen palisade with evenly spaced bastions. *State:* NHL.

VIGO COUNTY

Terre Haute. **CONDIT HOUSE,** 629 Mulberry St. on Indiana State University campus, 1860. Brick, 2 1/2 stories, modified rectangle, hipped and gabled roof sections, interior chimneys, bracketed cornice and paneled frieze, pedimented center entrance pavilion with transom over door and balcony, flanking porches with square columns, stone lintels; reconstructed rear wing; restored, 1960's. Italianate. House remained in Condit family for nearly a century; now president's home for Indiana State University. *State.*

Terre Haute. **DEBS, EUGENE V., HOUSE,** 451 N. 8th St., 1885. Frame, clapboarding; 2 1/2 stories, modified rectangle, gabled roof sections, interior chimneys, replacement corner porch, projecting side section, bracketed cornice. Home of Eugene Debs, founder of industrial unionism in the U.S., who helped organize the American RR. Union, which successfully struck against James J. Hill's Great Northern RR. in 1894, and the Industrial Workers of the World; Socialist Party's Presidential candidate 5 times between 1900 and 1920. Museum. *Private:* NHL.

Terre Haute. **DRESSER, PAUL, BIRTHPLACE,** 1st and Farrington Sts., Early 1850's. Brick, 2 stories, rectangular, gabled roof, interior end chimneys, center door with transom in 3-bay facade, segmental arches over 2nd-floor windows; porch with turned posts, frame kitchen ell, side stairs and entrance; 2nd story added, 19th C.; moved and restored. Example of pre-Civil War workingman's home, the birthplace of Paul Dresser, composer of state song and popular songwriter known as the "King of Tin Pan Alley"; also home of his brother, author Theodore Dreiser. Museum. *Private.*

Terre Haute. **SAGE-ROBINSON-NAGEL HOUSE,** 1411 S. 6th St., 1868. Brick, 2 stories, modified L shape, hipped roof, bracketed cornice with paneled frieze, off-center porch with paired square pillars, entrance with fanlight, segmental and round arched windows with label molds, off-center 1st-floor bay; late-19th C. additions. Well-preserved Italianate style house of the period. Museum. *County.*

Historical Places

Terre Haute. **STATE BANK OF INDIANA, BRANCH OF (MEMORIAL HALL),** 219 Ohio St., 1832–1834, Edwin J. Peck, builder-architect. Stucco, 2 stories, rectangular, gabled roof, pedimented Doric entrance portico; large addition, 1920's. Greek Revival. City's oldest commercial building; built as branch of Second State Bank of Indiana. *Private.*

WARRICK COUNTY

Newburgh vicinity. **ROBERTS-MORTON HOUSE,** 1.5 mi. E of Newburgh on IN 662, 1834. Stone (ashlar facade, random ashlar elsewhere), 2 stories, modified rectangle, gabled roof, 2 sets of paired end chimneys with connecting parapets, center 2-tier pedimented portico, main entrance with fanlight and side lights; 1-story wing added, portico reconstructed, early-20th C. Federal and Greek Revival elements. Built for Gaines Head Roberts, county judge and state senator. *Private; not accessible to the public:* HABS.

WASHINGTON COUNTY

Salem. **HAY-MORRISON HOUSE,** 106 S. College Ave., 1824. Brick, 1 story, L-shaped, gabled roof, interior end chimneys, box cornice, side and end entrances with transom; later frame rear ell. Small house built as grammar school, where noted state educator John I. Morrison taught; later as residence, was birthplace of John Milton Hay, ambassador and U.S. Secretary of State under 2 Presidents. Museum. *Private.*

WAYNE COUNTY

Centerville. **CENTERVILLE HISTORIC DISTRICT,** Bounded by the corporation line, 3rd and South Sts., and Willow Grove Rd., 19th C.. Town district featuring numerous 2-story early–mid-19th C. brick structures among more than 100 historic buildings; includes many row houses, some with archways leading through to rear. Greek Revival and Italianate elements common. Among early chartered towns in state, along old National Road; several taverns remain from the stage stop days. *Multiple public/private:* G.

Fountain City. **COFFIN, LEVI, HOUSE,** 115 N. Main St., 1827. Brick, painted; 2 1/2 stories, L-shaped, gabled and shed roof sections, 3 interior chimneys, simple cornice with end returns, front center door; rear porch removed. Greek Revival elements. Home of Levi Coffin, leader in the operation of the Underground RR., who later devoted his efforts to aiding freedmen. *Private; not accessible to public:* NHL.

Richmond. **OLD RICHMOND HISTORIC DISTRICT**, Roughly bounded by C & O Railroad, S. 11th, South A, and alley S of South E St., 19th C.. District comprising the original plat of Richmond (1816); includes residences, churches, and other 19th C. buildings. Numerous buildings served Richmond's German and free black communities and several were used to harbor runaway slaves. *Multiple public/private.*

Richmond. **STARR HISTORIC DISTRICT,** Roughly bounded by N. 16th, E and A Sts., and alley W of N. 10th St., 19th C.. Residential district containing variety of Victorian period buildings. Location of homes of many of the state's business and industrial leaders. *Multiple public/private.*

CONSTITUTION

Approved in Convention at Indianapolis,
February 10, 1851

Adopted by the Electorate, effective November 1, 1851

As Amended through 1988

ARTICLE 7.
Judicial.

§ 4 Jurisdiction of supreme court

Section 4. The Supreme Court shall have no original jurisdiction except in admission to the practice of law; discipline or disbarment of those admitted; the unauthorized practice of law; discipline, removal, and retirement of justices and judges; supervision of the exercise of jurisdiction by the other courts of the State; and issuance of writs necessary or appropriate in aid of its jurisdiction. The Supreme Court shall exercise appellate jurisdiction under such terms and conditions as specified by rules except that appeals from a judgment imposing a sentence of death, life imprisonment or imprisonment for a term greater than fifty years shall be taken directly to the Supreme Court. The Supreme Court shall have, in all appeals of criminal cases, the power to review all questions of law and to review and revise the sentence imposed.

(History: As Amended November 8, 1988).

ARTICLE 15.
Miscellaneous.

§ 8 Repealed

(Repealed November 8, 1988).

CONSTITUTION OF STATE OF INDIANA
1851

ARTICLE.
1. BILL OF RIGHTS.
2. SUFFRAGE AND ELECTIONS.
3. DISTRIBUTION OF POWERS.
4. LEGISLATIVE.
5. EXECUTIVE.
6. ADMINISTRATIVE.
7. JUDICIAL.
8. EDUCATION.
9. STATE INSTITUTIONS.

ARTICLE.
10. FINANCE.
11. CORPORATIONS.
12. MILITIA.
13. MUNICIPAL DEBT.
14. BOUNDARIES.
15. MISCELLANEOUS.
16. AMENDMENTS.
    SCHEDULE.

PREAMBLE

To the end, that justice be established, public order maintained, and liberty perpetuated: WE, the People of the State of Indiana, grateful to ALMIGHTY GOD for the free exercise of the right to choose our own form of government, do ordain this Constitution.

ARTICLE 1
BILL OF RIGHTS

SECTION.
1. Natural rights.
2. Right to worship.
3. Freedom of thought.
4. No preference to any creed.
5. No religious test for office.
6. No money for religious institutions.
7. Competency of witness.
8. Oath, how administered.
9. Free speech and writing.
10. The truth in libel.
11. Unreasonable search or seizure.
12. Courts open—Due course of law—Administration of justice.
13. Rights of accused.
14. Former jeopardy—Self-incrimination.
15. Unnecessary rigor prohibited.
16. Excessive bail, punishment, and penalties.
17. Bailable offenses.
18. Reformation as basis of penal code.
19. Jury in criminal cases—Right to determine law and facts.
20. Trial by jury inviolate in civil cases.

SECTION.
21. Compensation for services or property.
22. Exemption—Imprisonment for debt.
23. Privileges equal.
24. Ex post facto laws—Laws impairing obligations of contract.
25. Taking effect of laws.
26. Suspension of laws.
27. Suspension of habeas corpus.
28. Treason.
29. Proof in treason.
30. Effect of conviction.
31. Right to assemble, instruct, and petition.
32. Right to bear arms.
33. Military subject to civil power.
34. Restrictions upon soldiers.
35. No titles of nobility, nor hereditary distinctions.
36. Emigration free.
37. Slavery prohibited.

Constitution

§ 1. Natural rights. — WE DECLARE, That all people are created equal; that they are endowed by their CREATOR with certain unalienable rights; that among these are life, liberty and the pursuit of happiness; that all power is inherent in the People; and that all free governments are, and of right ought to be, founded on their authority, and instituted for their peace, safety, and well-being. For the advancement of these ends, the People have, at all times, an indefeasible right to alter and reform their government. [As amended November 7, 1984.]

§ 2. Right to worship. — All people shall be secured in their natural right to worship Almighty God, according to the dictates of their own consciences. [As amended November 7, 1984.]

§ 3. Freedom of thought. — No law shall, in any case whatever, control the free exercise and enjoyment of religious opinions, or interfere with the rights of conscience.

§ 4. No preference to any creed. — No preference shall be given, by law, to any creed, religious society, or mode of worship; and no person shall be compelled to attend, erect, or support, any place of worship, or to maintain any ministry, against his consent. [As amended November 7, 1984.]

§ 5. No religious test for office. — No religious test shall be required as a qualification for any office of trust or profit.

§ 6. No money for religious institutions. — No money shall be drawn from the treasury, for the benefit of any religious or theological institution.

§ 7. Competency of witness. — No person shall be rendered incompetent as a witness, in consequence of his opinions on matters of religion.

§ 8. Oath, how administered. — The mode of administering an oath or affirmation, shall be such as may be most consistent with, and binding upon, the conscience of the person, to whom such oath or affirmation may be administered.

§ 9. Free speech and writing. — No law shall be passed, restraining the free interchange of thought and opinion, or restricting the right to speak, write, or print, freely, on any subject whatever: but for the abuse of that right, every person shall be responsible.

§ 10. The truth in libel. — In all prosecutions for libel, the truth of the matters alleged to be libellous may be given in justification.

§ 11. Unreasonable search or seizure. — The right of the people to be secure in their persons, houses, papers, and effects, against unreasonable search, or seizure, shall not be violated; and no warrant shall issue, but upon probable cause, supported by oath or affirmation, and particularly describing the place to be searched, and the person or thing to be seized.

§ 12. **Courts open — Due course of law — Administration of justice.** — All courts shall be open; and every person, for injury done to him in his person, property, or reputation, shall have remedy by due course of law. Justice shall be administered freely, and without purchase; completely, and without denial; speedily, and without delay. [As amended November 7, 1984.]

§ 13. **Rights of accused.** — In all criminal prosecutions, the accused shall have the right to a public trial, by an impartial jury, in the county in which the offense shall have been committed; to be heard by himself and counsel; to demand the nature and cause of the accusation against him, and to have a copy thereof; to meet the witnesses face to face, and to have compulsory process for obtaining witnesses in his favor.

§ 14. **Former jeopardy — Self-incrimination.** — No person shall be put in jeopardy twice for the same offense. No person, in any criminal prosecution, shall be compelled to testify against himself.

§ 15. **Unnecessary rigor prohibited.** — No person arrested, or confined in jail, shall be treated with unnecessary rigor.

§ 16. **Excessive bail, punishment, and penalties.** — Excessive bail shall not be required. Excessive fines shall not be imposed. Cruel and unusual punishments shall not be inflicted. All penalties shall be proportioned to the nature of the offense.

§ 17. **Bailable offenses.** — Offenses, other than murder or treason, shall be bailable by sufficient sureties. Murder or treason shall not be bailable, when the proof is evident, or the presumption strong.

§ 18. **Reformation as basis of penal code.** — The penal code shall be founded on the principles of reformation, and not of vindictive justice.

§ 19. **Jury in criminal cases — Right to determine law and facts.** — In all criminal cases whatever, the jury shall have the right to determine the law and the facts.

§ 20. **Trial by jury inviolate in civil cases.** — In all civil cases, the right of trial by jury shall remain inviolate.

§ 21. **Compensation for services or property.** — No person's particular services shall be demanded, without just compensation. No person's property shall be taken by law, without just compensation; nor, except in case of the

State, without such compensation first assessed and tendered. [As amended November 7, 1984.]

§ 22. **Exemption — Imprisonment for debt.** — The privilege of the debtor to enjoy the necessary comforts of life, shall be recognized by wholesome laws, exempting a reasonable amount of property from seizure or sale for the payment of any debt or liability hereafter contracted; and there shall be no imprisonment for debt, except in case of fraud.

§ 23. **Privileges equal.** — The General Assembly shall not grant to any citizen, or class of citizens, privileges or immunities which, upon the same terms, shall not equally belong to all citizens.

§ 24. **Ex post facto laws — Laws impairing obligations of contract.** — No ex post facto law, or law impairing the obligation of contracts, shall ever be passed.

§ 25. **Taking effect of laws.** — No law shall be passed, the taking effect of which shall be made to depend upon any authority, except as provided in this Constitution.

§ 26. **Suspension of laws.** — The operation of the laws shall never be suspended, except by the authority of the General Assembly.

§ 27. **Suspension of habeas corpus.** — The privilege of the writ of habeas corpus shall not be suspended, except in case of rebellion or invasion; and then, only if the public safety demand it.

§ 28. **Treason.** — Treason against the State shall consist only in levying war against it, and in giving aid and comfort to its enemies.

§ 29. **Proof in treason.** — No person shall be convicted of treason, except on the testimony of two witnesses to the same overt act, or upon his confession in open court.

§ 30. **Effect of conviction.** — No conviction shall work corruption of blood, or forfeiture of estate.

§ 31. **Right to assemble, instruct, and petition.** — No law shall restrain any of the inhabitants of the State from assembling together in a peaceable manner, to consult for their common good; nor from instructing their representatives; nor from applying to the General Assembly for redress of grievances.

§ 32. **Right to bear arms.** — The people shall have a right to bear arms, for the defense of themselves and the State.

§ 33. **Military subject to civil power.** — The military shall be kept in strict subordination to the civil power.

§ 34. **Restrictions upon soldiers.** — No soldier shall, in time of peace, be quartered in any house, without the consent of the owner; nor, in time of war, but in a manner to be prescribed by law.

§ 35. **No titles of nobility, nor hereditary distinctions.** — The General Assembly shall not grant any title of nobility, nor confer hereditary distinctions.

§ 36. **Emigration free.** — Emigration from the State shall not be prohibited.

§ 37. **Slavery prohibited.** — There shall be neither slavery, nor involuntary servitude, within the State, otherwise than for the punishment of crimes, whereof the party shall have been duly convicted. [As amended November 7, 1984.]

ARTICLE 2
SUFFRAGE AND ELECTIONS

SECTION.
1. Elections free and equal.
2. Qualifications of electors.
3. Soldiers — Seamen — Marines.
4. Residence.
5. [Repealed.]
6. Bribery a disqualification for office.
7. [Repealed.]
8. Disfranchisement.
9. Effect of holding lucrative offices.

SECTION.
10. Defaulters not eligible.
11. Pro tempore appointments.
12. Electors free from arrest.
13. Method of election.
14. Time of elections — Judges — Registration.

§ 1. **Elections free and equal.** — All elections shall be free and equal.

§ 2. **Qualifications of electors.** — Every citizen of the United States, of the age of eighteen (18) years or more, who has been a resident of a precinct thirty (30) days immediately preceding such election, shall be entitled to vote in that precinct. [As amended November 7, 1984.]

§ 3. **Soldiers — Seamen — Marines.** — No member of the armed forces of the United States, or of their allies, shall be deemed to have acquired a residence in the State, in consequence of having been stationed within the same; nor shall any such person have the right to vote. [As amended November 7, 1984.]

Constitution

§ 4. **Residence.** — No person shall be deemed to have lost his residence in the State by reason of his absence, either on business of this State or of the United States.

§ 5. [Repealed.]

§ 6. **Bribery a disqualification for office.** — Every person shall be disqualified from holding office, during the term for which he may have been elected, who shall have given or offered a bribe, threat, or reward, to procure his election.

§ 7. [Repealed.]

§ 8. **Disfranchisement.** — The General Assembly shall have power to deprive of the right of suffrage, and to render ineligible, any person convicted of an infamous crime.

§ 9. **Effect of holding lucrative offices.** — No person holding a lucrative office or appointment under the United States or under this State is eligible to a seat in the General Assembly; and no person may hold more than one lucrative office at the same time, except as expressly permitted in this Constitution. Offices in the militia to which there is attached no annual salary, shall not be deemed lucrative. [As amended November 7, 1984.]

§ 10. **Defaulters not eligible.** — No person who may hereafter be a collector or holder of public moneys, shall be eligible to any office of trust or profit, until he shall have accounted for, and paid over, according to law, all sums for which he may be liable.

§ 11. **Pro tempore appointments.** — In all cases in which it is provided, that an office shall not be filled by the same person more than a certain number of years continuously, an appointment pro tempore shall not be reckoned a part of that term.

§ 12. **Electors free from arrest.** — In all cases, except treason, felony, and breach of the peace, electors shall be free from arrest, in going to elections, during their attendance there, and in returning from the same.

§ 13. **Method of election.** — All elections by the People shall be by ballot; and all elections by the General Assembly, or by either branch thereof, shall be viva voce.

§ 14. **Time of elections — Judges — Registration.** — All general elections shall be held on the first Tuesday after the first Monday in November, but township elections may be held at such time as may be provided by law: Provided, that the General Assembly may provide by law for the election of all

Encyclopedia of Indiana

Judges of courts of general and appellate jurisdiction, by an election to be held for such officers only, at which time no other officer shall be voted for; and shall also provide for the registration of all persons entitled to vote. [As amended March 14, 1881.]

ARTICLE 3
DISTRIBUTION OF POWERS

SECTION.
1. Three departments.

§ 1. **Three departments.** — The powers of the Government are divided into three separate departments; the Legislative, the Executive including the Administrative, and the Judicial; and no person, charged with official duties under one of these departments, shall exercise any of the functions of another, except as in this Constitution expressly provided.

ARTICLE 4
LEGISLATIVE

SECTION.
1. The general assembly.
2. Number of members.
3. Term of office.
4. Filling vacancies.
5. Apportionment of representation.
6. [Repealed.]
7. Qualifications of members of assembly.
8. Privileges of members.
9. Sessions.
10. Officers — Procedure — Adjournment.
11. Quorum.
12. Journal.
13. Doors to be open.
14. Disorderly behavior punished.
15. Imprisonment for contempt.

SECTION.
16. Powers of each house.
17. Bills.
18. Reading and vote.
19. Subject matter of acts.
20. Plain wording.
21. [Repealed.]
22. Local or special laws forbidden.
23. Laws must be general.
24. Suits against the state.
25. Passage of bills.
26. Protest and entry.
27. Public laws.
28. Effective date of statutes.
29. Pay of members.
30. Members ineligible to certain offices.

§ 1. **The general assembly.** — The Legislative authority of the State shall be vested in the General Assembly, which shall consist of a Senate and a House of Representatives. The style of every law shall be: "Be it enacted by the General Assembly of the State of Indiana"; and no law shall be enacted, except by bill.

§ 2. **Number of members.** — The Senate shall not exceed fifty, nor the House of Representatives one hundred members; and they shall be chosen by the electors of the respective districts, into which the State may, from time to time, be divided. [As amended November 7, 1984.]

Constitution

§ 3. **Term of office.** — Senators shall be elected for the term of four years, and Representatives for the term of two years, from the day next after their general election. One-half of the senators, as nearly as possible, shall be elected biennially. [As amended November 7, 1984.]

§ 4. **Filling vacancies.** — The General Assembly may provide by law for the filling of such vacancies as may occur in the General Assembly. [As amended November 7, 1984.]

§ 5. **Apportionment of representation.** — The General Assembly elected during the year in which a federal decennial census is taken shall fix by law the number of Senators and Representatives and apportion them among districts according to the number of inhabitants in each district as revealed by that federal decennial census. The territory in each district shall be contiguous. [As amended November 7, 1984.]

§ 6. **[Repealed.]**

§ 7. **Qualifications of members of assembly.** — No person shall be a Senator or a Representative who, at the time of his election, is not a citizen of the United States; nor any one who has not been for two years next preceding his election, an inhabitant of this State, and, for one year next preceding his election, an inhabitant of the district, whence he may be chosen. Senators shall be at least twenty-five, and Representatives at least twenty-one years of age. [As amended November 7, 1984.]

§ 8. **Privileges of members.** — Senators and Representatives, in all cases except treason, felony, and breach of the peace, shall be privileged from arrest, during the session of the General Assembly, and in going to and returning from the same; and shall not be subject to any civil process, during the session of the General Assembly, nor during the fifteen days next before the commencement thereof. For any speech or debate in either House, a member shall not be questioned in any other place.

§ 9. **Sessions.** — The sessions of the General Assembly shall be held at the capital of the State, commencing on the Tuesday next after the second Monday in January of each year in which the General Assembly meets unless a different day or place shall have been appointed by law. But if, in the opinion of the Governor, the public welfare shall require it, he may, at any time by proclamation, call a special session. The length and frequency of the sessions of the General Assembly shall be fixed by law. [As amended November 3, 1970.]

The 1970 amendment to §§ 9 and 29 of Art. 4 also contained a schedule which read:

"SCHEDULE

"If at the time these amendments

become effective, the General Assembly has not fixed the length of time in days of the legislative session by law, any regular session of the General Assembly held thereafter and until the length and frequency of such sessions are fixed by law, shall begin from the date specified in Section 9 of Article 4 of this Constitution and shall continue for not more than sixty-one (61) session days. A session day is defined as any day in which either House of the General Assembly convenes. The Speaker of the House acting jointly with the President of the Senate, or if there be no President, the President Pro-Tem of the Senate, jointly may recess or adjourn a session for any period of time not to exceed twenty-one (21) days, during which time various standing committees of both Houses may meet at the call of the respective committee chairmen. No regular legislative session of the General Assembly may extend beyond the 30th day of April of the year in which it is convened."

The amendment to this section was proposed by Senate joint resolution No. 11, Acts 1967, ch. 394, p. 1386 and House joint resolution No. 10, Acts 1969, ch. 438, p. 1829 and was adopted by the people at the general election held on November 2, 1970, by a vote of 536,294 for and 408,158 against.

As originally adopted in 1851 this section read: "The sessions of the General Assembly shall be held biennially at the capital of the State, commencing on the Thursday next after the first Monday of January, in the year one thousand eight hundred and fifty three, and on the same day of every second year thereafter, unless a different day or place shall have been appointed by law. But if, in the opinion of the Governor, the public welfare shall require it, he may, at any time by proclamation, call a special session."

§ 10. **Officers — Procedure — Adjournment.** — Each House, when assembled, shall choose its own officers, the President of the Senate excepted; judge the elections, qualifications, and returns of its own members; determine its rules of proceeding, and sit upon its own adjournment. But neither House shall, without the consent of the other, adjourn for more than three days, nor to any place other than that in which it may be sitting.

§ 11. **Quorum.** — Two-thirds of each House shall constitute a quorum to do business; but a smaller number may meet, adjourn from day to day, and compel the attendance of absent members. A quorum being in attendance, if either House fail to effect an organization within the first five days thereafter, the members of the House so failing, shall be entitled to no compensation, from the end of the said five days until an organization shall have been effected.

§ 12. **Journal.** — Each House shall keep a journal of its proceedings, and publish the same. The yeas and nays, on any question, shall, at the request of any two members, be entered, together with the names of the members demanding the same, on the journal; Provided, that on motion to adjourn, it shall require one-tenth of the members present to order the yeas and nays.

§ 13. **Doors to be open.** — The doors of each House, and of Committees of the Whole, shall be kept open, except in such cases, as, in the opinion of either House, may require secrecy.

§ 14. **Disorderly behavior punished.** — Either House may punish its members for disorderly behavior, and may, with the concurrence of two-thirds, expel a member; but not a second time for the same cause.

Constitution

§ 15. Imprisonment for contempt. — Either House, during its session, may punish, by imprisonment, any person not a member, who shall have been guilty of disrespect to the House, by disorderly or contemptuous behavior, in its presence; but such imprisonment shall not, at any one time, exceed twenty-four hours.

§ 16. Powers of each house. — Each House shall have all powers, necessary for a branch of the legislative department of a free and independent State.

§ 17. Bills. — Bills may originate in either House, but may be amended or rejected in the other; except that bills for raising revenue shall originate in the House of Representatives.

§ 18. Reading and vote. — Every bill shall be read, by title, on three several days, in each House; unless, in case of emergency, two-thirds of the House where such bill may be pending, shall, by a vote of yeas and nays, deem it expedient to dispense with this rule; but the reading of a bill, by title, on its final passage, shall, in no case, be dispensed with; and the vote on the passage of every bill or joint resolution shall be taken by yeas and nays. [As amended November 7, 1984.]

§ 19. Subject matter of acts. — An act, except an act for the codification, revision or rearrangement of laws, shall be confined to one [1] subject and matters properly connected therewith. [As amended November 8, 1960; November 5, 1974.]

§ 20. Plain wording. — Every act and joint resolution shall be plainly worded, avoiding, as far as practicable, the use of technical terms.

§ 21. [Repealed.]

§ 22. Local or special laws forbidden. — The General Assembly shall not pass local or special laws:
Providing for the punishment of crimes and misdemeanors;
Regulating the practice in courts of justice;
Providing for changing the venue in civil and criminal cases;
Granting divorces;
Changing the names of persons;
Providing for laying out, opening and working on highways, and for the election or appointment of supervisors;
Vacating roads, town plats, streets, alleys and public squares;
Summoning and impaneling grand and petit juries, and providing for their compensation;
Regulating county and township business;
Regulating the election of county and township officers and their compensation;

Providing for the assessment and collection of taxes for State, county, township, or road purposes;

Providing for the support of common schools or the preservation of school funds;

Relating to fees or salaries: except that the laws may be so made as to grade the compensation of officers in proportion to the population and the necessary services required;

Relating to interest on money;

Providing for opening and conducting elections of State, county, or township officers, and designating the places of voting;

Providing for the same of real estate belonging to minors or other persons laboring under legal disabilities, by executors, administrators, guardians, or trustees. [As amended November 7, 1984.]

§ 23. **Laws must be general.** — In all the cases enumerated in the preceding Section, and in all other cases where a general law can be made applicable, all laws shall be general, and of uniform operation throughout the State.

§ 24. **Suits against the state.** — Provision may be made, by general law, for bringing suit against the state; but no special law authorizing such suit to be brought, or making compensation to any person claiming damages against the State, shall ever be passed. [As amended November 7, 1984.]

§ 25. **Passage of bills.** — A majority of all the members elected to each House, shall be necessary to pass every bill or joint resolution; and all bills and joint resolutions so passed, shall be signed by the Presiding Officers of the respective Houses.

§ 26. **Protest and entry.** — Any member of either House shall have the right to protest, and to have his protest, with his reasons for dissent, entered on the journal.

§ 27. **Public laws.** — Every statute shall be a public law, unless otherwise declared in the statute itself.

§ 28. **Effective date of statutes.** — No act shall take effect, until the same shall have been published and circulated in the several counties of this State, by authority, except in case of emergency; which emergency shall be declared in the preamble, or in the body, of the law.

§ 29. **Pay of members.** — The members of the General Assembly shall receive for their services a compensation to be fixed by law; but no increase of compensation shall take effect during the session at which such increase may be made. [As amended November 3, 1970.]

Constitution

§ 30. Members ineligible to certain offices. — No Senator or Representative shall, during the term for which he may have been elected, be eligible to any office, the election to which is vested in the General Assembly; nor shall he be appointed to any civil office of profit, which shall have been created, or the emoluments of which shall have been increased, during such term; but this latter provision shall not be construed to apply to any office elective by the People.

ARTICLE 5
EXECUTIVE

SECTION.
1. Governor.
2. Lieutenant-Governor.
3. Election.
4. Manner of voting.
5. Tie vote.
6. Contests.
7. Qualifications.
8. Persons ineligible.
9. Term of office.
10. Vacancies.
11. President pro tempore of senate.
12. Governor — Commander-in-chief.
13. Messages.

SECTION.
14. Bills signed or vetoed.
15. Information from officers.
16. Execution of laws.
17. Pardons and reprieves.
18. Vacancies filled by governor.
19. [Repealed.]
20. Change of meeting-place of assembly.
21. Duties of lieutenant-governor.
22. Pay of governor.
23. Pay of lieutenant-governor.
24. Ineligibility to other office.

§ 1. Governor. — The executive power of the State shall be vested in a Governor. He shall hold his office during four years, and shall not be eligible more than eight years in any period of twelve years. [As amended November 7, 1972.]

§ 2. Lieutenant-Governor. — There shall be a Lieutenant- Governor, who shall hold his office during four years.

§ 3. Election. — The Governor and Lieutenant Governor shall be elected at the times and places of choosing members of the General Assembly.

§ 4. Manner of voting. — Each candidate for Lieutenant Governor shall run jointly in the general election with a candidate for Governor, and his name shall appear jointly on the ballot with the candidate for Governor. Each vote cast for a candidate for Governor shall be considered cast for the candidate for Lieutenant Governor as well. The candidate for Lieutenant Governor whose name appears on the ballot jointly with that of the successful candidate for Governor shall be elected Lieutenant Governor. [As amended November 5, 1974.]

§ 5. Tie vote. — In the event of a tie vote, the Governor and Lieutenant Governor shall be elected from the candidates having received the tie vote by the affirmative vote in joint session of a majority of the combined membership of both Houses as the first order of business after their organization. [As amended November 5, 1974.]

§ 6. Contests. — Contested elections for Governor or Lieutenant Governor, shall be determined by the General Assembly, in such manner as may be prescribed by law.

§ 7. Qualifications. — No person shall be eligible to the office of Governor or Lieutenant Governor, who shall not have been five years a citizen of the United States, and also a resident of the State of Indiana during the five years next preceding his election; nor shall any person be eligible to either of the said offices, who shall not have attained the age of thirty years.

§ 8. Persons ineligible. — No member of Congress, or person holding any office under the United States or under this State, shall fill the office of Governor or Lieutenant Governor.

§ 9. Term of office. — The official term of the Governor and Lieutenant Governor shall commence on the second Monday of January, in the year one thousand eight hundred and fifty-three; and on the same day every fourth year thereafter.

§ 10. Vacancies. — (a) In case the Governor-elect fails to assume office, or in case of the death or resignation of the Governor or his removal from office, the Lieutenant Governor shall become Governor and hold office for the unexpired term of the person whom he succeeds. In case the Governor is unable to discharge the powers and duties of his office, the Lieutenant Governor shall discharge the powers and duties of the office as Acting Governor.

(b) Whenever there is a vacancy in the office of Lieutenant Governor, the Governor shall nominate a Lieutenant Governor who shall take office upon confirmation by a majority vote in each house of the general assembly and hold office for the unexpired term of the person whom he succeeds. If the general assembly is not in session, the Governor shall call it into special session to receive and act upon the Governor's nomination. In the event of the inability of the Lieutenant Governor to discharge the powers and duties of his office, the General Assembly may provide by law for the manner in which a person shall be selected to act in his place and declare which powers and duties of the office such person shall discharge.

(c) Whenever the Governor transmits to the President pro tempore of the Senate and the Speaker of the House of Representatives his written declaration that he is unable to discharge the powers and duties of his office, and until he transmits to them a written declaration to the contrary, such powers and duties shall be discharged by the Lieutenant Governor as Acting Governor. Thereafter, when the Governor transmits to the President pro tempore of the Senate and the Speaker of the House of Representatives his written declaration that no inability exists, he shall resume the powers and duties of his office.

(d) Whenever the President pro tempore of the Senate and the Speaker of the House of Representatives file with the Supreme Court a written statement suggesting that the Governor is unable to discharge the powers and duties of his office, the Supreme Court shall meet within forty-eight [48] hours to decide the question and such decision shall be final. Thereafter, whenever the Governor files with the Supreme Court his written declaration that no inability exists, the Supreme Court shall meet within forty-eight [48] hours to decide whether such be the case and such decision shall be final. Upon a decision that no inability exists, the Governor shall resume the powers and duties of his office.

(e) Whenever there is a vacancy in both the office of Governor and Lieutenant Governor, the general assembly shall convene in joint session forty-eight [48] hours after such occurrence and elect a governor from and of the same political party as the immediately last past Governor by a majority vote of each house. [As amended November 7, 1978.]

§ 11. **President pro tempore of senate.** — Whenever the Lieutenant Governor shall act as Governor, or shall be unable to attend as President of the Senate, the Senate shall elect one of its own members as President for the occasion.

§ 12. **Governor — Commander-in-chief.** — The Governor shall be commander-in-chief of the armed forces, and may call out such forces, to execute the laws, or to suppress insurrection, or to repel invasion. [As amended November 7, 1984.]

§ 13. **Messages.** — The Governor shall, from time to time, give to the General Assembly information touching the condition of the State, and recommend such measures as he shall judge to be expedient. [As amended November 7, 1984.]

§ 14. **Bills signed or vetoed.** — Every bill which shall have passed the General Assembly shall be presented to the Governor. The Governor shall have seven days after the day of presentment to act upon such bill.

(1) He may sign it, in which event it shall become a law.

(2) He may veto it:

(a) In the event of a veto while the General Assembly is in session, he shall return such bill, with his objections, within 7 days of presentment, to the House in which it originated, which House shall enter the objections at large upon its journals and proceed to reconsider the bill. If, after such reconsideration, a majority of all the members elected to that House shall approve the bill, it shall be sent, with the Governor's objections, to the other House, by which it shall likewise be reconsidered and, if approved by a majority of all the members elected to that House, it shall be a law. If such bill is not so returned by the Governor within 7 days of presentment, it shall be a law notwithstanding such veto.

(b) In the event of a veto after final adjournment of a session of the General Assembly, or during a temporary adjournment of a session, such bill shall be returned by the Governor to the House in which it originated on the first day that the General Assembly is in session after such adjournment, which House shall proceed in the same manner as with a bill vetoed before adjournment. If such bill is not so returned, it shall be a law notwithstanding such veto.

(3) He may refuse to sign or veto such bill in which event it shall become a law without his signature on the eighth day after presentment to the Governor.

Every bill presented to the Governor which is signed by him or on which he fails to act within said seven days after presentment shall be filed with the Secretary of State within ten days of presentment. The failure to so file shall not prevent such a bill from becoming a law.

In the event a bill is passed over the Governor's veto, such bill shall be filed with the Secretary of State without further presentment to the Governor: Provided, That in the event of such passage over the Governor's veto in the next succeeding General Assembly, the passage shall be deemed to have been the action of the General Assembly which initially passed such bill. [As amended November 7, 1972.]

§ 15. **Information from officers.** — The Governor shall transact all necessary business with the officers of government, and may require information in writing, from the officers of the administrative department, upon any subject relating to the duties of their respective offices.

§ 16. **Execution of laws.** — The Governor shall take care that the laws are faithfully executed. [As amended November 7, 1984.]

§ 17. **Pardons and reprieves.** — The Governor may grant reprieves, commutations, and pardons, after conviction, for all offenses except treason and cases of impeachment, subject to such regulations as may be provided by law. Upon conviction for treason, the Governor may suspend the execution of the sentence, until the case has been reported to the General Assembly, at its next meeting; when the General Assembly shall either grant a pardon, commute the sentence, direct the execution of the sentence, or grant a further reprieve. The Governor may remit fines and forfeitures, under such regulations as may be provided by law; and shall report to the General Assembly, at its next meeting, each case of reprieve, commutation, or pardon granted, and also the names of all persons in whose favor remission of fines and forfeitures were made, and the several amounts remitted: Provided, however, the General Assembly may, by law, constitute a council composed of officers of State, without whose advice and consent the Governor may not grant pardons, in any case, except those left to his sole power. [As amended November 7, 1984.]

§ 18. **Vacancies filled by governor.** — When, during a recess of the General Assembly, a vacancy shall happen in any office, the appointment to which is vested in the General Assembly; or when, at any time, a vacancy shall have occurred in any other State office, or in the office of Judge of any court; the Governor shall fill such vacancy, by appointment, which shall expire, when a successor shall have been elected and qualified.

§ 19. [Repealed.]

§ 20. **Change of meeting-place of assembly.** — Should the seat of government become dangerous from disease or a common enemy, the Governor may convene the General Assembly at any other place. [As amended November 7, 1984.]

§ 21. **Duties of lieutenant-governor.** — The Lieutenant Governor shall, by virtue of his office, be President of the Senate; have a right, when in committee of the whole, to join in debate, and to vote on all subjects; and, whenever the Senate shall be equally divided, he shall give the casting vote.

§ 22. **Pay of governor.** — The Governor shall, at stated times, receive for his services a compensation, which shall neither be increased nor diminished, during the term for which he shall have been elected.

§ 23. **Pay of lieutenant-governor.** — The Lieutenant- Governor while he shall act as President of the Senate, shall receive, for his services, the same compensation as the Speaker of the House of Representatives; and any person, acting as Governor, shall receive the compensation attached to the office of Governor.

§ 24. **Ineligibility to other office.** — Neither the Governor nor Lieutenant Governor shall be eligible to any other office, during the term for which he shall have been elected.

ARTICLE 6
ADMINISTRATIVE

SECTION.
1. Secretary, auditor and treasurer of state.
2. Designated county officers — Terms.
3. Other county and township officers.
4. Qualifications of county officers.
5. Residence of state officers.
6. Residence of local officers.

SECTION.
7. Impeachment of state officers.
8. Impeachment of local officers.
9. Vacancies in local offices.
10. County boards.
11. [Repealed.]

§ 1. **Secretary, auditor and treasurer of state.** — There shall be elected, by the voters of the state, a Secretary, an Auditor and a Treasurer of State, who shall, severally, hold their offices for four years. They shall perform such duties as may be enjoined by law; and no person shall be eligible to either of said offices, more than eight years in any period of twelve years. [As amended November 3, 1970.]

§ 2. **Designated county officers — Terms.** — There shall be elected, in each county by the voters thereof, at the time of holding general elections, a Clerk of the Circuit Court, Auditor, Recorder, Treasurer, Sheriff, Coroner and Surveyor, who shall, severally, hold their offices for four years; and no person shall be eligible to the office of Clerk, Auditor, Recorder, Treasurer, Sheriff, or Coroner more than eight years in any period of twelve years. [As amended November 7, 1984.]

§ 3. **Other county and township officers.** — Such other county and township officers as may be necessary, shall be elected, or appointed, in such manner as may be prescribed by law.

§ 4. **Qualifications of county officers.** — No person shall be elected, or appointed, as a county officer, who is not an elector of the county and who has not been an inhabitant of the county one year next preceding his election or appointment. [As amended November 7, 1984.]

§ 5. **Residence of state officers.** — The Governor, and the Secretary, Auditor and Treasurer of State, shall, severally, reside and keep the public records, books, and papers, in any manner relating to their respective offices, at the seat of government.

§ 6. **Residence of local officers.** — All county, township, and town officers, shall reside within their respective counties, townships, and towns; and shall keep their respective offices at such places therein, and perform such duties, as may be directed by law.

§ 7. **Impeachment of state officers.** — All State officers shall, for crime, incapacity, or negligence, be liable to be removed from office, either by impeachment by the House of Representatives, to be tried by the Senate, or by a joint resolution of the General Assembly; two-thirds of the members elected to each branch voting, in either case, therefor.

§ 8. **Impeachment of local officers.** — All State, county, township, and town officers, may be impeached, or removed from office, in such manner as may be prescribed by law.

§ 9. **Vacancies in local offices.** — Vacancies in county, township, and town offices, shall be filled in such manner as may be prescribed by law.

§ 10. **County boards.** — The General Assembly may confer upon the boards doing county business in the several counties, powers of a local, administrative character.

Constitution

§ 11. [Repealed.]

ARTICLE 7
JUDICIAL

SECTION.
1. Judicial power.
2. Supreme Court.
3. Chief Justice.
4. Jurisdiction of Supreme Court.
5. Court of Appeals.
6. Jurisdiction of Court of Appeals.
7. Judicial circuits.
8. Circuit courts.
9. Judicial nominating commission.
10. Selection of justices of the Supreme Court and judges of the Court of Appeals.
11. Tenure of justices of Supreme Court

SECTION.
and judges of the Court of Appeals.
12. Substitution of judges.
13. Removal of circuit court judges and prosecuting attorneys.
14. [Repealed.]
15. No limitation on term of office.
16. Prosecuting attorneys.
17. Grand jury.
18. Criminal prosecutions.
19. Pay.
20. [Repealed.]

§ 1. **Judicial power.** — The judicial power of the State shall be vested in one Supreme Court, one Court of Appeals, Circuit Courts, and such other courts as the General Assembly may establish. [As amended November 3, 1970.]

§ 2. **Supreme Court.** — The Supreme Court shall consist of the Chief Justice of the State and not less than four nor more than eight associate justices; a majority of whom shall form a quorum. The court may appoint such personnel as may be necessary. [As amended November 3, 1970.]

§ 3. **Chief Justice.** — The Chief Justice of the State shall be selected by the judicial nominating commission from the members of the Supreme Court and he shall retain that office for a period of five years, subject to reappointment in the same manner, except that a member of the Court may resign the office of Chief Justice without resigning from the Court. During a vacancy in the office of Chief Justice caused by absence, illness, incapacity or resignation all powers and duties of that office shall devolve upon the member of the Supreme Court who as senior in length of service and if equal in length of service the determination shall be by lot until such time as the cause of the vacancy is terminated or the vacancy is filled.

The Chief Justice of the State shall appoint such persons as the General Assembly by law may provide for the administration of his office. The Chief Justice shall have prepared and submit to the General Assembly regular reports on the condition of the courts and such other reports as may be requested. [As amended November 3, 1970.]

§ 4. **Jurisdiction of Supreme Court.** — The Supreme Court shall have no original jurisdiction except in admission to the practice of law; discipline or disbarment of those admitted; the unauthorized practice of law; discipline, removal and retirement of justices and judges; supervision of the exercise of jurisdiction by the other courts of the State; and issuance of writs necessary or appropriate in aid of its jurisdiction. The Supreme Court shall exercise appellate jurisdiction under such terms and conditions as specified by rules except that appeals from a judgment imposing a sentence of death, life imprisonment or imprisonment for a term greater than ten years shall be taken directly to the Supreme Court. The Supreme Court shall have, in all appeals of criminal cases, the power to review all questions of law and to review and revise the sentence imposed. [As added November 3, 1970.]

§ 5. **Court of Appeals.** — The Court of Appeals shall consist of as many geographic districts and sit at such locations as the General Assembly shall determine to be necessary. Each geographic district of the Court shall consist of three judges. The judges of each geographic district shall appoint such personnel as the General Assembly may provide by law. [As amended November 3, 1970.]

§ 6. **Jurisdiction of Court of Appeals.** — The Court shall have no original jurisdiction, except that it may be authorized by rules of the Supreme Court to review directly decisions of administrative agencies. In all other cases, it shall exercise appellate jurisdiction under such terms and conditions as the Supreme Court shall specify by rules which shall, however, provide in all cases an absolute right to one appeal and to the extent provided by rule, review and revision of sentences for defendants in all criminal cases. [As amended November 3, 1970.]

§ 7. **Judicial circuits.** — The State shall, from time to time, be divided into judicial circuits; and a Judge for each circuit shall be elected by the voters thereof. He shall reside within the circuit and shall have been duly admitted to practice law by the Supreme Court of Indiana; he shall hold his office for the term of six years, if he so long behaves well. [As amended November 3, 1970.]

§ 8. **Circuit courts.** — The Circuit Courts shall have such civil and criminal jurisdiction as may be prescribed by law. [As amended November 3, 1970.]

§ 9. **Judicial nominating commission.** — There shall be one judicial nominating commission for the Supreme Court and Court of Appeals. This commission shall, in addition, be the commission on judicial qualifications for the Supreme Court and Court of Appeals.

The judicial nominating commission shall consist of seven members, a majority of whom shall form a quorum, one of whom shall be the Chief Justice of the State or a Justice of the Supreme Court whom he may designate, who shall act as chairman. Those admitted to the practice of law shall elect three of their number to serve as members of said commission. All elections shall be in such manner as the General Assembly may provide. The governor shall appoint to the commission three citizens, not admitted to the practice of law. The terms of office and compensation for members of a judicial nominating commission shall be fixed by the General Assembly. No member of a judicial nominating commission other than the Chief Justice or his designee shall hold any other salaried public office. No member shall hold an office in a political party or organization. No member of the judicial nominating commission shall be eligible for appointment to a judicial office so long as he is a member of the commission and for a period of three years thereafter. [As amended November 3, 1970.]

§ 10. **Selection of justices of the Supreme Court and judges of the Court of Appeals.** — A vacancy in a judicial office in the Supreme Court or Court of Appeals shall be filled by the Governor, without regard to political affiliation, from a list of three nominees presented to him by the judicial nominating commission. If the Governor shall fail to make an appointment from the list within sixty days from the day it is presented to him, the appointment shall be made by the Chief Justice or the acting Chief Justice from the same list.

To be eligible for nomination as a justice of the Supreme Court or judge of the Court of Appeals, a person must be domiciled within the geographic district, a citizen of the United States, admitted to the practice of law in the courts of the state for a period of not less than ten (10) years or must have served as a judge of a circuit, superior or criminal court of the State of Indiana for a period of not less than five (5) years. [As amended November 3, 1970.]

§ 11. **Tenure of justices of Supreme Court and judges of the Court of Appeals.** — A justice of the Supreme Court or judge of the Court of Appeals shall serve until the next general election following the expiration of two years from the date of appointment, and, subject to approval or rejection by the electorate, shall continue to serve for terms of ten years, so long as he retains his office. In the case of a justice of the Supreme Court, the electorate of the entire state shall vote on the question of approval or rejection. In the case of judges of the Court of Appeals the electorate of the geographic district in which he serves shall vote on the question of approval or rejection.

Every such justice and judge shall retire at the age specified by statute in effect at the commencement of his current term.

Every such justice or judge is disqualified from acting as a judicial officer, without loss of salary, while there is pending (1) an indictment or information charging him in any court in the United States with a crime punishable as a felony under the laws of Indiana or the United States, or (2) a recommendation to the Supreme Court by the commission on judicial qualifications for his removal or retirement.

On recommendation of the commission on judicial qualifications or on its own motion, the Supreme Court may suspend such justice or judge from office without salary when in any court in the United States he pleads guilty or no contest or is found guilty of a crime punishable as a felony under the laws of Indiana or the United States, or of any other crime that involves moral turpitude under that law. If his conviction is reversed, suspension terminates and he shall be paid his salary for the period of suspension. If he is suspended and his conviction becomes final the Supreme Court shall remove him from office.

On recommendation of the commission on judicial qualifications the Supreme Court may (1) retire such justice or judge for disability that seriously interferes with the performance of his duties and is or is likely to become permanent, and (2) censure or remove such justice or judge, for action occurring not more than six years prior to the commencement of his current term, when such action constitutes willful misconduct in office, willful and persistent failure to perform his duties, habitual intemperance, or conduct prejudicial to the administration of justice that brings the judicial office into disrepute.

A justice or judge so retired by the Supreme Court shall be considered to have retired voluntarily. A justice or judge so removed by the Supreme Court is ineligible for judicial office and pending further order of the Court he is suspended from practicing law in this State.

Upon receipt by the Supreme Court of any such recommendation, the Court shall hold a hearing, at which such justice or judge is entitled to be present, and make such determinations as shall be required. No justice shall participate in the determination of such hearing when it concerns himself.

The Supreme Court shall make rules implementing this section and provide for convening of hearings. Hearings and proceedings shall be public upon request of the justice or judge whom it concerns.

No such justice or judge shall, during his term of office, engage in the practice of law, run for elective office other than a judicial office, directly or indirectly make any contribution to, or hold any office in, a political party or organization or take part in any political campaign. [As amended November 3, 1970.]

§ 12. **Substitution of judges.** — The General Assembly may provide, by law, that the Judge of one circuit may hold the Courts of another circuit, in cases of necessity or convenience; and in case of temporary inability of any Judge, from sickness or other cause, to hold the Courts in his circuit, provision may be made, by law, for holding such Courts. [As amended November 3, 1970.]

§ 13. **Removal of circuit court judges and prosecuting attorneys.** — Any Judge of the Circuit Court or Prosecuting Attorney, who shall have been convicted of corruption or other high crime, may, on information in the name of the State, be removed from office by the Supreme Court, or in such other manner as may be prescribed by law. [As amended November 3, 1970.]

§ 14. [Repealed.]

§ 15. **No limitation on term of office.** — The provisions of Article 15, section 2, prohibiting terms of office longer than four years, shall not apply to justices and judges. [As amended November 3, 1970.]

§ 16. **Prosecuting attorneys.** — There shall be elected in each judicial circuit by the voters thereof a prosecuting attorney, who shall have been

Constitution

admitted to the practice of law in this State before his election, who shall hold his office for four years, and whose term of office shall begin on the first day of January next succeeding his election. The election of prosecuting attorneys under this section shall be held at the time of holding the general election in the year 1974 and each four years thereafter. [As amended November 3, 1970.]

§ 17. **Grand jury.** — The General Assembly may modify, or abolish, the grand jury system. [As amended November 3, 1970.]

§ 18. **Criminal prosecutions.** — All criminal prosecutions shall be carried on in the name, and by the authority of the State; and the style of all process shall be: "The State of Indiana." [As amended November 3, 1970.]

§ 19. **Pay.** — The Justices of Supreme Court and Judges of the Court of Appeals and of the Circuit Courts shall at stated times receive a compensation which shall not be diminished during their continuance in office. [As amended November 3, 1970.]

§ 20. **[Repealed.]**

ARTICLE 8

EDUCATION

SECTION.
1. Common schools.
2. Common school fund.
3. Principal a perpetual fund — Appropriation of income.
4. Investment and distribution.
5. Reinvestment.

SECTION.
6. Counties — Liability.
7. Trust funds inviolate.
8. Superintendent of public instruction.

§ 1. **Common schools.** — Knowledge and learning, generally diffused throughout a community, being essential to the preservation of a free government; it shall be the duty of the General Assembly to encourage, by all suitable means, moral, intellectual, scientific, and agricultural improvement; and to provide, by law, for a general and uniform system of Common Schools, wherein tuition shall be without charge, and equally open to all.

§ 2. **Common school fund.** — The Common School fund shall consist of the Congressional Township fund, and the lands belonging thereto;

The Surplus Revenue fund;

The Saline fund and the lands belonging thereto;

The bank Tax fund, and the fund arising from the one hundred and fourteenth section of the charter of the State Bank of Indiana;

The fund to be derived from the sale of County Seminaries, and the moneys and property heretofore held for such seminaries;

From the fines assessed for breaches of the penal laws of the State; and from all forfeitures which may accrue;

All lands and other estate which shall escheat to the State, for want of heirs or kindred entitled to the inheritance;

All lands that have been, or may hereafter be, granted to the State, where no special purpose is expressed in the grant, and the proceeds of the sales thereof; including the proceeds of the sales of the Swamp Lands, granted to the State of Indiana by the act of Congress of the twenty-eighth of September, eighteen hundred and fifty, after deducting the expense of selecting and draining the same;

Taxes on the property of corporations, that may be assessed by the General Assembly for common school purposes.

§ 3. **Principal a perpetual fund — Appropriation of income.** — The principal of the Common School fund shall remain a perpetual fund, which may be increased, but shall never be diminished; and the income thereof shall be inviolably appropriated to the support of Common Schools, and to no other purpose whatever.

§ 4. **Investment and distribution.** — The General Assembly shall invest, in some safe and profitable manner, all such portions of the Common School fund, as have not heretofore been entrusted to the several counties; and shall make provision, by law, for the distribution, among the several counties, of the interest thereof.

§ 5. **Reinvestment.** — If any county shall fail to demand its proportion of such interest, for Common School purposes, the same shall be reinvested, for the benefit of such county.

§ 6. **Counties — Liability.** — The several counties shall be held liable for the preservation of so much of the said fund as may be entrusted to them, and for the payment of the annual interest thereon.

§ 7. **Trust funds inviolate.** — All trust funds, held by the State, shall remain inviolate, and be faithfully and exclusively applied to the purposes for which the trust was created.

§ 8. **Superintendent of public instruction.** — There shall be a State Superintendent of Public Instruction, whose method of selection, tenure, duties and compensation shall be prescribed by law. [As amended November 7, 1972.]

Constitution

ARTICLE 9
STATE INSTITUTIONS

SECTION.
1. Benevolent institutions.
2. Institutions for juveniles.
3. County farms.

§ 1. Benevolent institutions. — It shall be the duty of the General Assembly to provide, by law, for the support of Institutions for the education of the Deaf, the Mute, and the Blind; and for the treatment of the Insane. [As amended November 7, 1984.]

§ 2. Institutions for juveniles. — The General Assembly shall provide institutions for the correction and reformation of juvenile offenders. [As amended November 7, 1984.]

§ 3. County farms. — The counties may provide farms, as an asylum for those persons, who, by reason of age, infirmity, or other misfortune, have claims upon the sympathies and aid of society. [As amended November 7, 1984.]

ARTICLE 10
FINANCE

SECTION.
1. Assessment and taxation.
2. Payment of public debt.
3. Appropriations.
4. Statement of receipts and expenditures.
5. State debt prohibited — Exceptions.
6. County indebtedness for stock — State assumption of debts.
7. Wabash and Erie Canal.
8. Income tax.

§ 1. Assessment and taxation. — (a) The General Assembly shall provide, by law, for a uniform and equal rate of property assessment and taxation and shall prescribe regulations to secure a just valuation for taxation of all property, both real and personal. The General Assembly may exempt from property taxation any property in any of the following classes:

(1) Property being used for municipal, education, literary, scientific, religious or charitable purposes;

(2) Tangible personal property other than property being held for sale in the ordinary course of a trade or business, property being held, used or consumed in connection with the production of income, or property being held as an investment;

(3) Intangible personal property.

(b) The General Assembly may exempt any motor vehicles, mobile homes, airplanes, boats, trailers or similar property, provided that an excise tax in lieu of the property tax is substituted therefor. [As amended November 8, 1966.]

§ 2. **Payment of public debt.** — All the revenues derived from the sale of any of the public works belonging to the State, and from the net annual income thereof, and any surplus that may, at any time, remain in the Treasury, derived from taxation for general State purposes, after the payment of the ordinary expenses of the government, and of the interest on bonds of the State, other than Bank bonds, shall be annually applied, under the direction of the General Assembly, to the payment of the principal of the Public Debt.

§ 3. **Appropriations.** — No money shall be drawn from the Treasury, but in pursuance of appropriations made by law.

§ 4. **Statement of receipts and expenditures.** — An accurate statement of the receipts and expenditures of the public money, shall be published with the laws of each regular session of the General Assembly.

§ 5. **State debt prohibited — Exceptions.** — No law shall authorize any debt to be contracted, on behalf of the State, except in the following cases: To meet casual deficits in the revenue; to pay the interest on the State Debt; to repel invasion, suppress insurrection, or, if hostilities be threatened, provide for the public defense.

§ 6. **County indebtedness for stock — State assumption of debts.** — No county shall subscribe for stock in any incorporated company, unless the same be paid for at the time of such subscription; nor shall any county loan its credit to any incorporated company, nor borrow money for the purpose of taking stock in any such company; nor shall the General Assembly ever, on behalf of the State, assume the debts of any county, city, town, or township; nor of any corporation whatever.

§ 7. **Wabash and Erie Canal.** — No law or resolution shall ever be passed by the General Assembly of the State of Indiana, that shall recognize any liability of this State to pay or redeem any certificate of stock issued in pursuance of an act entitled "An act to provide for the funded debt of the State of Indiana, and for the completion of the Wabash and Erie Canal to Evansville," passed January 19, 1846, and an act supplemental to said act, passed January 29, 1847, which, by the provisions of the said acts, or either of them, shall be payable exclusively from the proceeds of the canal lands, and the tolls and revenues of the canal in said acts mentioned, and no such certificate or stocks shall ever be paid by this State [as adopted February 18, 1873].

§ 8. **Income tax.** — The general assembly may levy and collect a tax upon income, from whatever source derived, at such rates, in such manner, and with such exemptions as may be prescribed by law.

Constitution

ARTICLE 11
CORPORATIONS

SECTION.
1. Incorporation of banks.
2. General banking law.
3. Registry of notes.
4. Bank with branches.
5. Branches mutually responsible.
6. [Repealed.]
7. Redemption.
8. Holders' preference.
9. Interest.

SECTION.
10. [Repealed.]
11. Trust funds.
12. State not to be stockholder.
13. General laws.
14. Individual liability of stockholders — Legislature empowered to fix.

§ 1. **Incorporation of banks.** — The General Assembly shall not have power to establish, or incorporate, any bank or banking company, or moneyed institution, for the purpose of issuing bills of credit, or bills payable to order or bearer, except under the conditions prescribed in this Constitution.

§ 2. **General banking law.** — No banks shall be established otherwise than under a general banking law, except as provided in the fourth section of this article.

§ 3. **Registry of notes.** — If the General Assembly shall enact a general banking law, such law shall provide for the registry and countersigning, by an officer of State, of all paper credit designed to be circulated as money; and ample collateral security, readily convertible into specie, for the redemption of the same in gold or silver, shall be required; which collateral security shall be under the control of the proper officer or officers of State.

§ 4. **Bank with branches.** — The General Assembly may also charter a bank with branches, without collateral security as required in the preceding section.

§ 5. **Branches mutually responsible.** — If the General Assembly shall establish a bank with branches, the branches shall be mutually responsible for each other's liabilities upon all paper credit issued as money.

§ 6. **[Repealed.]**

§ 7. **Redemption.** — All bills or notes issued as money shall be, at all times, redeemable in gold or silver; and no law shall be passed, sanctioning, directly, or indirectly, the suspension, by any bank or banking company, of specie payments.

§ 8. **Holders' preference.** — Holders of bank notes shall be entitled, in case of insolvency, to preference of payment over all other creditors.

§ 9. **Interest.** — No bank shall receive, directly or indirectly, a greater rate of interest than shall be allowed, by law, to individuals loaning money.

§ 10. **[Repealed.]**

§ 11. **Trust funds.** — The General Assembly is not prohibited from investing the trust funds in a bank with branches; but in case of such investment, the safety of the same shall be guaranteed by unquestionable security.

§ 12. **State not to be stockholder.** — The State shall not be a stockholder in any bank; nor shall the credit of the State ever be given, or loaned, in aid of any person, association or corporation; nor shall the State become a stockholder in any corporation or association. [As amended November 7, 1984.]

§ 13. **General laws.** — Corporations, other than banking, shall not be created by special Act, but may be formed under general laws.

§ 14. **Individual liability of stockholders — Legislature empowered to fix.** — Dues from corporations shall be secured by such individual liability of the stockholders, or other means, as may be prescribed by law. [As amended November 5, 1940.]

ARTICLE 12
MILITIA

SECTION.	SECTION.
1. Organization.	4. Conscientious objectors.
2. Commander-in-chief.	5, 6. [Omitted.]
3. Adjutant general.	

§ 1. **Organization.** — A militia shall be provided and shall consist of all persons over the age of seventeen (17) years, except those persons who may be exempted by the laws of the United States or of this State. The militia may be divided into active and inactive classes and consist of such military organizations as may be provided by law. [As amended November 3, 1936 and November 5, 1974.]

§ 2. **Commander-in-chief.** — The Governor is Commander-in-Chief of the militia and other military forces of this state. [As amended November 5, 1974.]

§ 3. **Adjutant general.** — There shall be an Adjutant General, who shall be appointed by the Governor. [As amended November 5, 1974.]

Constitution

§ 4. Conscientious objectors. — No person, conscientiously opposed to bearing arms, shall be compelled to do so in the militia. [As amended November 5, 1974.]

§§ 5, 6. [Omitted by amendment.]

ARTICLE 13
MUNICIPAL DEBT

SECTION.
1. Limitation on indebtedness — Excess void.

§ 1. Limitation on indebtedness — Excess void. — No political or municipal corporation in this State shall ever become indebted in any manner or for any purpose to an amount in the aggregate exceeding two per centum on the value of the taxable property within such corporation, to be ascertained by the last assessment for State and county taxes, previous to the incurring of such indebtedness; and all bonds or obligations, in excess of such amount, given by such corporations, shall be void: Provided, That in time of war, foreign invasion, or other great public calamity, on petition of a majority of the property owners, in number and value, within the limits of such corporation, the public authorities, in their discretion, may incur obligations necessary for the public protection and defense, to such an amount as may be requested in such petition. [As amended March 14, 1881.]

ARTICLE 14
BOUNDARIES

SECTION.
1. State boundaries.
2. Jurisdictions.

§ 1. State boundaries. — In order that the boundaries of the State may be known and established, it is hereby ordained and declared, that the State of Indiana is bounded, on the East, by the meridian line, which forms the western boundary of the State of Ohio; on the South, by the Ohio river, from the mouth of the Great Miami river to the mouth of the Wabash river; on the West, by a line drawn along the middle of the Wabash river, from its mouth to a point where a due north line, drawn from the town of Vincennes, would last touch the north-western shore of said Wabash river; and, thence, by a due north line, until the same shall intersect an east and west line, drawn through a point ten miles north of the southern extreme of Lake Michigan; on the North, by said east and west line, until the same shall intersect the first mentioned meridian line, which forms the western boundary of the State of Ohio.

§ 2. **Jurisdictions.** — The State of Indiana shall possess jurisdiction and sovereignty co-extensive with the boundaries declared in the preceding section; and shall have concurrent jurisdiction, in civil and criminal cases, with the State of Kentucky on the Ohio river and with the State of Illinois on the Wabash river, so far as said rivers form the common boundary between this State and said States respectively.

ARTICLE 15
MISCELLANEOUS

SECTION.
1. Official appointments.
2. Duration of office.
3. Holding over.
4. Official oath.
5. State seal.
6. Commissions.

SECTION.
7. Areas of counties.
8. Lotteries prohibited.
9. Public grounds.
10. Tippecanoe Battle Ground.

§ 1. **Official appointments.** — All officers, whose appointment is not otherwise provided for in this Constitution, shall be chosen in such manner as now is, or hereafter may be, prescribed by law.

§ 2. **Duration of office.** — When the duration of any office is not provided for by this Constitution, it may be declared by law; and, if not so declared, such office shall be held during the pleasure of the authority making the appointment. But the General Assembly shall not create any office, the tenure of which shall be longer than four years.

§ 3. **Holding over.** — Whenever it is provided in this Constitution, or in any law which may be hereafter passed, that any officer, other than a member of the General Assembly, shall hold his office for any given term, the same shall be construed to mean, that such officer shall hold his office for such term, and until his successor shall have been elected and qualified.

§ 4. **Official oath.** — Every person elected or appointed to any office under this constitution, shall, before entering on the duties thereof, take an oath or affirmation, to support the Constitution of this State, and of the United States, and also an oath of office.

§ 5. **State seal.** — There shall be a Seal of State, kept by the Governor for official purposes, which shall be called the Seal of the State of Indiana.

§ 6. **Commissions.** — All commissions shall issue in the name of the State, shall be signed by the Governor, sealed by the State Seal and attested by the Secretary of State.

Constitution

§ 7. **Areas of counties.** — No county shall be reduced to an area less than four hundred square miles; nor shall any county, under that area, be further reduced.

§ 8. **Lotteries prohibited.** — No lottery shall be authorized; nor shall the sale of lottery tickets be allowed.

§ 9. **Public grounds.** — The following grounds owned by the State in Indianapolis, namely: the State House Square, the Governor's Circle, and so much of out-lot numbered one hundred and forty-seven, as lies north of the arm of the Central Canal, shall not be sold or leased.

§ 10. **Tippecanoe Battle Ground.** — It shall be the duty of the General Assembly to provide for the permanent enclosure and preservation of the Tippecanoe Battle Ground.

ARTICLE 16
AMENDMENTS

SECTION.
1. How made.
2. Separate vote.

§ 1. **How made.** — Any amendment or amendments to this Constitution, may be proposed in either branch of the General Assembly; and, if the same shall be agreed to by a majority of the members elected to each of the two Houses, such proposed amendment or amendments shall, with the yeas and nays thereon, be entered on their journals, and referred to the General Assembly to be chosen at the next general election; and if, in the General Assembly so next chosen, such proposed amendment or amendments shall be agreed to by a majority of all the members elected to each House, then it shall be the duty of the General Assembly to submit such amendment or amendments to the electors of the State; and if a majority of said electors shall ratify the same, such amendment or amendments shall become a part of this Constitution.

§ 2. **Separate vote.** — If two or more amendments shall be submitted at the same time, they shall be submitted in such manner that the electors shall vote for or against each of such amendments separately. [As amended November 8, 1966.]

SCHEDULE

Effective date of constitution. — This Constitution, if adopted, shall take effect on the first day of November, in the year one thousand eight hundred and fifty-one, and shall supersede the Constitution adopted in the year one thousand eight hundred and sixteen.

Continuance of former laws. — That no inconvenience may arise from the change in the government, it is hereby ordained as follows:

Laws continued. — First. All laws now in force, and not inconsistent with this Constitution, shall remain in force, until they shall expire or be repealed.

Proceedings continued. — Second. All indictments, prosecutions, suits, pleas, plaints, and other proceedings, pending in any of the courts, shall be prosecuted to final judgment and executions; and all appeals, writs of error, certiorari, and injunctions, shall be carried on in the several courts, in the same manner as is now provided by law.

Fines, bonds, and forfeitures — Insurance to state or county. — Third. All fines, penalties, and forfeitures, due or accruing to the State, or to any county therein, shall inure to the State, or to such county, in the manner prescribed by law. All bonds executed to the State, or to any officer, in his official capacity, shall remain in force, and inure to the use of those concerned.

Municipal acts continued. — Fourth. All acts of incorporation for municipal purposes shall continue in force under this Constitution, until such time as the General Assembly shall, in its discretion, modify or repeal the same.

Governor holds over. — Fifth. The Governor, at the expiration of the present official term, shall continue to act, until his successor shall have been sworn into office.

General assembly. — Sixth. There shall be a session of the General Assembly, commencing on the first Monday of December, in the year one thousand eight hundred and fifty-one.

Legislators hold over. — Seventh. Senators now in office and holding over, under the existing Constitution, and such as may be elected at the next general election, and the Representatives then elected, shall continue in office until the first general election under this Constitution.

First general election. — Eighth. The first general election under this Constitution, shall be held in the year one thousand eight hundred and fifty-two.

Election of state officers. — Ninth. The first election for Governor, Lieutenant Governor, Judges of the Supreme Court and Circuit Courts, Clerk of the Supreme Court, Prosecuting Attorneys, Secretary, Auditor and Treasurer of State, and the State Superintendent of Public Instruction, under this Constitution shall be held at the general election in the year one thousand eight hundred and fifty-two; and such of said officers as may be in office when this Constitution shall go into effect, shall continue in their respective offices, until their successors shall have been elected and qualified.

Continuance of officers. — Tenth. Every person elected by popular vote, and now in any office which is continued by this Constitution, and every person who shall be so elected to any such office before the taking effect of this

Constitution

Constitution, (except as in this Constitution otherwise provided,) shall continue in office until the term for which such person has been, or may be, elected, shall expire: Provided, that no such person shall continue in office, after the taking effect of this Constitution, for a longer period than the term of such office in this Constitution prescribed.

Oath. — Eleventh. On the taking effect of this Constitution, all officers thereby continued in office, shall, before proceeding in the further discharge of their duties, take an oath or affirmation to support this Constitution.

Vacancies. — Twelfth. All vacancies that may occur in existing offices, prior to the first general election under this Constitution, shall be filled in the manner now prescribed by law.

Submission of Thirteenth Article. — Thirteenth. At the time of submitting this Constitution to the electors for their approval or disapproval, the article numbered thirteen, in relation to Negroes and Mulattoes, shall be submitted as a distinct proposition, in the following form: "Exclusion and Colonization of Negroes and Mulattoes," "Aye" or "No." And if a majority of the votes cast shall be in favor of said article, then the same shall form a part of this Constitution; otherwise, it shall be void, and form no part thereof.

General submission. — Fourteenth. No Article or Section of this Constitution shall be submitted as a distinct proposition, to a vote of the electors, otherwise than as herein provided.

Perry and Spencer Counties. — Fifteenth. Whenever a portion of the citizens of the counties of Perry and Spencer, shall deem it expedient to form, of the contiguous territory of said counties, a new County, it shall be the duty of those interested in the organization of such new county, to lay off the same, by proper metes and bounds, of equal portions as nearly as practicable, not to exceed one-third of the territory of each of said counties. The proposal to create such new county shall be submitted to the voters of said counties, at a general election, in such manner as shall be prescribed by law. And if a majority of all the votes given at said election, shall be in favor of the organization of said new county, it shall be the duty of the General Assembly to organize the same, out of the territory thus designated.

Charter of Clarksville. — Sixteenth. The General Assembly may alter or amend the charter of Clarksville, and make such regulations as may be necessary for carrying into effect the objects contemplated in granting the same; and the funds belonging to said town shall be applied, according to the intention of the grantor.

Done in Convention, at Indianapolis, the tenth day of February, in the year of our Lord one thousand eight hundred and fifty-one; and of the Independence of the United States, the seventy-fifth.

GEORGE WHITFIELD CARR,
President, and Delegate
from the County of Lawrence.

Attest: WM. H. ENGLISH,
        Principal Secretary.

GEORGE L. SITES,
HERMAN G. BARKWELL, } Assistant Secretaries.
ROBERT M. EVANS,

Books about Indiana

Baker, Ronald L. and Marvin Carmony. *Indiana Place Names.* 1975.

Ball, T. H. *Northwestern Indiana from 1800 to 1900.* 1900.

Banta, Richard E. *Hoosier Caravan: A Treasury of Indiana Life and Lore.* 2d ed. 1975.

Barce, Elmore. *The Land of the Miamis.* 1922.

Black, Harry G. *Trails to Hoosier Heritage.* 1981.

Bloemaker, Al. *500 Miles to Go: The Story of the Indianapolis Speedway.* 1961.

Bole, John Archibald. *The Harmony Society.* 1904.

Burnet, Mary Q. *Arts and Artists of Indiana.* 1921.

Carty, Mickey D. *Searching in Indiana: A Reference Guide to Public and Private Records.* 1939.

Cauthorn, Henry S. *History of the City of Vincennes.* 1902.

Cavinder, Fred D. *The Indiana Book of Records, Firsts, and Fascinating Facts.* 1985.

Cockrom, William M. *Pioneer History of Indiana; Including Stories, Incidents, and Customs of the Early Settlers.* 1980.

Encyclopedia of Indiana

Cottman, George S. *Centennial History and Handbook of Indiana.* 1915.

Dean, Linda. *Indiana Folklore: A Reader.* 1980.

Dunn, Jacob P. *True Indian Stories.* 1908.

Engel, J. Ronald. *Sacred Sands: The Struggle for Community in the Indiana Dunes.* 1983.

Esarey, Logan. *The Indiana Home.* 2d ed. 1953.

Fatout, Paul. *Indiana Canals.* 1972.

Federal Writers' Project. *Indiana: A Guide to the Hoosier State.* 1941.

Funk, Arville L. *A Sketchbook of Indiana History.* 1969.

Gass, William H. *In the Heart of the Heart of the Country.* 1968.

Goodrich, Dewitt C. and Charles R. Tuttle. *An Illustrated History of the State of Indiana.* 1875.

Hawkins, Hubert H. *Indiana's Road to Statehood: A Documentary Record.* 1964.

Hedge, Christine. *A Guide to State Forests, State Parks, Reservoirs.* 1987.

Jonsson, Ingrid E. *Refererence Guide to Indiana.* 1977.

Kellar, James H. *An Introduction to the Prehistory of Indiana.* 1983.

Levering, Julia H. *Historic Indiana.* 1909.

Bibliography

Lindley, Harlow. *Indiana as Seen by Early Travelers.* 1916.

Lynd, Robert. *Middletown: A Study in Contemporary American Culture.* 1929.

Madison, James H. *Indiana through Tradition and Change: A History of the Hoosier State and its People, 1920-1945* (The History of Indiana, Vol.V). 1982.

--*The Indiana Way: A State History.* 1986.

Noland, Jeannette C. *Hoosier City, the Story of Indianapolis.* 1943.

Oskinson, John M. *Tecumseh and His Times.* 1938.

Phillips, Clifton J. *Indiana in Transition: The Emergence of an Industrial Commonwealth 1880-1920* (The History of Indiana, Vol. IV) 1968.

Pumroy, Eric and Paul Brockman. *A Guide to the Manuscript Collection of the Indiana State Historical Society.* 1986.

Rudolph, L.C. and Judith E. Endelman. *Religion in Indiana: A Guide to Historical Resources.* 1986.

Shumaker, Arthur. *A History of Indiana Literature: With Emphasis on the Authors...Writing Prior to World War II.* 1962.

Simons, Richard S. *The Rivers of Indiana.* 1985.

Stampp, Kenneth. *Indiana Politics during the Civil War.* 1949. rpt. 1978.

Tesich, Steve. *Summer Crossing.* 1982.

Encyclopedia of Indiana

Troyer, Byron L. *Yesterday's Indiana.* 1975.

VanderMeer, Philip R. *The Hoosier Politician: Officeholding and Political Culture in Indiana 1896-1920.* 1985.

West, Jessamyn. *The Massacre at Fall Creek.* 1975.

Wilson, William E. *Indiana, a History.* 1966.

INDEX

Abbey Press, 298
Abbot
　Edward, 53
Abolition, 70,71, 200, 333
Abraham Lincoln Hall, 244
Academy of Music, 348
Acton, 139
Adams, 139
Adams County, 15
Ade
　Ella M., 110
　George, 83, 156, 232, 247, 271
Adena Culture, 37, 341
Adjutant General, 125
Administration
　Department of, 125
Advance, 139
Aeronautics
　Department of, 125
Aging
　Department of, 125
Agricultural Conservation and Adjustment Administration, 114
Agriculture
　Department of, 125
Air Pollution Control
　Department of, 125
Akron, 139
Albany, 140
Albion, 140
Alcoa, 192
Alcoholism
　Department of, 126
Alexander
　Sarah, 93
Alexandria, 140
Alfordsville, 140
Alice of Old Vincennes, 327
Allen, 141
Allen County, 15
Allen County-Fort Wayne Historical Society Museum, 199
Allen
　John, 141
Allison Mansion, 364
Allouez
　Father, 47, 77
Altona, 141

Ambia, 141
Amboy, 141
American and State Federations of Labor, 74
American Baseball League, 308
American Can Company, 146
American Colonies, 62
American Commercial Barge Line, 229
American expansion, 62
American Federation of Labor, 82, 353
American Fur Company, 306
American Legion, 113, 116, 350
American Legion Memorial Park, 220
American Railway Union, 82, 315, 353
American Relief Administration, 109
American Revolution, 44, 52, 55, 59, 168, 181, 198, 202, 208, 211, 219,236, 250, 288, 301, 304, 311, 331
American Settlement, 53
American Sheet and Tinplate Company, 190
American Steel Foundries, 215
Amish, 207, 209, 238, 245, 265, 305, 332
Amishville, 141, 149
Amo, 141
Amsden
　Mary, 96
Anderson, 63, 141
Anderson College, 142
Anderson
　Deliah, 88
　John, 293
Andersontown, 142
Andrews, 143
Angel Mounds, 191, 193, 324, 379
Angel Mounds State Memorial, 143, 191
Angola, 143
Anthony
　Susan B., 315
Anti-Gambling Laws, 107
Appeal to the Great Spirit, 264
Appleseed
　Johnny, 199
Arcadia, 144
Archaic Stage, 37, 38

443

Encyclopedia of Indiana

Archives & Records
  Department of, 126
Argos, 144
Arkla Air Conditioning, 192
Arlington, 144
Arnold's Creek Embayment, 292
Art Association of
  Indianapolis, 82
Artifacts, 38
Arts & Humanities, 126
Ashford
  Ellen Lane, 93
Ashley, 145
Assembly of 1861, 71
Athenaeum (Das
  Deutsche Haus), 348, 365
Athletics
  Department of, 126
Atkins
  E.C., 81
Atlanta, 145
Atlantic Ocean, 23
Atterbury State Fish
  and Game Area, 187
Attica, 145
Attorney General, 126
Atwood, 145
Auburn, 145
Auburn-Cord-Duesenberg
  Museum, 146
Audit, 126
Audubon
  James, 268
Augsburg Svenska Skola, 286
Augsburg Swedish School, 286
Augustine Homestead, 267
Aurora, 146
Austin, 146
Automobile, 74
Automobile Racing, 83
Avilla, 146
Avoca, 146
Avoca State Fish Hatchery, 147
Ayres, L.S., Annex
  Warehouse, 365
Ayres Memorial Library, 322
Azabia, 173

Backous
  Mary Josephine, 108
Bailly, Joseph,
  Homestead, 372
Bain
  Katherine, 111
Bainbridge, 147

Baker Park, 268
Baker
  Conrad, 97, 99
Baldwin Steam Locomotive, 212
Baldwin
  Abel, 259
Ball Brothers, 263
Ball State Gallery, 264
Ball State University, 264
Ball
  Patty, 95
Baltimore & Ohio
  Railroad, 205, 256, 265
Baltimore Colts, 85
Bank of the United States, 68
Bank of Vincennes, 79
Banking
  Department of, 126
Bankrupcy, 80
Baptists, 69, 78
Barbee
  Clarissa, 87
Bargersville, 147
Barnum
  Abel, 140
Barrett-Gate House, 269
Bartholomew, 147
Bartholomew
  Joseph, 147
Bass Lake, 147
Bass Lake Hatchery, 147
Bass Lake State Beach, 147
Batesville, 147
Battle Ground, 147
Battle of Fallen Timbers, 42
Battle of —
  Corydon, 175
  Fallen Timbers, 42,
  57, 78, 198
  New Orleans, 226
  Thames, 63, 79
  Tippecanoe, 61, 79, 147,
  180, 184, 277, 283, 308,
  317, 331, 337, 340
Baxter Prohibition Law, 99
Bayard
  Samuel, 193
Bayh
  Birch Evan III, 122
  Marvella, 122
Bean Blossom Overlook, 334
Bear Creek Canyon, 145
Bear of Blue River Trail, 304
Beard
  Charles A., 309

Index

Beatty Memorial Hospital, 336
Beaver Bend, 220
Beaver Prairie, 261
Beck's Mill, 148, 300
Beck
  George, 148
Beckner-Nelson House, 144
Bedford, 148
Beech Creek, 211
Beech Grove, 148
Beecher
  Henry Ward, 80
Bell Creek, 182
Belleville, 149
Ben Hur, 157, 176
Ben Hur Museum, 176
Benedictine Saint Meinrad
  Archabbey, 298
Benjamin Harrison
  Memorial Home, 149
Benton, 149
Benton County
  Country Club, 201
Benton House, 365
Benton
  Thomas Hart, 149, 151
Bentonville, 149
Berne, 149
Berry
  John, 142
Bethany Park, 156
Bethel College, 255
Bethlehem Steel, 286
Beveridge
  Albert J., 83, 84
Beverly Shores, 150
Bicknell, 150
Biddle's Island, 150
Biddle
  Judge Horace, 150
Bieger House, 374
Bierce
  Ambrose, 189
Big Blowout, 225
Big Blue River, 150
Big Creek, 228, 287
Big Four
  Railroad Company, 226
Big Monon Creek, 288, 337
Big Pine Creek, 284
Big St. Joseph Station, 306
Big Wyandotte Cave, 342
Bigger
  John, 91
  Samuel, 91

Billie Creek Village, 294
Billy Sunday Tabernacle, 341
Biograph Theater, 84
Birch Creek, 169
Birdseye, 151
Black Hawk's War, 80
Black Horse Troop, 178
Black Population, 75
Black
  F. A., 140
  Glenn A., 143
Blackford, 151
Blake
  Thomas H., 88
Blizzard, 85
Block Brothers, 185
Bloomfield, 151
Bloomingdale, 151
Bloomington, 92, 94, 151
Blue Jacket, 57
Blue River, 152
Bluffton, 152
Boggstown, 152
Bondholders, 67
Bonesteel
  Luke, 172
Bonneyville Mill, 155
Boon
  Jesse, 88, 153
  Kessiah, 88
  Ratliff, 88, 153
Boone, 152
Boone Grove, 153
Boone's Pond State
  Fishing Area, 153
Boone
  Daniel, 152, 310
  Squire, 310
Boonville, 153
Borden, 153
Borden Institute, 356
Boston, 154
Boswell, 154
Bouquet
  Colonel, 51
Bourbon, 154
Bowels
  Dr. William A., 204
Bowen
  Otis R., 120, 122
  Vernie, 120
Bowles Spring, 204
Bowling Green, 154
Boyd
  Catharine, 105

Encyclopedia of Indiana

Brackbill
  Lottie, 117
Branch
  Elliott, 110
  Emmett, 110
Brandt Campanile, 323
Brandywine Creek, 212, 216
Branigin
  Elba, 118
  Roger D., 118
Branson
  Clo, 116
Brazil, 154
Bremen, 155
Bridgeport, 155
Bridgeton, 155
Brimfield, 155
Bringhurst, 155
Bristol, 155
Bristow, 155
British, 44
Brittania Club, 348
Broadview, 156
Brockway Glass Company, 240
Bronson Cave, 156
Brook, 156
Brooker
  Esther, 90
Brooklyn, 156
Brookston, 156
Brookville, 90, 91, 156
Brookville Reservoir, 157
Brower
  Ann Beckner, 293
Brown, 157
Brown County, 10
Brown County Art Gallery, 265
Brown County Artists'
  Colony, 265, 314
Brown County State
  Park, 35, 152, 158,
  221, 265, 334
Brown-Kercheval House, 374
Brown
  Henry, 267
  Jacob, 157
  James A., 190
  James B., 158
  Maude L., 115
  Minerva, 102
  Phebe Ann, 89
  William Otterbein, 276
Browne
  Thomas M., 99
Brownsburg, 158

Brownstown, 159
Brownstown State
  Fishing Area, 159
Bruce
  William, 159
Bruceville, 159
Brush
  Charles F., 328
Brute
  Bishop Gabriel, 49, 69, 80
Bryan
  Henry, 165
  William Jennings, 200, 253
Buck Creek, 159, 182, 250
Buckongahelas, 57
Budget, 126
Buffalo Trace, 148, 159, 326
Bundle
  David, 231
Bunker Hill, 160
Burbank
  Lucinda, 97
Burdette Park, 193
Bureau of Mines, 30
Burial, 39
Burket, 160
Burkhardt
  Mary Ann, 112
Burlington, 160
Burnettsville, 160
Burney, 160
Burns Ditch, 286
Burns Harbor, 160
Burnside
  Gen. Ambrose, 243
Bush Creek State Fish
  and Wildlife Area, 160, 161
Busseron Creek, 312
Butler, 161
Butler University, 81,
  350, 352
Butler
  Amos, 157
  Charles, 67
Butlerville, 161
Buzzard Roost Overlook, 221

Cabin Creek, 79
Cagles Mill Flood Control
  Reservoir, 290
Cagles Mill Reservoir, 337
Calkins
  William, 101
Calton
  Ann, 106

Index

Calumet, 82
Calumet Industrial
  District, 160
Cambridge City, 161
Camby, 162
Camden, 162
Camp Creek, 260, 261
Campbellsburg, 162
Camper's Roost, 285
Canal House, 359
Cannelburg, 162
Cannelton, 162
Cannelton Cotton Mill, 162
Canning, 146
Canterbury College, 179
Cape Canaveral, 256, 309
Capone
  Al, 335
Carbide and Carbon
  Chemicals Corporation, 339
Carbon, 163
Carbon Company, 272
Carey
  Rose Alice Smith, 103
Carlisle, 163
Carlos, 163
Carmel, 163
Carmelite Monastery, 345
Carpenter Bodyworks, 256
Carpenters Union, 353
Carroll, 164
Carroll County Country
  Club, 182
Carroll County Historical
  Society, 182
Carroll
  Charles, 164
Carthage, 164
Cascade Park, 261
Cass, 164
Cass County Historical
  Museum, 246
Cass
  Lewis, 164
Castle
  Rhoda, 104
Castleton, 164
Cataract Falls, 277
Cathedral of Immaculate
  Conception, 200
Cave River Valley, 162
Cavelier
  Robert, 48, 77
Caves—
  Marengo, 9

Wyandotte, 9
Cayuga, 165
Cedar Creek, 181, 333
Cedar Grove, 165
Cedar Lake, 165
Centennial Exposition, 83
Centennial Park, 285
Center Point, 165
Center, The, 140
Centerville, 165
Centerville
  Historic District, 381
Central Canal, 249
Central Library, 350
Central Normal College, 108, 179, 236
Chaffee
  Warren, 140
Chain O' Lakes State
  Park, 140, 166, 271, 332, 342
Chalmers, 166
Champaign County, 106
Chandler, 166
Chapel of the
  Resurrection, 323
Chapman
  John, 199
Charles II, 47
Charlestown, 166
Charlottesville, 167
Chase
  Benjamin, 103
  Ira, 103, 104
  William M., 202
Chautauqua, 253
Chautauqua Bible
  Conference, 341
Chesterfield, 167
Chesterton, 167
Chicago Century of
  Progress, 150
Chief Menominee Monument, 285
Child Labor Law, 107
Child Welfare
  Department of, 127
Children's Museum in
  Indianapolis, 260
Cholera, 191
Cholera epidemic, 299
Chrisney, 167
Christ Church
  Cathedral, 350, 366
Christ of the Ohio, 320
Christianity, 42, 47, 141

Encyclopedia of Indiana

Christy Woods, 264
Church of God, 142
Church of the Holy Family. 274
Churubusco, 167
Chute
  Charlotte, 98
Cicero, 168
Cicero Creek, 318
Cincinnati Arch, 177
Circus Hall of Fame. 282
Citizens' Bank. 105
City Coal Mine, 312
City Market, 348. 366
City-County Building, 350
Civil Defense
  Department of, 127
Civil Rights, 118
Civil Rights Commission, 119
Civil War, 70, 71. 72, 74,
  81, 96, 97, 98, 100, 102,
  103, 105, 108, 148, 175,
  198, 202, 235, 236, 243,
  246, 267. 268, 290, 296.
  324, 325. 333. 336
Clark, 168
Clark County, 78, 87
Clark Memorial, 208
Clark State Forest, 168, 180
Clark's Grant, 58. 168
Clark
  Daniel, 179
  George Rogers. 44.
  45, 53. 77. 168.
  208, 290, 312. 326
Clarks Hill, 168
Clarksburg, 168
Clarksville, 168
Clay, 169
Clay City, 169
Clay County, 99
Clay
  Henry, 159, 169
Claypool, 169
Clayton, 169
Clear Creek, 169
Clear Creek Park, 291
Cleo Rogers Memorial
  Library, 173
Clerk of the House. 127
Clermont. 170
Cleveland
  Grover, 99
Clifford, 170
Clifty Creek, 170, 181
Clifty Falls, 170

Clifty Falls State
  Park, 170, 229. 249
Clinton, 170
Clinton
  DeWitt, 170. 171
Clothing, 38
Cloverdale. 171
Coal City, 171
Coal Creek, 200
Coal Mining, 76
Coal Strike, 82. 85
Coatesville, 171
Coca-Cola Bottling, 192, 322
Coffin
  Levi, 200
  Levi, House. 382
Coke Production, 28
Cold Water Spring, 147
Colfax, 171
College Park. 353
College Park Life
  Insurance Company. 353
Collegeville. 171
Collins School, 275
Colonial Dames Harmonist
  Museum House. 269
Columbia, 172
Columbia City, 107. 171
Columbian Park. 237
Columbus, 95. 172
Commerce
  Department of, 127
Community Affairs
  Department of, 127
Concordia College, 199
Condit House, 379
Confederacy, 71, 73
Conflict of Interest, 127
Conn
  Charles G., 188
Conner Prairie, 173
Conner
  William, 142, 173
Connersville, 173
Connor
  John, 174
  William, 272
Conrad
  David, 240
Constitution Elm, 174
Constitutional Convention, 80
Consumer Affairs, 127
Continental Congress, 54, 224
Converse, 174

448

Index

Conwell
 James, 241
Cook
 Caroline, 95
 John E., 95
Cool Lake Park, 243
Coquillard
 Alexis, 79, 306
Corn Island, 168
Corn Production, 81
Cornelius Westfall, 316
Cornell, William,
 Homestead, 358
Corrections
 Department of, 128
Cortland, 174
Corunna, 174
Corydon, 65, 72,
 78, 89, 174, 346
Corydon Capitol State
 Memorial, 175
Corydon Historic District, 360
Costigan
 Francis, 239
Council Oak, 48, 77, 306
Council of Municipal
 Performance, 351
Counties —
 Adams, 15
 Allen, 15
 Brown, 10
 Crawford, 9
 Dearborn, 11
 Floyd, 10
 Gibson, 16
 Jackson, 10
 Knox, 41
 Kosciusko, 15
 Lake, 8
 Lawrence, 11
 Monroe, 11, 16
 Owen, 11
 Porter, 8
 Posey, 7, 41
 Randolph, 7, 16
 Ripley, 11
 Scott, 10
 Sullivan, 41
 Vanderburgh, 41
 Vigo, 9
 Warrick, 9
 Washington, 10, 11
County Log Jail, 212
Court Administration, 128
Courthouse Tower Tree, 212

Covered Bridge Festival, 279
Covington, 175
Cowles Bog, 184
Craig
 Bernard, 116
 George N., 116, 117
Crandall, 176
Craven
 Jennie, 108
Crawford, 176
Crawford County, 9
Crawford Upland, 177
Crawford
 William, 176
Crawfordsville, 96, 176
Croghan
 George, 50, 52, 77
Cromwell, 177
Crooks-Anderson House, 294
Crosley Fish and
 Wildlife Area, 177
Crossroads of America, 4
Crothersville, 177
Crown Hill Cemetery, 366
Crown Point, 178, 238, 253
Crown Point-Lowell
 Race Course, 247
Cubberley
 Ellwood Patterson, 143
Culbertson Mansion, 266, 359
Culver, 178
Culver Bird Sanctuary, 178
Culver Military
 Academy, 116, 178
Cumberland Road, 161
Cummins Diesel Engine
 Company, 173
Cummins Engine Factory, 173
Cummins
 W. W., 190
Cynthiana, 178

D. A. Beyson, 82
Daily Art Collection, 151
Dale, 178
Daleville, 178
Dallin
 Cyrus, 264
Dan Patch, 277
Dana, 179
Danville, 179
Darlington, 179
Darlington Covered Bridge, 180
Das Deutsche Haus, 348

Encyclopedia of Indiana

Data Processing
  Department of, 128
Daviess, 180
Daviess
  Joseph Hamilton, 180
Deam Lake State
  Recreation Area, 180
Dean
  James, 194
Dearborn, 180
Dearborn County, 11
Dearborn
  Gen. Henry, 180
Debs
  Eugene V., 74, 81,
  82, 83, 315, 353
  Eugene V., House, 380
Decatur, 181
Decatur
  County Courthouse, 358
Decatur
  Stephen, 181
Decker, 181
Declaration of
  Independence, 164,
  216, 224, 296
Deer Creek, 164, 182
DeKalb, 181
DeKalb
  Baron, 181
Delaware, 41, 42, 182
Delaware County Fair, 264
Delco Battery, 263
Delphi, 182
Delta Queen, 249
Deming Park, 316
Demotte, 182
Denver, 182
Department of
  Conservation, 33, 109
Department of
  Corrections, 117
Department of Health, 117
Department of
  Natural Resources, 119
Department of Revenue, 116
Department of
  the Interior, 34
Department of
  Veteran Affairs, 116
DePauw University, 69,
  80, 109, 211
Depression, 74, 112
Deputy, 183
Derby, 183

Desegregation, 84
Desiderata, 315
Developmental Disabilities, 128
Devil's Backbone, 183
Diana of the Dunes, 273
Digby
  William, 236
Dillin
  S. Hugh, 84
Dillinger
  John, 84, 178, 345
Dillsboro, 183
Dillsboro Sanatorium, 183
Dimension Stone, 31
Disciples of Christ, 69
Discrimination, 85
Distilling, 211
Division of Labor, 114
Doans Creek, 211
Dogwood Festival, 276
Dolfuss
  Patricia, 120
Donaldson Cave, 309
Doud
  Louise, 119
Douglas
  Lloyd C., 171
Dowling Park, 216
Draft, 72, 83
Dreiser
  Theodore, 81, 145, 315
Dresser
  Paul, 5, 145, 315
  Paul, Birthplace, 380
Drexel Hall, 290
Drought disaster, 85
Drug Abuse
  Department of, 128
Dublin, 183
Dubois, 183
Dubois
  Toussaint, 184
Duck Creek, 181, 190, 249
Dugger, 184
Dumont
  John, 91
Dune Acres, 184
Dunehilda, 273
Dunkerson
  Louise, 121
Dunkirk, 184
Dunlap, 184
Dunning
  James, 93
  Paris C., 93

Index

Dunreith, 184
Dunseth Planetarium
 and Museum, 327
DuPont, 72, 185
Durbin
 William, 105
 Winfield, 105
Dyer, 185

E.I. duPont de Nemours
 and Company, 166
Eagle Fall Creek, 250
Earl Park, 185
Earlham, 185
Earlham College, 80, 185, 291
Early Wheels Museum, 316
Early Woodland Stage, 38
East Chicago, 185
East Grey, 186
Eaton, 186
Eavleo
 George, 220
Eckerty, 186
Eclipse, 192
Economic Development
 Department of, 128
Economy, 187
Economy Task Force, 120
Edger
 Elizabeth, 109
Edgerton, 187
Edgewood, 187
Edinburg, 187
Education (Higher), 128
Education (Primary, Secondary,
 & Vocational), 128
Education Center, 350
Edwards
 Helene, 116
Edwardsport, 187
Eel River, 15, 187
Eggleston
 Edward, 81, 325
 Edward and George
 Cary, House, 376
Ehrmann
 Max, 315
Elberfield, 188
Elections, 129
Electra Memorial, 163
Electrical Energy, 28
Eli Lilly & Co., 352
Eli Lilly Company
 Biological Laboratories, 212
Elihu Stout's Print Shop, 234

Elizabeth, 188
Elizabethtown, 188
Elk Creek State Fish
 and Game Area, 188
Elkhart, 188, 189
Elkhart Academy, 209
Elkhart County River
 Preserve, 189
Elkhart Institute
 of Technology, 189
Elkhart River, 189
Elkhart River
 Hydroelectric Canal, 189
Ellets
 Edward, 189
Ellettsville, 189
Elliott
 Israel, 165
Elmhurst Mansion, 174
Elnora, 189
Elston
 Joanna, 97
Elwood, 190
Emens Auditorium, 264
Emlow's Mill, 227
Empire State Building, 148
Employment Security
 Division of, 129
Empson
 Inez, 118
Enabling Act, 64, 87
Energy
 Department of, 129
Engle
 William, 140
English, 190
English
 William Hayden, 190
Enterprise, 214
Environmental Affairs
 Department of, 129
Environmental groups, 27
Equal Rights Amendment, 121
Erie Canal, 340
Erie Investments, 121
Ernie Pyle Rest Park, 179
Etna Green, 190
Evans
 Robert M., 191
Evansville, 98, 191
Evansville Metal Products, 121
Evansville Post Office, 377

Encyclopedia of Indiana

Fables in Slang, 156
Fairfax State Recreation
  Area, 194, 257
Fairland, 194
Fairmount, 194
Fairview Park, 194
Fall Creek, 219, 249, 340
Falls of the Ohio, 58
Falls Park, 280
Farm Credit Administration, 119
Farmers, 64
Farmers and Mechanics Bank, 79
Farmersburg, 194
Farmland, 195
Fayette, 195
Federal Courts Building, 350
Federal Land Bank, 119
Federal Security
  Administration, 113
Federal-State Relations, 129
Federation of
  German Societies, 348
Ferdinand, 195
Ferdinand Railroad Company, 195
Ferdinand State
  Fish Hatchery, 196
Ferdinand State Forest, 196
Fessler
  Alice, 115
Festival Music Theater, 199
Festival of Arts
  and Crafts, 296
Field Artillery, 113
Fifteenth Amendment, 73
Fillmore, 196
Finance
  Department of, 129
Firearms, 50
First —
  American flag in Indiana, 45
  American settlement in
    Northwest Territory, 45
  Automatic potato digger, 216
  Automatic traffic signal, 163
  Belt railroad in U.S., 82
  Black major in State, 76, 84
  Board of Education, 94
  Capital of Indiana
    Territory, 208
  Cavalry of Indiana
    Volunteers, 98
  Christian church, 172
  Church in Indiana, 77
  Coal mined in State, 80
  Coeducational school, 79
  Compulsory education
    law passed, 82
  Democratic Convention
    in Indiana, 79
  Denominational college
    in Indiana, 79
  Federal land sale, 78
  Free kindergarten, 79
  Free school, 79
  General Assembly of
    Indiana Territory, 197
  Governor of Indiana
    Territory, 58
  Indiana regiment, 96
  Indianapolis 500 auto
    race held, 83
  Industrial union in U.S., 82
  Interurban car, 82
  Large coal mine, 81
  Mail delivered by air, 81
  Mansion in Indiana, 327
  Medical Society in State, 79
  Methodist Church in
    Indiana, 166
  Newspaper in State, 78
  Newspaper in Territory, 225
  Normal school in Indiana, 160
  Oil well in State drilled, 82
  Permanent settler
    in Indianapolis, 79
  Permanent white
    settlements in Indiana, 49
  Professional football
    team, 216
  Protestant church
    in Indiana, 78
  Railroad track in State, 80
  Sale of town lots
    in Indianapolis, 79
  Scientific archaeological
    excavation, 83
  Settler in Brown Township, 158
  Source of water supply, 154
  Stage line in Indiana, 79
  State election, 79
  State Fair, 80, 94
  State Federation of
    Labor in U.S., 82
  State General Assembly, 79
  State primary held, 83
  Steam train, 80
  Streetcars in State, 81
  Territorial delegate
    to the U.S. Congress, 278
  Territory election, 78

Index

Theatrical performance
  in Indianapolis, 79
U.S. senator from
  Indiana, 79
Union Station in U.S., 80
War memorial in U.S.
  dedicated to peace, 181
White man to explore
  Indiana, 48
Women's club in U.S., 81
First Methodist
  Church of Indiana, 211
Fish & Game
  Department of, 129
Fish Creek, 181
Fisher
  Carl G., 212
Fishers, 196
Fishers Station, 196
Fishing, 37
Flat Rock, 196
Flatrock Creek, 181, 296, 304
Fletcher
  Eliza, 104
Flint & Walling, 231
Flood, 146, 242, 280
Flood Control Commission, 116
Floods, 84, 85, 108, 191
Flora, 196
Floyd, 196
Floyd County, 10
Floyd
  Col. Davis, 197
  Col. John, 196
Floyds Knobs, 197
Flying Squadron, 106
Food & Drugs
  Department of, 129
Food Conservation
  Committee, 110
Food Production
  Administration, 114
Forest, 197
Forestry
  Department of, 130
Former Vandeburgh County
  Sheriff's Residence, 378
Fort Ancient Culture, 40
Fort Benjamin Harrison, 197
Fort Branch, 197
Fort Dearborn, 334
Fort Defiance, 56
Fort Flora, 332
Fort Greenville, 56
Fort Harrison, 61, 62, 79

Fort Miami, 49, 51,
  52, 77, 78, 198
Fort Montgomery, 233
Fort Ouiatenon, 49,
  52, 236, 237, 377
Fort Patrick Henry, 54
Fort Pitt, 51
Fort Recovery, 56
Fort Sackville, 53, 54
Fort Sumter, 71
Fort Vallonia, 322
Fort Vincennes, 49
Fort Wayne, 49, 57, 58,
  62, 63, 77, 78, 79,
  80, 92, 101, 107,
  146, 197
Fort Wayne Art Institute, 199
Fort Wayne Bible School, 199
Fort Wayne City Hall, 355
Fort Wayne Civic Theater, 199
Fort Wayne School
  of Fine Arts, 199
Fort Wayne Treaty, 60
Fort
  Cephas, 197
Fortville, 197
Foulke
  William, 291
Fountain, 200
Fountain City, 200
Fountain
  Maj., 200
Fourteen Mile Creek, 167
Fourteenth Amendment, 73
Fowler, 200
Fowler
  Moses, 201
  Moses, House, 376
Fowlerton, 201
France Park, 246
Frances Slocum State
  Forest, 201
Frances Slocum State
  Recreation Area, 328
Francesville, 201
Francis Slocum Trail, 250
Francis Vigo Chapter of the
  Daughters of the American
  Revolution, 214
Francis
  Zula, 118
Francisco, 201
Franke Park, 200
Frankfort, 201
Franklin, 202

Encyclopedia of Indiana

Franklin College, 69, 80, 118, 119, 202
Franklin County Seminary, 359
Franklin
 Benjamin, 202, 203
Frankton, 203
Freckles, 207, 244
Fredericksburg, 203
Free public school system, 80
Free-Soilers, 71
Freelandville, 203
Freetown, 203
Fremont, 204
French, 43
French and Indian
 War, 44, 48, 77
French Catholic, 69
French Jesuits, 43, 47
French Lick, 204, 275
French Lick Springs Hotel, 204
French Lick-Sheraton Hotel, 204
Friends Church, 151
Friends' Boarding School, 291
Fudge Indian Mounds, 341
Fullenwider
 Lucinda, 104
Fulmer
 Christian, 330
Fulton, 204
Fur traders, 48

Gable Town, 179
Gage
 General, 52
Gale
 Thomas, 143
Galena, 205
Galey
 Martha, 109
Galveston, 205
Gambler's Row, 242
Gamelin
 Antoine, 55
Garrett, 205
Gary, 205
Gary Land Company, 206
Gary
 Judge Elbert H., 205
Gas City, 206
Gaston, 207
Gates
 Benton, 115
 Ralph F., 115
Gem City, 145
Gemini, 328

Gene Stratton Porter
 State Memorial, 207, 314
General Assembly, 67, 84
General Land Office, 92, 99
General Motors, 142
General Services
 Department of, 130
General Strike, 84
Geneva, 207
Gentry
 James, 207
Gentryville, 207
Geology
 Department of, 130
George Rogers Clark
 Memorial, 111, 234
George Rogers Clark
 National Historic Park
 and Memorial, 208, 362
George
 King, 77
Georgetown, 208
Georgetown Reservoir, 208
German Ridge, 221
Gibault
 Pierre, 53
Gibson, 208
Gibson County, 16
Gibson
 John, 64, 160, 208
Gill
 E. Gurney, 291
Gilmore
 Cornelius, 143
Glacial Kame Culture, 37, 38
Glancy
 Lydia, 113
Glass Museum, 184
Glen Miller Park, 291
Glendale State Fish and
 Wildlife area, 208, 332
Glenwood, 209
Godfrey
 Francois, 282
Godfroy Reserve, 259
Godfroy
 Francois, 259
Goethe Link Observatory, 260
Gold Creek, 156
Goldsmith, 209
Gompers
 Samuel, 353
Goodlands, 209

Index

Goodrich
  James P., 109
  John, 109
Goodwin Funeral
  Home Museum, 202
Goodyear Tire
  and Rubber Company, 166
Gootee
  Thomas, 247
Goshen, 209
Goshen College, 209
Gosport, 209
Government Spending, 121
Governor's Cup, 249
Governor's Mansion, 348
Grabill, 210
Graham Creek, 230
Gramelspacher-Gutzweiler
  House, 227
Grand Army of the Rebublic, 81
Grandview, 210
Grange, 73
Granger, 210
Grant, 210
Grant
  Capt. Samuel, 210
  Moses, 210
Grass
  Daniel, 294
Grassy Fork Fish Hatchery, 260
Gray
  Isaac P., 100
  John, 100
Great Depression, 76,
  84, 114, 150, 165,
  173, 294, 335, 347
Great Spirit Manitou, 293
Green
  Seth, 163
  William, 353
Greenburg, 66
Greenburg Reservoir
  State Fishing Area, 213
Greencastle, 90, 211
Greendale, 211
Greene, 211
Greene
  Gen. Nathaniel, 211
Greene-Sullivan
  State Forest, 211
Greenfield, 95, 212
Greenhorn Valley, 158
Greens Fork, 213
Greensboro, 212
Greensburg, 212

Greentown, 213
Greentown Glass
  Museum, 213, 235
Greenville, 213
Greenville Treaty Line, 321
Greenwood, 213
Griffin, 213
Griffith, 214
Grisell
  Samuel, 281
Grissom Air Force Base, 282
Grissom
  Virgil "Gus", 256,
  309, 328
Gross Income Tax, 84
Grouse Ridge, 173
Grouseland, 78, 214, 234, 327
Gulf of Mexico, 18, 23

H. Vance Swope
  Memorial Art Gallery, 302
Hackleman Log Cabin, 296
Hackleman
  Pleasant A., 296
Hagerstown, 214
Hahn, 121
Haines
  Leslie, 163
Halleck Student Center, 290
Halleck
  Charles, 290
Hamburg Exposition, 94
Hamilton, 214
Hamilton College, 94
Hamilton County
  Circuit Courthouse, 272
Hamilton
  Alexander, 215
  Henry, 45, 52, 77
Hamlet, 215
Hamlet
  John, 215
Hammer's Mill, 162
Hammond, 215
Hammond
  Abram A., 95
  George, 215
  Nathaniel, 95
Hancock, 216
Hancock
  John, 216
Handicapped, 130
Handley
  Harold L., 117
  Harold W., 117

Encyclopedia of Indiana

Hanly
　Elijah, 106
　James Franklin, 106
Hanna, 216
Hanna
　Samuel, 140
Hannegan
　Edward A., 175
Hanover, 216
Hanover College, 69,
　79, 98, 101, 216
Hardin Ridge, 221
Hardin
　John, 78
Harding
　Warren, 83, 110
Hardinsburg, 216
Hardy Lake State
　Recreation Area, 216
Harlan, 217
Harmar
　Josiah, 56
Harmonie State
　Recreation Area, 217
Harper
　Ida Husted, 315
Harris
　Benjamin, 82
　Eliza, 281
　Nora, 114
　William, 158
Harrison, 217
Harrison County, 10, 72, 78
Harrison County Fair, 175
Harrison Park, 225
Harrison
　Benjamin, 149, 349
　Benjamin, House, 366
　William Henry, 58, 68, 78,
　80, 147, 160, 174, 209,
　214, 217, 229, 237,
　317, 326, 340
　William Henry, Home,
　(Grouseland), 362
Harrison-Crawford State
　Forest, 217
Hart's Ford, 218
Hart
　David, 218
Hartford City, 151, 218
Hartmar, 78
Hartsville, 218
Hartsville College, 218
Harvard Graduate School of
　Business Administration, 121

Harvard Law School, 112
Harvard University, 119
Harvest Homecoming, 266
Hatcher
　Richard D., 84
　Richard H., 76
Haubstadt, 218
Havenhurst Golf Course, 269
Hawkins
　John, 161
Hay House, 300
Hay-Morrison House, 381
Hay
　Ann Gillmore, 87
　John, 299
Hayes Office, 312
Hayes
　William H., 312
Haynes
　Elwood, 82, 234, 287
Hayswood Nature Reserve, 175
Hazardous Materials, 130
Hazeldon Home, 156
Hazelton, 218
Hazelton
　Jarvis, 218
Health
　Department of, 130
Hebron, 218
Heekin Park, 264
Heiliger
　Kathryn, 117
Helm
　Leonard, 53
Helmer, 218
Helmsburg, 218
Heltonville, 219
Hemlock, 219
Hendricks, 219
Hendricks
　John, 98
　Thomas, 96, 98, 212, 304
　William, 79, 88, 219
Henry, 219
Henry County
　Historical Museum, 268
Henry County
　Memorial Park, 268
Henry
　Patrick, 53, 219
Henryville, 219
Herschell
　William, 308
Hess Manufacturing Company, 156
Hicksite Friends'

456

Index

Meeting House, 291
Higgins
  Mary, 96
High Mary, 224
Highland, 219
Highland Cemetery, 306
Highland Park, 235
Highway Safety
  Department of, 130
Highways
  Department of, 131
Hill Greenhouses, 291
Hill
  Samuel, 258
Hillenbrand II
  John, 122
Hillforest (Forest Hill), 357
Hills
  Glenn, 115
Hillsboro, 220
Hindostan Falls, 252, 305
Hindostan Falls
  State Fishing Area, 220
Hispano-American Center, 348
Historic Madison, 248
Historic Preservation
  Department of, 131
Historical Museum, 182
Historical Museum of
  Wabash Valley, 316
Historical Society
  of Washington County, 300
Hoagland, 220
Hobart, 220
Hochstetler
  Rose M., 121
Hog Back Ridge, 304
Hog Creek, 331
Hog raising, 81
Hohman, 215
Hohman Inn, 215
Hohman
  Ernest, 215
Holcomb
  Research Institute, 352
Holland, 220
Holliday
  John, 81
Holmes
  Ensign, 51
Holton, 220
Homann
  Virginia, 118
Home Corner, 221
Home Packing Company, 315

Honey Creek, 325
Honeywell Auditorium, 328
Honeywell Gardens, 328
Honig
  George, 294
Hoosier Boy, 292
Hoosier Dome, 85
Hoosier Hills, 168,
  180, 219, 290
Hoosier National
  Forest, 148, 221, 265
Hoosier Schoolmaster, 325
Hoover
  Herbert, 110
Hope, 221
Hopewell Culture, 37, 39, 262
Houck
  John, 297
House of Tomorrow, 150
Houses, 41
Housing
  Department of, 131
Hovey Lake, 221
Hovey Lake State Fish
  and Game Area, 221, 222
Hovey Lake State
  Game Preserve, 262
Hovey
  Abiel, 102
  Alvin P., 102, 103
Howard, 222
Howard County, 111
Howard County Historical
  Museum, 235
Howard Home, 357
Howard Shipyards, 169, 229
Howard Steamboat Museum, 169
Howard
  Tilghman A., 222
Howe, 222
Howell
  Mary, 111
Hubbard
  Frank McKinney,
  "Kin", 83
Hudson, 222
Huffman
  Henry, 195
  Nancy, 100
Human Rights
  Department of, 131
Hunt
  Eliazer, 224
Hunters, 37
Huntertown, 222

Encyclopedia of Indiana

Hunting, 37, 42
Huntingburg, 222
Huntingburg Country Club, 223
Huntington, 223
Huntington College, 223
Huntington Reservoir, 223, 224, 331
Huntington
   Samuel, 223, 224
Huntley Creek, 183
Huntsville, 224
Huron, 41
Hurst
   Ann Renick, 93
Hutchenson
   Big Bill, 353
Hymera, 224

Ice Age, 7, 24
Idaville, 224
Illinois Glacier, 334
Illinois Oil Basin, 192
Illinois River, 15, 23
Illinois Territory, 58, 78
Immaculate Conception Convent and Girl's Academy, 195
Immigrants—
   British, 44
   Danish, 74
   Dutch, 219
   English, 3, 65
   French, 43
   French Jesuits, 43
   German, 74, 147, 195, 222, 227, 274, 348
   Hungarian, 74
   Irish, 65, 348
   Italian, 74, 233, 347
   Polish, 74
   Scandinavian, 233
   Scotch-Irish, 65
   Scottish, 65
   Slavic, 233
   Swedish, 74
   Swiss, 65, 78, 149
Independent Party, 73
Indian Creek, 211, 217
Indian Hills Golf Course, 243
Indian Knoll Culture, 37, 38
Indian Mound Cemetery, 165
Indian Ridge Lake Country Club, 220
Indian Springs, 319
Indian Tribes—
   Algonquian, 60

Angel Mounds, 143
Artifacts, 38, 148, 235
Arts and Crafts, 40
Black Hawk's War, 80
Burial Customs, 38
Chieftains, 57
Christianity, 42, 43
Clothing, 38
Delaware, 41, 42, 59, 60, 61, 63, 78, 79, 87, 168, 174, 182, 188, 263, 272, 304
Delaware chief, Anderson, 141
Delaware language, 188
Delaware trail, 275
Delaware village, 141
Eel River village, 78
Fishing, 37
Food, 42
Great Lakes, 47
Housing, 41
Hunting, 37, 42
Huron, 41
Illinois, 48, 77, 306
Iroquois, 48
Iroquois nation, 47
Kethtippecanunk, 78
Kickapoo, 41, 62, 185
Kickapoo chief, Parish, 185
Lafayette village, 78
Lake, 56
Land, 2, 43
Language, 41
Les Gros chief, 238
Mascontin, 41
Miami, 41, 48, 57, 59, 60, 61, 63, 77, 78, 79, 87, 89, 144, 150, 153, 164, 172, 198, 201, 246, 259, 293, 306, 339
Miami chief, Green, 213
Miami chief, Kokomo
Miami chief, Little Turtle, 41, 56, 78, 79, 172, 198
Miami Confederacy, 79
Miami, Eel River, 56
Miami village, 281, 340
Mississippi Mound Builders, 167
Mississippi mounds, 143, 324
Moravian Mission, 38, 42
Mounds, 142, 164, 173, 241, 253, 321, 335, 341
Munsee, 263
Munsee campsite, 264
No'Kamena, 150

Index

Northern tribes,62
Ottawa, 44
Ottawa chief, Pontiac, 44, 51, 77
Ottawa-Ojibway-Potawatomi Confederacy, 51
Ouiatenon village, 49
Piankeshaw, 41, 78
Potawatomi, 41, 43, 60, 62, 63, 67, 79, 80, 87, 89, 91, 144, 145, 188, 198, 246, 253, 268, 293,303, 322, 339
Potwatomi chief, Menominee, 285
Potawatomi chief, Shipshewana, 305
Potawatomi village, 285
Religious Ceremonies, 38
Seneca, 51
Shawnee, 59, 60, 63, 79, 147, 164, 214, 236, 255, 283, 317
Shawnee chief, Elkhart, 255
Shawnee chief, Tecumseh, 2, 59, 79, 237
Shawnee Confederacy,61
Shawnee Prophet, Tenskwatawa, 59, 79, 147, 236, 317
Shipshewana, 305
Simon Pokagon, 285
Treaty, 42, 43
Topenbee, 145
Villages, 42, 258
Village, Prophet's Town, 60
Wabash, 60
Wabash Confederacy,56
War Dances, 61
Wea, 56, 57, 59, 77, 79, 87
Winamac, 340
Winnebago, 41
Women, 42
Woodland mounds,262
Wyandotte, 60, 160, 342
Wyandotte chief, Burlington, 160
Indiana News, 83
Indiana Academy of Science, 81
Indiana admitted to Union, 79
Indiana Asbury College, 69, 101
Indiana Asbury University, 80
Indiana Asylum for the Education of the Deaf, 92
Indiana Baptist Convention, 69

Indiana Baptist Manual Labor Institute, 69, 80, 202
Indiana Beach, 259
Indiana Board of Agriculture, 110
Indiana Boy's School, 284
Indiana Central College, 149
Indiana Coal Association, 27
Indiana Colonization Society, 79
Indiana Constitutional Convention, 89, 91, 98
Indiana Convention-Exposition Center, 350
Indiana Deep Waterway Commission, 109
Indiana Department of Conservation, 207
Indiana Department of Natural Resources, 34, 343
Indiana Dunes National Lakeshore, 36, 85, 150, 225
Indiana Dunes State Park, 19, 36, 216, 225, 286, 323, 330
Indiana Education Society, 80
Indiana Fair Employment Commission, 118
Indiana Farm Bureau, 114
Indiana Forestry Association, 33
Indiana General Assembly, 183
Indiana Harbor, 185
Indiana Harbor Canal, 84
Indiana Historical Bureau, 83
Indiana Historical Society, 143
Indiana Hospital for the Insane, 93
Indiana Institute of Technology, 199
Indiana Limestone Corporation, 148
Indiana Masonic Home, 202
Indiana Militia, 90
Indiana National Bank, 351
Indiana Plan, 84
Indiana Railway Museum, 212
Indiana Seminary, 79, 94
Indiana Soldiers and Sailors' Monument, 101
Indiana Soldiers' and Sailors' Children's Home, 233
Indiana State Beach, 303
Indiana State Board of Agriculture, 99
Indiana State College, 93

Encyclopedia of Indiana

Indiana State Fairgrounds, 106
Indiana State House, 100
Indiana State Museum, 367
Indiana State Soldiers
 Home Historic District, 377
Indiana State Teachers
 College, 81
Indiana State
 University, 193, 316
Indiana State University
 Stadium Golf Course, 316
Indiana Steel and
 Wire Company, 263
Indiana Supreme Court, 230
Indiana Territory, 58,
 59, 63, 78, 87, 88,
 174, 208, 214, 225,
 287, 326
Indiana Territory State
 Memorial, 225
Indiana Toll Road, 116, 144
Indiana Tumbler and
 Goblet Company, 213
Indiana University, 80, 81,
 84, 110, 117, 143,
 151, 186, 235, 260
Indiana University,
 Bloomington, 122, 266
Indiana University Law
 School, 112
Indiana University
 School of Medicine, 121, 352
Indiana University,
 Southeast, 266
Indiana University-Purdue
 University, 352
Indiana University-South
 Bend, 306
Indiana Vocational
 Technical College, 193
Indiana Women's Prison, 345
Indianapolis, 65, 66, 225
Indianapolis 500 auto race, 83,
 86, 307, 345
Indianapolis Athletic Club, 348
Indianapolis Center of
 Advanced Research, 352
Indianapolis Conference of
 Indiana, 82
Indianapolis Episcopal
 Diocese, 349
Indianapolis Journal, 82
Indianapolis Land Office, 90
Indianapolis News, 81, 84
Indianapolis Roman

Catholic Archdiocese, 350
Indianapolis Speedway, 29, 212
Indianapolis Symphony
 Orchestra, 345
Indianapolis Union
 Railroad Station, 367
Industrial School for
 Girls, 106
Industrialization, 75
Ingalls, 226
Ingalls
 M.E., 226
Inland Steel Corp., 74, 82, 185
Insurance
 Department of, 131
Integration, 84
Internal Improvements Board, 90
Internal Improvements
 Program, 92
International Business
 Machine, 211
International Center, 348
International Harvester
 Company, 199
International Packing
 Company, 261
International St. Lawrence
 Waterways Commission, 109
Interstate 69, 144
Ireland, 226
Ireland
 Merritt W., 171
Iron Brigade, 161
Iron production, 83
Iroquois River, 15, 23, 226
Irwin Union Bank, 173
Irwin's Sunken Gardens, 173
Island Branch, 292
ITT Business and
 Technical Institute, 193

J.F.D. Lanier
 State Memorial, 239
J.W. Davis Company, 316
Jack D. Diehm Museum
 of Natural History, 199
Jackson, 226
Jackson County, 10
Jackson State Forest, 159
Jackson
 Andrew, 92, 226
 Edward, 111
 Presley, 111
 Samuel D., 116

Index

Jackson-Washington
 State Forest, 226
Jackson-Washington
 State Park, 226
Jacksonian Democratic Party, 68
James Dean Gallery, 194
James Walsh & Company
 Distillery, 211
James Whitcomb Riley
 Memorial Park, 212
James Lake, 227
James
 Mary Ann, 103
Jameson
 Pamela Bledsoe, 96
Jamestown, 227
Jaqua
 Eliza, 101
Jasonville, 227
Jasper, 227, 228
Jasper Country Club, 228
Jasper Dutch, 227
Jasper Municipal Golf
 Course, 228
Jasper Summer Theater, 227
Jasper-Pulaski Fish
 and Wildlife Area, 228, 253
Jay, 228
Jay
 John, 228
Jefferson, 228
Jefferson County Jail, 361
Jefferson Party, 68
Jefferson Proving Ground, 161
Jefferson
 Thomas, 228, 229
Jeffersonville, 64, 229
Jenkins
 Lieutenant, 51
Jennings, 230
Jennings County Historical
 Society Museum, 324
Jennings
 Jacob, 87
 Jonathan, 64, 79,
 87, 88, 167, 230
Jog Rock, 284
John Birch Society, 345
John Fitzgerald
 Kennedy Memorial Bridge, 230
Johnny Appleseed
 Memorial Park, 355
Johns-Manville Company, 140
Johnson, 230
Johnson

Adam, 267
Ban, 308
John, 230
Jones
 Col. Willam, Home, 208
 Eleanor, 91
 James G., 192
 James W., 191
 Obadiah, 230
 Samuel, 331
Jonesboro, 230
Jonesville, 230
Jordan
 Vernon E., 85
Joseph Moore Museum, 291
Judson, 231
Judson
 George, 155
Jug Rock, 177, 231, 252, 305
Jug Rock Park, 284
Julian House
 George W., 166
Julian, George W., 73
Junction Railroad, 262
Juvenile Delinquency
 Department of, 131

Kadley
 Paul, 260
Kankakee Marshes, 238, 241
Kankakee River, 15,
 20, 23, 43, 231
Kankakee State Recreation
 Area, 231
Kankakee Swamp, 101
Kankakee Valley, 18
Kansas-Nebraska Bill, 71
Kaskaskia, 77
Keewaskee, 316
Kekionga, 198
Kelly's Livery Stable, 277
Kemper House, 349
Kempton, 231
Kendall
 Amos, 231
Kendallville, 231
Kendrick Memorial
 Hospital, 260
Kennard, 111, 232
Kennedy
 Mary, 87
Kentland, 232
Kern
 John Worth, 105, 106
Kewanna, 232

461

Encyclopedia of Indiana

Keystone, 82
Kickapoo, 41
Kilbuck Creek, 182, 249
Kilsoquah, 293
Kimmel, 232
Kimmell Park, 327
Kimsey
   Lois, 108
King's Mine, 288
Kingman, 232
Kingsbury, 232
Kingsbury State Fish
   and Wildlife Area, 232
Kingsford Heights, 233
Kinsey
   Alfred, 84
Kintner-Withers
   Plantation House, 236
Kirk's Popcorn Company, 155
Kirklin, 233
Kirklin
   Nathan, 233
Kissinger
   John R., 223
Knight
   Bobby, 85
   Jonathan, 233
Knights of Labor, 82
Knights of the
   Golden Circle, 72, 81
Knightstown, 101, 233
Knightsville, 233
Knobs, The, 197, 233
Knobstone Escarpment, 266
Know-Nothing Party, 71
Knox, 233, 234
Knox County, 41, 78
Knox
   Henry, 234
Kokomo, 234
Kokomo Reservoir, 235
Kopper Kettle Restaurant, 262
Kosciusko, 235
Kosciusko County, 15
Kosciusko
   Gen. Thaddeus, 235
Kouts, 235
Kraft Foods, 232
Ku Klux Klan, 75,
   83, 84, 272, 345
Kunderd Gladiolus Farm, 184

L'Enfant
   Pierre Charles, 346
L.C.C. Association

Golf Course, 319
La Crosse, 236
La Fontaine, 237
La Fontaine
   Francis, 223
La Paz, 240
La Porte, 240
La Porte County Farm Bureau
   Co-op Association, 295
La Salle, 48, 49, 77
La Salle
   Robert Cavalier, Sieur de, 43,
   48, 77, 306
Labor conflicts, 74
Labor disputes, 84, 104
Labor movement, 74
Labor strikes, 83, 84
Labor unions, 74
Labor
   Department of, 131
Laboratory Building, 268
Laconia, 236
Ladoga, 236
LaFayette, 49, 236
Lafayette Park, 288
Lafayette Springs, 163
Lafayette
   Marquis de, 195,
   236, 237, 238
Lagrange, 237
Lagro, 238
Lain Technical Institute, 193
Lake, 238
Lake County, 8
Lake County Courthouse, 363
Lake County Jail, 178
Lake Front Park, 216
Lake Plain, 8
Lake Village, 239
Lakes—
   Bar-K, 313
   Bass, 147, 234
   Beaver, 261
   Beaver Dam, 228
   Bixler, 232
   Blue, 167
   Briarwood, 184
   Bruce, 232
   Byrd's Echo, 314
   Cataract, 171, 211, 288, 290
   Cedar, 336
   Cedarville, 210
   Chrisney City, 167
   County Line, 184
   Cree, 232

Index

Crooked, 144
Cypress, 302
Diamond, 244
Dietz, 165
Dilldear, 183
Dogwood, 332
Downing, 245
Dugger Boat, 184
Edgewood, 211
Elk Creek, 300
Emma, 319
Erie, 23, 47, 49, 80, 329
Fish, 209
Fletcher, 204
Freeman, 303
Galacia, 207
Gordon's, 262
Hamilton, 214
Hardy, 217
Heaton, 189
Hi-Pit, 184
Hickory Grove, 287
Hog, 295
Holland, 220
Hoon, 237
Hovey, 263
Huntingburg, 223
James, 227, 243, 285, 311
Jewell, 156
John Hay, 300
Kilgore, 322
Knob, 227
Koontz, 311
Labline Bed, 302
Larwill, 241
Lenape, 227
Lost, 193
Manitou, 204, 293
Mansfield, 211
Marsh, 237
Maxinkuckee, 144, 178, 252
Michigan, 1, 7, 15, 17, 18, 22, 23, 36, 74, 79, 116, 117, 150, 167, 184, 185, 205, 225, 238, 240, 247, 273, 286, 298, 306, 338
Mississinewa, 255, 289
Mohee, 218
Monroe, 152, 257
Mont Longnecker, 341
Myers, 285
North, 316
Ontario, 48
Papakeechee, 333
Paradise, 312
Pay, 284
Pine, 322
Placid, 218
Pleasant, 239
Pretty, 285
Rainbow, 207
Riddle, 239
Robinson, 241, 283
Round, 232
Royer, 237
Salamonie, 247
Salinda, 300
Saugany, 295
Shady, 308
Shafer, 303
Shakamak, 303
Shipshewana, 305
Silver, 144
Simonton, 189
South, 316
Spring Valley, 278
Stephen's, 245
Sylvan, 295
Thompson Bed, 337
Tippecanoe, 243
Tolling Timbers, 295
Troy Cedar, 241
Tucker, 278
Twin, 285
Twin Hills, 246
Walter's, 204
Walton, 278, 316
Wapler, 245
Wawasee, 15, 314
Wible, 232
Winona, 341
Wipporwill, 324
Wofal, 296
Wolf, 209
Laketon, 239
Lakeville, 239
Land Grants, 52
Land Speculators, 68
Land Tax, 64
Landers
  Franklin, 101
Lands, 43
Lane
  Henry Smith, 71, 96, 97, 99
  James, 96
Lanesville, 239
Langford
  James, 294
Langlois Creek, 223

Encyclopedia of Indiana

Language, 41
Lanier
  James F.D., 239
  James F.D., Home, 248
Laotto, 239
Lapaz, 240
Lapel, 240
Larwill, 241
Lasalle Fish and
  Wildlife Area, 241
Late Prehistoric Stage, 37
Laughery Creek, 180, 273
Laulewasikau, 59, 60
Laurel, 241
Laurel Feeder Dam, 338
Laurel Hill, 241
Law Enforcement Planning, 131
Lawrence, 241, 242
Lawrence County, 11, 320, 327
Lawrence County Historical
  Museum, 148
Lawrence
  James, 242
Lawrenceburg, 101, 105, 242
League Park, 199
Leavenworth, 242
Lebanon, 242
Ledgerwood
  Samuel, 163
Leeper Park, 307
Leesburg, 243
Legal Division
  Army Transport Corps, 119
Legionnaire's Disease, 85
Legislative Research, 132
Leo, 243
Les Gros, 238
Leslie
  Daniel, 112
  Harry G., 112
Letters Ford, 243
Levenworth
  Seth M., 88
Levering
  John, 276
Lew Wallace Study, 176
Lewis
  John L., 353
Lewisville, 243
Lexington, 243
Liberal Republicans, 100
Liberty, 91, 243
Liberty Mills, 244
Library Park, 318
Library Services

  Department of, 132
Licensing (Corporate), 132
Licensing (Occupational
  & Professional), 132
Lick Creek, 151, 218, 249
Lick Creek Friends Church, 203
Lieber State Park, 171
Lieber
  Col. Richard, 309
Lightning Dude Ranch, 234
Ligonier, 244
Lilly Endowment, 348, 352
Lilly Foundation, 143
Limberlost Cabin, 207, 244
Limberlost State
  Memorial, 207, 244
Limberlost Swamp, 207, 244
Lincoln Boyhood National
  Memorial, 244, 308, 374
Lincoln Boyhood National
  Memorial Park, 245
Lincoln Heritage
  Trail, 193, 244
Lincoln Library and Museum, 199
Lincoln National Life
  Foundation, 199
Lincoln Pioneer
  Village, 245, 294
Lincoln State Park, 244,
  245, 309
Lincoln
  Abraham, 81, 153, 159,
  207, 227, 244, 245,
  276, 294, 299, 343
  Nancy Hanks, 244
Linden, 245
Lindley
  William, 299
Lindsay
  John, 172
Linton, 245
Linton Conservation
  Ponds, 245
Lion Club Memorial, 343
Lipschitz
  Jacques, 269
Liquor Control
  Department of, 132
Little Cedar Grove
  Baptist Church, 157
Little Clifty Creek, 170
Little Monon Creek, 256, 337
Little Pigeon
  Creek, 184, 308, 331
Little Pigeon Roost, 62

Index

Little Theater Society
of Indiana, 83
Little Turtle, 41, 42,
56, 57, 59, 60, 62, 79
Little Turtle State
Recreation Area, 223
Little Wyandotte Cave, 342
Little York, 245
Living Historical Farm, 244
Living Light, 223
Lizton, 245
Lockerbie Square, 349
Lockerbie Square Historic
District, 367
Lockyear College
of Business, 193
Logan
James, 246
Logansport, 66, 78, 99, 246
Logansport State
Hospital, 246
Long Beach, 246
Longlois Creek, 139, 276, 334
Loogootee, 247
Losantville, 247
Lost Bridge State
Recreation Area, 238,
247, 299
Lost River, 246
Lost River Acres, 278
Lowell, 247
Lowell Bridge, 173
Lowry's Station, 275
Lusk Home and Mill Site, 372
Lutheran University
Association, 323
Lydick, 247
Lyell
Sir Charles, 268
Lynd
Helen Merrell, 264
Robert, 264
Lynn, 248
Lynnville, 248
Lynnville Park, 248
Lyons, 248

MacLaine
Shirley, 249
MacLean
J. Arthur, 83
Macy, 248
Macy
William, 195
Madison, 66, 88, 248, 249

Madison Academy, 79
Madison County
Historical Society, 275
Madison Historic District, 361
Madison
James, 249
Madonna of the Trails, 291
Maennerchor, 348
Mail Fraud, 110
Mammoth Internal
Improvement Bill, 67, 80
Manchester College, 293
Mann Site, 373
Mansfield Reservoir, 288, 337
Mapes
Arthur Franklin, 6
Maples, 183
Mardi Gras, 50
Mardis
Josephine, 119
Marengo Caves, 9, 176
Maria Creek, 234, 312
Marion, 250
Marion College, 113, 250
Marion County, 65
Marion County Jail, 350
Marion
Gen. Francis, 250
Market Square Arena, 350
Markle, 251
Markle
John, 251
Markleville, 251
Marquette Park, 206
Marquette
Pere Jacques, 47, 206, 306
Marshall, 251, 252
Marshall County Historical
Society and Museum, 285
Marshall County Jail, 370
Marshall
Daniel, 107
John, 252
Thomas Riley, 107, 108, 171
Martin, 252
Martin State Forest, 252, 305
Martin
Dean, 249
Maj. John T., 252
Martinsville, 112
Mary Gray Bird Sanctuary, 172
Mascontin, 41
Mass Production, 74
Mass Transit
Department of, 132

Encyclopedia of Indiana

Matter Park, 250
Matthews Mansion, 189
Matthews
 Claude, 104
 Thomas, 104
Maumee River, 15, 23
Maurice Thompson
 Birthplace, 327
May
 Edwin, 6
McBrides's Bluff, 252
McCormick's Creek
 State Park, 36, 277, 308
McCray Refrigerators, 231
McCray
 Greenberry, 109
 Warren, 109, 111
McCulloch
 Carleton, 110
McCullough Park, 264
McCullough
 Bertha, 106
McDonald
 Joseph, 96
McFadden's Landing, 262
McFadden
 Andrew, 262
McGary
 Hugh, 191
McGill Manufacturing
 Company, 322
McGuffey Readers, 80
McGwinn's Village, 253
McNutt
 John, 112
 Paul, 112, 114, 202
Mead Johnson
 and Company, 192
Medaryville, 253
Medical Examining Board, 105
Medora, 253
Mellott, 253
Melodeon Hall, 373
Memorial Coliseum, 199
Memorial
 Community House, 339
Memorial Park, 296
Menne
 James H., 85
Mennonite Book Concern, 150
Mennonite Church, 149
Mennonites, 209
Mental Health
 Department of, 132
Mentone, 253

Merchants National Bank, 351
Meredith
 Solomon Concise, 161
Merom, 253
Merom Institute, 253
Merrifield Park, 255
Merrill
 Dudley, 254
Merrillville, 253
Mesker Park, 193
Mesker Zoo, 193
Messner
 Dan, 277
Methodist Ashbury College, 92
Methodist Church, 241, 323
Methodist Episcopal Church, 281
Methodist Home, 202
Methodists, 69
Metro Bus System, 347
Mexican Border campaign, 111
Mexican War, 69, 96, 102
Mexico, 254
Meyer
 Magdalena, 114
Miami, 41, 43
Miami County Historical
 Museum, 282
Miami Indians, 41
Miami State
 Recreation Area, 255
Miami University, 97
Michigan and Erie Canal, 313
Michigan Central Railroad, 7
Michigan City, 66
Michigan City Lighthouse, 364
Michigan Road, 66,
 79, 89, 90, 233, 240
Michigan Road Tollhouse, 368
Michigan Territory, 164
Mid-America World
 Trade Association, 120
Middlefork Reservoir, 291
Middletown, 264
Middletown in
 Transition, 264
Midwest Steel, 286
Miles Laboratories, 188
Milhouse Home, 324
Milhouse
 Joshua, 161
Military Park, 368
Mill Creek, 167,
 219, 277, 288, 337
Miller
 Sarah, 97

Index

Millhousen, 254
Milligan Park Gold Course, 177
Millrace, 173
Mills, 347
Mills
  Alexander, 163
Milltown, 254
Milroy, 254
Milroy Park, 290
Milroy
  Gen. Robert, 290
  Samuel, 182
Milton, 255
Milville Lock, 338
Mine Inspection and Safety, 82
Minerva Club, 81
Mining Disaster, 312
Mining
  Department of, 132
Mishawaka, 255
Mishawaka Children's
  Museum, 255
Miss Liberty, 346
Mississinewa Dam and
  Reservoir, 255, 289, 328, 329
Mississinewa River, 41, 255
Mississippi Culture, 37
Mississippi River, 15, 23, 44
Mississippi Valley, 48
Missouri Compromise, 71
Mitchell, 256
Mitchell Plain, 176, 221
Mitchell
  William, 231
Mix
  Lorinda, 103
Modoc, 256
Mongo Reservoir, 237
Monon, 256
Monon Corporation, 256
Monon Railroad, 81, 165, 256
Monroe, 256, 257
Monroe County, 11, 16
Monroe Dam and Reservoir, 194, 221, 257, 280, 337
Monroeville, 257
Monrovia, 257
Monte Cassino Chapel, 298
Monterey, 257
Montezuma, 258
Montgomery, 258
Montgomery County, 104
Montgomery
  Gen. Richard, 258
Monticello, 259

Montpelier, 259
Monument Circle, 346, 349
Moody Bible Institute, 165
Moody
  William Vaugh, 308
Moore
  James, 197
  Philip, 259
  Samuel, 260
Mooreland, 259
Moores Hill, 259
Mooresville, 260
Moravian Missionaries, 141
Moravians, 221
Morgan, 260
Morgan Manor, 193
Morgan Packing Company, 146
Morgan's Raiders, 324
Morgan
  Eliza, 99
  Gen. Daniel, 260
  John Hunt, 72, 81, 100, 324
  Martha, 112
Morgan-Monroe State Forest, 260
Morgantown, 261
Morningside, 261
Morocco, 261
Morris-Butler House, 368
Morrison Creek, 303
Morrison
  Lt. John, 303
Morristown, 261
Morse
  Samuel, 251
Morton
  James, 97
  Oliver P., 71, 81, 97, 98, 99
Motor Vehicles
  Department of, 133
Mounds State Park, 142, 157, 250, 262, 364
Mount Ayr, 262
Mount Calvary Cemetery, 223
Mount Summit, 262
Mount Tom, 225
Mount Vernon, 102, 262
Mount
  Atwell, 104
  James A., 104
Mulholland Museum, 232
Muncie, 263
Munster, 264
Muscatatuck Fish
  Management Headquarters, 264
Muscatatuck State Park, 264

467

Encyclopedia of Indiana

Myers
  William R., 103

Nabisco, 261
Nancy Hanks Lincoln Hall, 244
Napoleon, 265
Nappanee, 265
Nashville, 265
Natchez, 229
National and Hoosier Cup, 264
National Flower Show, 223
National Greenback Party, 73
National Guard, 104
National Highway System, 121
National Historic Landmark, 349
National Historic Site, 300
National Register of
  Historic Landmarks, 350
National Register of
  Historic Places, 146, 166
National Republican
  Convention, 71
National Road, 66, 79,
  183, 233, 315, 334, 346
Natural gas, 82, 210
Natural Resources
  Department of, 133
Navarre
  Pierre F., 306, 307
Neely
  Ruth, 112
New Albany, 94, 266
New Albany-Paoli
  Toll House, 205
New Augusta, 266
New Carlisle, 267
New Castle, 267
New Chicago, 268
New France, 47
New Harmony, 79, 268
New Harmony
  Historic District, 373
New Harmony State Memorial, 193
New Haven, 269
New Market, 270
New Middletown, 270
New Palestine, 270
New Paris, 270
New Philadelphia, 105
New Purchase, 65
New Richmond, 270
New Ross, 270
New Salisbury, 271
New York Central
  Railroad, 188, 215

Newberry, 267
Newburgh, 267
Newpoint, 270
Newport, 270
Newport Army
  Ammunition Plant, 85
Newton, 271
Newton
  John, 271
Nicholson
  Meredith, 82, 176, 349
Nixon
  Richard, 161
Noble, 271
Noble
  James, 79, 272
  Noah, 90, 91, 271
  Thomas, 90
Noblesville, 272
Noblesville Milling
  Company, 272
North American House, 324
North
  Rachel, 93
Northern Indiana Historical
Society Museum, 307
Northwest Boundary
  Dispute, 176
Northwest Territory, 1, 2,
  44, 45, 58, 63, 78,
  208, 234, 306, 326
Northwestern Christian
  University, 81
Northwood Institute, 335
Norway Dam, 303
Nuclear Energy
  Department of, 133

Oakdale Plant, 318
Oakland City, 272
Oakland City College, 272
Oaktown, 272
Oberholtzer
  Madge, 272
Oberlin College, 285
Occupational Safety & Health
  Department of, 133
Octogenarian Museum, 250
Odon, 273
Office of Agricultural
  War Relations, 114
Office of Labor
  Commissioner, 105
Ogden Dunes, 273
Ohio, 273

Index

Ohio & Mississippi
 Railroad, 302
Ohio County Courthouse, 292
Ohio County Historical
 Society, 292
Ohio River, 1, 7, 9,
 10, 11, 14, 16, 18,
 22, 23, 40, 42, 273
Ohio River Basin, 274
Ohio River
 Navigation Project, 274
Ohio University, 91
Ohio Valley, 38,
 44, 52, 77, 191
Oil & Gas
 Department of, 133
Old Cathedral, 326
Old Clarksville Site, 356
Old Flat Belly, 333
Old French Cemetery, 326
Old Monon Park, 165
Old North Church, 150
Old Northwest, 208
Old Rappite Fort Granary, 269
Old Richmond
 Historic District, 382
Old Sauk Trail, 254, 336
Old State Bank, 362
Old Town Pump, 154
Old Tunnel Mill, 167
Old Vanderburgh
 County Courthouse, 378
Olde Blue River Festival, 203
Olde Towne, 246
Oldenburg, 274
Oliver
 James, 81
Oliver, Joseph D.,
 House (Copshaholm), 375
Ombudsman, 133
Onward, 274
Oolitic, 274
Orange, 275
Ordinance of 1787,
 58, 63, 64
Orestes, 275
Orland, 275
Orleans, 275
Orr Iron Company, 121
Orr
 Robert D., 121
 Samuel Lowry, 121
Osceola, 276
Osgood, 276
Ossian, 276

Ottawa, 44
Otter Creek, 177
Otterbein, 276
Otwell, 276
Ouabache State Recreation
 Area, 152, 276, 335
Ouiatonon, 58
Our Sunday Visitor, 223
Overbeck House, 162
Overbeck Museum, 162
Owen, 277
Owen County, 11, 108
Owen's Creek, 78
Owen
 Abraham, 277
 David Dale, 268
 Robert Dale, 71, 79, 178, 268
Owen-Putnam State Forest, 277
Owens-Corning Fiberglass
 Corporation, 322
Owens-Illinois
 Glass Company, 207
Owensville, 277
Oxford, 277

Pacific Theater, 120
Paleo-Indian Stage, 37
Paleo-Indians, 37
Paleozoic Era, 13
Palmyra, 278
Panhandle Railroad, 203
Paoli, 278
Paoli Turnpike, 205, 213
Paragon, 278
Parameter
 Lydia, 92
Parish Grove, 185, 228
Parke, 278
Parke County Covered
 Bridge Festival, 258, 294
Parke County Maple Fair, 294
Parke
 Benjamin, 278
Parker City, 279
Parker
 Andrew, 195
 Richard, 195
Parks
 Alice, 110
Parks
 Department of, 133
Patoka, 279
Patoka River, 9
Patoka State Fish
 and Wildlife Area, 279

Encyclopedia of Indiana

Patriot, 280
Patterson
  Martha, 107
Paul House, 248
Paul Revere House, 150
Paul Tillich Park, 269
Paul
  Ann Parker, 89
Paynetown State
  Recreation Area, 257, 280
Peace Monument, 181
Pei
  I.M., 172
Pekin, 280
Pence, 280
Pendleton, 280
Pendleton Town Hall, 281
Pendleton
  Thomas, 280
Penn Central Railroad, 304
Penn
  William, 281
Pennsylvania College, 97
Pennsylvania Railroad, 215
Pennville, 281
People's Party, 71
Perry, 281
Perry County, 10
Perry
  Oliver H., 281
Perrysville, 281
Personnel
  Department of, 134
Peru, 281
Peter Morgan Greenhouses, 223
Peter-Paul Candy Factory, 202
Petersburg, 282
Peterson
  Christopher D., 85
  Frances, 102
Petroleum, 81
Phelps
  John, 163
Piankashaw, 41
Pierceton, 282
Pierro
  Don, 77
Pigeon Creek, 191, 208,
  283, 298, 311, 323, 331
Pigeon River, 283
Pigeon River State
  Fish and Game Area, 237
Pigeon River State Fish
  and Wildlife Area, 283
Pigeon Roost Massacre, 79

Pigeon Roost State
  Memorial, 283
Pike, 283
Pike State Forest, 283
Pike
  Gen. Z.M., 283
Pine Creek, 149
Pine Village, 284
Pinnacle, 177, 231, 252, 305
Pinnacle, The, 284
Pioneer Cemetery, 234
Pioneer Mothers'
  Memorial Forest, 221
Pipe Creek, 203, 249
Pittsboro, 284
Pittsburgh of the West, 315
Pittsburgh Plate Glass
  and Window Glass, 190
Pittsburgh Screw
  and Bolt Corporation, 206
Plainfield, 284
Plainville, 284
Pleasant Lake, 284
Plummer Creek, 211
Pluto Spring, 204, 275
Plymouth, 284
Pokagon State Park, 144,
  218, 227, 285, 311
Pokagon
  Simon, 285
Pokeberry Creek, 184
Poland, 285
Police
  Department of, 134
Pollution, 84
Pond Grove, 276
Poneto, 286
Pontiac, 44, 51, 77
Populist Party, 73
Port of Indiana, 286
Portage, 286
Porter, 286
Porter Beach, 184
Porter County, 8
Porter County Fair, 323
Porter County Historical
  Society Museum, 323
Porter County
  Municipal Airport, 323
Porter, Gene Stratton, Cabin
  (Limberlost Cabin), 355
Porter, Gene Stratton,
  Cabin (The Cabin in
  Wildflower Woods), 371
Porter Memorial Hospital, 323

Index

Porter Park, 286
Porter's Cave, 278
Porter
  Albert G., 101
  Cole, 282
  Gene Stratton, 19, 152, 181, 207, 244, 335
  Thomas, 101
Portland, 287
Posey, 287
Posey County, 7, 40
Posey
  Thomas, 64, 87, 287
Poseyville, 287
Post Office, 350
Potawatomi, 41, 43
Potawatomi Inn, 285
Potawatomi Park, 307
Pottery, 40
Powell
  Simon, 161
Prairie Creek Reservoir, 264
Presbyterian Academy, 105
Presbyterian Westminster Village, 213
Presbyterians, 69, 79
Priest Magazine, 223
Prince
  Capt. William, 288
Princeton, 287
Printing & Publishing
  Department of, 134
Prist
  Cora I., 109
Probation & Parole, 134
Proclamation of 1763, 51
Product Analysis and Research Industries, 121
Proffit-Morgan House, 282
Prohibition, 107, 211
Property Tax Relief, 121
Prophet, The, 59, 61, 63
Prophet's Town, 60, 61, 237
Propylaeum, The 349, 369
Proserpine Spring, 204
Province of Quebec, 52
Provolot
  Ezekiah, 295
Public Defender, 134
Public Utilities, 134
Public Welfare Programs, 76
Public Works
  Department of, 134
Pucket, 194
Pulaski, 288

Pulaski
  Casimir, 288
Pulitzer Prize, 75, 83, 84, 85
Pullman Strike, 82
Pumpkin Vine Pike, 234
Purchasing
  Department of, 135
Purdue University, 82, 110, 112, 119, 237, 336
Purdue University Veterinary School, 117
Purdue
  John, 336
Purdue-North Central, 336
Puterbaugh Museum, 282
Putnam, 288
Putnam
  Israel, 288
  Rufus, 78
Pyle
  Ernie, 179

Quaker, 200, 203, 291
Quaker Trace, 321
Quakers, 68, 73, 80, 157, 161, 185, 187, 194, 309, 335
Quebec Act, 77
Quebec Act of 1774, 52
Quincy, 184

Raccoon, 316
Raccoon Creek, 152, 155, 236, 258, 270, 278, 288, 295, 337
Raccoon Lake State Park, 279
Raccoon Lake State Recreation Area, 288, 294
Railroads, 70
Railroads
  Division of, 135
Rain Tree County, 219
Raintree Lake Park, 301
Ralston
  Alexander, 346
  John, 108
  Samuel M., 106, 108, 243, 308
Ramp Bridge, 158
Ramsey, 289
Randolph, 289
Randolph County, 7, 15, 79
Randolph
  Thomas, 87

Rapp
  George, 268
Rapp-Maclure Mansion, 269
Rappite Cemetery, 269
Rappite Community House, 269
Rappite Society, 268
Rappites, 79
Ray
  James Brown, 89
  William, 89
Rea Park Golf Course, 316
Real Estate, 135
Reconstruction, 73
Red Bridge State
  Recreation Area, 255, 289
Red Key, 289
Red Rock Ranch, 336
Reed
  Dr. Walter, 223
Reeder Park, 258
Reelsville, 289
Reeves Octoauto, 173
Reforestation, 34
Refugee Resettlement
  Department of, 135
Regenstrief Institute
  for Health Care, 352
Reitz, John
  Augustus, House, 379
Religion, 69
Remington, 289
Reno Gang, 302
Rensselaer, 290
Rensselaer
  James Van, 290
Republic Steel, 206
Republican Party, 71, 81
Restored Labryinth, 269
Retirement, 135
Reynolds, 290
Richard Lieber
  State Park, 288, 290
Richardson Wildlife
  Foundation, 184
Richland, 290
Richland Creek, 211
Richmond, 290
Richmond Rose, 291
Riddle
  Mary, 90
Ridgeville, 292
Riley Homestead, 212
Riley
  James Whitcomb, 2,
  80, 82, 83, 212, 349

  James Whitcomb, House, 369
Ripley, 292
Ripley County, 11
Ripley County Historical
  Museum, 325
Ripley
  Gen. E. W., 292
Rising Sun, 292
River Cave, 162
Rivers—
  Allegheney, 273
  Anderson, 281,
    298, 308, 319
  Big Bayou, 214
  Big Blue, 216, 233,
    261, 267, 296, 304
  Big Sandy, 274
  Black, 208
  Blue, 176, 203, 217,
    219, 254, 299, 332, 339
  Cumberland, 274
  Deshee, 234
  East Fork, 337
  Eel, 15, 62, 78, 152, 164,
    169, 172, 182, 211, 219,
    235, 246, 277, 288,
    292, 329, 339
  Elkhart, 62, 188, 189,
    209, 231, 271, 295, 298
  Freeman, 259
  Grand Calumet, 186, 206,
    238, 286
  Great Miami, 338
  Green, 274
  Illinois, 23, 48,
    77, 226, 286
  Iroquois, 23, 171,
    228, 231, 271, 290
  Kanawaka, 273
  Kankakee, 20, 23, 43,
    48, 228, 231, 238,
    240, 271, 286, 297,
    301, 306, 311
  Lick, 275, 278
  Little, 223, 293
  Little Blue, 176
  Little Calumet, 206, 238, 286
  Little Elkhart, 237
  Little Vermillion, 270
  Lost, 246, 252,
    275, 278, 332, 335
  Maumee, 15, 23,
    57, 67, 78, 141,
    197, 269, 298
  Miami, 273

Index

Mississinewa, 41, 79, 182, 186, 201, 210, 230, 237, 250, 255, 289, 292, 329
Mississippi, 15, 16, 23, 44, 48, 49, 96, 274
Monongahela, 273
Muscatatuck, 226, 264, 301, 332
Muskingum, 273
Ohio, 1, 7, 9, 10, 11, 14, 16, 18, 22, 23, 40, 47, 58, 63, 77, 78, 79, 80, 84, 89, 152, 167, 168, 170, 176, 177, 191, 192, 196, 210, 211, 216, 217, 228, 229, 230, 242, 248, 262, 267, 273, 280, 281, 287, 292, 294, 308, 313, 314, 317, 319, 320, 323, 325, 329, 331, 333, 346
Patoka, 9, 183, 208, 227, 275, 279, 283, 341
Pigeon, 237, 283
Salamonie, 151, 223, 228, 259, 281, 287, 299, 329, 331, 334
Scioto, 273
Shafer, 259
St. Joseph, 41, 48, 57, 77, 78, 141, 155, 181, 188, 189, 197, 255, 276, 283, 297, 298, 306
St. Mary's, 15, 57, 78, 139, 141, 181, 197
Tennessee, 274
Tippecanoe, 60, 78, 164, 204, 235, 237, 252, 257, 259, 288, 303, 317, 332, 337, 340
Vermillion, 324
Wabash, 1, 7, 9, 15, 16, 18, 22, 23, 24, 26, 41, 48, 56, 59, 60, 62, 63, 67, 77, 78, 79, 139, 145, 152, 170, 175, 208, 214, 217, 223, 234, 236, 238, 246, 251, 253, 255, 258, 268, 270, 273, 278, 281, 287, 299, 314, 317, 320, 324, 325, 328, 329, 331, 334, 336, 337, 340

West Fork, 337
White, 9, 16, 22, 23, 24, 59, 141, 142, 147, 151, 152, 159, 177, 180, 181, 182, 183, 187, 208, 209, 211, 214, 218, 220, 226, 230, 234, 241, 242, 246, 247, 249, 250, 252, 256, 260, 262, 267, 277, 278, 282, 283, 289, 305, 308, 330, 332, 337, 340, 341, 342, 343, 345, 347
Whitelick, 156, 219, 260, 284
Whitewater, 11, 156, 161, 173, 180, 187, 195, 202, 213, 214, 255, 289, 290, 320, 333, 335
Wildcat, 222
Yellow, 233, 252, 284, 297, 311
Yukon, 229
Riverside Park, 216
Roachdale, 292
Roann, 292
Roanoke, 293
Roanoke Classical Seminary, 293
Robert E. Lee, 192, 229
Robert Fulton, 192, 204
Roberts-Morton House, 381
Robertson
    Oscar "Big O", 345
Robinson
    Solon, 178
Roche
    Kevin, 172
Rochester, 293
Rockefeller
    John D., 339
Rockfield, 294
Rockville, 294
Rodehever
    Homer, 341
Roebuck
    Alvah, 216
Rolling Prairie, 295
Roman Catholic Church, 69
Rome City, 295
Roofless Church, 269
Roosevelt
    Franklin D., 84
Rose Polytechnic Institute, 82, 316
Rosedale, 295

Encyclopedia of Indiana

Roseland, 295
Rossville, 295
Roth Museum, 187
Royal Center, 295
Rudd-Miller House, 193
Rudolph Schwartz, 262
Rugg
  Samuel L., 181
Rum Village Park, 307
Ruritan Park, 258
Rush, 296
Rush County Fair, 296
Rush County Historical
  Museum, 296
Rush
  Dr. Benjamin, 296
Rushville, 91, 296
Rushville's East
  Hill Cemetery, 296
Russellville, 296
Rustic Furniture Company, 117

Saarinen
  Eero, 172
  Eliel, 172
Sackville, 326
Saddle Lake, 221
Sage-Robinson-
  Nagel House, 380
Sakamak State Park, 303
Salamonia, 299
Salamonie Dam
  and Reservoir, 328
Salamonie Forest
  State Recreation Area, 299
Salamonie Reservoir, 224,
  238, 299, 331
Salamonie River, 299
Salamonie River State
  Forest, 238, 247, 299, 328
Salem, 72, 299
Salem Grammar School, 300
Salisbury, 97
Salisbury Courthouse, 166
Salt, 256
Salt Creek, 158, 242, 274, 337
San Pierre, 300
Sanborn, 300
Sand Creek, 181, 230
Sander Wood
  Engraving Company, 286
Sanders
  Zeralda, 91
Santa Claus Land, 300
Saratoga, 300

Sargent
  Winthrop, 78, 234
Sauk Trail, 295
Sault Saint Marie, 47
Scales Lake Fish Hatchery, 301
Scales Lake State Beach
  and State Park, 301
Scales Lake State Forest, 153
Schererville, 301
Schmidt Cabinet Company, 216
Schneider, 301
Schofield Mansion, 248
School for Blind, 80
Schricker
  Christopher, 114
  Henry F., 114
Scott, 301
Scott County, 10
Scott
  Caroline Lavinia, 149
  Charles, 56, 78, 301
  Sarah, 108
Scottish Rite Cathedral, 350
Scottsburg, 301
Scribner House, 266
Seagram
  Joseph E., 211
Seaman
  Rachel, 93
Second Presbyterian Church, 80
Secretary of State
  Office of, 135
Secretary of the Senate, 135
Securities
  Division of, 135
Sedgewick
  Elizabeth, 90
See, 157, 191, 207, 237, 326
Seelyville, 302
Selective Service, 83
Sellersburg, 302
Selma, 302
Selmier State Forest, 302
Settlers, 89, 346
Seventh-Day Adventists, 168
Sewall
  May Wright, 82
Sextoauto, 173
Seymour, 302
Shades State Park, 177,
  302, 333
Shaefer's Beach, 221
Shafer Reservoir, 303
Shakamak State Park, 224, 227
Sharpsville, 303

474

Index

Shedtown, 263
Shelburn, 303
Shelby, 304
Shelby County
  Historical Society, 304
Shelby
  Isaac, 304
Shelbyville, 98, 304
Sheldon-Swope Art Gallery, 316
Sherer
  Nicholas, 301
Sheridan, 304
Shipshewana, 305
Shirley, 305
Shoals, 305
Shrewsbury House, 248
Shrine of the
  Sorrowful Mother, 274
Sidneyham, 155
Sieberling Mansion, 360
Sigler
  Jacob, 203
Sign Crafters, 121
Silurian Period, 13
Silver Creek, 168, 302
Silver Lake, 305
Simmer
  Eva, 107
Sinatra
  Frank, 249
Single G, 161
Sippy
  Dr. Joseph, 139
Sisters of St. Francis
  Convent and Academy, 274
Sixth Judicial Court, 92
Ski Valley, 240
Skyline Drive, 159, 226
Slavery, 55, 58, 64, 200
Sloan House, 266
Slocum
  Frances, 201
Small Eagle Creek, 343
Smith
  Jeremiah, 281
Social Democratic Party, 82
Social Security, 84
Social Services
  Department of, 136
Socialist Movement, 74
Socialist Party
  of America, 353
Society of Friends, 69
Soldiers and
  Sailors Monument, 262, 346

Soldiers' Orphan Home, 101
Solid Waste Management
  Department of, 136
Some Came Running, 249
Somerville, 306
Sommers
  Matilda, 98
Sonntag-Bayard-Kiechle
  House, 193
South Bend, 48, 63, 66, 306
South Gleason Park, 206
South Milford, 307
South Side Park, 288
South Whitley, 307
Southport, 307
Spanish-American War, 82,
  105, 110, 202
Sparks
  Eliza, 105
Speakman House, 292
Speedway, 307
Spencer, 308
Spencer
  Spier, 308
  S.C., 140
Spencerville, 309
Spiceland, 309
Spiceland Academy, 309
Spring Hills Golf Course, 214
Spring Mill State Park, 36,
  152, 156, 256, 309
Spring Valley State
  Fish and Wildlife Area, 310
Springer
  Raymond E., 114
Springport, 310
Sprinkle
  John, 267
Sprinklesburgh, 267
Spurgeon, 310
Squatters, 58
Squire Boone
  Caverns, 175, 217, 310
St. Anthony, 297
St. Bernice, 297
St. Benedict's College, 199
St. Clair
  Arthur, 55, 78
St. Francis College, 199
St. Francis Xavier, 49
St. John's Catholic Church, 350
St. Joe, 297
St. John, 297
St. Joseph, 77, 297
St. Joseph Courthouse, 307

475

St. Joseph River, 15.
 23, 41, 297
St. Joseph Valley, 47
St. Joseph's College, 171
St. Joseph's Indian
 Normal School, 361
St. Lawrence Basin, 306
St. Lawrence River, 15
St. Lawrence Valley, 47
St. Mary's College, 307
St. Mary's River, 15, 298
St. Mary-of-the-Woods, 80
St. Mary-of-the-Woods
 College, 316
St. Meinrad, 298
St. Meinrad's College, 81
St. Peter's Church, 258
St. Paul, 299
Stage Lines, 66
Stage Route, 79
Standard Coal Company, 327
Standard Life
 Insurance Company, 112
Standard Oil, 74, 339
Standard Oil Company, 82
Standard Steel
 Spring Company, 206
Stanford University, 143
Star City, 310
Starke, 311
Starke
 Gen. John, 311
Starr Historic District, 382
Starve Hollow State
 Forest, 311
State Bank, 92
State Bank of Indiana, 80
State Bank of Indiana,
 Branch of (Memorial Hall), 381
State Bird, 5
State Board of
 Agriculture, 80, 94
State Board of Education, 103
State Board of Health, 82, 101
State Capital, 89
State Capitol Building, 6
State Constitution, 79,
 94, 121
State Department
 of Geology, 81
State Department of
 Public Welfare, 84
State Flag, 2
State Flower, 5
State Historical Society, 79

State Hospital for Insane, 80
State Language, 6
State Line House, 185
State Lottery, 85
State Militia, 72
State Mineral, 6
State Motto, 4
State Name, 1
State Nickname, 2
State Office Building, 350
State Park System, 108
State Poem, 6
State Revenue, 64
State Roads, 67
State School for Deaf, 80
State Seal, 4
State Seminary, 79
State Soldiers and
 Sailors Monument, 369
State Soldiers' Home, 336
State Song, 5
State Spiritualist
 Association, 167
State Symbols, 1
State Tree, 5
State Workmen's
 Compensation Act, 83
State-Local Relations, 136
Statehood, 87
Statehouse, 82
Statehouse at Corydon, 64
Staunton, 311
Steamboat Festival, 229
Steel Production, 83, 261
Steele
 Theodore Clement, 314
 Theodore Clement, House
 and Studio, 356
Steinmann
 Elizabeth, 121
Stephenson
 D.C., 75, 83, 272
Sterling Brewers, 121
Steven Memorial Museum, 300
Stewart
 William, 154
Stilesville, 311
Stinesville, 312
Stone Quarrying, 76
Stone
 Cornelia, 102
 Nathan, 165
Storyland Zoo, 307
Storytelling Festival, 155

Index

Stout
  Daniel, House, 371
  Elihu, 225, 327
Strawberry Festival, 162, 350
Strawboard Company, 272
Strawtown, 215
Strip Mine Reclamation
  Program, 27
Strip Mining, 26
Studebaker, 76, 80
Studebaker Brothers
  Manufacturing Company, 306
Studebaker
  Clement, 306
  Henry, 306
Stueben, 311
Stueben
  Baron, 311
Sugar Creek, 149, 152, 170, 180, 216, 258, 278, 303, 304, 316, 320
Sugar Creek Canoe Race, 303
Sugar Creek Park, 212
Sullivan, 312
Sullivan County, 40
Sullivan County Park, 312
Sullivan
  Daniel, 312
Sulphur Springs, 312
Summitville, 313
Sunday
  "Billy", 253, 341
Sunman, 313
Surplus Property
  Department of, 136
Sutton
  Isaiah, 184
Swayzee, 313
Swearington
  Catherine Stull Van, 90
Sweetser, 313
Switz City, 313
Switzerland, 313
Switzerland County Historical
  Society Museum, 325
Sylvan Lake, 313
Syracuse, 314

T.C. Steele State
  Memorial, 314
Taggart
  Thomas, 204
Tannehill
  W. M., 90
Tariff, 68

Tarkington
  Booth, 82, 349, 350
Taverns, 66
Tax Reform, 84
Taxation & Revenue
  Department, 136
Taylor University, 322
Taylor
  Waller, 79
  Zachary, 79
Teachers' Seminary, 80
Teagarden
  Ann Todd, 276
Teamsters Union, 353
Tecumseh, 1, 59, 60, 61, 62, 63, 79, 237, 246
Tecumseh Trail Rest Park, 336
Tell City, 314
Tell City Chair Company, 314
Tell
  William, 314
Temperance, 106
Ten O'Clock Line, 159, 209
Tennyson, 314
Tenskwatawa, 237, 317
Terre Haute, 60, 80, 92, 314
Territorial Capital, 327
Territorial Capitol of Former
  Indiana Territory, 363
Territorial Legislature, 64
Territory, 55
Territory Northwest of
  the River Ohio, 78
Texas Declaration
  of Independence, 69
Text
  Esther French, 91
Textbooks
  Department of, 136
Thomas
  Jesse Brooks, 157
Thompson
  Dr. John K., 276
  Jane, 98
  Maurice, 176, 327
Thorntown, 316
Tilden
  Samuel J., 99
Timber, 81
Timolatin
  Kathleen, 113
Tip-Top Creamery, 327
Tippecanoe, 316, 317
Tippecanoe Battlefield, 236, 377

Encyclopedia of Indiana

Tippecanoe Battlefield
 State Memorial, 237, 317
Tippecanoe County, 112
Tippecanoe County
 Courthouse, 376
Tippecanoe County
 Historical Museum, 237
Tippecanoe Place
 (Studebaker House), 375
Tippecanoe River, 15, 317
Tippecanoe River
 State Park, 288, 318, 341
Tipton, 318
Tipton Knoll, 173
Tipton Till Plain, 8, 148, 318
Tipton
 John, 147, 172, 318
Tobin
 Dan, 353
Todd
 Jr., John, 77
Tolliver Swallowhole, 246
Topeka, 319
Tornadoes, 85, 216
Tourism
 Department of, 136
Tousey
 Miranda, 101
Townsend
 Clifford, 84, 113
 David, 113
Tracy, 251
Trafalgar, 319
Traffic Safety Commission, 116
Trail Creek, 319
Trail of Death, 285
Trailblazer Railroad, 327
Transportation
 Department of, 136
Transylvania University, 92
Treasurer
 Department of, 137
Treaty, 42, 43
Treaty Elm, 163
Treaty of 1783, 55
Treaty of Alliance, 53
Treaty of Fort Wayne, 59, 60
Treaty of Ghent, 63
Treaty of Greenville, 57,
 58, 60, 78, 145, 172
Treaty of Paradise Springs, 328
Treaty of Paris, 44,
 45, 50, 77, 326
Treaty of St. Mary's, 79, 263
Treaty of Wabash, 79

Trenton Oil and Gas, 182
Trenton's Field, 28
Tri-County Fish and
 Wildlife Area, 319
Tri-State University, 143
Tribune, 178
Trinity Springs, 305, 319
Troy, 319
Tucker
 Ralph, 117
Tumbling Waters Cave, 278
Turkey Creek, 235, 318
Turkey Run Inn, 320
Turkey Run State Park, 36,
 279, 294, 320
Turman Gallery of
 Fine Arts, 316
Turnverein, 348
Twin Caves, 309, 320
Twin Creek, 332
Tyson
 Mike, 86

U.S. Army Medical Corps, 120
U.S. Courthouse
 and Post Office, 370
U.S. Electric
 Carriage Company, 268
U.S. Forest Service, 34
U.S. Geological Society, 81
U.S. Geological Survey, 269
U.S. Gypsum Company, 305
U.S. Highway 50, 33
U.S. Land Office, 78
U.S. Steel Corporation, 74, 83,
 205, 206, 238
Uhl Pottery Works, 223
Ulen, 320
Unagusta Furniture
 Corporation, 117
Unclaimed Property
 Division of, 137
Uncle Tom's Cabin, 281
Underground Railroad, 71,
 79, 151, 200, 243,
 271, 292, 333, 335
Unemployment, 122
Unemployment Compensation, 84
Unemployment
 Division of, 137
Union, 64, 72, 96, 97, 98, 320
Union City, 100, 321
Union Depot, 81
Union Mills, 321

Index

Union Sanitary
  Manufacturing Company, 272
Union Station, 351
Uniondale, 321
United Mine Workers
  Union, 74, 82, 85, 353
United States Census Bureau, 229
Universal, 321
Universe Room, 328
University of Evansville, 193
University of Indiana, 112, 116, 119, 120
University of Indiana
  at Bloomington, 120
University of
  Indiana Law School, 113
University of Notre
  Dame, 80, 258, 285, 307
University Square, 350
Upland, 321
Upper Mississippi River, 16
Urbana, 322
Urch Plow, 192

V-J Day, 113
Vail
  Edward, 240
Valley Belle, 338
Valleys —
  Ohio, 38, 44
  Wabash, 40
Vallonia, 322
Valparaiso, 322
Valparaiso Glacial
  Moraine, 323
Valparaiso Technical
  Institute, 323
Valparaiso University, 322
Van Buren, 323
Van Buren
  Martin, 69
Van Slyke
  Peter, 151
Vance
  Samuel, 242
Vanderburgh, 323
Vanderburgh County, 41
Vanderburgh County Republican
  Central Committee, 121
Vandiver
  William E., 85
Veraestau, 357
Vermillion, 324
Vernon, 324
Vernon Creek, 230, 324

Versailles, 72, 324
Versailles State
  Park, 220, 292, 325
Veterans' Affairs
  Department of, 137
Vevay, 325
Viele-Koch House, 193
Vietnam, 120
Vigo, 325
Vigo County, 9
Vigo
  Francis, 54, 160, 325
  Francis, 54
Village of Squirrel Creek, 292
Vincennes, 58, 64, 77, 326
Vincennes Historic
  District, 363
Vincennes Land Office, 191
Vincennes Roman
  Catholic Church, 77
Vincennes University, 78, 87, 225, 327
Vincennes
  Francois Morgane de, 77, 326
Vinegar Mill, 264
Virgil I. Grissom
  State Memorial, 327
Virginia Cession, 168
Vital Records & Statistics, 137
Vonnegut
  Kurt, Jr., 345
Voting, 64

Wabash, 328, 329
Wabash and Erie Canal, 65, 67, 79, 80, 89, 145, 164, 166, 180, 182, 191, 198, 201, 236, 238, 249, 258, 269, 273, 282, 298, 315, 328, 329, 332, 342
Wabash College, 80, 107, 177
Wabash County
  Historical Museum, 328
Wabash Fire and
  Casualty Company, 115
Wabash Lowland, 220, 329
Wabash Manual Labor College, 80
Wabash Railroad, 336, 340
Wabash River, 1, 7, 9, 15, 16, 18, 22, 23, 24, 41, 329
Wabash University, 69
Wabash Valley, 9, 40
Wabash Valley Golf Club, 207

479

Encyclopedia of Indiana

Wakarusa, 330
Waldron, 330
Walker
 James H., 330
Walkerton, 330
Wallace, 330
Wallace Circus Farm, 282
Wallace
 Andrew, 91
 Ben, 282
 David, 91
 Joanne "Josie", 122
 Lew, 82, 157, 176
Walton, 330
Wanatah, 330
War Manpower Commission, 113
War of 1812, 62, 157, 198, 246, 283, 292, 343
War Risk Insurance Bureau, 115
Warnecke
 John Carl, 172
Warner Gear Division, 263
Warren, 331
Warren County Bar, 106
Warren
 Daniel, 163
 Joseph, 331
Warrick, 331
Warrick County, 88
Warrick
 Capt. Jacob, 331
Warrior's Island, 54
Warsaw, 332
Washington, 332
Washington Country Club, 332
Washington County, 10, 11
Washington Park, 186
Washington
 George, 56, 176, 235, 236
Water Pollution Control
 Department of, 137
Water Resources
 Division of, 137
Waterloo, 333
Waterways, 67
Watson
 James, 107
Wattles
 John, 278
Waveland, 333
Wawaka, 333
Wawasee Fish Hatchery, 314
Wawasee lake, 333
Wawasee State Fish Hatchery
 and Fishing Area, 333

Wawasee
 Chief, 314
Way
 Amanda, 183
Wayne, 333
Wayne County
 Historical Museum, 291
Wayne
 Anthony, 42, 56, 78, 198, 333
Waynetown, 334
Weed Patch Hill, 158, 334
Weese
 Harry, 172
Weights & Measures
 Division of, 137
Weir Cook
 Municipal Airport, 352
Welfare
 Department of, 138
Wells, 334
Wells County, 82
Wells County
 Historical Museum, 152
Wells County State
 Game Farm, 276
Wells
 William H., 334
Welsh
 Matthew, 118
Wendell Wilkie Grave
 and Memorial, 296
Wepecheange, 223
Werline and Halbieb
 Horse Auction, 296
West Baden, 275
West Baden Springs, 335
West Baden Springs Hotel,
 (Northwood Institute
 of Indiana), 335, 371
West College Corner, 335
West Harrison, 335
West Lafayette, 336
West Lebanon, 336
West Point, 91
West Terre Haute, 336
Westendorf
 Thomas Pain, 284
Western Hills Golf Course, 300
Westfield, 335
Westinghouse Electric, 263
Westport, 336
Westville, 336
Wheat Production, 81
Wheatfield, 336
Wheatland, 99, 337

Index

Whetzel Trace, 337
Whetzel
  Jacob, 337
Whig Convention, 80
Whig Party, 68, 92
Whirlpool Corporation, 192
Whitcomb
  Edgar D., 119
  James, 92, 93
  John, 92, 119
  Martha, 104
White, 9, 337
White Lick Creek, 158
White River, 9, 15,
  22, 23, 24, 42, 337
White River Basin, 337
White Water State Park, 157
White
  Isaac, 337
  John, 140
Whiteland, 337
Whitestown, 338
Whitewater Canal, 80,
  157, 161, 241, 338
Whitewater Canal Company, 174
Whitewater Canal
  Historic District, 360
Whitewater Canal
  State Memorial, 338
Whitewater River, 11, 338
Whitewater State Park, 244,
  321, 338
Whitewater Valley, 63, 338
Whiting, 82, 338
Whiting Park, 339
Whitley, 339
Whitley County
  Historical Society, 171
Whitley County Hospital, 172
Wiggin's Point, 254
Wiggins
  Jeremiah, 254
Wigwam Convention, 81
Wilbur Wright
  State Memorial, 339
Wilbur Wright State
  Recreation Area, 339
Wildcat Creek, 164, 170,
  213, 234, 295, 317, 318
Wildflower Woods, 207
Wilkie
  Wendell, 296
Wilkinson, 340
Wilkinson
  James, 56, 78

Rosa, 112
Willard Library, 379
Willard
  Ashbel, 94, 95, 97
Williams Dam State
  Fishing Area, 340
Williams
  George, 99
  James D., 99, 100
Williamson
  Ellen, 92
Williamsport, 340
Williamsport Falls, 340
Willkie
  Herman F., 190
  Wendell L., 84, 190
Willow Prairie, 204
Willow Slough, 261, 340
Willow Slough State
  Recreation Area, 340
Wilson
  Woodrow, 107
Winamac, 340
Winamac
  Chief, 340
Winchester, 341
Winchester Speedway, 341
Windfall, 341
Wingate, 341
Winnebago, 41
Winona Lake, 341
Winslow, 341
Winter
  Ezra, 208
Winterble
  Barbara, 118
Winterheimer
  Catherine, 97
Wolcott, 342
Wolcottville, 342
Wolf Lake, 342
Wolf Lake Park, 216
Woman's Prison, 82
Women, 42, 138
Woodburn, 342
Woodland Indians, 262
Woodland Park, 286
Woodland Stage, 37
Woodrow Wilson, 171
Woodruff Place, 350, 370
Woodruff
  James O., 350
Worden
  James, 140
Workers' Compensation, 138

Workingmen's Institute
  Library, and Museum, 269
Workmen's Compensation Law, 108
World War I, 75, 83, 109,
  110, 111, 113, 115,
  202, 255, 272, 315, 348, 350
World War II, 114, 116,
  117, 118, 119, 121,
  179, 202, 227, 244,
  338, 347, 349
World War Memorial, 350
Worthington, 342
Worthington
  Hannah, 100
Wright
  John, 93
  Joseph A., 93
  Orville, 339
  Pearl, 120
  Wilbur, 267, 339
Wyandotte, 342
Wyandotte Cave, 9, 175, 176
Wyatt Seed Company, 282

Yale University, 121
Yellowood State Forest, 265, 343
Yellowood State Park, 343
Yeoman, 343
Yorktown, 343
Young
  John, 328
Youngstown Sheet
  and Tube Company, 185

Zimmerman Art Glass
  Factory, 175
Zionsville, 343

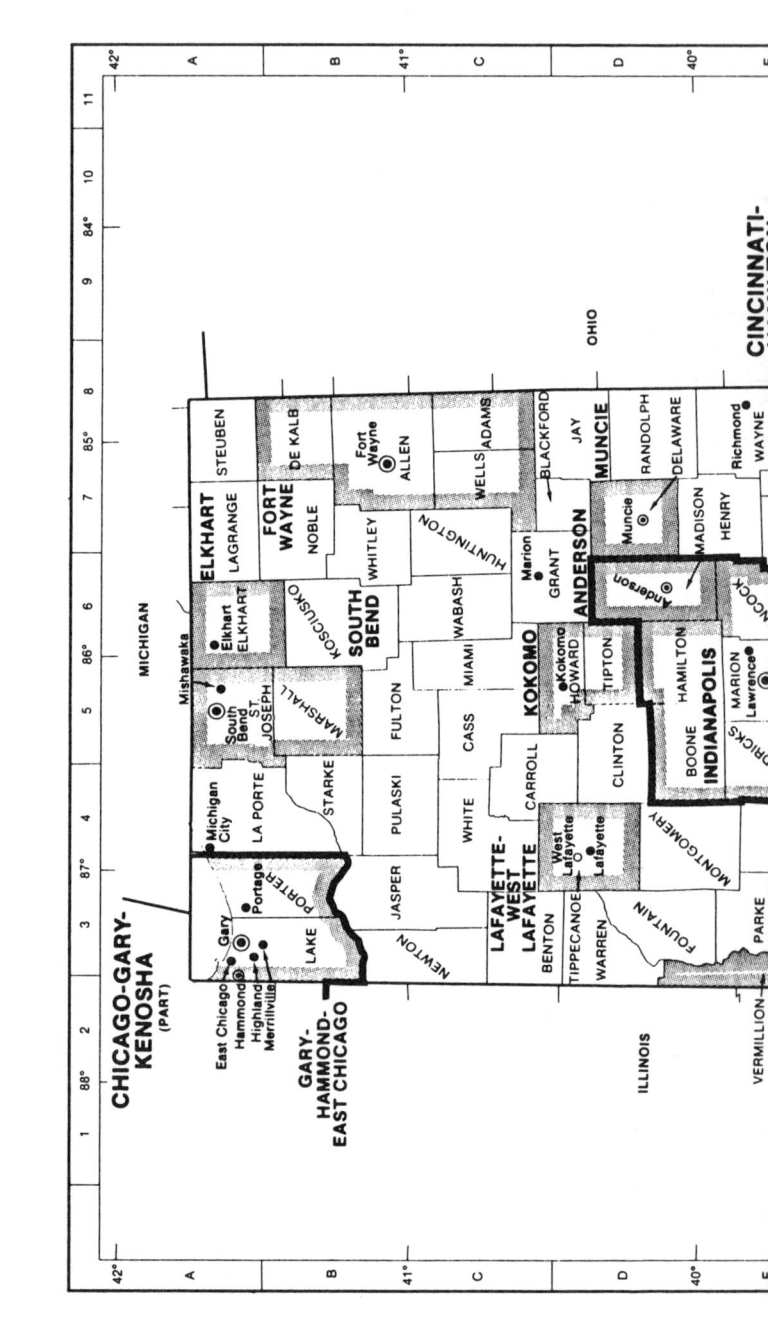

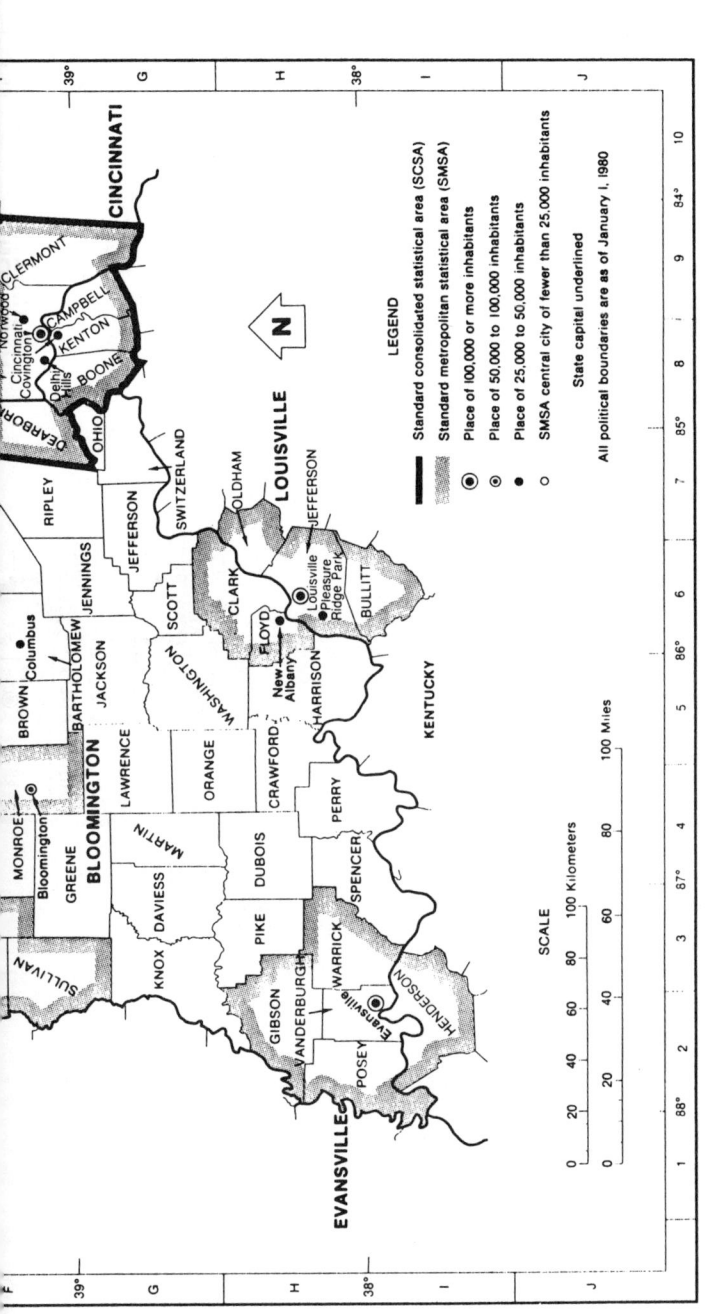